Washington Irving
and the Fantasy of Masculinity

THE WASHINGTON MONUMENT, RICHMOND, VA.
THOMAS CRAWFORD, SCULPTOR

From a Photograph & Drawing made for Irving's Washington, by J. W. Ehninger, N.Y.

NEW YORK. G. P. PUTNAM.

Washington Irving and the Fantasy of Masculinity
Escaping the Woman Within

Heinz Tschachler

McFarland & Company, Inc., Publishers
Jefferson, North Carolina

Also by Heinz Tschachler
and from McFarland

*George Washington and Political Fatherhood:
The Endurance of a National Myth* (2020)

George Washington on Coins and Currency (2020)

*The Monetary Imagination of Edgar Allan Poe:
Banking, Currency and Politics in the Writings* (2013)

The Greenback: Paper Money and American Culture (2010)

This book has undergone peer review.

Frontispiece: Thomas Crawford, Washington Memorial, Richmond, Virginia, in Washington Irving, *Life of George Washington*, vol. V (New York: Putnam, 1859), p. 351 (author's collection).

ISBN (print) 978-1-4766-8666-0
ISBN (ebook) 978-1-4766-4507-0

Library of Congress and British Library
cataloguing data are available

Library of Congress Control Number 2021062281

© 2022 Heinz Tschachler. All rights reserved

*No part of this book may be reproduced or transmitted in any form
or by any means, electronic or mechanical, including photocopying
or recording, or by any information storage and retrieval system,
without permission in writing from the publisher.*

On the cover: a portrait of Washington Irving, 1825, artist Charles Turner,
copy after Gilbert Stuart Newton (National Portrait Gallery, Smithsonian Institution)

Printed in the United States of America

*McFarland & Company, Inc., Publishers
Box 611, Jefferson, North Carolina 28640
www.mcfarlandpub.com*

... forming that manliness and independence of character which it has ever been my ambition to acquire.

—Washington Irving, letter to William Irving, Jr., August 1, 1804

Contents

Acknowledgments	ix
Prologue	1
ONE. Anima Consciousness and Archetypal Masculinities	13
TWO. "Because it was fun": Whimsicality, Gentility, and the Loss of Communal Manhood	44
THREE. Rip Van Winkle, Ichabod Crane, and Other Troubled Masculinities	74
FOUR. "Dear old romantic Spain": Purloined Heroes	105
FIVE. On the Prairies and in the West: Manhood Wrapped in the Nation's Flag	138
SIX. *Life of George Washington*: Manly Perfection in the Father of His Country	167
Epilogue	197
Chapter Notes	211
Bibliography	263
Index	267

Acknowledgments

THIS BOOK WAS NOT ALWAYS EASY TO WRITE, not least because concepts like anima and animus, or femininity and masculinity too easily suggest fundamental and supposedly immutable dualisms and, worse, a form of biological determinism that is not only out of fashion but has become simply untenable. It was, therefore, absolutely essential to always be on guard against distortions and biases, reminding myself and potential critics that C.G. Jung himself was not a strict adherent to a bipolar mode of thinking. Although he distinguished male and female principles, Jung accepted an inherent mixture of masculinity and femininity within each human psyche, arguing that the archetypes of anima and animus existed to degrees in all people. Every individual, then, displays a mixture, a continuum perhaps of masculine and feminine principles. Moreover, it is now generally accepted that these principles are not "universal," in the sense that they are always and everywhere constructed in the same way, translating into recognizable gender roles. Concepts like femininity and masculinity are ascriptive and culturally relative, embedded in culture-specific symbolic systems.

I am not a trained psychoanalyst, and therefore often depended on the advice of mentors and colleagues, as well as on scholarship that places the anima/animus scheme in perspective. I have tried to be quite scrupulous about acknowledging specific aid both in my notes and in the bibliography. More comprehensively, I am grateful to Miles White for reading portions of the manuscript and helping me think through the central questions of the book at a crucial state. I also thank Franz K. Stanzel, Jürgen Peper, Walter Grünzweig, Dan Shanahan, Sean Cubitt, Alex Hunt, Andrew Bourque, and Jessa Krick for responding to my requests for information or indulging my incessant tossing out of ideas. I would also like to acknowledge here the efforts of students in my graduate seminar on American Masculinities, especially Andrea Ettinger, Lisa Kazianka, Martina Maierbrugger, Doroteja Perse, and Aislinn Piball. Shauna Bennis, Vanessa Erat, László Bernáth, Brigitte Pasterk, and Paulina Stec took part in my graduate course in early anthropology. I profited from their good efforts as well. Finally, I thank Stefan "Steve" Rabitsch, for imparting valuable comments and providing moral as well as material support, and, beyond that, for remaining a steadfast friend, an inspiring colleague, and an intellectual companion.

My formal acknowledgments go to the friendly and efficient staff of the library and interlibrary loan desks at the University of Klagenfurt, who went out of their way to keep the flow of books running during the difficult time of the Covid-19 pandemic. At McFarland, I have had the good fortune to work with David Alff on four books. Thus, I give up on finding some new way to say what a great editor David is, but I must thank him for taking charge of the Irving project once it arrived at McFarland and shepherding it through with care and precision until it went to print. Working with David and the entire production team at McFarland is a sheer joy. I am grateful to all of these good people for their dedication to this project, much as I greatly appreciate the work of two anonymous readers for McFarland. The finished product is not their responsibility, but it bears their fingerprints throughout. They will know where to find me when it's time to return the favor. Returning the favors bestowed on me by my wife, Gerhild, will be beyond my capacities forever. While at first she didn't much like the idea of me writing another book in my retirement, in the end she not only kept encouraging me in my efforts but also became my first and best reader.

Prologue

DURING MY LONG CAREER AS A TEACHER, Washington Irving had been a fixture in my American culture classes for many years. Students, graduate and undergraduate alike, generally took well to Irving's sketches and stories. They even loved "The Legend of Sleepy Hollow," which they could relate to thanks both to the 1999 movie with Johnny Depp and to the 2013 crime/horror series of that name. They likewise were able to make sense of "Rip Van Winkle," engaging with the protagonist's disorientation as well as the fairy-tale style. "Tales of the Alhambra" would make them dreamy, perhaps because I was able to draw on my personal experience from various visits to this enchanted place. I was less successful with "The Devil and Tom Walker," which students found too outlandishly fantastic, and Irving's satirical wit utterly beyond them. As I was then at work on a cultural history of America's money, I was adamant. My students just had to read the story, if only grudgingly. My engagement with the nation's monetary history also meant that a book project on Irving had to be shelved, and I had to content myself with an article on racial and ethnic stereotyping in his writings. Nevertheless, the Irving project did begin to acquire some contours, as vague as they at first were. I was intrigued that Irving had written a five-volume biography of George Washington, a work that engaged him for many years and became his last literary effort, the "crowning effort" of his career.[1] Browsing through the *Complete Works*, I also found that George Washington was in good company. Christopher Columbus, Mahomet, Boabdil, John Jacob Astor, Captain Benjamin Bonneville and, not to forget, Oliver Goldsmith, had also become subjects of Irving's historical biographies.

The question why Irving had chosen such subjects puzzled me. Had he been drawn to the Great Men theory of history? According to that theory, which today has fallen into disrepute but was in great vogue during Irving's lifetime, history is a drama of personalities, centered around individuals imbued with moral qualities that make them molders of history, movers and shakers. Irving saw the publication of Thomas Carlyle's famous book, *On*

Heroes, first published in 1841 and kept in print throughout the century.² He lived through the hype about Napoleon Bonaparte, whom he characterized as a "noble fellow" even after his final defeat at Waterloo, just as he fell for William the Conqueror, Admiral Nelson, whose fleet he saw at Messina in January 1805, Andrew Jackson, Aaron Burr, or, in the 1840s, General Espartero, Spain's tyrannical Regent, and, equally tyrannical, Prime Minister Joaquin Narváez.³ Irving was personally acquainted with a number of military and naval men, raving over Stephen Decatur's naval victory at Algiers, and, in addition, writing sketches of four naval heroes of the War of 1812—James Lawrence, William Burrows, Oliver Hazard Perry, and David Porter.⁴ However, the historical biographies form only part of Irving's oeuvre.

Irving also published a substantial body of writings under pseudonyms or fictitious narrator-figures—most notably, Jonathan Oldstyle, Diedrich Knickerbocker, Geoffrey Crayon, and Fray Antonio Agapida. One can only speculate about Irving's decision to do so, but a reasoned guess is that the quaint, old-fashioned faces that he turned to the world concealed something, as most affectations conceal something eventually, even though they do not at first sight. Irving was terrified of harsh criticism and failure, and so he heaped layer upon layer—real author, fictitious author, narrator, sometimes more than one. As a result, there is no presence in these writings of Irving as a fully developed personality, as if the world had been too much for him. Although Irving's liberal use of pseudonyms may well speak to his love of theatricals, Oldstyle, Knickerbocker, Crayon, and other figures are like so many masks behind which a fragile author could hide, shields with which to protect a delicate and vulnerable self and simultaneously to evoke curiosity about the writer's true identity.

The psychoanalyst James Hillman has called the practice of writing under pseudonyms or fictitious narrator-figures "protective mimicry," describing it as "an *attachment* to something or someone else to which it is echo." Hillman, who is Jungian trained, relates the practice to an "anima-consciousness," by which he means a consciousness that looks inward, one that is devoted, yet labile, generous and generative, yet reserved, shy, shameful, retreating, pure, veiled, a consciousness that does not soar but stays attached, has depth and receptivity, hovers and flutters, butterfly-like, harboring low-flying dreams. In short, it is a consciousness that is made up by feminine personality components.⁵ Reading Hillman, I felt I was on to something, even though I was still wary, for, "A good answer must be reinvented many times from scratch."⁶

And one day I found out what the matter was. The igniting spark was a visit to Austrian artist André Heller's imaginative *ANIMA GARDEN* near Marrakesh, Morocco, in the fall of 2018. This opulent, five-acre garden, which had opened only in 2016,⁷ provided an enchanting walk-through tableau vivant, full of bewitching and, at times, unsettling aromas, of sounds and colors that were at one and the same time harmonious and dissonant. I became enthralled by the garden's playfulness, the boundless nuances of inspiration, magic and wonder, its layout yielding to disinterested pleasure and loveliness. This was an experience that provided nourishment for the soul, joy, healing, and inspiration, while its beauty and sensuality, the intensity of color, aroma, and hearing left the visitor amazed and astonished. All in all, this artificial environment in a desert country is a territory of happiness and inner peace, a magical pasture of ideas.

The companion book to the Anima garden contains a poem generally ascribed to Samuel Taylor Coleridge, "What if you slept":

> What if you slept
> And what if
> In your sleep
> You dreamed
> And what if
> In your dream
> You went to heaven
> And there plucked a strange and beautiful flower
> And what if
> When you awoke
> You had that flower in your hand
> Ah, what then?[8]

When I read the poem, I was instantly reminded of Washington Irving at the Alhambra. Looking, from his window, into the garden of Lindaraxa, he had written to his brother Peter in June 1829: "I have nothing but the sound of water, the humming of bees, and the singing of nightingales to interrupt the profound silence of my abode; and at night, stroll until midnight about the galleries overlooking the garden and the landscape, which are now delicious at night from the brightness of the moon." Small wonder then, that he added, "I am now determined to linger here until I get some writing under way connected with the place, and that shall bear the stamp of real intimacy with the charming scenes described."[9]

It was easy, in the quiet haunt of André Heller's garden, to give myself to daydreaming, to half-dreaming moods of mind, wavering between conscious and unconscious, to musings, inspirations, perhaps even quests. At the same time, it was as if there remained to the perceived images an unknowable, unfathomable depth. Thus, I began to think of the garden as an experimental station for the hereafter, a curative, therapeutic stay for the soul. I'm saying "soul" deliberately, for the name Heller chose for his botanical stage—"*ANIMA*"—in Latin means "soul." But "anima" is also a term that is central to Jungian psychology. The anima, like its masculine counterpart, the animus, is understood as a psychological function that takes on a personality, a personality that behaves as if it were an inner personality, exhibiting traits that are lacking in the outer personality. In this sense, Heller's *"retour du paradis"* constitutes a manifestation of the anima archetype, echoing the image of the artist's "femininity."[10]

André Heller spent his entire fortune (and a considerable one for all that) on his Moroccan garden, resources that he used only too happily, as if they had only waited to be converted into the tools and aids necessary for the project. A commentator once called the garden a "majestic antithesis to a savings agreement."[11] Indeed the place is a wholesome refuge from a dog-eat-dog world, a world of machos, warlords, rogues, autocratic leaders, and political desperadoes, of freebooters and hicks for whom climate change or the Covid-19 pandemic is mere fake news and whose utter indifference to the future of this earth and its inhabitants is enough to make anyone miserable and despairing. The impending environmental and human catastrophe excepting, nineteenth-century America was not much different. In such a world, there simply was no place for Washington Irving, who throughout his life suffered from what he called his "sensibility" and who summed up the American writer's dilemma in the following words: "Unqualified for business in a nation where everyone is busy; devoted to literature where literary leisure is confounded with idleness, the man of letters is almost an insulated being, with few to understand, less to value, and scarcely any to encourage his pursuits."[12]

Those of his contemporaries who did understand, value, and encourage Irving generally found him full of geniality and charm, with more than one professing to love him for his *"bonhomie."*[13] As a writer, too, Irving has been characterized as all sweetness and light, a "gentle humorist" in Henry Wadsworth Longfellow's memorable words.[14] And in a late-nineteenth-century monograph on Irving, Charles Dudley Warner wrote, "His books are wholesome, full of sweetness and charm, of humor without any sting, of amusement without any stain; and their more solid qualities are marred by neither pedantry nor pretension."[15] Even Irving's earlier writings like *Salmagundi* or *A History of New York*, as bitingly satirical and ironic as they are, are completely devoid of malice or hatred. By the same token, his piece on "English Writers on America," which he included in *The Sketch Book*, is a model of conciliatory grace at a time when tensions between Britain and the United States had reached a new height. Irving himself contributed much to the public image of an amiably reasonable disposition, writing, in the preface to *Tales of a Traveller*, that he was "for curing the world by gentle alternatives, not by violent doses; indeed, the patient should never be conscious that he is taking a dose."[16]

Irving's writings, his reputation and image, together with the impressions I took away from the *Anima Garden*, had an afterlife of their own. I dreamed. Slowly a fertile thought would form in my brain. Then no longer a dream but rather a complex idea, the accidental out-birth of "spontaneous variation" in my brain.[17] I realized that Irving, like André Heller, must have been an anima persona, one whose "feminine" style of behavior was characteristic of his ego identity. A "feminine" style of behavior, Jungian analysts would say, is first and foremost characterized by receptivity, by an openness not least towards the irrational, and by an ability to give to events the significance of "soul."[18] For a male anima persona, the relation to the anima is truly unique in that the anima attains a rare degree of reality. This necessarily happens at the expense of the masculine side. Normally in the development of masculine ego-consciousness the feminine aspects are left behind; they become part of the unconscious, waiting to be integrated in the course of a man's lifetime. An anima persona, however, seems unable to identify with his own masculinity. If Irving was such a persona, his conflicted self must become visible, together with attempts to resolve the conflict. As I will try to show, Irving spent his long career as a writer searching for and making visible various forms of masculinity. What he left behind is a veritable gallery of male characters—quaint and old-fashioned narrators like Jonathan Oldstyle, Geoffrey Crayon or Diedrich Knickerbocker, anxious and troubled characters like Ichabod Crane, Rip Van Winkle, Wolfert Webber or Tom Walker, purloined heroes like Columbus, Mahomet, Boabdil, the last of the Moorish sovereigns of Granada, or the residents, past and present, of the Alhambra, Native Americans, fur traders and trappers and western heroes like J.J. Astor and Captain Bonneville, the gentle Oliver Goldsmith and, finally, George Washington, the ultimate American hero.

If the cast of memorable characters in Irving's sketches and stories is practically all male, by the time he arrived in Spain, in 1826, women had ceased being of any real importance to his work, as he eagerly embraced the lives of questing and conquering heroes—real men like Columbus, Mahomet and, above all, George Washington, the protagonists of his historical biographies. It has puzzled (and angered) numerous critics that female characters remain lone exceptions in Irving's writings, and in such as there are—like the Wife, who is all "sweetness and good humour," or the Widow, with her "enduring tenderness [...] to her son"[19]—we will be hard pressed to make out any redemptive or emancipatory powers behind their all-too apparent submissiveness. The same may be said about the "late Margaret Miller Davidson," whose *Biography and Poetical Remains* Irving published in 1841, and which his biographer crudely dismissed as "a devastating proof that Irving had gone quite to seed."[20] On the other end of the spectrum, Dame Van Winkle and Tom Walker's wife are but caricatures, and

Katrina Van Tassel, the object of Ichabod Crane's ill-begotten desires, very much resembles a not-too-bright village coquette. No wonder that Irving has been accused of simply reproducing a frankly avowed system of gender hierarchy, with the "fair sex" under the thumb of the "noble sex."[21] Other critics, in contrast, have tried to exonerate Irving from charges of misogyny, insisting on his hints that he was not suited for male society, that he felt shouldered aside by men and could only flourish and expand his powers in the company of women. Irving, these critics said, would crave women's "tea and sympathy," and rhapsodize over the redemptive powers of marriage against communal breakdown and psychological ruin.[22]

On the other hand, did Irving not simply relocate patriarchy to more secure grounds when he singles out the "proud, hardy, frugal and abstemious" Spanish peasants, whose "half-wild" manner Irving had come to admire during his years in Spain?[23] And when, moreover, in the 1830s these patriarchal Spaniards re-emerged as stereotypical "Noble Savages" on the prairies of his own country? The view that there is a palpable masculine bias in Irving's literary productions cannot be so easily dismissed. The Osages' "Roman countenances" as well as the likable folks represented as Rouseauvian *hommes naturels*, not to mention the significant masculine achievements traits of his other male heroes—his Columbus appears as an exemplar of "what human genius and laudable enterprize may accomplish," while his Washington is said to have been graced by "fewer inequalities and a rarer union of virtues than perhaps ever fell to the lot of one man"—point to principles, mental powers, abstractions, and fixed meanings, including courage, in short, to "spirit." And "spirit" is what "animus" originally meant in Latin, which seems reason enough to explore Irving's male characters in terms of "animus images" or "animus archetypes," born as they were from their author's deeply felt psychological needs.[24]

About a year after my visit to the *Anima Garden*, I had accumulated quite a corpus of materials, even though the thoughts and ideas were still fragmentary and disparate. It was, in fact, not until I was done with my writings on George Washington that I was able to muster the unhurried leisure to tie up all these loose ends as well as to take stock of my mind's "selective industry"[25] that had led me to choose as a topic Irving's search for patterns of achieved masculinity. That was in 2020. The year not only brought stay-at-home orders and the lockdown of libraries but also pushed me to the point when the easy, exhilarating confidence that surrounds the start of any book is followed by those terrible long moments when the words refuse to come and crushing doubts rush in to fill the void. Most of these doubts stemmed from my use of the Jungian concepts of anima and animus. I do not here use these concepts in strictly Jungian terms as descriptions of personal experiences; instead, I use them as notions, as ideas by means of which I'm making observations, lenses through which I try to come to an understanding of Washington Irving and his works.[26] But notwithstanding my engaging in critical phenomenology rather than in empirical phenomenology, in my worst fears I would hear someone saying that, after all, the response to the matters and issues here represented may have just happened to proceed from the given observer's countertransference, that is, from his own entanglement in them, or else from his intellectual extravagance, or both.

It certainly would be intellectually extravagant to posit a fundamental and immutable dualism between male and female, masculine and feminine. Jung was invariably attacked for his intellectual oppositionalism, which would bring him dangerously close to biological determinism.[27] But for Jung, male and female, masculine and feminine were biological metaphors for psychic conditions.[28] He called anima and animus archetypes because he saw them as the essential building blocks in the psychic structure of every man and woman, the basis for instinctive, unlearned behavior patterns that are common to all humankind and that manifest themselves in human consciousness in certain typical ways.[29] Clearly, the concepts of "anima" and "animus" speak to the spirituality of their author, for whom the spiritual world was the real world, while the material world at best was its corrupt shadow. This may seem outlandish, though there is no way to prove that the opposite position, which awards causal priority to the material world, is correct.[30] In this book, I do not see instinctual behavior patterns as exclusively determined by the sexual characteristics they represent. Just as important are the experiences a person has had in the course of his or her life, that is, all kinds of socially and culturally determined behavior patterns which relate intrapsychic dynamics to the social and cultural organization of their production. Yet there were more instances when I would say to myself, is this right? Is this helpful or is it taking me down a blind alley I don't want to end up in? How helpful is it to search for and explain "patterns," even though often when I found one, I was expecting it to flow into and out of the next? Mindful of Irving Berlin's caution against certainties or "historical inevitability," I eventually learned to beware of what appeared like "irresistible rhythms."[31] Especially seductive was the "rhythm" of the gradual evolution of archetypal masculinities in Irving's writings. Upon closer inspection, however, anima-driven sentimentalizations would appear to alternate or exist side by side with figures clothed in the rhetoric of tough masculinity, and more often than not in one and the same work.

Now that the balloon of my mind has been put into its narrow shed, it but remains to spread out my argument, which in rough outline looks something like this: I begin, in Chapter One, by addressing the purportedly "enigmatic quality of Washington Irving's real self."[32] The enigma dissolves once we remind ourselves that this genial and charming man throughout his life retained a decidedly feminized masculinity, enshrined forever in Gilbert Stuart Newton's portrait of 1820, which foregrounds classical traits of what Jungian psychoanalysts call the anima archetype. Irving was dominated by the anima to such an extent that he remained out of touch with his masculine strength. Stuck in the mold of an anima-ego, he rejected the images of manhood that were projected upon him, by his father, the first representative of the animus image the child encounters, as well as by society at large. The traumatic conflict between inner self and socially sanctioned self would have a paralyzing effect on most people. But Irving was an artist and thus took inspiration to heightened creativity. The animus images projected upon him became his masculine "shadow," his unwanted and unloved characteristics. Irving would work through them in his writings, which we may see as self-representations of internal psychic processes. Altogether, the line-up of male figures in his writings—his masculine archetypal images—served not so much to articulate his social and political ideals as to transform a sense of his own precarious form of male selfhood, his imperfectly realized masculinity, together with his purportedly female defects. Additionally, the transformation included the very profession Irving had chosen for himself, writing, which at the time was generally seen as a manipulative manifestation of effeminacy.

Chapter Two begins with Irving's literary debut at age twenty, as Jonathan Oldstyle, which reflects both the author's "theatrical" temperament and his easy-going sense of humor. In 1807, Irving wrote as "Will Wizard, Esq.," commenting on the stage, morals, manners, and politics for *Salmagundi*. No less satirical, albeit more serious was *A History of New York*. Written and published under the pseudonym of Diedrich Knickerbocker in 1809, the book became a literary sensation. In a Swiftean vein, it satirizes Thomas Jefferson in the description of William Kieft, second governor of New Amsterdam. At the time Irving's political leanings were mildly federalist and, like many Federalists, he looked critically upon Jefferson's anti-urban, anti-speculative creed, much as he distrusted the idealistic Jeffersonian sensibility that sought to give political power also to the underclasses. By 1813, Irving's mood had shifted. He had begun to fear and despise "the all pervading commonplace" in "a nation where every one is busy."[33] In compensation for the desperate competitiveness he saw around him, Irving began to incorporate in his writings various redemptive ideals of manhood, which mostly he drew from English models—sentimentalism, Shandyism, the polite and satirical models he found in Joseph Addison, with a dose of Jonathan Swift, and all under genteel control. These models had long been defunct in England, though they lingered on in America. As masculine archetypes, these residual figures—especially Squire Bracebridge and

Geoffrey Crayon—are expressive of a sense of decline and nostalgia for an anterior moment when masculinity seemed secure and unscathed by competitive individualism and naked self-interest. These figures constitute both a fantasied retreat from and a compensatory response to the forces of the new economy, of commerce and market corruption, even though the fantasy could offer, at best, partial or temporary comfort.

By the time of the *Sketch Book*, entrepreneurial capitalism was beginning to effect new relations to property and money and, concomitantly, to spawn new classes of people whose property consisted not of land and other tangible assets but rather of paper and credit. With these self-made men came unstable and volatile forms of personality. Economic success or the lack thereof no longer was a matter of one's station in life; instead, success and, more importantly, failure redounded to the individual.[34] In the culture, the most dramatic representations of the faith that constructs economic striving as a moral imperative were anxious and troubled masculinities. In Irving's writings, these masculinities appear as some of his best-known characters, most notably Rip Van Winkle, Ichabod Crane and, to a lesser extent, Tom Walker and Wolfert Webber. They faithfully register the psychological and human costs of an ideology centered on economic ambition as the hallmark of the good life. Chapter Three links Irving's writings to the increasingly nervous, anxious, hysterical, even panicky form of masculinity emerging in early nineteenth-century America.

Masculine archetypes of the like of Crayon or Bracebridge could offer, at best, partial or temporary comfort in view of the evils of commerce and market corruption. Hence Irving had to turn elsewhere in order to transform the desperate competitiveness he saw around him. Chapter Four leads us to Spain, where Irving lived from 1826 and which provided him with another chance to mining the past. Bringing together romance and history allowed Irving both to paint Spain as a "proud, magnificent civilization," thus to latch on to the knightly ideal of chivalry, and to express his disgust at utilitarian modern civilization. His writings from that period are chockfull of chivalric masculinities. The noble qualities he ascribed to his heroes—such as the courage, moral restraint, and strong will of a Christopher Columbus—correspond to an ideal or complete vision of masculinity. Elsewhere in his Spanish period, Irving and his alter ego, Geoffrey Crayon, merge into what might be called the archetypal romantic tourist, indulging in the charms of storied and poetical association.

For the subjects of antebellum America, the world of established hierarchies and stability, of civilized urbanity and perfection, of patrician refinement and elegance, no longer existed. In its stead, there now was a dynamic and increasingly aggressive world of individual liberty and acquired status. That world belonged to professional, bureaucratic and commercial middle classes—classes which Irving, who always aspired to be a well-heeled gentleman, rarely if ever felt at home in. Nevertheless, he approvingly, albeit erringly, portrayed a typical representative of the new middle classes in his book on John Jacob Astor and the fur trade. The portrayal did nothing to dispel Irving's concerns about masculine achievement. Altogether in his western writings—the subject of Chapter Five—Irving showed a profound ambivalence about the course of American history and the constituent elements of an American identity. His writings may seem imperialist, though they nonetheless represent a significant clue to a society that was itself absorbed in imperialist conquest. Irving thematized that conquest also in his book on Captain Bonneville, and he received a first-hand experience on the prairies, where he had hoped to find the genuine article as he romantically embraced the concept of the natural man. If he found masculine achievement in various Indigenous people, his fellow Americans of the frontier were utterly unsuitable as archetypes of achieved masculinity.

Irving already had scoured England and Spain, reinventing a form of aristocratic patriarchy in a bid to compensate for the loss of idyllic relations and traditional simplicities. In this project, he typically anchored achieved manhood in various pasts. Each of these pasts served as an anterior moment when masculinity seemed secure, though as I show in Chapter Six, none more than the national past. By casting his epic biography of George Washington in the form of a dramatic narrative in the American romantic tradition, Irving constructed an ideal vision of masculine achievement in the realm of truth and unswerving principles. His Washington, who outmasculinizes all other Irvinian archetypes, takes a heroic stand against an unjust colonial regime and, just as heroically, against incompetent and self-serving politicians, disgruntled farmers, factions in his cabinet, and divisiveness in the nation at large. The very words and phrases Irving used in his final portrayal of America's revolutionary hero and first president—"a rarer union of virtues," "example," "paternal appeal"[35]—speak to an intensified ideology of manhood, one that celebrates a manliness not to be found in a world dominated by "bullyboys" who set the pace and the model for manhood in the marketplace and whom the social structure no longer restrained.[36] As a compensatory response to perceived threats of dispossession, loss, bruising defeats, and humiliation, George Washington's archetypal masculinity provided genteel readers with moral simplicities to steer their lives by, if not to save the entire nation, which by the time the final volume of *Life of George Washington* was published already was at the brink of Civil War.

This book, which has taken on the lineaments of a "deep biography,"[37] explores Washington Irving's jostling with ideologies of manhood in a highly conflicted emotional drama about the successful life. Like other men who were becoming frustrated by efforts to keep up with the relentless pressure to modernize, Irving was obsessed with being a man, and, suffering from his perceived femininity, throughout his career as a writer was questing for the self-image of a man whose masculinity seemed secure. He finally found it in George Washington, whose image allowed him to come to terms with his own purportedly "female" defects, especially his shyness and uncertainty, which was in perpetual conflict with the confident public image he habitually projected or felt he had to project. In the Epilogue, I summarize Irving's visions of achieved manhood as a writer's way of overcoming, thanks to his creative powers, the constellated predicaments of his inner life. These predicaments were rooted both in Irving's biography and in the collective problems of the culture surrounding him. Altogether, Irving had to cope with his personal as well as his writerly fears of not somehow being able to win a place among other men, fears of his own "female" defects as well as rage against the relentlessly modernizing United States and against the country's social structure. Though a participant himself, Irving was deeply suspicious of the marketplace where the Irving family business had failed and where he himself had almost failed as a writer (or had in fact, as he purportedly had "written himself out" by the 1820s). Always uneasy about the forced compromises and self-diminishments of middle-class life, once the excitement of his return home in 1832 had worn off he was merely disgusted by "the all pervading commonplace," denouncing it as his country's "curse."[38]

ONE

Anima Consciousness and Archetypal Masculinities

In 1809, Washington Irving turned twenty-seven. What was he to do with his life? How was he to make a living? He had published, had achieved a measure of fame, but this was not yet the time for professional writers. Faced with the question about what *sort* of man he wished to be, he transferred to the offices of Judge Josiah Hoffman, a former attorney general of New York, a leading New York federalist, and a wealthy landowner and real estate speculator. Irving was unenthusiastic about becoming a lawyer, but he put his shoulder to the wheel, not least because he had decided he wanted to marry Matilda Hoffman, the judge's younger daughter. A lawyer at least was a profession, unlike an existence as a writer, and it also was a role one played in social life. Choice of an occupation then was fraught with latent gender meaning. The law, as well as politics and business, at the time were marked "male," but a career as a writer, in what Irving called the "labour of headwork," was generally seen as a manipulative manifestation of effeminacy. Poetry was more highly regarded, and the masculinity of the great English Romantics (Wordsworth, Coleridge, Shelley, Byron) was never in dispute. Novels, however, were the domain of women, in England especially, where women had made the Gothic mode their own. An American male, self-convicted of feminine qualities, thus was usually also troubled by fears that he might be a failure, dysfunctional, even non-existent.[1]

Irving loathed studying law and was admitted to the bar and, later, accepted into his brother Peter's law office only by acts of mercy. And business? "By all the martyrs of Grub Street," he wrote his friend Henry Brevoort, "I'd sooner live in a garret, and starve into the bargain, than follow so sordid dusty, and soul-killing a way of life, though certain it would make me as rich as Croesus, or John Jacob Astor himself!"[2] Irving was utterly disinclined to bind his "*indolent and restive habits* to the plodding routine of traffic."[3] Clearly, then, business and the law were diametrically opposed to his innermost life, the less conscious part of himself. That life was dominated by the "anima," his inner "femininity," to use the Jungian terms,[4] so much so that it thwarted all his good intentions to become a respected man of the law or a stolid businessman.

Jungian psychoanalysis has it that we derive our personality, or, rather, our consciousness of ourselves as a personality "primarily through the influence of quasi-personal archetypes."[5] Archetypes can be understood as symbols, ideal examples, models, prototypes, or patterns of a set of psychic qualities and characteristics. They belong to the individual consciousness as well as to the collective unconscious, forming a link between the personal and the impersonal, the conscious and the unconscious. Archetypes are impersonal, unvisualized structures that manifest themselves only through the internal, subjective awareness, that is, through introspection, of images and ideas, as well as of ritualistic gestures. Put more simply, archetypes map unconscious events onto types or patterns of behavior which, once they become conscious, take the form of images.[6] According to Jung, one archetype is feminine and the other masculine, hence anima and animus. With the majority of men, the anima archetype is an *un*conscious femininity, unconscious because the feminine is left behind in the development of masculine ego-consciousness. There are, however, exceptions, most notably among writers and artists. For these men, the inner anima often acquires an unusual degree of reality. Such men, C.G. Jung wrote, are "characterized by identity with the anima."[7]

When the anima enters conscious personality, it becomes visible in overt social behavior, which necessarily manifests itself in a variety of contrasexual traits. Washington Irving was no exception. According to his biographer, Irving loved theatricality, loved to perform, go to the theater and to the opera. He also tried himself at a few pieces of drama, including a translation into English of Carl Maria von Weber's 1821 opera *Der Freischütz* (*The Marksman* or *The Freeshooter*).[8] Some of the dramas were turned into (unsuccessful) plays, and Irving, when he was living in Paris, even saw some of his characters in both amateur and professional theatricals. He gave up theatrical experiments only when his financial needs became too overwhelming. Still, he considered, about 1824–25, to become a dramatist himself.[9] There is even a factual connection to opera, pointed out by Stanley Williams, who hints at the possibility that Irving, through "The Phantom Ship," a tale collected in *Bracebridge Hall* of 1822, helped to suggest Richard Wagner's *Der fliegende Holländer* (*The Flying Dutchman*).[10]

Irving's penchant for theatricality also connects to his cravings for admiration, applause, and praise. If he invented, lived into, or even played other characters, he did so from a firm belief that these characters were more admirable than himself. No wonder that he often hid behind his own creations, making use of "protective mimicry," a practice that directly relates to his "anima-consciousness."[11] Anima-consciousness is deeply receptive; it looks inward; it is a consciousness that does not soar but stays attached. In this regard, inventing other characters or hiding behind them really is a search for one's true self. What writers (as well as actors or artists in general) rarely, if ever, understand is that all of their creations have always existed within themselves. If this were not so, the psychoanalyst Erika Freeman remarked, they would not be able to play them or create them in words.[12] It took Washington Irving almost a lifetime to figure that out, if he ever did.

There is another aspect to anima-consciousness. It is devoted, yet labile, generous and generative, yet reserved, shy, shameful, retreating, pure, veiled; it has depth and receptivity, it hovers and flutters, butterfly-like, harboring low-flying dreams.[13] To C.G. Jung, a personality governed by anima-consciousness is "gushing, soulful, aesthetic, oversensitive, etc.— in a word, *effeminate*."[14] Irving's apparent effeminacy—or, in more cautious terms, androgyny[15]—is captured paradigmatically in various paintings. One is a portrait which John Wesley Jarvis took in 1809, shortly after the untimely death of Matilda Hoffman. According to Pierre Munro Irving, who saw it at his uncle's house at Sunnyside, the portrait was "remarkable for its expression of pensive refinement."[16] The other portrait worth mentioning in this context is Gilbert Stuart Newton's of 1820, which shows Irving at age 37. The vivid look and the tousled hair then were the trademark of the romantic artist; the fur-lined overcoat he's wearing is green, the life-color, the anima color.[17]

Irving had been sent to England in 1815 to supervise the Liverpool branch of the family business, which had suffered significant losses due to the embargoes during the War of 1812. He did his best to salvage the company, which nevertheless went bankrupt in 1819, a belated casualty of the war and a great blow to Irving. The author of the farcical *History of New York* and also well known for *Salmagundi*, he now was jobless, with little prospect of employment. Brother William therefore urged him to return to America, waving the prospect of political appointment for him (another "male" pursuit). Washington, claiming that his talents were "merely literary,"[18] turns down the offer, stays in Europe, where he makes any number of friends, among them the painters Charles R. Leslie and Gilbert Stuart Newton.[19] Newton was a nephew of Gilbert Stuart, famous for his portrait of George Washington, the one that still stares at us from the $1 bill. Irving loved Newton's portrait, and he later kept it in his Sunnyside house. From the beginning, he admired the painter's gift for seeing colors, which makes Newton's portrait so unlike the one done in 1833 by Irving's other friend, Leslie, which gives a more relaxed and slightly melancholic image, more realistic perhaps, more mature, and truer to Irving's public image as a cultivated Man of Feeling, Mackenzie-like.[20] Newton's portrait, in contrast, is more energetic, even enthusiastic, and it makes Irving look as if he were given to "camping"—which is an old slang word for making a parade of effeminacy.

Effeminacy and effeminate, the adjective related to it, means visible in feminine forms. Jungian psychoanalysts think about these forms as anima projections or, more specifically, projections of the anima archetype. This does not mean that "the archetype is constituted like that *in itself*."[21] Although anthropomorphic, the feminine archetype is an impersonal rather than a personal archetype of the psyche. Jungian tradition therefore speaks of "the anima" (as well as of "the animus") rather than of "my anima" or "my animus."[22] The anima is, then, a form of psychic life, an "*a priori* element in [a person's] moods, reactions, impulses, and whatever else is spontaneous in psychic life. It is something that lives of itself, that makes us live; it is a life behind consciousness that cannot be completely integrated with it, but from which, on the contrary, consciousness arises."[23]

Both the Jarvis and the Newton portraits foreground classic traits of the anima archetype, showing forth the reality of the anima to an otherwise unbelieving world. The anima is visible not only in Irving's dress, but also in a variety of animatic compass points—in his mannerisms, his sensitiveness and gentleness, his "pleasant humor" and "melancholy tenderness" as well as in his "touches of sentiment."[24] These characterizations date from 1859, following Irving's death. A generation earlier, Emily Foster, Irving's Dresden flame of 1823 (who soon after became Mrs. Fuller), found him "most interesting, dark, hair of a man of genius waving, silky, & black, gray eyes full of various feeling, & an amiable smile." Emily's sister, Flora Foster (later Mrs. Dawson), too found Irving's smile "one of the sweetest I know, but he can look very, very sad [...] oppressed with morbid feelings." Above all, she recalled him as "an admirable *relater*," a man who made the entire family feel. "Never beat a more kindly heart than his."[25]

Irving knew that one must look with one's heart in order to see to the bottom of the soul. He had a warm, open ability to suspend judgment and take people at their own valuation, finding friendliness wherever he went. Like Henry Mackenzie's Man of Feeling or his own Dolph Heyliger, whose good nature is enough to secure a measure of felicity life, Irving embodied a "softened masculinity." As a seasoned traveler, his method mostly relied on chance, the accident of the road, bestowing dignity, respect, spirituality, and love to those he chanced upon. He also had a thoroughly empathetic feeling into other cultures and their differences—the Dutch in his native Hudson Valley, English country squires, the Spanish peasantry, the French along the Mississippi, the Native Americans out west. Last but not least, he fed his feeling for other cultures through the study of folktales, legends, and myths, as well as his interest in history, in all kinds of pasts, which he attempted to recover through his work, trying to save us, as Andrew Burstein remarked, "from despair."[26]

To the extent that Irving's sense of personal identity was rooted in the anima, the result was a kind of feminized male ego in which the anima played a dominant role. There is, however, also a dangerous, menacing, even demonic side to an anima-ego, ready to unleash forces one is unable to control. As Jung suggested, the anima makes us not more conscious but less, flourishing in states of drowsiness and mood, illusions and follies, leading us to chasing ephemera, even inviting madness. Succumbing to the power of the anima is, in a way, comparable to emasculation.[27] And, on occasion Jung even discusses male homosexuality as anima identification.[28] Unsurprisingly perhaps, critics have invariably tried to trace at least a latent homosexuality in Washington Irving.[29] The evidence that is customarily cited is the fact that following the death, in 1809, of Matilda Hoffman, the young woman he had thought of marrying, Irving never again had a serious relationship with a woman.

Scholars have been extremely fond of mulling over the question whether Irving's life-long bachelorhood was caused by grief, or whether he simply used Matilda's death as a ruse, when in actual fact he must have been relieved that he was "off the hook." Matilda's early death at age seventeen occasioned a mere bald diary entry for 1809, "Mat. Died in April," a sixteen-page manuscript fragment written in Dresden in 1823, in which he vents his grief to Mrs. Foster and her daughters, in particular Emily, and a brief lament, inserted into his French journal at a later time: "She died in the flower of her youth & of mine but she has lived for me ever since in all woman kind."[30] Following Matilda's death, Irving left New York for the Van Ness estate at Kinderhook. When he returned in the summer, "the poignancy of his grief had worn away," his nephew wrote much later, though his face still "retained the trace of melancholy feelings."[31] This may well have been so, but Irving also sat down to write *A History of New York*, a literary hoax under the authorship of the fictitious Diedrich Knickerbocker, a comic old bachelor and whimsical crank. It is impossible to determine whether Irving applied himself to *A History* in order to recover from grief, whether "off the hook" meant that he now was free to pursue his literary career, or whether he really was a homosexual, the "gay bachelor."[32]

There is precious little evidence of Irving really having been a "gay bachelor." To be sure, he had any number of male friends. But the channels of intimacy between men were different then, as were notions of homoerotic contact.[33] Moreover, wherever Irving went, in Europe or in America, it was the women he looked at most closely and lovingly. And there were attachments galore throughout Irving's life to other women—an inconclusive list would contain Mary Fairlie of New York, the original of "Sophie Sparkle" in *Salmagundi*; Rebecca Gratz in Philadelphia; or Jean Jeffrey Renwick. Romantic story and gossip also connected Irving—the eligible and charming bachelor—with the Empress Maria Louisa, Theodosia Burr (Aaron Burr's pampered daughter), Madame de Bergh, Madame de Staël, Antoinette Bolviller, or Mary Godwin Shelley, the poet's widow (whose interest in him he scorned).[34] These were lively, independent women of character and substance, women to flirt or dance with, but not women to love or marry. Of course, there were such women, but what Irving really sought in women was "innocent perfection." Only by giving himself over to a retrogressive pull, Andrew Burstein suggests, could Irving fantasize about marrying them.[35] Such fantasies reveal that Irving had found a relation to the inner anima, to his own femininity, and had ceased to project the anima upon real women.[36] A final point. As eligible and charming Irving was as a bachelor, his conservative nature told him that he lacked the financial resources for setting up in marriage. As he wrote to his sister Sarah in 1842, he had "no great idea of bachelorhood," but had remained single, not through "choice" but through "providence," which had "thwarted the warm wishes of my heart."[37]

While a discussion of Irving's purported homosexuality, whether latent or not, does not lead anywhere, a discussion of his bachelor status might be fruitful, insofar as it resolved the dominant projection of the anima to the point when it became Irving's ego identification. To fully accept the anima would have been difficult, as it would have entailed taking up something that he had learned to consider inferior, if not dangerous. A bachelor did not then carry quite such an opprobrium. A bachelor in the nineteenth century was "a liminal figure," one who could either be critiqued as a failure from a heteronormative perspective or celebrated as an exemplar of individualism and, by extension, as an authoritative cultural commentator.[38] In sociological terms, a bachelor, unlike a man or a woman, had no practical function. Therefore, bachelorhood could lend itself to authorship as a form of surrogate indispensability, and the "bachelor aesthetic" of Irving's writings especially of the 1820s testifies to this. As for Irving himself, who in 1829 declared himself "an absolute old Bachelor," he was always at risk of being most "*uncharitably* charged" with all kinds of "rusty unaccommodating habits."[39] His insistence that he had remained a bachelor not through "choice" but through "providence," leaving him lonely and painfully unmarried, therefore should be seen as a moralistic parable, an example of the "bachelor sentimentalism" current at the time.[40]

"There is no character in the comedy of human life that is more difficult to play well, than that of an old Bachelor," Irving wrote in a sketch called "Bachelors."[41] The messiness of the bachelor image shows the extent to which Irving's gender performance was at odds, or at least confused. We might even say that his self was bipolar. On one hand there was the feminine or effeminate style in his behavior, which, contrary to nineteenth-century gender norms, constituted Irving's actual ego identity. On the other hand, there was his literary output, which focused on manhood and masculine achievement. Manhood and masculine achievement should be seen as Irving's ineradicable masculine "shadow," his undeveloped characteristics, which could have become part of his conscious self but which he rarely acknowledged and often rejected. (More of that anon.) A letter he wrote home from his first European journey bears out this fundamental conflict. The self-reliance imposed on him on the trip, he wrote, would "tend to forming that manliness and independence of character which it has ever been my ambition to acquire."[42] The braggadocio as well as the overblown stories about attending lectures on "botany, chemistry, and different other branches of science" did not fool brother William. Washington had raved too much about the Scala in Milan, and he had waxed equally enthusiastic about the abundance of theaters and operas in Paris and, later, in London.[43] William saw only too clearly that Washington's *real* motivation was "good company," an "evil" that "is now without remedy."[44]

The "evil" that allegedly was "without remedy" was, of course, Irving's anima-consciousness, forever at odds with social demands, the pressure to "act like a man." Manhood, after all, is not simply a reflection of an irreducible core of sexual identity but is, rather, the approved way of being an adult male in a given society. Being a man, for better or worse, means being socially useful. Irving's yearning for "manliness and independence of character" thus correlates with a social imperative that was deeply ingrained in his male consciousness and in perpetual conflict with the feminine components of his personality.[45] By assuming that manhood ideologies are adaptations to social environments, we also must acknowledge that whatever archetypes there are in the male image (Irving's own as well as the images he made up in his writings), they are largely culturally constructed as symbolic systems.

We see things differently if we focus on individual self-identity or on intrapsychic processes. For Jung, traits that belong to a manhood ideology translate into a man's ego. Behind the ego is the animus, standing in as the ego's archetype. The ego may be wise, heroic, hardworking, physically powerful, or courageous in *content*, but as a psychic *function* it relates to the animus. There is a caveat, though: the ego cannot have a valid identity of its own. Rather, it is bound up in tandem with the anima, the soul, the lunar consciousness, passiveness, receptivity, the feminine. In this sense, anima and animus are bound up as a pair, even a "divine pair [...] the divine syzygy [...] 'gods' in fact."[46] Is this what Irving had sensed when, borrowing from Shakespeare's *Hamlet*, he ruminated about "the divinity that dwells in us"?[47] Be that as it may, in Irving's case manhood and masculine achievement were *un*developed and *un*acknowledged characteristics, and thus should be seen as his ineradicable masculine "shadow." The "shadow" is generally described as all those characteristics that a person wishes to hide from others as well as from himself or herself, hence what is morally repressed. Of course, one may project the shadow, so that an individual sees his or her own hidden features in another person, whether real or imagined.[48] Yet as Jung also said, individuation, that life-long process leading a human being to the unification of his or her personality, requires the integration of one's shadow, whether masculine or feminine.[49] Elsewhere, Jung uses "recognition" for integration.[50] He also speaks of "relativizing" the unconscious, making it conscious so that it is no longer unknown (although it at the same time remains unknowable).[51] For a writer like Irving, this meant integrating (recognizing, relativizing) his unwanted, suppressed masculinity by giving it a satisfactory shape through writing and, in doing so, winning a place among other men.

In order to achieve integration, various ritual processes offer themselves. One such process is "active imagination." Technically, "active imagination" is a conscious, focused way of assimilating unconscious content into a wakeful state. The idea, Jung wrote, is to bring into focus an image, a voice, or a figure of one's inner world and then to enter into interaction with that image, voice, or figure.[52] These images, voices, or figures of one's inner world constitute archetypal contents. Such contents, Jung argued, express themselves predominantly in metaphors so that their meaning (the "unknown third thing") can make an appearance, can become subject to the conscious self only "in the course of amplification," that is, through the use of the use of mythic, historical, and cultural parallels. "Amplification" thus is a way of thinking that proceeds by way of analogy, parallel and imaginative elaboration.[53] It can take the form of dialogue, of arguing with oneself, or else of writing down one's thoughts, the voices one hears, or the images one sees in the course of what Jung described as a "fantasy journey."[54] A related technique is "admiration," that is, to establish contact with men "we can look up to." Such men are not always available, but we can "read their biographies and become familiar with their words and deeds."[55] Another psychoanalytical tool for working with one's unconscious is "acting 'as if,'" that is, getting into a character, acting like the character, or moving and talking like that character. In real life, it might mean acting like a selfless and wise king even if one is feeling lousy—that is, following a "fake it until you make it" philosophy.[56]

"Active imagination," "invocation," "admiration," and "acting 'as if'" give reality to interaction with the unconscious, enabling us to reconstruct personal belief, "psychological faith," that is, a belief in a personified world.[57] All these techniques rely on what Jung called the "spontaneous amplification of the archetypes," and they suited only too well Irving's "temperamental substitution of dreams for realities," as Stanley Williams disparagingly wrote.[58] Put more benignly, Irving became Irving through working with his unconscious, what he understood as "realis[ing] daydreams and turn[ing] a shadow into substance."[59] Giving life to voices and images, acting as if he were Knickerbocker or Crayon, invoking and deeply admiring George Washington led to psychological faith and, consequently, to a sense of personality. There is an intriguing passage in a letter Irving wrote to his brother Peter in 1829: "In all my writings I have to be governed by a certain tact which I cannot well explain. I feel how a thing ought to be done and how I can render it effective, and if I go counter to this feeling I am likely to come off lamely; yet I cannot reduce this feeling to any rule or maxim by which I can make my plan comprehended in its essential points by others."[60] And how should he? The "feeling" Irving seems unable to put into rational language belongs to a transient world, to those "half-dreaming moods of mind" he refers to in one of his earlier sketches.[61]

In "certain half-dreaming moods of mind," the passage runs, "we may indulge our reveries and build our air-castles undisturbed."[62] What Irving describes here is an experience of self-hypnosis, an experience that facilitates tapping into the unconscious.[63] Some of these "dreams" still exist at the moment of awakening, telling us that internal stimuli, as aids to the conscious imagination, represent a part of us that we should not dismiss as irrelevant.[64] In Irving's instance, it would have been the contents of the psychological function of the animus that he brought to light, into words, into personified figures.[65] These personifications speak to Irving's constructive way of dealing with his own shortcomings; they were operational, assertive, creative, in short, inspirational. Unsurprisingly, therefore, Irving felt that the figures he created were no longer fantasies but were, rather, "dreams turned into realities."[66] As he lived into his characters, they became individualized into distinct personalities. In his fictional writings, he took his fantasies to shift attention from the ordinary flow of reality, the ugly manhood he perceived around him. There would be lampooning of middle-class New Yorkers, political satire, attacks on money-grubbing Yankees; also there would be loving descriptions of what was attractive in England, and, not to forget, eulogies of "dear old romantic Spain." In his historical biographies, fantasy too made him act, not as a sober and rational historian, but by way of recreating history imaginatively. Irving's refusal to sacrifice masculine archetypes to recorded events eventually transformed his ensemble of historic characters into "great men," heroes, larger-than-life figures whose masculine achievements he commemorated and celebrated. As Jung once said, "In his real form [the animus] is a hero, there is something divine about him."⁶⁷

Lest this appear as too much psychoanalytical lingo, let's go back to Shakespeare, who, Irving remarked late in his life, "has a phrase for everything."⁶⁸ Towards the end of *A Midsummer Night's Dream*, Theseus, Duke of Athens, delivers some potent lines about the imagination:

> The poet's eye, in a fine frenzy rolling,
> Doth glance from heaven to earth, from earth to heaven;
> And, as imagination bodies forth
> The forms of things unknown, the poet's pen
> Turns them to shapes, and gives to airy nothing
> A local habitation and a name.⁶⁹

Never mind that Theseus, the rationalist, does not think too highly of the imagination's worth and importance, pronouncing that, "The lunatic, the lover, and the poet, / Are of imagination all compact."⁷⁰ Shakespeare's own ironic distance from such thoughts is evident from the fact that Theseus is not having the final word, which is given to the King and Queen of the Fairies.

Irving too wanted to "look at things poetically, rather than politically," as Geoffrey Crayon, "the author," states in *Bracebridge Hall*, adding that his "only aim" was "to paint characters and manners. I am no politician."⁷¹ Irving's purpose thus seems clear. Techniques such as "active imagination," "invocation," "admiration," and "acting 'as if'" became decisive factors in the process of integration, of resolving his inability to identify with his own masculinity. We know the result—all kinds of masculine archetypes who populate Irving's writings as so many "shapes" from "airy nothing" given "local habitation and name." Yet archetypes are not just elicited by use of the imagination. They may also be projected under the impact of exterior events, they may manifest themselves in connection with events of one's innermost life, or they may appear in dreams.⁷² There are no records of Irving's dreams, though he did reveal much about his innermost life, his morbid sensitiveness, streaks of depression and what he once described as "a melancholy that corrodes the spirits & seems to rust all the springs of mental energy."⁷³

As for exterior events, there were negative ones such as the hostile reviews of *Tales of a Traveller*, but also literary influences such as Addison's *Spectator* essays, Oliver Goldsmith, Henry Mackenzie's *The Man of Feeling*, Sir Walter Scott's historical romances, histories of the wars on the Spanish peninsula, or the biographies of George Washington, John Marshall's or Jared Sparks's. In each instance, Irving's male figures, although fantasies, were real psychic processes that were happening to him personally. Of course, as a writer he would look on from outside, yet at same time he was an active figure in whatever drama was unfolding, "just as if [he] were one of the fantasy figures."[74] As we will see, almost all of these instantiations of archetypal masculinity were but adumbrations, not of Irving himself but of how he did not want to be or—especially with George Washington—of what he wanted to be, of his ideal self, as a hero, befitting high drama.

Working with one's unconscious is hard work, requiring a lot of discipline. The journals Irving kept for many years testify to this. And so, of course, do his published works. His tales, histories, biographies and legends are elegantly written, and while Irving made it all look easy, it had always been the result of patient and diligent labor. "I should like," he wrote to Henry Brevoort, "to write occasionally for my amusement, and to have the power of throwing my writings either into my portfolio, or into the fire. I enjoy the first sketching down of my ideas, but the correcting and preparing them for the press is irksome, and publishing is detestable."[75] In fact, writing rarely flowed with ease; inspiration often was a struggle, and there were long periods of writer's block. Nor were there any preeminent American men of letters to flatter and curry favors from. But what about Irving the man?

Many of Irving's contemporaries saw in him a talented, charming, and easygoing man of letters, a wealthy bachelor and gentleman, though that was only the image he projected or felt he had to project to the public. Irving also was gushing, soulful, receptive, aesthetic and, above all, oversensitive. But often enough he was petty and jealous, erratic and moody, a lazy malcontent and loiterer who was utterly unable to make up his mind. The essayist Donald Grant Mitchell, at the centennial celebration of Irving's birth in 1883 came forth with the following account: "At times— rare times, it is true—I have seen this most amiable gentleman manifest a little of that restive choler which sometimes flamed up in William the Testy,—not long-lived, not deliberate—, but a little human blaze, of impatience at something gone awry."[76] In the account of Irving's overprotective nephew, Pierre Munro Irving, this estimate is still much more restrained: "An impatience of restraint, a love of leisure and of ample freedom, a hatred of all tasks upon time or talent, were characteristic of the author, and would no doubt incline him at first to chafe at these trammels of official station, which he was bound to respect, and would not willingly slight."[77]

Overall, then, as a character Irving seems to just lend himself to becoming the subject of an emotional history. Yet the "enigmatic quality of Irving's real self," which made at least one of his later editors throw up his hands in despair, seems much less enigmatic if we bear in mind that Irving throughout his life retained his feminized masculinity, remaining out of touch with his masculine strength because he was dominated by the anima.⁷⁸ Irving's apparent effeminacy (or rather, his insufficiently developed masculine ego) was, I am suggesting, his "basic fault," the conflict he had to work on throughout his life.⁷⁹ Irving may not have been aware that the anima belonged to him as his feminine personality components; or else, he may have found it difficult to relate to the inner anima, his own femininity. It was as if to escape the woman within that he joined the New York State Militia after the British invasion of Washington, DC, in August 1814.⁸⁰

Clearly, then, there existed a compensatory relationship between the persona, the image Irving presented to the world, and his inner life.⁸¹ As a result, we have all kinds of questing and conquering heroes. These heroes were projections of Irving's unconscious, symbols of transformation, evidence of the close link between compensatory contents and psychological self-guidance.⁸² The figures of achieved masculinity Irving created may have been guides, torchbearers who point or lead the way,⁸³ yet Irving for the most part was unable or unwilling to follow, to fully immerse himself in their world. They merely represent the totality and wholeness that Irving the man never achieved. What remained was a longing for wholeness, for significant masculine achievement and responsible social maturity, for winning a place among other men. On hindsight, Irving's career as a writer resembles a kind of *bildungsroman*, a process of intellectual and emotional development in which any number of imagined masculinities unfold themselves. It is even possible to discern something of a trajectory, if not an evolutionary history, albeit a pretty checkered and uneven one, of his masculine archetypes. At the beginning there is, necessarily, the typical pattern of conflict followed by resistance, the setting of boundaries and the creation of distance. The trajectory or arc therefore begins with rather derivative and unimaginative shapes resembling theatrical stock characters, together with troubled and anxious masculinities. More formative and creative masculinities were to follow, which became fully developed and projected onto historical persons after the personal crisis he went through in the early 1820s. But all these figures, be they sentimental men of feeling, dysfunctional shadows or figures clothed in the rhetoric of tough masculinity, speak to Irving's deep need to integrate into himself (and, on occasion, ward off) what his creations represented.

Scholars have repeatedly described Irving's career in terms of a "quest" or "pilgrimage" of some kind. Stanley Williams, for instance, explains Irving's extensive travels as a quest for suitable material that he could use in his writings, traveling on once he had harvested a country, a mere "prospector on the trail of literary gold."⁸⁴ In contrast, Jeffrey Rubin-Dorsky sees Irving's European travels as a form of "psychological pilgrimage."⁸⁵ But what pilgrimage? What quest? And why? For Rubin-Dorsky, Irving's European years present an Eriksonian "identity crisis" of searching for a lost home.

Traumatized by the ruin of the family business, Irving belonged "to no real place in time," and so became a "displaced self adrift in a mutable world."[86] The conjunction of travel and writing was not accidental. It made it possible for Irving to build his career as a writer on all kinds of evasion—evasion of his country, of his own masculinity, of his financial embarrassments, and of his occupation itself. There are numerous instances of Irving's defensive insistence of being an American despite the fact of his living abroad; there are also numerous instances of his hiding behind a narrator-persona; and there are, finally, numerous instances of his pretending to be an amateur rather than a professional writer, feigning surprise in the face of success.[87]

Yet despite, or even because of, all these disclaimers, of the apparent aimlessness or casualness of travels, and of the wish to appear as an amateur, Irving had an "acute longing for stability."[88] Stability is a clue. Irving may well have seen his career as a writer in terms of an escape from financial embarrassment. Yet his pilgrimage, I argue throughout, also was a quest for his own imperfectly realized masculinity, a quest for male images that would take the form of various masculine archetypes. In the long run, that quest would help him find a part of himself, an antidote to his sensibility, his emotional response to loss, deprivation, and mourning, his effeminacy. We can only speculate about the causes of Irving's effeminacy, his unmanly softness and delicacy. The most plausible cause is a love problem of long standing, especially the missing love of the father. Boys need and crave love from their fathers, not least physical expressions of the father's affection for them. Irving's father was a Scotch Presbyterian deacon, stern and severe, and quite incapable of that kind of love. More than anything, Irving recalled the tediously religious regime in his home with lingering bitterness: "When I was a child religion was forced upon me [...] I was made to swallow it whether I would or not, and that too in its most ungracious form [...] until I was disgusted with all its forms and observances."[89]

For the rest of his life, Irving recalled the Deacon and his lessons with derision: "When I was young," his nephew heard him say, "I was led to think that somehow or other everything that was pleasant was wicked."[90] And when in his recollections Irving describes his father in family prayers, he delivers almost a caricature of pious rhetoric and religious fervor.[91] It is no surprise that the Christmas Eve which his alter ego, Geoffrey Crayon, spends at the manor house of a prototypical English country gentleman turns into a lesson of a domestic policy, a policy that was "to make his children feel that home was the happiest place in the world."[92] No wonder also that late in his life, Irving joins the Old Dutch Church in Tarrytown, an Episcopal church, in defiance of his Presbyterian father. Finally, when his father died, on October 25, 1807, Irving did not write a word regarding the parent's death, then or later.[93]

Masculine identification in a boy develops partly as a result of the boy's identification with the father, the representative of the animus image, and the resulting feeling that he is included in the world of men as a man among men, socially useful. Irving's unfulfilled needs thus would lead to uncertainty in the developing ego of the boy about his own masculinity, an inability to identify with his own masculinity. Although the brothers—especially William, Peter, and Ebenezer—took over, it was the father who failed as a model, failed in shaping Washington's male gender identity.[94] Nevertheless, there is more in Irving's writings, both published and unpublished, than merely an unstillable ache for a weak, absent, or otherwise problematic father who made him feel belittled and unproductive. For young Irving, there also was the mother, Sarah Irving, who often served as a primary parent, especially when the Deacon was away. More kindly tempered, mother Sarah provided not just basic physical care, but, on the strength of the notion that woman was the embodiment of virtue, a notion she had fully internalized, also became a moral teacher.[95]

Irving was strongly attached to his mother and always spoke of her with veneration. However, Sarah Irving had seven other children to look after. Moreover, she may well have cut him off from too much of his budding masculinity, the kind of boyish masculinity that tracks dirt into the house, uses dirty words, and struts about like a bantam rooster. At such times, Pierre Munro Irving imagines, his mother would look at him and exclaim: "Oh, Washington! If you were only good!"[96] When such signs of masculinity are squashed, a boy, especially a sensitive youngster, may lose touch with that side of himself as a result.[97] Unable to separate himself psychologically from his mother, young Irving would remain unreceptive to the social demands for gender-appropriate behavior, the demands for a purely masculine image, with its emphasis on aggressivity, productivity, responsibility, and engagement. Altogether in Irving, unfulfilled needs, for primitive masculine development as well as for masculine affection from the father would thicken into an unholy alliance that manifested itself in a lack of confidence in his instinctual masculine side and a wish to escape to all sorts of tension-free idylls.

Irving's lack of confidence in his instinctual masculine side cannot be separated from his guilt about writing, because Irving believed it, or believed society believed it, to be a feminine occupation. In a story he included in *Tales of a Traveller*, the young hero, Buckthorne, confesses, "with shame," to have been "an incorrigible laggard. I have always had the poetical feeling, that is to say I have always been an idle fellow and prone to play the vagabond."[98] Buckthorne's father disinherits the son on the grounds that poetry was "a cursed sneaking, puling, housekeeping employment, *the bane of all true manhood.*" When Buckthorne later regains his legacy, Doubting Castle (as Irving calls it with tongue in cheek), he repents and renounces "the sin of authorship." Authorship is a "sin" because it was believed to give in to passivity and dependence rather than to assert one's manhood in the specifically American style of work and materialism. The conflict ultimately was unresolvable. The tone and direction of Irving's writings from beginning to end therefore were motivated by one single motive—the struggle of a man seeking to escape from "the woman within" even as he tried to appease her.[99]

The "woman within" no doubt manifested itself in Irving's personal shyness and uncertainty, causing a perpetual conflict with the confident public image he habitually projected or felt he had to project. Irving was aware of the dilemma, as he repeatedly complained that throughout his life he suffered from his "sensibility."[100] A man in perpetual crisis, he read Burton on melancholy, quoted passages on the sensitive mind, "the soul of sensibility,"[101] and lamented that he could not be like his father or his practical brother Ebenezer. At other times, he denounced the imaginative mind, his outward-turned melancholy, and he suffered from bouts of depression that lasted, sometimes, for weeks (not months, not years). Criticism hurt him terribly, he was paralyzed with fear of his readers, even of his friends, and he constantly questioned his own abilities.[102] He also habitually relied on sources—stories and legends he read or was told, other books, for instance of voyages and discoveries, even newspapers—rather than on his own creative abilities. Irving clearly was an observer, not a participant, a "mere spectator of other men's fortunes and adventures," of customs and scenes, all of which would add to his "stock of knowledge."[103] In his published works at least, he rarely looked inward, so that we find little self-searching or speculation.

Irving's mind, Stanley Williams found, "was peculiarly sensitive to adversity. For, as real misfortunes, an unsuccessful book or a disastrous investment, punished him more keenly than men of stouter nerves, so, also, the ordinary penalties of living wore him down more readily."[104] Among these "ordinary penalties of living" was a mysterious malady or indisposition of the legs and ankles, which Irving invariably felt fettered by, like a reined-in horse chafing at its bit. "It was not a dangerous, but a cruel, tormenting malady, incapacitating and seemingly endless," his biographer concluded.[105] Indeed, there was worse. There was a second ailment Irving suffered from during his final years—asthma, "the precursor and probably the cause of the enlargement of the heart which brought about Irving's death."[106] Leaving aside bodily torments, in the early 1820s the realization that he now was a man in middle age only compounded Irving's miseries. "We look forward to better hours," he clumsily wrote in his German journal in September 1823. "What better times can I hope / My sunny days of youth are oer...."[107] When Irving wrote this, he was struggling with what was to become *Tales of a Traveller*, a miscellany of anecdotes, tales, and impressions from his life in France and Germany, and his travels on the Continent.

The plan had been to produce another *Sketch Book*, this time with material collected during his German tour. In preparing for that tour, which lasted from July 1822 to the fall of 1823, Irving even began studying German as early as 1818.[108] Once on the continent, he instantly began laying up a stockpile of accounts of people, legends, and countries; he even bought the Grimms' *Deutsche Sagen* in Dresden, reading them in Paris.[109] Yet in Dresden, the original plan began to unravel. Irving arrived on November 28, 1822, and stayed for eight months, a favorite at the court of Frederick Augustus, King of Saxony, and the darling of the family of Mrs. John Foster, an Englishwoman residing there with her children. Socializing at the expense of writing took its toll. Irving crashed once he arrived in Paris, on August 3, 1823. "Woke at 4 oclock," he wrote into his journal a week later, "with a strange horror on my mind—a dread of future evil—of failure in future literary attempts—a dismal foreboding that I could not drive off by any effort of reason."[110] Nervously exhausted, anxious, and depressed, often unable to sleep or waking up in middle of the night, in December 1823 he abandoned the "idea of a plan" that had "dawned" on him, and spontaneously decided to "arrange the Mss. on hand so as to make 2 vols of Sketch Book."[111] In his reply to a letter from John Murray, his London publisher, Irving wrote on March 25, 1824: "I have the materials for two volumes nearly prepared, but there will yet be a little rewriting and filling up necessary. I hope however to lay the work before you in the course of six weeks. I think the title will be 'Tales of a Traveller, by Geoffrey Crayon, Gent.'"[112]

By the time Irving contracted with Murray, in late May of 1824, the manuscript was still unfinished.[113] The book finally appeared in August 1824. Its reception devastated Irving. Critics viciously attacked him for his alleged adulation of British aristocracy, a veneration that to many readers seemed like groveling before gentility. Democratic reviews were particularly unforgiving, as was James Fenimore Cooper, who professed to be thoroughly disgusted.[114] But not only was Irving's credit with critics entirely gone. Already the toilsome composition of *Traveller* had bedeviled him. His creative powers seemingly exhausted, he did not write anything for some time; money-wise, too, he was in dire straits, compounded by the failure of some of his investments.[115] Thus, he scribbled in his notebook, probably in the late summer of 1825:

> Oh heart weighed down by the pressure of a thousand cares, and humbled by the remembrance of a thousand errors and saddened by a thousand griefs and losses and disappointments, why doest thou still presume to hope. Behold the sweetness and freshness and fragrance of life is over; what remains is seared

and withered, and colourless. If the morning could not yield thee full delight what canst thou expect from the arid and sultry noon or the chill of gloomy evening.[116]

Such words are but symptoms of a break-down, of feeling spaced-out and down-hearted, of weary resignation, and apathy, as if Irving was facing an abyss, a void, experiencing the world as cold, empty, and gray. There is also the feeling that he was cut off from himself, that he was not real, that the world was not real but as if behind a veil or glass wall, there and not really there, no longer personally significant, himself no longer personally involved with or attached to it, nor with or to himself. Psychoanalysts describe a dissociative condition of this kind as "depersonalization" or "derealization," adding that it typically occurs after a long period of intellectual labor, or else at the end of a love-affair.[117] Irving surely had exhausted himself intellectually. However, there had not been a real love-affair in his life then, though he was devastated when Emily Foster, the eighteen-year-old daughter of the Mrs. Foster he had met in Dresden, rejected his proposal of marriage.[118]

Frequently, "depersonalization" or "derealization" mark a turning point, an awakening to spontaneous activity beyond the reach of one's personal will. C.G. Jung's diagnostic rhetoric seems helpful: "[A]t the climax of the illness, the destructive powers were converted into healing forces. This is brought about by the archetypes awaking to independent life and taking over the guidance of the psychic personality, thus supplanting the ego with its futile willing and striving. [...] He has regained access to the sources of psychic life, and this marks the beginning of the cure."[119] In Irving's case, intellectual exhaustion, morbid introspection, and the rejection of his proposal of marriage would have provoked such a turning point. The same is true of the singularly hostile reviews of his *Tales of a Traveller*, which brought about a turning point in his literary career, accompanied by deep regrets that he had not "been imperiously bound down to some regular and useful mode of life [and] the habits of business."[120] Had Irving somehow "lost" his anima-consciousness? Or, had his suppressed masculinity gained the upper hand, making him sick and tired of being a "sissy" writer (the term is David Leverenz's), unable or unwilling to join the rough play of "real" men? "Do not seek to feed the imagination," he warned his nephew Pierre Paris Irving.[121] Clearly, Irving didn't know whether the year 1825 marked for him a beginning or an ending. But with the familiar weakness of the anima ego, he resolved that it was an ending.

In 1825, while Irving was in the middle of his personal crisis, Rembrandt Peale completed his *Pater Patriae* portrait of George Washington. In the same year, Irving was struck by the idea, vague and tentative at first, of writing a biography of the man he had been named after and who allegedly even laid his hands on him when a mere child. Thus, the idea of a Washington biography may well have occurred to Irving in his formative years, when he grew up in a New York City that was still unmistakably marked by the American Revolution. As a matter of record, in July 1825 Archibald Constable, an Edinburgh publisher, directly approached Irving about a Washington biography, just as he was about to finish reading John Marshall's *The Life of Washington*.[122] Although Irving instantly made some notes, he declined the offer, concluding, "I feel myself incapable of executing my idea of the task. It is one that I dare not attempt lightly. *I stand in too great awe of it.*"[123]

Still, Irving's reading of Marshall's *Life*, together with the idea of himself writing a book on Washington amounted to a tender awaking of the archetype of dutiful masculinity. But a real change of direction came from another side, by way of an invitation to go to Spain, a true godsend.[124] Shortly before Irving decided to go to Spain, where in 1826 he became attached to the American embassy in Madrid, the Paris publisher Galignani asked him to write a biography of Byron, who had just died. The project never materialized, though in 1829, when Irving was forty-six years old, Galignani published *The Life and Voyages of Christopher Columbus*, the first of the historical biographies and under his own name, and in 1831, *Voyages and Discoveries of the Companions of Columbus*. Irving continued studying Spanish history and legend, working on *Legends of the Conquest of Spain*, *The Alhambra*, and *Mahomet*.

In Spain, Irving found a new purpose in life and, equally important at the time, a way out of the financial hardship he had been suffering from after the speculative failure of 1825. Spain, Stanley Williams comments, proved to be a true "turning point" in Irving's long life.[125] It is not entirely clear what Williams meant by this; most likely, the comment refers to Irving's turning to history, producing historical biographies rather than fictional sketches. The change certainly unleashed Irving's creative powers. Importantly, it enabled him to produce new projections of masculine achievement. There was Columbus, the admiral, followed by Mahomet, the warrior-prophet, Boabdil, the last of the Moorish sovereigns of Granada, the residents, past and present, of the Alhambra, as well as the "proud, hardy, frugal and abstemious" Spanish peasants in general.[126] Irving returned to America on May 21, 1832, after an absence of seventeen years.

New York welcomed its native son, with a public dinner given in his honor. In August he began a trip to the Oklahoma Territory, which resulted in *A Tour of the Prairies*. In it, he found nobility in Native Americans' "Roman countenances," much as he found genuine manhood in hardy trappers and fur traders, as well as, later, in pioneers of westward expansion such as J.J. Astor and Captain Bonneville. In 1835, Irving bought an estate near Tarrytown, which eventually became his "Sunnyside." Five years later, at age fifty-seven, Harper of New York published *Life of Oliver Goldsmith*, the biography of a quite different masculine hero, cast very much in the image of Geoffrey Crayon, and of Irving himself. In the same year, Irving took up his life of Washington, only to interrupt the work again when in 1842 he was appointed United States Minister to Spain. He had many regrets about his having to give up literary matters, so when he returned to Sunnyside in the fall of 1846, he at once took the biography, "my history," as he had come to call it, in hand again. Irving's Washington, the result of some "happy magic," as George Bancroft admiringly wrote, became the ultimate American hero, a chivalric knight reverentially cast in "a dramatic narrative in the tradition of American Romanticism."[127]

Early critics often had difficulty separating Irving the man from Irving the writer—"The life of Washington Irving was one of the brightest ever led by an author," wrote Richard Henry Stoddard, an early Irving biographer.[128] As years passed and Irving's celebrity personality faded into the background, critics often began to review his writings as all style, no substance. "The man had no message," pronounced critic Barrett Wendell. "From beginning to end he was animated by no profound sense of the mystery of existence."[129] To be sure, Irving was no philosopher of history who would struggle with the question whether history had any meaning or whether its goal was the unstoppable development of humankind. He did, however, probe into what it means to be a man and to attempt to win a place among other men, which seems proof enough of a sense of the mystery of existence. Seen in their totality, Irving's masculine archetypes constitute personifications of his own creative powers that, Jung would have said, wanted union with him. The plurality of masculine archetypes, his "guardian angels,"[130] should not surprise us. "The animus," Jung wrote, "does not appear as one person, but as a plurality of persons."[131]

The notion of plurality is repeated over and over again in Jung's writings. "[N]ot so much a unity as a plurality," he wrote in *Civilization in Transition*. And in the later *Alchemical Studies* we read, "As it is made up of a plurality of preconceived opinions, the animus is far less susceptible of personification by a single figure but appears more often as a group or crowd."[132] Quite similarly, Emma Jung wrote, "An archetype, such as the animus represents, will never really coincide with an individual man.... Individuality is not in any way typical...."[133] Archetypes resemble character *types*, which may well be symbolic forms of *ideal* gender roles. Individuality, in contrast, is essential in fiction, as it creates a plausible plot. Jungian psychoanalysts, too, look at individuals as always comprised of patterns of behavior and thought, energies perhaps, in varying degrees. This thought is the basis also of the mythopoetic framework that Robert Moore and Douglas Gillette created in the heyday of the 1990s Men's Movement. Moore and Gillette understand the mature masculine psyche in terms of four major archetypes: the "King" (the energy of just and creative ordering, of wisdom, selflessness, and benevolence), the "Warrior" (the energy of aggressive but nonviolent action, of courage, and the ability to bear pain), "the Magician" (the energy of initiation and transformation, of guidance to these processes, of knowledge and skill), and the "Lover" (the energy that emotionally connects one to others and the world, empathetic and brimming with vitality and sensitivity).[134]

Maturity is only the full and highest expression of the four archetypes as Moore and Gillette delineate them. There are also, on the downside, dysfunctional shadows of each archetype, and always in active and passive forms.[135] In addition, each archetype has an immature "boyhood" form, again paired with two dysfunctional shadows.[136] In one form or the other, the four major archetypes, together with their dysfunctional shadows and childhood emanations, already appeared in Joseph Campbell's groundbreaking study of comparative mythology, *The Hero with a Thousand Faces*.[137] But whereas Campbell's archetypal figures are male as well as female, *King, Warrior, Magician, Lover* was written as a kind of self-help manual to help men express their "mature masculine potentials." In order for a man to achieve mature masculine strength and energy, he must, Moore and Gillette pronounce, be in touch with all four major archetypes. In addition, maturity requires an "adequate connection with the inner *feminine*," meaning that mature masculinity is not abusive or domineering, but generative, creative, and empowering of the self and others.[138]

One can relate to Moore and Gillette's framework on a personal level, yet the categories are abstract and conceptual, and they cannot be proven or disproven. Moreover, labels like King, Warrior, Magician, Lover, etc., classify a character, who thus becomes part of a lifeless taxonomy. Yet a text's unity lies not in its origin but in its destination. We can adequately understand neither Irving's male characters nor Irving the man without reference to time, history, and the emotions they elicit (which may or may not echo, parallel, or diverge from the emotions we experience in other areas of our lives). Both Irving's male characters and Irving the man unfolded slowly, over the years, and always within contexts, of Irving's biography (Irving never fully connected with the inner feminine but throughout his life rather struggled to escape from it), as well as of the various social, political, and cultural environments. It is one thing to say, for instance, that Rip Van Winkle epitomizes "the ego arrested at the infantile level in an Oedipal situation," as Rip passes "from childhood to second childhood with next to nothing in between." It is, however, quite another thing to argue that Rip as well as others of Irving's fictional heroes represent "childish, primitive images of what America could not assimilate into the national self-image."[139]

Looking at the plurality of masculine archetypes in Irving's writings (there is indeed a plurality, though there are not nearly as many of these "faces" as in Joseph Campbell's pioneering study), we see that the process leading him to a better understanding of himself, to self-awareness, if not self-transformation, was slow and convoluted, making the writer appear unstable, mutable, and incomplete. For *The Conquest of Granada*, published in 1829, Irving once again used a pseudonymous author, Fray Antonio Agapida. When his London publisher, John Murray, used Irving's full name instead, an angry response followed: "By inserting my name in the title page as the avowed author, you make me personally responsible for the verity of the fact and the soundness of the opinions of what was intended to be given as a romantic chronicle."[140] *The Conquest of Granada* purports to be a chronicle based on old Spanish historians, but, Irving wrote, it was intentionally "colored and tinted by the imagination so as to have a romantic air, without destroying the historical basis or the chronological order of events."[141] Withdrawals from the realities of the present into the traditions and legends of the past are characteristic of anima-writing, of tales, legends, fairytales, the marvelous, magic, enchantment, a truly romantic polyphony. Irving's anima-writing reached an apex in 1832 in *The Alhambra: A Series of Tales and Sketches of the Moors and Spaniards*, and once again under the authorship of "Geoffrey Crayon."

Washington Irving, incurable romanticist that he was, saw everything as "different." Looking, from his window at the Alhambra, into the garden of Lindaraxa, he wrote to his brother Peter: "I have nothing but the sound of water, the humming of bees, and the singing of nightingales to interrupt the profound silence of my abode; and at night, stroll until midnight about the galleries overlooking the garden and the landscape, which are now delicious at night from the brightness of the moon."[142] Even more tellingly, in a letter to Henry Brevoort he enthuses about his present location as "one of the most remarkable romantic and delicious spots in the world. [...] when I am not occupied with my pen, I lounge with my book about these oriental apartments. [...] It absolutely appears to me like a dream; or as if I am spell bound in some fairy palace."[143]

References to dreaming abound in Irving's writings. As early as 1810 he had confided to his journal: "I never think of those dreams of fairy land without a confidence that there is something in store for mankind infinitely more delightful than any thing we can conceive of the kind."[144] In 1816, he wrote to Brevoort from England that he now had entered "the dreams of fairy land."[145] And in *The Sketch Book* he gushes about "certain half-dreaming moods of mind," as they allow him to "steal away from the noise and glare, and seek some quiet haunt."[146] One of these haunts, though not necessarily a quiet one, was New York harbor, where Irving, in the guise of Crayon, would "wander about the pier heads in fine weather, and watch the parting ships, bound to distant climes. With what longing eyes would I gaze after their lessening sails, and waft myself in imagination to the ends of the earth."[147] And looking back on his voyage to Europe, the author, real or fictitious, characterizes himself as "one given to day dreaming and fond of losing himself in reveries."[148] Irving would always come back from his excursions into the realm of the imagination, though never empty-handed. He would return full of suggestions, truths, even visions that complemented the mundane, rational everyday world.

Fantasy-images, we've seen, can be explained as products of the anima, thus of a psychological function.[149] However, the anima is not just a personal thing, but can also be seen as a cultural factor, shaping personal expression as such. Put simply, Irving's anima-type was shaped to a great extent by the culture he grew up and lived in. In that culture—*vide* Gilbert Stuart Newton's portrait—romanticism was a determining factor. The classicists had seen the individual in relation to society (or, even, God). It was other people (or God) that provided them with a sense of self or selfhood, for instance by pronouncing, "well done!" or, "Thou shalt not…!" The great Romantics, in their rejection of society, their own, rapidly modernizing one, that is, had to ask themselves who shall we turn to in order to get a sense of self? Failing all previous choices, they would turn to nature, the cultures of the Orient, Italy, Spain or Greece, non-hegemonic social strata like peasants, an idealized past, an imaginary future, or their innermost self—all to be approached with feeling or empathy, *Einfühlung* in German.

We are learning nothing new about Irving when we discover that he too was familiar with the writings of many of the Romantics, especially British ones like Wordsworth, Coleridge, Scott, Byron, and Shelley, or German ones like Hoffmann, Tieck, Wieland, Fouqué, Nachtigal (who wrote as "Otmar"), and the brothers Grimm.[150] Irving's interest in popular tales, folklore, legends, and myths also is notorious. He reveled in a pantheon of giants, dwarfs, gnomes, phantom warriors, wild huntsmen, sailors and pirates, even the devil.[151] He also glorified peasants and similarly marginalized groups, whose communal life he felt was "nature-given," unlike life in "artificial" society. In addition, Irving had a romantic fondness for battles, together with much experience in describing them in his writings on Spain. Romanticism also means a longing for something indefinable and extraordinary (what Friedrich Schlegel called *Sehnsucht*)—including an extraordinary hero. Irving too dreamed of virtuous (and heroic) individuals whose masculine achievement consisted in preserving the patrician valuation of traditional culture over mere business and populist politics, while he also dreamed of revaluing culture by investing the capital, drawn from a usable past, of American manhood.

If Irving's indebtedness to romanticism seems beyond dispute, his "glorification of manhood" has been attacked as "a reactionary rather than a radical romanticism."[152] However one defines radical romanticism, it clearly involves a genuinely political sense. Inspiration would come from ethical concerns, not sentimentalism. It is impossible, for instance, to conceive of Irving dying, like Byron, in the cause of Greek liberty.[153] Irving did not stay at home, writing odes to Greece, but he hid himself in the Alhambra, feeding his imagination with Spanish legends which a poor squatter from the palace told him. And really, Irving had no patience with a faceless "*World Spirit*" (Hegel's "*Weltgeist*") tirelessly working, through various agents of enlightenment, towards the unstoppable realization of reason and liberty. While he was partial, in his writings as well as privately, to a few "great men," he had little good to say about the working classes or, for that matter, the "lower orders" in general. Least of all did he see fit to invest a female figure with emancipatory powers. Irving's whole sense of self focused on the manhood and masculinity he believed he lacked and could not be compensated for by something which he believed or had been made to believe was somehow inferior. At best, women formed a kind of afterthought, as is evident from the words of Geoffrey Crayon, who in many ways was Irving's alter ego, a projection of his anima-ego: "I profess not to know how women's hearts are wooed and owned. To me they have always been matters of riddle and admiration."[154]

As we have seen, there were two types of women in Irving's universe, independent women of character and substance, and women who embodied innocent perfection. If Irving was able to flirt or dance with the former, with the latter he could fantasize about marrying them. Such fantasies extend to the writings, which are rooted in a male/female scheme that faithfully reproduces the separation of spheres in which "the workplace was masculinized, the home feminized."[155] In keeping with the dominant ideology, Irving reproduced the current system of gender hierarchy, which probably was made worse by his idealizations of women's boundless capacities for love and devotion, and his metaphoric praise for the redemptive powers of marriage against communal breakdown and psychological ruin. The hollow ring of the following passage from "The Wife" bears this out: "There is in every true woman's heart a spark of heavenly fire, which lies dormant in the broad daylight of prosperity; but which kindles up, and beams and blazes in the dark hour of adversity. No man knows what the wife of his bosom is—no man knows what a ministering angel she is—until he has gone with her through the fiery trials of this world."[156] Such fantasies of womanhood seem outmoded and sexist, as in fact they are. Moreover, they appear utterly immature, fantasies of infantile regression, the outpourings of a child yearning, not for the actual mother but for the feminine energy of the mythic "Great Mother," nurturing, infinitely good, and infinitely beautiful.[157]

On a more mundane level, Irving's fantasies of womanhood also register the drastic change in social conditions that came about from the time of the American Revolution to about 1850, especially for men. Many men then felt that they were not suited for male society, that they were shouldered aside by other men and could only flourish and expand their powers in the company of women. They would crave women's "tea and sympathy," and rhapsodize over the redemptive powers of womanly virtues—"piety, purity, submissiveness, and domesticity," to use the words of a contemporary—against communal breakdown and psychological ruin inherent in an economy based on speculation and ruthless enterprise.[158] Irving's readers would rave about stories like "The Broken Heart," "The Pride of the Village," "The Widow and Her Son," "Annette Delarbre," or "The Wife."[159] Sentimental stories of women drowning themselves when wronged in their first love, of women tenderly supporting their worn-down husbands or sons and displaying fortitude in the face of overwhelming disasters, had a tremendous appeal in nineteenth-century America. But already in *The Sketch Book*, there is a sense of uneasiness. Irving never explicitly wrote about it, but he did pull away from wives, marriage, and mothers, towards associations of men with fellow men, most of them bachelors. Hence we have sketches like "The Angler," "A Bachelor's Confessions" or, later, the group of jolly burghers around Diedrich Knickerbocker, idling away their days fishing off Manhattan's east side—and swapping stories.

As Irving was growing uneasy with womanhood and femininity, all kinds of stories or collective fictions entered the culture about what it meant to be male. Yet despite Irving's rootedness in his anima-identity, his response was not to validate, or at least give substance to, a sense of alienation.[160] On one hand, he created a veritable club of unproductive refugees from marriage, as well as of comic, not fully developed men, who are futilely looking for treasure or a profitable match. On the other hand, he would, faithfully following his role model, Sir Walter Scott, produce romantic histories replete with often improbable adventures.[161] Yet the heroes of these romances of manly conquerors, exalted as they are as gallant warriors, great men imbued with moral qualities that make them molders of history, movers and shakers, remain stranded in the past or, rather, in a past that only existed in the form that their author's romanticizing imagination produced.[162] Always the antiquarian, Irving appreciated anything old, but from an aesthetic perspective, without entering into the sociological, political, or philosophical. More often than not, therefore, reality and romance become indistinguishable. As Irving, hiding behind Geoffrey Crayon, wrote in *The Alhambra*, the ancient palace's power consisted in "clothing naked realities with the illusions of the memory and the imagination."[163]

Irving's troubled masculinity, we have seen, owes a good deal to the distorted animus image his father projected upon him. In more general terms, manhood must be seen as the approved way of being an adult male in a given society, a social imperative or normative idea. We can trace Irving's troubled masculinity to a male-role stress sanctioned by the specifically American style of materialism and hard work, a role stress that involved suppressing human feelings of vulnerability and denying emotional connection and gentleness.[164] The socially ascribed male gender identity became deeply ingrained in Irving's consciousness and always was at odds with the feminine components of his personality. Manhood ideologies, David Gilmore contends, always are adaptations to social environments.[165] Seen in this light, many of the masculine archetypes in Irving's disenchanted cosmos are intrinsic to the modern world. Anxious, troubled, sentimental, or heroic, they constitute a code form of the experience of modernity and thus serve as powerful warnings of the evils of capitalism, of humankind's enslavement to the shallow enjoyments of the modern world, and of men's surrender to the contractual qualities of mere exchange and naked self-interest.

There appears to be a clear link between the free and unimpeded expansion of industrial capitalism, the longing for true heroes casting a shadow, and a veritable masculinity crisis.[166] From its beginnings in the northern United States, industrial capitalism reshaped the entire nation in the course of a half century. This was not a marginal change, but a fundamental one. Within a dozen or so decades, the shift from a land to a cash and credit economy led to an economic boom (and bust) that meant westward expansion, the development of a national transportation system, accelerating urban growth and industrialization, extensive domestic and overseas commerce, and an almost exponential expansion of banking and finance. In short, America became a "scrambling, individualistic, acquisitive society."[167] The transformation had dramatic consequences for the meanings of manhood. As radically new notions of self and subjectivity emerged, traditional forms of male identity construction, especially those based on landed property, were marginalized and became irrelevant. Personality now meant providing for oneself, the acquisition of money, paid work, and personal achievement. For the "self-made man," only success and failure counted.[168]

By 1830 or so, an ideology of "self-made manhood" had become the dominant cultural form, especially in the Northeast, where it had driven out the older ideologies of genteel patriarchy and artisan independence.[169]

Most visibly, a self-consciously self-made middle class, consisting of entrepreneurial managers and professionals, themselves in opposition to wage laborers and others with little education and even less tradition, won cultural and economic power from small patriarchal shopkeepers and artisans and a patrician class that also included merchants like the Irvings.[170] Washington Irving saw the new power of the rising middle classes with fear and loathing. "Happy he who shuns business," he wrote into his notebook during his residence in Paris in 1825, translating from Horace's *Epodes*.[171] Irving was not the only writer who broke with the rising middle classes because he could not bring himself to like their ways. However, he never went as far as Herman Melville, whose "Bartleby, the Scrivener" (1853), an elaborate fantasy of regression, mercilessly dissects what in modern parlance has become known as "bullshit jobs,"[172] together with the downward slide into mediocrity and bored stolidity. Instead, Irving responded to the devastations of a life in which individuals were becoming, in the words of Alexis de Tocqueville, "strangers one to the other,"[173] by seeking compensation, which customarily took the form of a nostalgic look backward and the creation, from an imagined past, of larger-than-life masculinities. Thus, any anti-capitalist thrust Irving was nursing inexorably propelled him towards historical and, more often than not, mythic figures.

If the masculine archetypes in Irving's writings were to secure an antithesis to the cultural malaise of his time—the experience of modernity and of men's surrender to the contractual qualities of mere exchange and naked self-interest—Irving the writer at the same time was, as he wrote to Henry Brevoort in 1828, "most anxious for success."[174] A year later, we find him "nestled" in Granada's famous Alhambra castle—"one of the most remarkable, romantic, and delicious spots in the world"—at work on a second edition of *Columbus* that, along with other literary schemes, "will secure me a moderate independence for the remainder of my existence."[175] Ten years before, he had written to his brother Ebenezer that, as regards his literary career, he'd be content "to produce articles from time to time that will be sufficient for my present support, and form a stock of copyright property, that may be a little capital for me hereafter."[176] It appears that Irving knew full well that he was writing under a new economic and social regime, one that emphasized, paradoxically, the possibility of upward mobility for everyone, including himself.

There is no doubt that Irving was himself a self-made man, a self-maker who was fending for himself and trying to find his own way in the world. His life story, Brian Jay Jones writes, "is the kind on which America was built and thrives: a likeable, average man does something no one has ever done before and becomes very, very famous."[177] So famous that *Harper's New Monthly Magazine* in 1851 called him the "patriarch of American letters."[178] It is also a matter of record that Irving's friend Henry Wadsworth Longfellow, in a December 15, 1859, commemorative speech before the Massachusetts Historical Society, urged his audience not to forget that Irving had been "the first to win for our country an honorable name and position in the History of Letters."[179] Longfellow's words would have pleased Irving, who always wanted to be regarded as a gentleman author whose writings rise above the squalor of the marketplace. But Irving was perfectly capable of denouncing the world of commerce as "sordid dusty, and soul-killing" while simultaneously partaking in the family business, investing in a French steamboat enterprise, Bolivian copper mines, insurance companies, American railroads and western lands for speculation.[180] His desire to make money clearly is at odds with the denial, even denigration as demeaning, of making money in his writings. But the ideal of gentleman author was never a reality for Irving, who, unlike writers before him, had no family wealth, personal estate, or patronage to sustain him if he simply dabbled or wrote for pleasure. This middle-class son of a New York merchant had to write for a living.[181]

Whatever literary reputation Irving acquired during his lifetime, it was hard earned. His tales, histories, biographies and legends are elegantly written, and while Irving made it all look easy, it had always been the result of patient and diligent labor. The easy look is telling: Irving wished to be known as a writer whose "literary reputation" depended on *not* writing "for profit."[182] A professional masquerading as amateur, Irving evaded or disguised just those restrictions imposed by the patrician or genteel duties which he celebrated in print. He would sit down in his lodgings and send out stories and sketches to compete, as he himself was forbidden or had himself forbidden to do, in the markets of the masculine world. In fact, Irving was perfectly at home in economic relations of different social formations—from publishing to book trade to libraries, and so on.[183] Legendary are his feuds with publishers over money, which began when David Longworth in 1807 secured the copyright to *Salmagundi*.[184]

Equally legendary are Irving's schemes to exploit loopholes of copyright. Since international copyright laws were vague and nearly nonexistent at the time, Irving would provide American publishers with prepublication copy of a British publisher's work—and vice versa. In this way, he would secure a nearly simultaneous copyright of his works on both sides of the Atlantic.[185] By 1840, Irving's patience was running thin. Literature, he was convinced, could prosper only if there were guarantees that writers' copyrights were protected. "If the copyright law remains in its present state," he wrote historian William H. Prescott, "our native literature will have to struggle with encreasing [sic] difficulties. No copyright to protect it in England and an influx of foreign and cheap literature to drown it at home."[186] Irving followed this up with an open letter in *Knickerbocker* magazine in which he publicly endorses copyright legislation pending in Congress.[187]

In antebellum America, literature was becoming a commodity; it was also inevitably becoming a form of public relations. Irving perceived this clearly, and he became a master of public relations. Nothing, of course, beats the buzz he created for *A History of New York*. With publication pending, Irving had his friends James Paulding and Henry Brevoort prepare a number of squibs, a series of notes in the newspapers designed to catch the public's attention and get it to purchase the book. "DISTRESSING," screamed a headline in the October 26, 1809, issue of the *New York Evening Post*. The rest of the text was a missing person's report for "a small elderly gentleman [...] by the name of KNICKERBOCKER," together with the request that other newspapers also run the notice. Several newspapers ran the report over the next few days, without, of course, anyone reporting seeing the gentleman. Until November 6, that is, when "a traveller" declared that the said gentleman had been seen "by the passengers of the Albany Stage." Accordingly, measures were taken to have Knickerbocker returned safely to the Columbian Hotel, his reputed lodgings. On November 16, a notice by the hotel's "landlord" in the *Evening Post* said that "a *very curious kind of written book*" had been found in the gentleman's room and that, should he not return and pay his bill, the book would be disposed of. Curiosity and anticipation had reached a new pitch when the *Evening Post* on November 29 announced that "Innskeep & Bradford have in the press and will shortly publish, A History of New York, in two volumes, duodecimo. Price three dollars."[188]

A History of New York was finally published on December 6, 1809, in time for the bicentennial of Hendrick Hudson's famed voyage to "Manahatta." The performance of the book had the kind of response a modern marketing company could only dream of. For Irving, mere publicity was not enough, though. Shortly after the publication of *The Sketch Book*, he famously (and quite bluntly) told a correspondent, "If the American public wish to have a literature of their own, they must consent to pay for the support of authors."[189] Irving proved true to his words. He had originally published *The Sketch Book* in installments but kept the copyright and later published the new work himself—at a total of $5.37 per copy, which was a very high price when most novels sold for less than two dollars. Irving marketed *The Sketch Book* a second time as a single volume both in England and in the United States. Overall, he had good reason to think that in the future he'd be able to support himself through writing. Nevertheless, in 1828 he wrote Thomas Aspinwall, his London agent, "I am not a man of business, and am easily perplexed in money matters."[190] This is not entirely convincing, for by the summer of 1835, the American edition of his first *Crayon Miscellany*—it contained *A Tour on the Prairies*—netted him almost $4,000, about $90,000 today. In addition, his brother Ebenezer had negotiated an agreement with the publishers to extend their exclusive publishing rights for another seven years for an annual payment of $1,150. Irving was relieved to know that he had a regular source of income for at least the next few years. He also had enough to acquire the small farmhouse at Tarrytown that he eventually transformed into his Sunnyside home.

Fortunately for Irving, his books sold extremely well. "Of all American authors," Henry C. Carey wrote in 1853, "those of school-books excepted, there is no one of whose books so many have been circulated as those of Mr. Irving. Prior to the publication of the edition recently issued by Mr. Putnam, the sale had amounted to some hundreds of thousands, and yet of that edition, selling at $1.25 per volume, it has already amounted to 144,000 volumes."[191] Once Putnam had started with the Author's Revised Edition (ARE) in 1848, Irving did even better. In Pierre Munro Irving's estimate, the sum total realized by his uncle for copyrights in America was some $63,000 prior to 1843, but the total receipts from Putnam's between 1848 and Irving's death in 1859 were some $88,000, plus additional revenue from 1859 through 1863 of some $34,000.[192] It is no surprise that Irving, in a letter to George P. Putnam of December 27, 1852, thanked his publisher profusely: "You called [my writings] into active existence, and gave them a circulation that I believe has surprised even yourself. In rejoicing at their success, my satisfaction is doubly enhanced by the idea that you share in the benefits derived from it."[193]

Irving's writings may have been commercially successful, yet nowhere does he come up with real solutions to the pressing problems of his time. Stanley Williams, writing in the 1930s, was especially critical of Irving's apparent indifference to and neglect of the most urgent social and political issues. For Williams, the problem with Irving was that he wrote "out of the past," and loved, as Irving himself had written, "to wander over the scenes of renowned achievement—to tread, as it were, in the footsteps of antiquity—to loiter about the ruined castle—meditate on the falling tower—to escape, in short, from the common-place realities of the present, and lose myself among the shadowy grandeur of the past."[194] Williams might just as well have pointed to another sketch, in which Irving confessed to his love of "stepping back into the regions of antiquity, and losing myself among the shades of former ages."[195] Never mind that these are actually the words of Geoffrey Crayon, but Crayon was Irving's alter ego, his "protective mimicry," in James Hillman's words.[196] As a pseudonym for the author, the charming voice of the man of feeling (like the voice of Diedrich Knickerbocker, the irreverent antiquarian and whimsical crank) allowed

Irving to step back from his own writing by claiming anonymity, preserving his anima-ego while evoking curiosity about the author's identity, and simultaneously avoiding any hint of business acumen and political convictions.

Avoidance was exactly what the real Irving in 1823 defined as his aim in writing: "I prefer summon[ing] up the bright pictures of life that I have witnessed and dwelling as much as possible on the agreeable." Writing therefore meant "an activity in my imagination [...] apt to soften and tint up the harshest realities."[197] For Irving, among these "harshest realities" were not just business and politics but also the "vulgarity" of the underclasses. His private writings are peppered with contemptuous remarks about various manifestations of the new rabble: "I shook hands with the mob—whom my heart abhorreth," he wrote to Miss Mary Fairlie in May 1807, on the occasion of elections in New York. Irving, basking in the initial glow of *Salmagundi*, sneered at newly enfranchised constituencies in terms of "small beer or tobacco" and an altogether "nauseous piece of business," an "abomination" included.[198] And in the April 4, 1807, issue of *Salmagundi*, he, ever in opposition against Thomas Jefferson and the Jeffersonians, describes the political system of his country as "*mobocracy*." Also telling is an entry into "Notes and Extracts, 1825": "Incessant industry is not conducive to happiness—Men labour because they have no other occupation—In interval they are brutes & get intoxicated—but a well educatd man mingles study with labour." Last but not least, there is Irving's dismissal, in *Life of George Washington*, of frontier squatters as "lawless intruders."[199] Irving was not alone in his dislike of the underclasses. The idea of a manly cultural elite rooted in the tradition of classic civic virtue was a pretty conventional patrician fantasy of the time, shared by Whig leaders and their supporters alike.[200] Like most of them, Cooper included,[201] Irving never saw the lower orders as a source of energy. For him, they were rather a source of barbarism that needed to be checked by all means whatsoever.

There is another problem. No matter how "active," Irving's anima-consciousness, which would spawn his masculine archetypes, was essentially the imagination of an individual, not of a collective subject. Yet individuals have not been known to effect significant changes. Unsurprisingly, Irving's male heroes are exiled from the present as he brings the imagined masculinities near. Constructing ever so many masculine archetypes in conjunction with the unloved present necessarily resulted in a skewed relationship, a fantasied retreat from and a compensatory response to the forces of the new economy and the ensuing cultural malaise. As Irving selects his masculine archetypes, he sanitizes them, so that they appear, especially in the bio-histories, as complete and stable. In actual fact, they are but results of complex projections, invoking a partial, idealized past that is merged with dissatisfaction with the present. Idealization of the past and dissatisfaction with the present were there from the beginning, together with attempts at achieved manhood. In the following chapter, "Whimsicality, Gentility, and the Loss of Communal Manhood," I will show how Irving tried to create an *American* masculinity from English models—sentimentalism, Shandyism, polite and other satirical models, and all under genteel control.

Two

"Because it was fun"

Whimsicality, Gentility, and the Loss of Communal Manhood

IN 1802, AARON BURR, a leading figure in New York politics, established a daily newspaper, the *Morning Chronicle*. The paper was managed and edited by Peter Irving, whom Burr considered literary as well as loyal. Peter's engagement no doubt precipitated Washington Irving's literary debut at age twenty. But it was Burr, who was too important a figure for Irving to ignore. Burr was one of the "people of substance" Irving always felt drawn to.[1] The masculinity he delineates in his early writings is, however, a far cry from the larger-than-life figures of his later writings. There is no King archetype here, no energy of just and creative ordering, of wisdom and selflessness, and benevolence. On the contrary. "If the observations of an old odd fellow are not wholly superfluous," began a letter in the November 15, 1802, edition of the *Chronicle*, "I would thank you to shove them into a spare corner of your paper." Until February 1, 1803, the *Chronicle* published nine letters by Irving, each signed "Jonathan Oldstyle." The "Letters," which Stanley Williams decided were "worthless as literature,"[2] attracted generally favorable notice. Irving did not include them in the Author's Revised Edition of 1848, though, and their only appearance in book form during his lifetime was in two pirated editions of 1824, which first gave the series its present title, *Letters of Jonathan Oldstyle, Gent*. Oldstyle primarily may have satisfied Irving's "theatrical" temperament. "Adopting a new persona [such as Oldstyle] appealed to his love of all things theatrical," Brian Jay Jones writes in his popular biography. "He became Oldstyle because it was *fun*."[3] Not only, of course. Yet there was more to Irving's choice of a name for the persona he created. By the time of his literary debut, the depiction of a form of masculinity unscathed by the forces of commerce and market corruption seemed much less problematic than in his later writings. For, Oldstyle is not simply Oldstyle, but Jonathan Oldstyle, *Gent*, the "Gent." having been introduced in Letter VI, in which Oldstyle's friend, Andrew Quoz, writes a letter *to* "Jonathan Oldstyle, Gent."[4]

In 1824, the title *Letters of Jonathan Oldstyle, Gent.* presumably was chosen in analogy to "Geoffrey Crayon, Gent.," whom Irving had been using as the name of the pseudonymous author from the *Sketch Book* through *Tales of a Traveller*. "Oldstyle" is not just a whimsical throwback to a time when use of pseudonyms was characteristic for periodic contributors in Addisonian journals.[5] The "odd old fellow" in the guise of an "uninterested spectator" (an unmistakable allusion to the tremendously popular *Spectator* as well as a form of Irvinian self-revelation) is, above all, a gentleman who abhors "the people," for instance those unruly and rowdy theatergoers on the gallery. And he bemoans the fact that young men today "no longer aim at the character of *pretty gentlemen*."[6] True to his conviction that today's youths are in need of being taught the elements of polite education, in Letter VI Oldstyle reads to his cousin, Jack Stylish, from Chesterfield's *Letters to His Son*. Philip Stanhope, 4th Earl of Chesterfield, wrote some 400 letters to his son. Most of them were written between 1746 to 1754, like the one Irving copied into his notebook in 1825: "Good manners are to particular societies what good morals are to society in general, their cement and security [...] *Good Breeding* the result of much good sense, some good nature and a little self denial for the sake of others, and with a view to obtain the same indulgence from them."[7]

A gentleman is "a man whose conduct conforms to a high standard of propriety or correct behavior," we learn from the *Merriam-Webster Dictionary*, as well as "a man of independent means who does not engage in any occupation or profession for gain."[8] Oldstyle is such a dignified gentleman or, at least, he purports to be one. Crotchety, odd, and injured, "nursing [his] wounded shin,"[9] he is unable to walk, literally as well as figuratively. He is the King archetype's passive shadow, the "weakling." From the perspective of a genteel patriarch, he observes with a mix of wonder, awe, and sadness the changing society around him. His observations, in the first letter, are lighthearted, concerning only the fashion of the day, which he dismisses as mere "puppyism."[10] The tone takes a more serious turn in the letters to follow. In Letter VI, for instance, Oldstyle's friend Andrew Quoz warns him not to be too severe on stage actors. "I would not for the world," Quoz begs, "that you should *degenerate* into a critic. The critics, my dear Jonathan, are the very pests of society: they rob the actor of his reputation; the public of their amusement: they open the eyes of their readers to a full perception of the faults of our performers, they reduce our feelings to a state of miserable refinement, and destroy entirely all the enjoyments in which our coarser sensations delighted."[11]

At the end of Letter VIII, Oldstyle wonders why Quoz should suspect him of turning critic, as he had already formed on opinion of critics as "the most 'presumptuous,' 'arrogant,' 'malevolent,' 'illiberal,' 'ungentleman-like,' 'malignant,' 'rancorous,' 'villainous,' 'ungrateful,' 'crippled,' 'invidious,' 'detracting,' 'fabricating,' 'personal,' 'dogmatical,' 'illegitimate,' 'tyrannical,' 'distorting,' 'spindle-shanked moppets, designing villains, and upstart ignorants.'"[12] In a previous letter Oldstyle had agreed with Quoz that, "As the actor is the most meritorious and faultless, so is the critic the most cruel and sanguinary character in the world." One needs but substitute "author" for "actor" to get a sense of how acutely aware Irving was of the rising influence of critics in what was fast becoming a publishing industry. And how foresighted—as if he had foreseen the hostile criticism later hurled at *Tales of a Traveller*. "All trades must live," Quoz's letter continues, "and, as long as the public are satisfied to admire the tricks of the juggler [...] whoever attempts to undeceive them, does but curtail the pleasures of the latter, and deprive the former of their bread." This is either a plea for what the Romantics called the "willing suspension of disbelief," or an instance of registering the breakdown of distinctions between an interior, feeling subject and a superficial social self. If the latter is true, a critic would be the Magician archetype's active shadow, a detached manipulator whose selfhood emerges in relation to the new speculative economy, a man who, as Teresa Goddu put it, "seemingly fashions himself out of nothing [and thus is] an apparition."[13]

In the final letter, printed in the *Morning Chronicle* of April 23, 1803, Oldstyle professes to be surprised at a new piece of legislation that bars duelists from public offices as well as from exerting their voting rights. For Oldstyle, the change amounts to a "catastrophe": "Spirit of chivalry, whither hast thou flown!" he exclaims in melancholy bewilderment. Conjuring up the "Shade of Don Quixote"—"dost thou not look down with contempt on the degeneracy of the times!"—Oldstyle, together with his sister, mourns to see "the last spark of chivalric fire thus rudely extinguished."[14] As long as the "gallantry of former days" lasted, there was a "genuine politeness and polished ceremony with which duels were conducted [...] when that gentlemanly weapon, the *small sword*, was in highest vogue." In contrast, duels fought with pistols are neither "well-bred" nor are they conducted in a "gentlemanly manner" but have become, rather, "blunt, unceremonious affairs." Remembering his "youthful days," Oldstyle here disagrees with Quoz, who believes that fighting with pistols is more civilized, considering that duelists are usually content with only one discharge, and tend to be rather awful shots, so that the persons who are in real danger are the seconds.

That was not always the case, though. Just over a year after the final letter was printed, Alexander Hamilton and Aaron Burr met on the dueling grounds at Weehawken, New Jersey, to fight the final skirmish of a long-lived political and personal battle. Their seconds had tried without success to settle the matter amicably, and so each of the two combatants fired a shot from a .56 caliber dueling pistol. Burr was unscathed, but Hamilton fell to the ground mortally wounded. He died the next day, July 12, 1804, and Burr would be charged with two counts of murder. By that time, Irving already had embarked for a two-year long trip to Europe. His brothers, concerned over his health and general well-being, financed the trip that took him through France, Italy, Switzerland, Belgium, Holland, and England. Though the journal Irving kept reads much like Sterne's *A Sentimental Journey through France and Italy* (1768), punctuated by wishes "that I had some one with me," the actual trip was decidedly different, full of a disquieting urgency.[15]

During his "*gallop through Italy*" (as his brother William morosely called it), Irving would rave about the Scala in Milan, and he would wax equally enthusiastic about the abundance of theaters and operas in Paris and, later, London.[16] He also tremendously enjoyed the company he met, the smart, talented, and refined young gentlemen he met in Rome, like Washington Allston, who almost made him decide to turn painter.[17] Or else, John Vanderlyn, a young American painter he met in Paris and whose drawing of Irving at age twenty-two is the first known portrait we have of him. The portrait, for which Irving had engaged a tailor and boot maker "to rig me out," as he said, "*a la mode de Paris*,"[18] shows an elegant, handsome young man in a dark coat and a cravat tied neatly at his neck. The aquiline nose, thin, somewhat pursed lips, dark, heavy-lidded eyes, sideburns curving down his cheeks, and curly hair brushed forward, falling across his forehead, later made Pierre Munro Irving remark that there was little likeness. At the time, however, Irving probably loved the pose of a typical nineteenth-century European gentleman.[19]

Irving returned to America in March 1806. His native New York had changed, "improved," as many officials would have it. There were new clubs, parlors, public gardens, fashionable shops and, not to forget, the Park Theater, purchased by John Jacob Astor and John Beekman in 1805 and now being renovated under the guidance of its new manager and Irving's friend, the actor Thomas Cooper. And there was, again, "good company," allowing Irving to form all kinds of masculine attachments. Within weeks of his return home, he fell in with a group of smart, literate, and extremely social young gentlemen he referred to as "the nine Worthies," or—since membership often crept above nine—"the Lads of Kilkenny."[20] When he was not frolicking with the "Lads," Irving was in Judge Josiah Hoffman's offices, preparing for his bar examination. It was slow going, and at times the sheer tedium drove this aspiring gentleman into fits of silliness. Irving hoped to take the bar exam in August of 1806, though he continually postponed it in favor of dining, conversation, theater, and other distractions. When he was finally admitted, in November 1806, it clearly was "more through courtesy and desert," for his performance was dismally bad.[21] Fortunately, even "d----d little" knowledge of the law was enough to earn him the title of "Esquire" and a welcome into the Wall Street offices of his brother Peter, who probably regretted his decision from the moment his younger brother entered the door.

Although for the next decade, "lawyer" would be Irving's formal occupation, he soon diverted his attention to a literary scheme he and James Kirke Paulding had cooked up in a frolicsome mood over drinks. The two soon located another accomplice for their project, David Longworth, a local printer with a good sense of humor. On January 24, 1807, the first issue of their collaboration reached the hands of unsuspecting New Yorkers: *Salmagundi; or, the Whim-Whams and Opinions of Launcelot Langstaff, Esq. and Others*. The opening remarks made the intention abundantly clear—"simply to instruct he young, reform the old, correct the town and castigate the age," with the addendum that, "we have no doubt that the whole town will flock to our exhibition."[22] The authors were right; New York had never seen anything like it. Already the first issue went back to press seven times. Over the next thirteen months, from January 1807 to January 1808, Irving, Paulding, Longworth and, occasionally, William Irving, Jr., altogether produced twenty-five issues of *Salmagundi*.

For the most part, *Salmagundi* was simply funny gossip and silly stories, but every once in a while, the satire bit. Thomas Jefferson, his Democratic-Republicans, and his red pants bore the brunt of the writers' attacks. If the satire was motivated politically (Jefferson had been re-elected to the presidency in 1805), there was another side to the authors' gentlemanly attitude: Irving and Paulding absolutely refused to have anything to do with money, and so Longworth eventually secured the copyright—and the profits—for himself.[23] Even so, Irving was much displeased when Paulding between May and September 1820 brought out a second series of *Salmagundi* on his own. Irving now considered the original "a juvenile production [...] full of errors, puerilities & impertinences."[24] He had had few regrets over its demise, in January 1808, though New York continued to be his muse and the subject of his first real book and first national success. As we will see, *A History of New York* was to liberate Irving from dreaded middle-class existence and factual reality, at the same time as it opened opportunities for dreaming himself into being a gentleman, creating an *American* masculinity from English models—sentimentalism, Shandyism, polite and other satirical models, and all under the genteel control of a moderate Federalist.[25]

A History of New York was released to the public on December 6, 1809, St. Nicholas Day. It became an instant success, to which the elaborate newspaper hoax concerning the disappearance of "Diedrich Knickerbocker," the purported author, in October and November, certainly contributed.[26] Book IV of *A History* is titled "Containing the Chronicles of the Reign of William the Testy." In a passage that Irving added to the Author's Revised Edition of 1848, a seemingly rhetorical question immediately catches the eye: "For what is history, in fact, but a kind of Newgate calendar, a register of the crimes and miseries that man has inflicted on his fellowman?" History or, rather, historiography, the passage continues,

> is a huge libel on human nature, to which we industriously add pager after page, volume after volume, as if we were building up a monument to the honor, rather than to the infamy of our species. If we turn the pages of these chronicles that man has written of himself, what are the characters dignified by the appellation of great, and held up to the admiration of posterity? Tyrants, robbers, conquerors, renowned only for the magnitude of their misdeeds, and the stupendous wrongs they have inflicted on mankind—warriors, who have hired themselves to the trade of blood, not from motives of virtuous patriotism, or to protect the injured and defenceless [sic!], but merely to gain the vaunted glory of being adroit and successful in massacring their fellow-beings![27]

Hegel would have shrugged off a "register of crimes and miseries." For this philosopher, who was Irving's senior by only thirteen years, all history's "misdeeds" and "wrongs" were but the workings of the "*World Spirit*" ("*Weltgeist*"), propelled forward precisely by such agents' negativity—by their murderous violence and destruction, hostilities and wars, greed and competition—until it reached its goal, the realization of reason and liberty, the reconciliation of the divine with the world ("*die Versöhnung des Göttlichen mit der Welt*"). Not so Washington Irving. He was no philosopher of history, and he never struggled with the question whether history had any meaning or whether the goal of a progressing "*World Spirit*" was the development of humankind. As if in anticipation of Theodor Adorno, for whom the Hegelian paradigm collapses into the category named Auschwitz,[28] there is, in Irving's satire, no achieved masculinity in history's "great men," to use the parlance of the time. History's "great men," Irving contends, were merely "driven by ambition." If they serve "as food for the historian," there is no feast. On the contrary. Like "those swarms of flies, which are so often execrated as useless vermin [...] so those heroes, who have been such scourges to the world, were bounteously provided as themes for the poet and historian, while the poet and the historian were destined to record the achievements of heroes!"[29]

It is difficult to imagine a crueler way to introduce the book's real villain—Thomas Jefferson, whose political views Irving found objectionable and whom he, like a reborn Swift, satirically portrays in the guise of Wilhelmus Kieft aka William the Testy, the colony's second governor. Irving had satirized Jefferson already in *Salmagundi*, both as a person and through references to his policies. In *History of New York* he launched a much fuller attack, casting, in truly mock-heroic fashion, Jefferson as the petty ruler of a petty colony, a dandified yet timid and whimsical creature, of a wavering disposition and with a weakness for flattery, a man who trusted his feelings and imagination rather than his reason and thus could easily be accused of effeminacy, of unmanly softness and delicacy—exactly the qualities Irving himself was most vulnerable in and thus may have felt compelled to attack in self-defense.[30]

Because of revisions, changes, and additions, the 1848 edition lost much of its federalist bias, including many of the anti–Jeffersonian references. We therefore need to turn to Book IV of the 1809 edition in order to savor "some of the best political satire ever written by an American."[31] In an "animated speech on the affairs of the province," which opens by "a very sonorous blast of the nose, according to the usual custom of great orators," Kieft/Jefferson "soon worked himself into a fearful rage against the Yankees, whom he compared to the Gauls who desolated Rome, and the Goths and Vandals who overran the fairest plains of Europe." The Yankees, the narrator, Diedrich Knickerbocker, thunders, had insolently "encroached upon the territories of New Netherlands [...] commenced the town of New Plymouth, and planted the onion patches of Weathersfield under the very walls, or rather mud batteries of Fort GOED HOOP."[32] In order to drive the Yankees from the land, Kieft "had been obliged to have recourse to a dreadful engine of warfare, lately invented, awful in its effects, but authorized by dire necessity. In a word, he was resolved to conquer the Yankees—by proclamation!"[33]

The "proclamation," Kieft assures the colonial council, "would at once exterminate the enemy from the face of the country, and he pledged his valour as a governor, that within two months after it was published, not one stone should remain on another, in any of the towns which they had built."[34] The worthy council "remained for some time silent, after he had finished; whether struck dumb with admiration at the brilliance of his project, or put to sleep by the length of his harangue, the history of the times doth not mention."[35] Needless to say, all attempts to fight "by proclamation" come to naught. Though the document "was perfect in all its parts, well constructed, well written, well sealed, and well published," its addressees did not stand in awe of it but, instead, "treated it with the most absolute contempt, applied it to an unseemly purpose, which shall be nameless, and thus did the first warlike proclamation come to a shameful end—a fate which I am credibly informed, has befallen but too many of its successors."[36] Though Irving here dishes up the lingering regional conflict between New York and New England, that is, between the different cultures of Yankees and Yorkers, the idea of "fighting by proclamation" makes sense only in the context of his anti–Jeffersonian prejudices. As Irving wrote his *History*, France and England were at war. Since neither side respected American neutrality, Jefferson issued a proclamation asserting the right of neutrals. The proclamation, together with legislation passed by Congress at Jefferson's behest (the Non-Importation Act of 1806 and the Embargo Act of 1807), backfired. International trade was shut down. Smuggling became much more difficult, if not impossible. Merchants—like the Irvings—were particularly hard hit (if not entirely ruined) by the embargo. At first, merchants made use of loopholes in the law; next, they turned to wholesale smuggling. In May 1808, Washington Irving traveled with his brother Peter to Montreal. Jefferson's embargo prevents him from taking the $9,000 in silver he is carrying into Canada. Irving buys cashier's receipts in Burlington, Vermont, in the hope that he would be able to exchange them for cash in Montreal.[37]

Irving had no sympathy for the Jeffersonians' belief that the welfare of the country meant "economy" aka "penny-pinching," which he had learned would lead to weak, ineffective, and cowardly government. He also had come to believe the Louisiana Purchase of 1803 a folly, clamoring that the newly acquired territory could not be governed. Altogether, Irving looked upon Jefferson's politics, especially foreign politics, as timid, misguided, and ineffectual. The deeper meanings of Jeffersonianism, in particular the civic vision upon which the early republic was based, Irving never seemed to have grasped or appreciated. Nor did he fully understand its aftermath, Jacksonian democracy, though he would come to speak admiringly about Jackson as a model masculine hero. As a moderate federalist under the influence of Judge Hoffman, Irving strongly believed in politics without conflict and, therefore, without parties, a dream he might have gleaned from George Washington's Farewell Address of 1796. Although Washington never mentioned Thomas Jefferson in his address, references to organized political opposition as "artificial" and "intolerable" were plainly directed against him.[38]

Irving too fell for the idea of an organic, well-ordered society, within which existed a natural harmony of interests. It was easy for him to see Jefferson as the originator of the factionalism of the early republic. In *A History*, there is, then, an unvarnished attack on the origin of political parties. In the 1809 edition, the parties are called, respectively, "*Square head*" and "*Platter breech*"—"the former implying that the bearer was deficient in that rotundity of pericranium, which was considered as a token of true genius—the latter, that he was destitute of genuine courage."[39] The satire draws on Johann Kaspar Lavater's physiognomy and the craniology (actually, cranioscopy) of Franz Joseph Gall, both methods to determine human personality and character traits, as well as mental and moral faculties, on the basis of external features, one's physiognomy or the shape of one's skull.[40]

Beginning with the first revision of 1812, Irving cloaked his satire of the origin of political parties in the form of Kieft's edict against the use of tobacco. In the 1809 edition, Kieft's misguided plan had led to riots, depicted in terms of "as violent a turmoil as the gravity of [the populace's] constitutional gravity would permit—a mob of factious citizens had even the hardihood to assemble around the little governor's house [and] fell to smoking with a determined perseverance."[41] There was worse to come, though, in the form of the rise of new political parties. Instead of the quarrel of the "*Square heads*" and "*Platter breeches*" we now have the long-pipes (the traditionalists) and the short-pipes (the loyal followers of Kieft's compromise) and, as a third party, the "*Quids*," who took to chewing tobacco.[42] The parties' worthy representatives were giving Kieft a hard time already in the original edition. "Whichever way he turned himself he was beleaguered and distracted by petitions of 'numerous and respectable meetings,' consisting of some half a dozen scurvy pot-house politicians—all of which he read, and what is worse, all of which he attended to."[43]

Irving is just as ungenerous to ordinary people. Though politically powerless, the "populace [...] like a true mob, did their best to help along public affairs; pestering their governor incessantly, by goading him on with harangues and petitions, and then thwarting [Kieft's] fiery spirit with reproaches and memorials, like a knot of Sunday jockeys, managing an unlucky devil of a hack horse."[44] The situation was not going to change, and political parties were here to stay, through the reign of Peter Stuyvesant, whose governing council (read, Congress) Irving lampoons as hopelessly inadequate, "visited by that talking endemic so universally prevalent in this country, and which so invariably evinces itself, wherever a number of wise men assemble together, breaking out in long, windy speeches, caused, as physicians suppose, by the foul air which is ever generated in a crowd."[45] Debates are, of course, a special case, and Irving, albeit unwittingly, sounds truly prophetic: "Whatever was proposed by a Square head, was opposed by the whole tribe of Platter breeches, who like true politicians, considered it their first duty to effect the downfall of the Square heads—their second, to elevate themselves, and their third, to consult the welfare of the country."[46]

By 1809, much of Jefferson's popularity was gone, mostly in the wake of the Non-Intercourse Act, passed by Congress in the last sixteen days of his presidency. To Irving's delight, the Federalists won control of the state legislature of New York for the first time in ten years in April 1809. Two years before, in 1807, they had received a severe drubbing by the Jeffersonians. This was a hurtful experience, since Irving had thrown himself into the election in Manhattan, in which Judge Hoffman was running as a Federalist candidate for a seat in the state assembly. As he reported to Mary Fairlie, an attractive and witty woman, who proved the ideal partner in a flirtatious correspondence in early 1807, Irving then felt truly sorry for his "forlorn brethren the Federalists," and he also commented on the election itself with a mixture of disgust and amusement: "I drank beer with the multitude, and I talked handbill fashion with the demagogues, and I shook hands with the mob—whom my heart abhorreth."[47]

Henry Seidel Canby, writing in the early 1930s, argued that Federalism "was essentially an aristocratic ideal struggling to adapt itself to the conditions of a republic and the equalities of a new country."[48] Federalism's "aristocracy" thus was not one of birth but of achievement. The Federalists' ideal state was run by a government of the best. Federalists also demanded respect for what had been tried, and they had a profound distrust of anything new, plus hatred and contempt for the vulgar, the "mob." To Canby, "Irving as the arch–Federalist of American literature is much more interesting than Irving as a custodian of the romantic movement in America."[49] While there is undeniably a romantic haze over many of Irving's writings, his true inspiration was not at all literary. Irving, Canby wrote, "spoke for the nostalgia of the Federalists [...] As a romantic [Irving] is humble and usually derivative, but as an American and as a federalist he speaks in his own right, and had a motive to speak well."[50]

Canby's estimation of Irving's politics may be too one-sided, yet it is refreshing to see him standing up in defense of Washington Irving at a time when, as we will see, his reputation was at a low point. Yet Irving was more of a political chameleon than loyal to a political party. If anything, his politics makes more sense in terms of his masculine attachments, people of substance like Judge Hoffman, Walter Scott, or the Duke of Gor, to name just a few. Between 1807 and 1809, Irving's political opinions were anti–Jeffersonian; by 1848, when he was at work on the Author's Revised Edition, they would have been anti–Jacksonian as well. Tellingly, he left the "Newgate calendar" passage in, as applying equally well to Jackson, the second Jefferson.[51] Nevertheless, it was in the earlier edition of *A History* that Irving gave full vent to his distrust of democracy and his conviction that a government by the people would become mere demagoguery and mob rule. Already the description of Peter Stuyvesant's council is as ungenerous as can be:

> Like a ward committee of political cats, who, when engaged in clamorous gibberings, and caterwaulings, eying one another with hideous grimaces, spitting in each other's faces, and on the point of breaking forth into a general clapper-clawing, are suddenly put to scampering rout and confusion by the startling appearance of a house-dog—So was the no less vociferous council of New Amsterdam, amazed, astounded, and totally dispersed, by the sudden arrival of the enemy.[52]

The enemy, in this instance, are the English, about to take over the Dutch colony. While the colony's worthy representatives simply run away, the "sovereign people all crowded into the market place, herding together with the instinct of sheep who seek for safety in each others company, when the shepherd and his dog are absent and the wolf is prowling round the fold." The shepherd, whose absence the people bewail, is Peter Stuyvesant, "the lion hearted Peter," the last of the Dutch governors.[53] Stuyvesant is no "restless and fidgeting" Kieft but, as we learn in an earlier chapter,

> a tough, sturdy, valiant, weatherbeaten, mettlesome, leathernsided, lion hearted, generous spirited, obstinate, old "seventy six" of a governor [...] a man, or rather a governor, of such uncommon activity and decision of mind that he never sought or accepted the advice of others; depending confidently upon his single head, as did the heroes of yore upon their single arms, to work his way through all difficulties and dangers.

Among the "enlightened vulgar," however, many accused the "great Peter [...] of entertaining highly aristocratic sentiments, and of leaning too much in favour of the patricians." If Stuyvesant seems a Federalist *avant la lettre*, this is no coincidence. George Washington, too, was invariably accused of aristocratic, if not of monarchist, sentiments during his presidency.[54]

There are, of course, differences between Stuyvesant aka "the high minded Pieter *de Groodt*," and America's first president. Whereas George Washington allegedly mastered his personal passions by adopting the virtues of Cato, Addison's Cato, that is,[55] Stuyvesant, upon the imminent arrival of the British forces, gives full vent to his choleric spleen. He locks himself in, refuses "to be broken in by what he esteemed a 'rascal rabble,'" and finally dissolves the whole council, "by kicking them down stairs with his wooden leg."[56] Of course, the colonists pronounce Stuyvesant's eruption as "tyrannical, unconstitutional, highly indecent, and somewhat disrespectful." A meeting is called to make the insults public, which has

> a violent effect upon the sensibility of the people, as it came home at once, to that delicacy of feeling and jealous pride of character, vested in all true mobs; and there is no knowing to what act of resentment they might have been provoked, against the redoubtable Hard-koppig Piet—had not the greasy rogues been somewhat more afraid of their sturdy old governor, than they were of St. Nicolas, the English—or the D---l himself.[57]

Although it is the adventurism of Stuyvesant, that "imp of fame and prowess,"[58] which brings about the ruin of Dutch New York, Knickerbocker does not see him as the tyrant he in reality is, the King archetype's active shadow. Knickerbocker steadfastly venerates Stuyvesant as a national hero, who ratifies the capitulation in style. Standing at "his little garret window in grim silence," the document is

> hoisted to him on the end of a pole, and having scrawled his name at the bottom of it, he excommunicated them all for a set of cowardly, mutinous, degenerate

platter-breeches—threw the capitulation at their heads, slammed down the window, and was heard stamping down the stairs with the most vehement indignation. The rabble incontinently took to their heels; even the Burgomasters were not slow in evacuating the premises, fearing lest the sturdy Peter might issue from his den, and greet them with some unwelcome testimonial of his displeasure.[59]

Over the years, Irving's instincts must have told him that times had changed, and resentments against the existence of political parties were no longer opportune or politically correct. Instead, the 1848 revision of the *A History of New York* echoes the Panic of 1837. Americans in 1848 would remember that the depression continued for years after 1837, and that in 1846 the Democrats had reinstituted Van Buren's independent treasury, to keep surplus federal money in government vaults and not in the private banks that had issued such a flood of inflationary paper money. By developing a new wrongheaded "improvement" for the Dutch colony (the introduction of paper currency, that is, something that never occurred historically), Irving reminds his readers of the days before 1837, rife with easy money and speculation. When Peter Stuyvesant, the Dutch governor who has "old-fashioned notions in favor of gold and silver," insists that only these metals be legal tender, he all but resembles a seventeenth-century Andrew Jackson. It had been Jackson who in 1836 had issued the so-called Specie Circular, which prohibited the use of "those rags of paper currency" to purchase public land in the West. Jackson must have known that the sudden shift to hard money would hurt speculators, but so what?[60]

In the 1848 Author's Revised Edition, Irving eliminated a great deal of his anti-republicanism, as well as references that were either dated or politically and socially inappropriate. Gone were, *inter alia*, a reference to yellow fever in New York City, to the very cold winter of 1804–1805, uncomplimentary references to the American navy, General Wilkinson, and Thomas Jefferson's speeches, as well as a long attack on general politics.[61] As a result of these changes, the 1848 edition lost much of its federalist bias, which Irving feared might offend new readers. He did, however, retain much of the anti-mob rhetoric, as if to defy an age that celebrated the common man.[62] And he retained passages of racial stereotyping, as when he depicts blacks in their conventional role as domestics. A typical Dutch household, for instance, is said to include "some old crone of a negro, who was the oracle of the family,—and who, perched like a raven in a corner of the chimney, would croak forth for a long winter afternoon, a string of incredible stories about New England witches—grisly ghosts—horses without heads—and hairbreadth escapes and bloody encounters among the Native Americans."[63]

One may, with a measure of good will, see such passages as belonging to Irving's light burlesque comedy set in the Golden Age of Dutch New York under its first governor, Wouter Van Twiller.[64] In that age, there were "neither public commotions, nor private quarrels, neither parties, nor sects, nor schisms; neither prosecutions, nor trials, nor punishments; nor were there counsellors, attornies, catch-poles or hangmen."[65] Yet the charming voice and good humor of Diedrich Knickerbocker reach beyond the irreverent antiquarian. Knickerbocker traces the history of New Netherlands with scarcely any reference to the commercial motives upon which the growth of these colonies had in historical fact been based. Instead, "*tranquility* and *repose* reigned throughout the province." An old burgher, for instance, "would set in perfect silence, puffing his pipe, looking in the fire with half shut eyes, and thinking of nothing for hours together," and even the "Burgomaster smoked his pipe in peace." Knickerbocker, the comic old bachelor, here conjures up an idyll of masculine idleness and goodwill, "a sweet and holy calm" that was far removed from both the law and the intrusiveness of women, who kept their homes "constantly in a state of inundation, under the discipline of mops and brooms and scrubbing brushes."

By 1848, the views expressed by Knickerbocker seemed dated and Irving was quite aware that his detractors could accuse him of lack of patriotism.[66] Moreover, Irving no longer was a relatively unknown writer of twenty-six, but a revered American man of letters who had become acquainted with more than one president, a former diplomat, and an international celebrity. And he was sixty-five years old. His youthful anger had disappeared with success. Irving was careful not to criticize political parties too harshly, and even the republican form of government is given a measure of respectability. Revisions, changes, and additions produced a dramatic alteration of tone. Altogether, the *History* of 1848 is a vastly different book from the 1809 version that Irving wrote as a young man. This fact constituted an editorial conundrum. While James Tuttleton, in order to retain "the original flavor," chose to reproduce the 1809 edition for the Library of America, the editors of the *Complete Works* used the 1848 Author's Revised Edition, arguing that this constitutes a text "which theoretically the author would approve."[67]

Irving no doubt would also approve of the London *Athenaeum*'s verdict of 1829: "'Knickerbocker's History of New York,'" the paper bubbled in 1829, "was an honest and manly attempt to found an American literature. Those who read it must have exclaimed involuntarily 'Yes, this is the work which was wanted. The umbilical cord is severed. America is indeed independent.'"[68] Yet *A History of New York* is not built on the heroic model of history to which the founding generation subscribed, and which Irving's contemporaries may have longed for. Rather, it resembles a jeremiad directed against official history. America, readers were to understand, had been built solely on the unwarranted seizure of Native American land in a history of murder, theft, and fraud legitimized by legal authority. "What right," a question in the final chapter of Book I runs, "had the first discoverers of America to land, and take possession of a country, without asking the consent of its inhabitants, or yielding them an adequate compensation for their territory?"[69] The most striking word here is "consent," a reference to America's sacred document, the Declaration of Independence, which accused King George III, the "Royal Brute" according to Thomas Paine, of taxing his "children" without "the consent of the governed."[70] The British government saw things differently, arguing that Parliament had every right to tax the colonies. Perhaps for that very reason, Irving employs a legal device, which, in its insidious aping of such grandees as Hugo Grotius, Samuel Pufendorf, Emer de Vattel, and William Blackstone, reflects his own studies and practice of law between 1799 and 1809. Though Irving never made the law fully his own, he cleverly constructs a case that concedes to Europeans every right to claim Indigenous lands as their legitimate property.[71]

Firstly, we learn, Europeans have the right of discovery of an uninhabited territory. Since the Indigenous population exhibited only "barbarism" and "imbecility," rejecting decent clothes and decent money, they obviously were "totally beneath the human character."[72] Second comes the right acquired by the cultivation of land. Again, the Native Americans failed. On good authority, therefore, they "*deserve to be exterminated as savage and pernicious beasts.*" Third comes "scientific" classification, which invested with the rights of ownership those Europeans who came to settle and cultivate; in contrast, those whose lives were "vagabond, disorderly, unrighteous" had no rights. Following a truly perverse logic, Europeans were only taking possession of "what, according to the aforesaid doctrine, was their own property." Worse, any opposition constituted a violation of those rights for which the Indigenous people deserved to be punished. The logical conclusion is, then, that "they ought to be exterminated."[73] Once again, Irving sounds truly prophetic. As we will see in Chapter Five, from the 1830s the identical conclusion was part of the rhetoric of proponents of Indian removal and westward expansion, of Andrew Jackson, Lewis Cass, or Thomas Hart Benton.

In the 1848 revision, Manhattan becomes the "promised land" for the Dutch settlers, here rendered as "pilgrims." Irving's replay of the Puritans' errand into the wilderness is, however, only marginally more peaceful than the one that took place further north. While some of the Dutch pilgrims wanted to shoot the Native Americans who opposed their landing, most of them paid for the land they bought, though what they offered was a mere pittance, thus tricking the Indigenous people completely.[74] The worthy Dutch colonists therefore can no longer be separated, even ironically, from other colonial groups, past or present. Desire for Native American land, regardless of its provenance, is the expression of "the spirit of 'annexation,'"[75] a spirit that in 1845 had annexed Texas and that in 1848 was fighting a war with Mexico in order to add large chunks of territory to the United States. Yet as soon as Irving introduced the word "annexation," he quickly retreats from any connection with contemporary America and its putative "manifest destiny" and inserts a paragraph identifying two historic figures who, as explorers, resemble Lewis and Clark rather than, say, Generals Winfried Scott or Zachary Taylor.[76]

Indeed, by the time of the ARE, Irving had "mellowed and softened a good deal," which in a reply to his nephew's comment the uncle ascribed to "the effect of age and improved taste combined."[77] Irving's readers too had watched the author take on the persona of the completely apolitical Geoffrey Crayon. And they had had their goodly doses of Diedrich Knickerbocker, the "poor old gentleman" whose "head was a little cracked," as the fictitious landlord of the Independent Columbian Hotel characterizes him.[78] Moreover, Knickerbocker's time, we learn in *The Sketch Book*, "might have been much better employed in weightier labours [than writing]." Once again, Irving's deep-felt need to find for himself a place among other men, shines through loudly and clearly. The crotchety, rough-and-tumble, comic old bachelor, we know, was one of Irving's alter egos, "apt to ride his hobby in his own way" and "never intend[ing] to injure or offend."[79] Tellingly, at the end of *A History of New York* Knickerbocker, whose "strong, vigorous, and manly style" had found the admiration of reviewers, confesses that he looks upon the world "with the most perfect good nature," and whose "only sorrow is, that it does not prove itself worthy of the unbounded love" he bears it.[80]

Geoffrey Crayon too is an essential part of Irving's complicated persona. "Well-read, well-traveled, and clever," as Brian Jay Jones describes him, Crayon was

> the kind of person you longed to chat with, dine with, or sit with at the theater. Elegant, self-deprecating, and never one to make himself more interesting than his stories, Crayon, readers were convinced, *was* Washington Irving. Crayon represented everything Irving would have *liked* to have been. In fact, Irving so successfully blurred the line between author and pseudonym that the polished, erudite, confident Geoffrey Crayon became the public persona of the nervous, insecure Washington Irving—one Irving would cultivate and protect for the next forty years.[81]

Irving had chosen his pen name with good reason. "Geoffrey" is an obvious homage to Chaucer, the great storyteller, whose *Canterbury Tales* remind us that Irving too wrote tales, narratives, usually of something remarkable, and mostly told in the third person, and with elements of an oral tradition. "Crayon," however, references to another writing style, the sketch. I shortly will have more to say on the sketch as the ideal vehicle to express one's status anxiety. At this point, it is worth noting that Irving had been making sketches—literally depicting people and places with a crayon, a waxy charcoal-based pencil—ever since he first traveled abroad in 1803. For him, they were the equivalent to the "thumb-sketches" from which a painter makes lager compositions, and thus he chose to title his first collections of stories a "sketch book."[82]

But not only is Irving's writing pictorial. Irving was most sympathetic to painters. He studied in New York with a drawing-master when he was young and, as his pencil sketches show, he had a real talent for drawing. While in Rome, he became friends with the painter Washington Allston, who praised his sketches and urged him to become a painter. Irving seriously thought about this for a few days, then abandoned the idea, though he always remained drawn to painters. Shortly after Matilda Hoffman's death, in 1809, Irving met John Wesley Jarvis, an aspiring painter, who took his likeness and whom Irving personally liked. Among his closest friends in England were the painters Charles R. Leslie and Gilbert Stuart Newton. In Spain, Irving met and befriended another painter, David Wilkie, later Sir David Wilkie. And he would meet over dinner with the great Emanuel Gottlieb Leutze.[83] This leaves us with the "Gent." As a short form of gentleman, "Gent." signals that a literary work was the product, not of a professional writer but of a gentleman-amateur, a singular producer known from a preindustrial mode of production and, for many readers of the nineteenth century, the object of desires and longings. Crayon's was, of course, more the charming voice of a man of feeling. Crayon above all enabled Irving to affect a patrician disdain for the "sordid dusty, and soul-killing" world of business, a world that he himself belonged to but did not feel at home in, from his imagined world.[84]

The *real* Irving, of course, was neither Crayon nor Diedrich Knickerbocker, the pretended author figure he had developed for *A History of New York*. Irving "was both—gruff yet graceful, blustering yet charming, crass but classy. And where Crayon made it all look easy, Knickerbocker knew it was hard work. The cultivated Crayon may have become the public personality, and Knickerbocker the private workhorse, but it was Irving alone who had earned the success and reputation."[85] There is, nevertheless, a deep and abiding connection between Geoffrey Crayon's (the Gent's) and "the late" Diedrich Knickerbocker's avoidance of money and Irving's own need to dissociate himself from his own commercial motive while rendering their voices profitable. The very title pages of Irving's books, John McWilliams concludes, "allow the reader to forget that, if the reader wishes to absorb the good humor, kindly feeling and self-protective melancholy of Diedrich Knickerbocker and Geoffrey Crayon, he must first buy Washington Irving's book."[86] This was not a conscious ploy to divert readers' attentions. There always remained, behind the cloak, Irving's anima-identity. Crayon as well as Knickerbocker are projections of this, insisting again and again that they write only to stimulate a benevolent view of human nature, only to arouse good feelings among sensitive men and women of good will.

Irving finally brought together the author Washington Irving and his pseudonymous creations in an introductory letter to the *Knickerbocker Magazine* in March 1839. The letter, purportedly written by Crayon, describes how as a youth he (Crayon) had met Diedrich Knickerbocker while Knickerbocker was doing antiquarian research at Wolfert's Roost, Wolfert Acker's seventeenth-century house, which we can clearly recognize, nowadays, as Irving's Sunnyside.[87] There are also good literary reasons why Irving cultivated and protected Crayon and Knickerbocker for so many years. Their third-person voices gave him a way of steadying textual contradictions. They permitted him a greater range of sympathies and muted his various antagonisms. Though Crayon as narrator edges toward an uncritical fascination with the past, Irving does not continually force the past to center stage. Instead, he grants his characters a sustained amplitude of sympathy. By the same token, Knickerbocker's penchant for stories about buried treasure at one point is belittled as mere "brain fever," which in turn makes us pity rather than envy Wolfert Webber.[88]

Put another way, Irving fictionalized himself so as to partially undermine his own authority. Clearly, his anima-identity had not yet morphed into the "Magician's" energy of initiation and transformation, of guidance to and knowledge of model masculinities. This would come later, especially with *Life of George Washington*.[89] In Irving's earlier writings, the numerous references to "old legends" or "old stories" all emphasize the authenticity of the narrated events, yet the narrators are either dead (like "the late" Diedrich Knickerbocker) or separated from readers by space or time. Represented as works of antiquarianism, fueled by a feeling for the historical and poetical, the marvelous and the enchanted, Irving's fictional writings after *A History of New York* are mediated through voices from a distant land who haunt libraries, town meetings, Spanish or Moorish palaces, or old French villages to collect touching anecdotes about the past. Their production thus reproduces the fundamental characteristics of a modern consumer society, production from a distance. *Sketch Book*, *Bracebridge Hall*, and *Tales of a Traveller*, as well as a number of the Spanish writings, are the works of an American living abroad that became bestsellers in the United States, far away from the scene of their production. They were made possible largely because of the revolution in transportation, which allowed increasingly large numbers of people to travel, and by a revolution in the readership, which had become a mass, replacing the "happy few" of the eighteenth-century elites.[90]

The "Christmas" section of the *Sketch Book* faithfully registers these changes. Crayon indulges in sentimentality, proclaiming his admiration for the antique, the customary, the unregulated. Indeed, the long descriptive passages in the "Christmas" section are all about a landed patriarchy whose feudally guaranteed continuity of a family, conceived as a web of property and class relations, works to provide a framework of temporality for Crayon. It is as if Irving had seen, like Tocqueville after him, that the material conditions in the United States made community (or the family) less capable of narrating beyond the individual life.[91] The "Christmas" section is no exception in this regard. In "The Legend of Sleepy Hollow" we observe the community's forceful expulsion of the Yankee capitalist aggression that Ichabod Crane represents. And in the "Money Diggers" section of *Tales of a Traveller*, Irving included the genteel Dutch burghers as an extended family of sorts. Thus, it is not a singular story, of Tom Walker or Wolfert Webber, so much as the community that's important for the tales. Through the community's successful resistance to capitalist acquisitiveness the tales reaffirm rural, precapitalistic values at the same time as they position an unwanted self-reliant masculinity in the new social regime of a market-based economy.

However, reaffirmation of precapitalistic values and rejection of entrepreneurial masculinity only compensate for the commercialization of all walks of life. Instead of offering viable alternatives, they inscribe the loss they mean to recover. This is especially true of the "Englishness" of *The Sketch Book*, whether originating from books or personal experience. That "Englishness" is "a purely imaginary construct that replaces the sense of home grounded on experience and perpetuated by actual memory."[92] As a construct, it is bound to meet with disappointment; on the other hand, it constitutes a link between *The Sketch Book*, the somewhat later *Bracebridge Hall*, and Irving's earlier writings, *Jonathan Oldstyle, Salmagundi*, and *A History of New York*. Irving, upon travelling to Europe, did not quite close "one volume of the world and its concerns."[93] Though Jeffrey Rubin-Dorsky writes that the purpose of the *Sketch Book* was "somehow to get inside the timelessness of England via an imaginative projection into the very fiber of its cultural and spiritual heritage,"[94] it is worth pointing out that four sketches are American and that, in addition, there is an entire American section in *Tales of a Traveller*. Nevertheless, the bulk of the sketches and tales remains English, and *Bracebridge Hall* is even more of an English work, with only one sketch, "Dolph Heyliger," set in America. In each instance, "imaginative projection" means that the old is appreciated from an aesthetic perspective, without entering into the sociological, political, or philosophical. America, in contrast, sometimes serves as a point of reference for liberty, innocence, and hope for the future. Crayon's romantic escape thus made an attractive contrast with America as a country "where history was, in a manner, in anticipation; where everything in art was new and progressive, and pointed to the future rather than to the past; where, in short, the works of man gave no ideas but those of young existence, and prospective improvement."[95]

America's future was not without its problems, though. American society in the early nineteenth century was no longer a given, but in flux, and highly divisive. The expansion of entrepreneurial capitalism was becoming an article of faith, and economic striving a moral imperative. Irving, faced with a bewildering, rapidly industrializing world, was aware of this, and, using his animatic compass points, he would write up against it throughout his career. More than anything, he registered the eclipse of "communal manhood" by "self-made manhood," to use E. Anthony Rotundo's terms.[96] The old paradigm of "communal manhood" was rooted in the life of the community and the qualities of a man's character; in contrast, the new paradigm of "self-made manhood" came to be based on individual achievement, direct action, entrepreneurial competition and, on the downside, profound anxieties. It is only logical, therefore, that the predominant theme in *Sketch Book* is "mutability." An idealized European past that focuses on the way of life of a privileged elite serves as a model of stability and equilibrium. Tellingly, in "English Writers on America" Crayon uses an architectural metaphor to capture England's stability as a force his own country would do well to emulate: "[I]t is in the moral feeling of the people that the deep foundations of British prosperity are laid; and however the superstructure may be time worn, or over run by abuses, there must be something solid in the basis, admirable in the materials, and stable in the structure of an edifice that so long has towered unshaken amidst the tempests of the world."[97] Disappointment is bound to follow suit. The onset of capitalism—and with it, modernity—saps every tradition of its vital force. England no longer "was itself," Crayon learns from young Squire Bracebridge, its cherished traditions lost within the past and no longer functioning on their own accord in the present.[98]

Crayon's main objective, we learn from "The Author's Account of Himself," was "to wander over scenes of renowned achievement—to tread, as it were, in the footsteps of antiquity—to loiter about the ruined castle—to meditate on the falling tower—to escape, in short, from the common-place realities of the present, and lose myself among the shadowy grandeur of the past."[99] The "common-place realities of the present" were part of life in the metropolis, where the frenzy of entrepreneurial activity that came with the rise of modern capitalism threatens the genteel patriarch's control. The untrammeled concern with commerce that Crayon finds in "a[n] immense metropolis like London is calculated to make men selfish and uninteresting[....] They present but the cold superficies of character—its rich and genial qualities have no time to be warmed into a flow."[100] For "rich and genial qualities" one had to turn to the English countryside, which for Crayon functions as the seat of moral order and social harmony. The English countryside's "great charm," he exclaims in "Rural Life in England," "is the moral feeling that seems to pervade it. It is associated in the mind with ideas of order, of quiet, of sober well-established principles, of hoary usage and reverend custom. Every thing seems to be the growth of ages of regular and peaceful existence."[101]

In contrast to the competitive frenzy of urban life, country life is a haven for the anima consciousness. Its very "regularity" allows for carefully modulated modes of social interaction. In the country, the "man of refinement [...] finds nothing revolting in an intercourse with the lower orders[....] He lays aside his distance and reserve, and is glad to wave the distinctions of rank, and to enter into the honest, heartfelt enjoyments of common life."[102] By portraying the relationships between "the lower orders" and the aristocracy as fundamentally beneficial to all, Crayon transforms a relation of rule into a familial relation, a relation which he depicts as a happy instance of benevolent paternalism. The *Sketch Book* of 1820 abounds with this form of traditional manhood, in particular as it is expressed in the longing for a period when the men of the landed gentry embodied a high-minded "statesmanship," acting (or at least seeing themselves) as the nation's "natural" leaders.[103] This is perhaps most evident in the figure of the Squire of Bracebridge, whom we meet in the book's extended "Christmas" section. As the Squire's son explains to the touring Crayon,

> My father, you must know, is a bigoted devotee of the old school, and prides himself upon keeping up something of the old English hospitality. He is a tolerable specimen of what you will rarely meet with now-a-days in its purity, the old English country gentleman; for our men of fortune spend so much of their time in town, and fashion is carried so much into the country, that the strong rich peculiarities of ancient rural life are almost polished away.[104]

Squire Bracebridge is an advocate both of "chivalry" and of the avoidance of "modern effeminacy and weak nerves."[105] This makes him one who—like the young George Washington—took "honest Peacham for his text book, instead of Chesterfield." As a "worthy old cavalier," the Squire is "happy himself, and disposed to make all the world happy." In this, he is probably closest to Baltus Van Tassel in terms of the propertied masculinity Irving offers in the *Sketch Book*. And there is more. The "hardy exercises" that come with life in the English countryside "produce also [...] a manliness and simplicity of manners, which even the follies and dissipations of the town cannot easily pervert, and can never entirely destroy." Thus, instead of the "softness and effeminacy" of city-dwellers, country gentlemen can boast of "elegance and strength, [and] a robustness of frame and freshness of complexion."

The authentic life of achieved manhood that Crayon imagines here coheres on the illusion of continuity in time as the basis of generational redefinition. As each successive head of the Bracebridge household has been "known simply by the appellation of 'The Squire'; a title which has been accorded to the head of the family since time immemorial,"[106] the reality of competitive individualism evaporates in the face of tradition, if not of timelessness. And, when raised to a cosmological level, it is also beyond dispute: "It was really delightful," Crayon tells us, "to see the old Squire, seated in his hereditary elbow chair, by the hospitable fireside of his ancestors, and looking around him like the sun of a system, beaming warmth and gladness to every heart."[107] Since the order is not made by humans, but is cosmological ("the sun of a system"), the social order of genteel patriarchy is also beyond dispute. It is an illusion of an atemporal stasis that Crayon values so highly in the system of squirarchy; sanctified by nature (and, by extension, its creator), achieved masculinity is its avatar.

Though Irving portrays Bracebridge's paternalism as kind and jovial, he also questions the extent to which a relation is still possible that "brought the peasant and peer together, and blended all ranks in one warm generous flow of joy and kindness."[108] The zealousness of the Squire to preserve tradition in itself carries with it the implication that traditions no longer function on their own accord but instead must be actively pursued. Tellingly, the Squire "regrets sometimes that he had not been born a few centuries earlier, when England was itself, and had its peculiar manners and customs."[109] The phrase "when England was itself" makes one suspect that England no longer *is* itself, that the Squire's honest practices are forever lost and no longer viable. Indeed, it seems as if the nobility as such had been hurled from the timeless space it claimed into the flow of time and history, where it survives as a mere relic of the past.

Signs of decay are everywhere in Crayon's depiction of the festive practices at Bracebridge Hall. The Squire, endeavoring to "follow up [...] the quaint customs of antiquity," does so only "at a humble distance" and by resorting to "make shifts."[110] Responsibility for the souring of the relationship between the peasants and the Squire is shown to lie with the peasants, though. As the Squire remembers, the last time he invited everyone into his manor hall, the peasants "did not understand how to play their parts in the scene of hospitality; many uncouth circumstances occurred; the manor was overrun by all the vagrants of the country, and more beggars drawn into the neighbourhood in one week than the parish officers could get rid of in a year."[111] The peasants' purported inability "to play their parts" signals both the breakdown of the atemporal domestic order the Bracebridges and, by extension, Crayon fantasies about, much as it points to the advent of capitalism as the originator of a script in which the peasants assume an array of new roles that disable the patriarchal economy. (American readers of the *Sketch Book* would remember these passages when news of the mayhem at Andrew Jackson's postinauguration party of March 4, 1829, reached an unbelieving nation.[112])

The peasants' new roles form part of Bracebridge's own analysis, which he "braces himself" for in order to enlighten the artless Crayon: "[W]e have almost lost our simple true-hearted peasantry. They have broken asunder from the higher classes, and seem to think their interests are separate."[113] The division of interest that the Squire deplores is the result of a number of transformations brought about by the emergence of capitalism—from fixed stations in life to self and self-interest; from a land-based economy to a cash economy; from ostensible timelessness to a vision of the future as a wide-open possibility. Crayon's rendering of English nobility on the edge of extinction thus is poignant. As narrator, he records the precise moment in history when entrepreneurial capitalism was destroying the conditions of possibility that allowed the nobility to exist as a moral and social authority. Irving makes the transformation clear in his vexed description of a "wealthy citizen" who has "amassed a vast fortune" and "purchased the estate and mansion of a ruined nobleman in the neighbourhood."[114] "[L]ooking about him with the pompous air of a man accustomed to rule on change and shake the stock market with a nod," the wealthy citizen embodies "the aspirings of vulgarity" that "thinks to elevate itself by humiliating its neighbor" and that Crayon (and Irving) associates with entrepreneurial capitalism. The purported vulgarity is even more striking in the depiction of the "aspiring citizen's" two sons, who seem to represent a posterity that, if anything, is even further removed from traditional masculinity. "They were arrayed in the extremity of the mode," Crayon describes the man's offspring, "with all that pedantry of dress, which marks the man of questionable pretensions to style. [...] Art had done everything to accomplish them as men of fashion, but nature had denied the nameless grace [of the] true gentleman."

Nouveau riche people, we are led to assume, may have bought up one of the mansions of a man called William Roscoe. Though praised by Crayon for his ability to maintain a "union of commerce and the intellectual pursuits," Roscoe has nevertheless been "unfortunate in business."[115] The result, Crayon soon learns, is that one of Roscoe's mansions has been sold off; worse still, his large library has "passed under the hammer of the auctioneer and was dispersed about the country." "The good people of the vicinity thronged like wreckers to get some part of the noble vessel that had been driven on shore," Crayon says, clearly disgusted by the mere exchange value assigned to Roscoe's literary collection. "We might picture to ourselves some knot of speculators debating with calculating brow over the quaint binding and illuminated margin of an obsolete author."

For David Anthony there is no doubt that Irving is making connections between Roscoe's compromised economic state and his own. "The scholar only knows how dear these silent, yet eloquent companions of pure thought and innocent hours become in the season of adversity," Crayon says, still speaking of Roscoe's books. "When all that is worldly turns to dross around us, these only retain their steady value."[116] Roscoe, modeled after a Liverpool banker, lawyer, abolitionist, and author of a book on Lorenzo de' Medici, is a figure who has become anachronistic both culturally and financially but who, Anthony points out, is of value for his very resistance to modernity. Like Rip Van Winkle, such men have woken from their extended slumber to find that they no longer fit into a society that has exchanged the "dignity" of an "aristocratic"/Federalist manhood rooted in property and the use value of things for the insubstantial paper money masculinity of the credit-based commercial world and its foundation of exchange value.[117]

There is a fervent eulogy on the use value of obsolete authors in "Westminster Abbey," one of the set pieces in *The Sketch* Book, in which Irving juxtaposes the tombs of the great men in England's history to the more modest and simple graves of the poets. While "the lives of literary men afford no striking themes for the sculptor," Crayon muses on the Poets' Corner, "the visitors to the abbey [nonetheless] remained longest about them. A kinder and fonder feeling takes the place of that old curiosity or vague admiration with which they gaze in the splendid monuments of the great and the heroic." If, therefore, visitors "linger about" the poets' graves as about "the tombs of friends and companions," the heroes' monuments at best elicit "empty names and sounding actions." The names of the latter perish "from record and recollection," so that their history is only "a tale that is told," while their monuments will become ruins.[118] Reading such lines we realize that Irving was still a long way off the great-deeds-and-great-men kind of manliness he would delineate in his later writings, seeking, instead, compensation for the commercialization of all walks of life in a kind of dead poets society.

The Irving of the 1820s still dreamed of genteel individuals that could preserve the patrician valuation of traditional culture over mere business and populist politics. Another good example is "The Spectre Bridegroom," the hero of a Gothic tale about a "tall, gallant cavalier"[119] who, though on an errand to bring news of the death of the destined bridegroom of the daughter of a wealthy baron, instantly wins the fair young lady's heart. The young man, rather than spoil the excitement of the family as well as of the guests, who are all waiting for the arrival of the real bridegroom, pretends to be a ghost and suddenly disappears—and takes the daughter with him. The two secretly marry. Upon their return, we see the young lady "mounted on a palfrey, attended by a cavalier on horseback [...] the Spectre Bridegroom [...] wonderfully improved in his appearance since his visit to the world of spirits. His dress was splendid, and set off a noble figure of manly symmetry." Needless to say, the baron, who is only too happy to have his daughter back, no longer has any objections to their union (even though the new bridegroom comes from a hostile house), and the "revels at the house were resumed."

Any regrounding of traditional culture in gentility, property, and social status only pastes over the fact that the genteel patriarchs had long started to lose their dominance. Derived as Irving's genteel patriarchs are from an earlier social formation, it seems easy to dismiss them as so many buffoons or clowns. Yet Irving's genteel patriarchs do not actually be*long* to a past era; they belong to Irving's anima-identity, and they are active in the cultural process of the present, hence "residual," to borrow Raymond Williams's term.[120] Williams describes as residual those beliefs, values, practices, or customs that are derived from an earlier stage of society, and thus reflect a very different social formation, together with different political and religious beliefs and values than the present. Importantly, residual beliefs often remain dominant long after the social conditions that made them dominant have disappeared (such as, for instance, today's assumptions by some people that men are inherently more important or intelligent than women). A residual relationship therefore does not denote something that is archaic, in the sense of recognizably belonging to a past era, but rather something that has been "formed in the past, but is still active in the cultural process, not only and often not at all as an element of the past, but as an effective element of the present."[121] Residual relationships, Williams goes on to say, can be oppositional to the dominant tendencies, in which case the dominant tries to forget or marginalize it. At times the dominant is successful, at times not. In addition, the dominant culture, when threatened by too many experiences that are interpretable in terms of past cultural formations and institutions weakening its legitimacy, incorporates residual elements into itself: "It is in the incorporation of the actively residual—by reinterpretation, dilution, projection, discriminating inclusion and exclusion—that the work of the selective *tradition* is especially evident."[122]

As effective elements of the present, residual figures like Squire

Bracebridge or the "Spectre Bridegroom" constitute both a fantasied retreat from and a compensatory response to the forces of the new economy, of commerce and market corruption, even though the fantasy could offer, at best, partial or temporary comfort. Such comfort can be gleaned from a notebook entry, probably from the summer of 1816, in which Irving, then living in England, compares the "settled and quiet habits" of the English to the "irregularity, impatience of restraint, the neglect and almost contempt for minor observances, the restless and sanguine spirit of the Americans." And, Irving added, "the speculative turn and proneness to hyperbole, with which Americans are charged, may be traced to the unsettled mode of their life."[123]

The Sketch Book established Irving as a celebrity writer. He was widely acclaimed on both sides of the Atlantic, though there were some reservations. Richard Henry Dana, for instance, deplored the lack of the "masculine" traits of Irving's earlier writings, with their "good bone and muscle." Finding fault with what most critics and readers crooned over, Dana dismissed *Sketch Book* as "feminine—*dressy*, elegant, and languid."[124] Dana's criticism was right to the point. It was a matter of the literary form Irving had chosen, the sketch. The sketch is humble, unpretentious, and self-deprecatory, the perfect medium for a writer who, stuck in his anima-identity, attempts "no lofty theme."[125] It is by definition short, pretends that it was produced at a single sitting, and makes no claim to last; it is, in Ann Douglas's words, "ultimately dispensable."[126] The apologetic tone, the attitude of humility indeed was essential to the career and art of the sentimentalist writer. Yet the apparent timidity of the sketch, its lack of pretension as art, is deceptive. Under the veneer of self-effacement lies a hidden animus, a rage, against the forces, social as well as personal, that humble the writer.[127] Geoffrey Crayon, Irving's persona, may be overtly emasculated, but he is covertly vengeful, carrying poison, though "the patient should never be conscious that he is taking a dose."[128]

Crayon's ambiguities reflect Irving's own aspirations and conflicts. Reading Dana's criticism, Irving must have writhed, though outwardly he remained unperturbed. He left for Paris in August 1820; when he returned to England in 1822, he published *Bracebridge Hall* towards the end of May, after which he went back to Paris, supervising the American edition. More American editions were to follow, through the Author's Revised Edition. This once again caused a considerable dilemma for the editors of critical editions. Which *Bracebridge Hall*, for instance, was to be used as copy-text? The original London edition or, rather, the Author's Revised Edition?[129] There were other problems as well. Living in England and also writing for an English audience, Irving nevertheless encouraged Americans to see the value of "gentlemen in three-cornered hats." If his benevolent, paternalistic masculinities resonate with an anachronistic idea of "Englishness," Irving nevertheless believed that they might be used as positive models in times that he or, rather, the woman within, experienced as unbearable. As he put it in "The Author," his intention was to give "new interest [...] to such topics."[130]

As he had confessed in *Sketch Book*, the Crayon of *Bracebridge Hall* likewise admits that his internalized image of "England"—a veritable "contagion" or "infection"—stems from books he had read while in America.[131] In this regard, his (or, rather, Irving's) "Englishness" should be seen, at least in part, as a form of transatlantic borrowing, and I draw my use of Irving's narrative strategy from C. Michael Hurst's essay, "Reinventing Patriarchy."[132] Irving may have drawn for his "Englishness" on the books he read in his native country, but there also was personal experience. According to Stanley Williams, the prototype for Bracebridge Hall was Aston Hall, in Birmingham, which during Irving's time was still in the countryside. Here had actually lived the Bracebridges, of an old Warwickshire family, long resident at Atherstone. Charles Holt Bracebridge was the last lineal descendant of the family that built "the Hall." Irving had visited Aston Hall in 1818, during his visit with the Van Warts (Henry Van Wart, an American expat, had married his sister, Sarah Sanders Irving, and eventually settled in Birmingham). Irving made ample notes during the visit, which he used for *The Sketch Book*. He used the same notes for *Bracebridge Hall*, adding embellishments from another manor house, Haddon Hall, which he visited with Charles Leslie in 1821.[133]

In *Bracebridge Hall*, Irving looks at England from two perspectives. In "The Author's Farewell," Crayon declares that he was born and raised in America, "the dear land that gave me birth."[134] Yet America was "a new country," and so he had been "educated from infancy in the literature of the old one," which provided for him "historical and poetical associations, connected with places, and manners, and customs of Europe." *Bracebridge Hall* thus is all about "recollected ideas" reflected and refracted in the "peculiarities which distinguish an old country."[135] Among these "peculiarities" are "the effects of hereditary rank." A gentleman thus endowed

> does not feel himself a mere individual link in creation, responsible only for his own brief term of being. He carries back his existence in proud recollection, and he extends it forward in honorable anticipation. He lives with his ancestry, and he lives with his posterity. To both does he consider himself involved in deep responsibilities. As he has received much from those that have gone before, so he feels bound to transmit much to those who are to come after him. His domestic undertakings seem to imply a longer existence than those of ordinary men; none are so apt to build and plant for future centuries, as noble-spirited men, who have received their heritages from foregone ages.[136]

It would be easy to dismiss such outpourings as willful blindness to social reality. But Crayon extenuates the ideological content by backpedaling: "Republican as I am by birth, and brought up as I have been in republican principles and habits, I can feel nothing for the servile reverence for titled rank, merely because it is titled."[137] The views expressed here continue to have power for one in search of the sort of manhood valorized in Squire Bracebridge—one that is unscathed by the forces of commerce and market corruption. What we see here is a peculiarly American redaction of Burkean conservatism. Compensatory, it marks a "nervous" Federalist effort to rely on a "gold standard" of male selfhood that is no longer in effect.[138] In other words, Crayon deploys the relays of sentimentality and sympathy in evoking nostalgia for the social cohesion of a Federalist-style community. Upon arrival in England, Crayon feels a stranger, but not because he is an American, hence different, but because the England he encounters does not quite jibe with the antiquated ideals that he—like many other Americans, including Irving himself—claimed as his own. What he sees in England are "signs of national old age, and empire's decay [...] crumbling monuments of the past."[139]

Crayon's account cannot really provide access to a timeless realm that contains "the unchanging foundations of all human endeavor."[140] What I am suggesting, therefore, is that Irving's sketches and tales seek to counter market panic and masculine anxiety by imagining an exchange value of "residual" gentility, one that would ensure what Joseph Fichtelberg called "a stable moral economy."[141] Residual as they are, the personalities of Crayon or Squire Bracebridge reflect an understanding that the account cannot be balanced, whether in the fictional worlds of moral economy nor in political economy. Moreover, Irving captures the past not through a factual exposition but through storytelling. By doing so, he transforms the active content of Old Federalism (or, if you like, Burkean Toryism), a verifiable historical phenomenon and potentially dangerous political force, in the way of progress by self-made men, into the passive content of reverie and daydream.

Being a writer endowed with a hypertrophic anima-consciousness for Irving came to mean making the best of a social reality of entrepreneurial capitalism and rugged individualism by living in dreamscapes of past cultures. In these dreamscapes Irving was able to reestablish a space of patriarchal control, a world in which not everything was for sale, alienable. This world was no longer outside but *within* the storytelling process itself. Yet to bring back, through storytelling, a time when land was not yet a commodity, not yet subject to speculation, had its price. Through the mode of storytelling Irving was able both to placate his woman within and to domesticate the social dislocations he was witness to. However, by obliterating the distinction between past and present, change itself becomes foreclosed. In the end, "mere business" (the acquisition of wealth, together with the speculative thrills this entails) is transformed into "inheritance," at the same time as mimesis (fictional realism) is transformed into fairy-tale. Crayon's entire narrative strategy depends on a legendary past, although the fantasy is often elided by the observational tone that frames many of the tales and sketches. As Michael Hurst concludes, "Insofar as the sketches adopt a tone of objectivity, however, they tend to cover over their fantastic origins, thereby reintroducing the illusion of atemporal stasis that Crayon valued so highly in the manor system."[142]

Faced with an incipient business culture in which ambitious males were setting postpatrician norms for manhood, Irving evolved premodern ways of deauthorizing conventional manhood, including his own authority. His relatively stable, simple duplicities presume a high degree of sympathy from his readers. Irving knew his audience, and he often writes as if he and his readers were in the same room. The datedness of his impassioned narrative style, however it diverges in resolving dependence on the market, suggests the common intensity in the writer's engagement with his contemporary world of genteel readers. When in "English Country Gentlemen," Squire Bracebridge laments the decline of the old order, we find, at best, merely dim echoes of the social changes that were rocking England. Moreover, there is a blithe disregard of the complex power relations that actually shaped life in the manor house. Instead, Crayon professes to not know "a more enviable condition of life, than that of an English country gentleman, of sound judgment and good feelings, who passes the greater part of his time on an hereditary estate in the country."[143]

Irving could never bring himself to describe the social upheavals in England, neither in *The Sketch Book* nor in *Bracebridge Hall*, let alone to analyze them.[144] The lacuna is hinted at in the "Author's Farewell" in *Bracebridge Hall*. "It will, probably, be said, too, by some, that I view England with a partial eye," Crayon begins clumsily. "Perhaps I do; for I can never forget that it is my 'father land.'"[145] Perhaps so, but Crayon is a citizen of the United States. Many of his commentaries on England therefore should be seen as Irving's attempts to contain the contradictory aspects of early nineteenth-century American selfhood, including of course his own. Clearly, the antagonism between communal manhood and the bristling egotism of the self-made man constituted such a contradiction. Gentleman Geoffrey Crayon stands for tradition, a time before a money economy, a time before rampant individualism, a time of patriarchy grounded in estates, families, and their durability, that is, in a system of hierarchy in which the normative order of gender and sex is oriented to the succession of fathers. Crayon, the bachelor, thus is not only the voice containing the contradictory aspects of American selfhood, but also the one to offer up the paternal role "as a way to transcend the selfishness of individual existence."[146]

In his later writings, Irving would invest this paternal role in the more or less perfectly realized masculinities of, for instance, Christopher Columbus and George Washington. In *Sketch Book* as well as in *Bracebridge Hall*, Irving still mourns the loss of "communal manhood," of a social formation in which a man's identity was inseparable from the duties a man owed to his community.[147] He registers the profound implications the shift in thinking from community to person had for notions of manhood. In fact, Irving idealized "communal manhood" just at the moment "when it was clearly being displaced by modernity."[148] Modern American men rejected the idea that they had a fixed place in any hierarchy; they ceased to see themselves as segments in an unbroken family line; and their zest for the marketplace and, later, the frontier, challenged the traditional disdain of the gentry for market interests and adventurism, a disdain, Gordon Wood explains, that also was "at the heart of classical republicanism."[149] In moral terms, the rejection of the here and now, which appears irredeemable, is a classic example of nostalgia. "Nostalgia," Linda Hutcheon explains, "is fundamentally conservative in its praxis, for it wants to keep things as they were—or, more accurately, as they are imagined to have been […] it is rarely the past as actually experienced, of course; it is the past as imagined, as idealized through memory and desire."[150] Put differently, the past is "memorialized" as past, crystallized into precious moments selected by memory. Memory, it is worth noting, sanitizes as it selects, making the past feel complete, stable, coherent, and safe from "the unexpected and the untoward, from accident or betrayal."[151]

Washington Irving, through Geoffrey Crayon, valorized and celebrated "residuals"—crusty, ludicrous, and whimsical throwbacks to yesteryear, who seem totally unfit for the present—to such an extent that the London *Gentleman's Magazine* wrote, "no such beings exist now a days."[152] What particularly angered reviewers was that the distresses English society was in at the time did not really concern Irving. They were a spectacle in which he had no part. His seeming indifference to the bad times, the despair in the countryside, the dire forebodings of the middle classes—all of which William Cobbett duly recorded[153]—led to more attacks from the democratic reviews. To be sure, Irving had commented on the "distress of the poor" in a letter written from Birmingham in 1816,[154] and in *Tales of a Traveller* he included a sketch about an "ignorant, self willed, and clownish" member of the gentry, a "Booby Squire." It was, however, not until 1829–1830, when Irving was attached to the American legation in London, that he directly addresses the appalling living conditions of English working classes and other living issues that would come out in the Reform Bill, though Irving was on his way to America before its passing.[155]

After the publication of *Tales of a Traveller*, critics even accused Irving of groveling before gentility. Irving "would strike out his best passage, dilute his best argument, or recant his sincerest opinion," the *Westminster Review* crabbed in October 1824, "in the fear of losing his next invitation to dinner he may expect from Grosvenor-square."[156] In the same spirit, an American critic called him a "mockbird" for not "startling" polite society, let alone "offending them with the intrusion of *a sentiment which can disturb the self-complacency*, which is their Elysium."[157] Irving resented the criticism, though he kept his convictions to himself, only confiding them to his notebook: "As to the idea that I have bowed to peers [...] I reject the calumny with scorn—It is true I have mingled with the nobility of the countries I have visited but it was on their own hospitable solicitations—and it is a low mind that can only think of mingling with nobility with bowing to it [...] I never sacrificed my independence...."[158]

We should look at the criticisms as well as on Irving's reaction as symptoms. The genteel patriarch still was a powerful ideal in antebellum America. It was, of course, an ideal inherited from Europe. At his best, the genteel patriarch represented a dignified aristocratic manhood, committed to the British upper-class code of honor and to a well-rounded character, with exquisite tastes and manners and refined sensibilities. This type of manhood was inseparable from property ownership and a benevolent patriarchal authority at home, including the moral instruction of one's sons. An entry in Irving's French journal for June 1825 testifies to his idealization of genteel patriarchs. Irving copied from an editorial in the London *Times* about the wealth of the peers in Britain's House of Lords, which "is wealth almost entirely confined to landed property: its immediate possessors have in few instances acquired it by their industry or talents." Though this leads to more "inertness [and] stagnation," it at the same time generates "more satisfaction [because] the greatness of every individual aristocrat who knows that he is already at the top of society & can be no personal gainer by change [is] favourable to the general stability of the commonwealth."[159] Reading these lines one begins to doubt whether the antiquarianism of *Bracebridge Hall* really is proof that, as Stanley Williams wrote, Irving's own feelings for old England had become exhausted.[160] Add to this what Irving, responding to "unfavourable representations" of him, wrote to Henry Brevoort from Madrid: "A man, however, must have firmness enough to pursue his plans when justified by his own conscience, without being diverted from them by the idle surmises and misconceptions of others."[161]

THREE

Rip Van Winkle, Ichabod Crane, and Other Troubled Masculinities

IRVING HAD SAILED TO ENGLAND IN MAY 1815, "adrift" and "weary of everything," especially of himself. Yet he was determined to leave behind the idle and meaningless life he had been leading in New York, and was ready, after his return, to "settle [himself] down to useful and honourable application."[1] As Geoffrey Crayon, the fictitious author of *The Sketch Book*, notes in "The Voyage," when his ship lost sight of America on her way to Europe, "it seemed as if I had closed one volume of the world and its concerns, and had time for meditation before I opened another."[2] As it was, the new volume came sooner than expected, and with pretty much the same "concerns." For, Irving decided to become a writer in order to achieve a "socially sanctioned identity."[3] The decision would allow him both to eschew male subject formation in terms of business and to imaginatively delineate all kinds of alternative masculinities, all in the project of integrating his own imperfectly realized masculinity. The original plan, however, had been to travel to Italy and Greece, to be financed by Irving's apparently prosperous brothers, the import merchants. Yet as soon as Irving arrived in England, he saw that the firm of P. & E. Irving was in serious trouble.[4] "We have," he wrote to his friend Henry Brevoort from Liverpool in January 1816, "in common with most American houses here, had a hard winter of it in money matters, owing to the cross purposes of last falls business, and have been harassed to death to meet our engagements. I have never passed so anxious a time in my life—my rest has been broken & my health & spirits almost prostrated...."[5]

The end of the War with England in 1815 had led to an unprecedented economic boom. Goods from Europe were cheap; American products, in contrast, reached high prices in Europe. Thus, American entrepreneurs found seemingly limitless opportunities for growth and investment. Additional fuel came from the sale of federal lands, which increased eightfold in

Three. Rip Van Winkle, Ichabod Crane, Other Masculinities

just five years. Moreover, the new steamboat technology made possible the widespread sales of imported goods and the transportation of produce to markets. All these opportunities resulted in increasing demands for capital. Yet capital was not to be had. Entrepreneurs therefore had to rely on credit, provided by willing bankers. And there were ever more of them, as bank charters were easy to obtain and bank notes easy to print. By 1819, America's economy had as its foundation a financial system that was itself floating on the airy promises of future profits rather than on a dependable system of value rooted in hard money and labor. Even the Bank of the United States, chartered in 1816 as the Second B.U.S., cashed in on the boom by overextending its own loan line, especially to banks in western states and territories. The policy gave rise to much bitterness and hostility, with the bank being denounced as a "monster" and a "hydra of corruption," while its directors were accused of "greed" said to echo the worst practices of European aristocracy. Not only had the bank's charter been "purposely contrived for *speculation*," the Philadelphia *Aurora* wrote in January 1818, but its directors were composed of "a majority of *brokers, shavers*, and *speculators*."[6]

By early 1819, the dire predictions of anti–B.U.S. financial doomsayers had proven painfully accurate. The Bank had run out of specie reserves and began calling in loans to commercial banks, requiring each bank to redeem its own notes. Although the process saved the B.U.S., commercial banks and their debtors were hit hard, especially after a collapse of commodity prices in Europe.[7] The result was the Panic of 1819, the first (though by no means the last) market collapse far-reaching enough to cause devastation on a widespread scale.[8] Almost overnight, businesses failed, property prices plummeted, and paper notes became devalued to the point of worthlessness; simultaneously, unemployment soared, and homelessness became acute. Within two years, John Quincy Adams wrote in his memoirs, immense fortunes were lost "in every part of the Union; enormous numbers of persons utterly ruined; multitudes in deep distress; and a general mass of disaffection to the government."[9]

The entire period, historians have shown, was marked by widespread economic insecurity and failure, as the increasing extension of paper forms of credit connected local communities and their inhabitants with distant, unseen markets, and as the value of paper currencies fluctuated with changes in those markets. "Wherever the market extended," Charles Sellers writes about the seemingly inevitable series of economic panics that rocked the nation during this period, "the remorseless process of debt liquidation chastened not only modest venturers, but also the apparently wealthy who had plunged and borrowed most recklessly. Specie to satisfy their creditors could not be had."[10] The historian Scott A. Sandage put it in this way: "Nineteenth-century Americans had to live in a new world where the sky was always falling. [...] From Wall Street to the muddiest rural lane, failure and the fear of it left a garrulous people at a loss for words."[11]

In his memoirs, John Quincy Adams depicts an unfortunate merchant (General Samuel Smith, the co-owner of one of the leading commercial houses in Baltimore) as "gone distracted" and "dangerously ill in bed."[12] Adams paradigmatically captured the distressed forms of masculinity emerging within an increasingly unstable paper economy, one that had done away with valuation based on "real" property, land and specie. Adams might as well have written about the "very nervous" Washington Irving on the brink of the bankruptcy of P. & E. Irving & Co. As Irving wrote to Henry Brevoort about the "humiliating alternative" of bankruptcy, "Various circumstances have concurred to render me very nervous and subject to fits of depression."[13] The bankruptcy was the result of Peter Irving's overpurchase of English goods for shipment to America at a time when the demand for such imports was declining as the United States was heading towards the Panic of 1819.[14] "In train" in January 1819, the bankruptcy finally went through less than a month later, when the official note appeared in the London *Times* of February 2, as well as in several other newspapers.[15]

The family company's bankruptcy, Irving wrote into his notebook, was "vile and sordid and humiliated me to the dust. I underwent ruin in all its bitterness & humiliation—in a strange land—among strangers."[16] As if this were not enough, Irving's brother Peter had become an invalid and required nursing, and his mother had died in April 1817. Especially during the first ten or so years of his prolonged stay in Europe—the period of *The Sketch Book, Bracebridge Hall*, and *Tales of a Traveller*—Irving was haunted by the twin specters of credit and debt. In November 1825, for instance, the London banking firm of Welles & Williams collapsed. The news was "disastrous," as Irving had extended to this house, in his brother Peter's behalf, a guarantee of two thousand pounds.[17] Three years later, he was still paying a "debt due the estate of S. Williams."[18] Irving, who always suffered from his purportedly female defects, must have felt all this particularly acutely, for, as Toby Ditz remarked, to become economically insolvent in this world was to become "unmanned" and "feminized."[19] Feeling wrapped in a "murky cloud" that threatened to "wither & blight" him, Irving went into a deep "gloom."[20] Yet, Haskell Springer notes, though at first Irving professed to be utterly incapacitated for "literary exertion," eventually he "made his escape from his emotional morass by writing."[21]

If only it had been that simple. It is true that at the time Irving was under considerable strain. But often his letters of self-confession were but convenient outlets for his appeals to friendship. A script that sees him merely "oppressed with morbid feelings" ignores his frequent returns to his more routine enthusiasm.[22] "Man must be aspiring," Irving had scribbled into his journal while on tour in Scotland in 1817, "ambition belongs to his nature. He cannot rest content but is continually reaching after higher attainments and more felicitous conditions. To rest satisfied with the present is a sign of an abject spirit."[23] The lines are characteristic of those ruminations on life that seemed addressed to Irving himself, showing neither dissatisfaction nor joylessness. Irving fretted about his professional future, and would continue to do so, but he never ceased to believe in his literary gift. In 1819–1820 Irving's gift resulted in *The Sketch Book*, the success of which, he thought, opened for him "an avenue to some degree of profit and reputation."[24] In addition, it brought him a letter from John Murray, the publisher, urging him "no longer to conceal his name from the world."[25] Irving may well have concealed his name from the world out of shame. As Andrew Kopec argues in a recent article, the ruin of the family business "threw into relief his own lack of ambition during an era in which ambition was becoming a social obligation."[26] Seen in this light, *The Sketch Book* would have been Irving's plan "to atone for his failure to act."[27] In the following I will extend Kopec's argument to show that, by choosing a career as a writer, Irving not only sought his own way to wealth but also found direction and purpose in his quest for his own imperfectly realized masculinity.

Just when Irving began composing *The Sketch Book* is impossible to say, though kernels and sometimes entire passages can be identified in a notebook titled "Notes While Preparing Sketch Book &c., 1817."[28] A letter to Brevoort of July 1817 likewise contains references to the book that would transform its author into a celebrity:

> I am waiting here to extricate myself from the ruins of our unfortunate concern, after which I will turn my back on this scene of care & distress. [...] I have a plan which, with very little trouble, will yield me [...] a sufficient means of support[....] I cannot at present explain to you what it is—you would probably consider it precarious, & inadequate to my subsistence—but a small matter will float a drowning man and I have dwelt so much of late on the prospect of being cast homeless & pennyless upon the world; that I feel relieved in having even a straw to catch at.[29]

Irving had no faith in paradise regained through commerce. His "Notes and Extracts, 1819–1823" contain a passage from Milton's *Paradise Regained*: "But these are false, or little else but dreams, / Conjectures, fancies built on nothing firm."[30] Irving registered the malaise of his time in "anxious masculinities," ineffectual and troubled characters like Rip van Winkle, Ichabod Crane, Tom Walker, his most unpleasant character, Wolfert Webber, as well as a number of other figures. All of them represent the masculine archetypes' dysfunctional shadows, displaying characteristics such as weakness, sadism, addiction, even impotence. In this sense, the characters that I will treat in this chapter stand in as the "universal heroes" (the term is Irving's)[31] that contemporary readers saw in them, and all of them testify, not to Irving's misogyny, but to the culture's obsession with—and anxieties about—gender and gender roles. These anxieties often made men turn against women, marriage, as well as anything that they believed to be effeminate. Beneath their anxieties and misogynous actions lurked a precarious form of masculinity, one that was no longer centered on an interior form of self-possession and inner being but was rather contingent on a commodified and often elusive, unstable, and volatile form of manhood. In a social world in which men were expected to constantly test and prove their manhood against external factors such as the whims of the marketplace, the prevailing feelings were marginality, doubt, insecurity, and fear. Especially when men came to link their sense of themselves as men to their work, that is, to their economic success, the relentless effort to prove their manhood left them vulnerable to shame and humiliation by other men. David Anthony has termed these men "paper money men," men who found themselves the victims of the new and unstable paper economy in the period from 1819 to 1857.[32]

This chapter considers the emotional dynamic that I see as the key to Irving's search for achieved manhood in the period through *Tales of a Traveller*. I argue that Irving, in his quest for a part of himself, would delineate all kinds of troubled masculinities. As we will see, it was not until he confronted George Washington's hypermasculine attributes that he found that part. Until then, the masculinities he created are but adumbrations, not of Irving himself but of how he wanted to be or how he did not want to be. The latter is especially true of the texts considered here, which share at their center a drama of humiliation, dispossession, and deviance, from which their voices recoil and diverge. Each of the stories under consideration reflects the vicissitudes of risk and competition, "the dislocations caused by the long-term transformations of markets from temporally and spatially delimited places and events into impersonal, unbounded, and abstract processes."[33] Story after story exposes conventional manliness as aggressive, insensitive, murderously dominant, as well as nervous and panicky. In this regard, Irving's anxious and troubled masculinities serve as crucial barometers for understanding his search for achieved manhood during the crisis of masculinity in the period leading up to and following the Panic of 1819.[34]

One of the earliest stories, in terms both of its composition and of its publication, is "Rip Van Winkle." Irving reportedly wrote it at great speed in June 1818 at the home of his sister Sarah Van Wart, in Birmingham.[35] When Irving sent the first number of the *Sketch Book* to his brother Ebenezer in New York on March 1, 1819, "Rip Van Winkle" was part of it. Ebenezer secured copyright, and C.S. Van Winkle of New York published the book on June 23, 1819, in 2,000 copies.[36] Prior to publication, Irving had

Three. Rip Van Winkle, Ichabod Crane, Other Masculinities 79

been deeply worried and anxious and nervous. In an emotional letter to Brevoort he expresses his "great diffidence" about his "re-appearance in literature" as well as being "conscious of [his] imperfections," which had been causing him "various cares and anxieties." Haunted by his anima-induced anxieties, he falls to defending the sort of writing he had produced:

> I have attempted no lofty theme, nor sought to look wise and learned, which appears to be very much the fashion among our American writers, at present—I have preferred addressing myself to the feeling & fancy of the reader more than to his judgment—My writing may appear therefore light & trifling in our country of philosophers and politicians—but if they possess merit in the class of literature to which they belong, it is all to which I aspire in the work.[37]

Irving need not have worried. *The Sketch Book* was an instant success. Already the first number was popular, even though many readers considered it too high-priced. Irving could relax. He had not failed. The pages of *Sketch Book*, dominated by Geoffrey Crayon, yielded a personal public history for its author, an affirmation that he had done interesting things that others—not least businesspeople, politicians, and other stay-at-home professionals—could only dream about. In America, Crayon became a favorite son. In England, too, William Godwin at once praised the sketches and tales, and both the *Kaleidoscope* and the London *Literary Gazette*, uninvited, republished them. Irving attended afternoon gatherings at the home of John Murray, who less than a year later became his publisher.[38] Weeping tears of happiness, Irving read and reread the incoming reviews, many of them forwarded from America by Brevoort, and he in all likelihood foresaw a rosy future moneywise. In America alone *The Sketch Book* brought him some $9,000 in two years, which is more than $200,000 in today's money and truly was "a princely sum for those times and circumstances."[39]

The immediate literary source of "Rip Van Winkle" was "Peter Klaus" in Otmar's *Volkssagen*, but also apparent in the story are Irving's own observations of Dutch families in New York, his reading from Johann Kaspar Riesbeck's *Travels through Germany*, and his interest in American and European folklore.[40] Given this genealogy and given Irving's "feminine" literary personality that was so averse to the market society dominated by bullying men, it is no surprise that Rip is anything but a "self-made man." Instead, he "harks back to a pre-capitalist era in which labor is regulated by the seasons rather than by the clock and marked by cooperation rather than competition, asceticism, and the single-minded pursuit of individual gain."[41] Rip never listens to exhortations to "industry," "persistence," "hard work," "unflagging efforts," or similar wisdoms. And, given as he is to "indolence" and "loafing," he also drinks. In terms of the culture's dominant views on socially useful manhood, Rip is ineffectual, inadequate, lacking vitality and vigor, traits that a nation bent on economic striving as an article of faith equated with vitality. A "want of achievement where achievement measured manhood," E. Anthony Rotundo argues, "was the paramount sign of failure. Moreover, in antebellum America, failure was viewed as a sign of poor character, especially of laziness and a tendency to vice and debauchery."[42]

The story's action begins somewhere around 1773 or 1774, when the country "was yet a province of Great Britain" and a portrait of King George III hangs in front of the tavern that Rip and his friends frequent. When Rip returns to the village after a twenty-year alcoholic reverie and confrontation with the homosocial world of the mountain trolls of Dutch ancestry, not only does he find George Washington's face on a sign in front of the Union Hotel but also stumbles upon a politician, "a lean bilious looking fellow with his pocket full of hand bills," while a villager wants to know whether he was a "Federal or Democrat."[43] These labels would have had little meaning before 1793. Now they pertain to pro–British or pro–French foreign policy, enough to eventually disrupt the harmony of the village community beyond the "disputatious tone" recorded by Rip, to the point where one-time friends would cross the street to avoid greeting a political foe. Rip's response to the villager's question, "I am a poor quiet man, a native of the place, and a loyal subject to the king—God bless him," results in a tumultuous uproar that nearly ends in mob violence: "A tory! A tory! A spy! A Refugee! hustle him! away with him!"[44]

Rip is a failure, but only when seen from within the paradigm of competitive individualism. For me, as well as for most commentators, Rip rather is an unbeliever, an almost self-conscious rebel, who—like Irving himself, who likewise kicked against the "unremitting industriousness"[45] of the middle-class life he knew—thinks that the game is not worth playing. Rip does not adhere to the expansion of capitalism as an article of faith, a faith that constructs economic striving as a moral imperative. To all this, he says no, though his naysaying is not nearly as conscious an act as Bartleby's "I prefer not to." Rip's naysaying rather is implicit, almost demure, and coming into sharper focus only through a comparison with his wife, Dame Van Winkle, to whose demands Rip simply "shrugged his shoulders, shook his head, and cast up his eyes" in response.[46] Dame Van Winkle, rather than meekly submit to a husband who fails to maintain his part by failing to provide economically for his family, excoriates Rip for his failure, thus dissolving the patriarchal order within the house. "Morning, noon, and night her tongue was incessantly going, and everything he did or said was sure to produce a torrent of household eloquence."[47] Finally, Rip, "reduced almost to despair," rebels against his wife's attempts to turn him into a virtuous, dutiful, well-mannered, and hard-working breadwinner. But the only alternative "to escape from the labor of the farm and clamor of his wife, was to take gun in hand and stroll away into the woods."[48]

Rip's movements, from his native village into the woods and back again, have been the subject of a plethora of interpretations. In one instance, Rip has been understood as a truly mythic, even archetypal figure who, following Joseph Campbell's *The Hero with a Thousand Faces*, becomes separated from the world, encounters a source of power, and finally returns.[49] Freudian interpretations, in contrast, extended from literary characters (Rip, Natty Bumppo, Daniel Boone) to American men in general, focusing on the avoidance of growing up and assuming responsibility. Put simply, males avoid direct confrontation with society but first evade and only then reunite with it. In this pantheon of misfits, Rip stands out as the prototype, the archetypal American male defining himself through flight and return. Importantly, that flight is often predicated on a desire to escape "female constraints."[50] Irving himself, we have seen, often felt that he had to flee from his own "woman within." What, then, is Rip's position in Irving's quest for his own imperfectly realized masculinity? Irving has Rip return as an old man whose lusty days are buried with the colonial past.

Yet when Rip wanders out of the woods after his long sleep, he is not only stranded in an alien environment; he quite literally has no home to return to. His old house is destroyed, "gone to decay—the roof fallen in, the windows shattered, and the doors off the hinges."[51] Rip's confrontation with a home that no longer guarantees patrimonial continuance is only the beginning of a process of destabilization that reaches a climax when he sees his own image in the face of his look-alike son, who during Rip's absence has matured into his dad's "precise counterpart [...] apparently as lazy and certainly as ragged." Utterly disoriented, Rip Sr. exclaims: "God knows [...] I'm not myself [...] I fell asleep on the mountain—and they've changed my gun—and every thing's changed—and I'm changed—and I can't tell what's my name, or who I am!" It is only after recognizing his daughter, Judith, that he is able to announce his own name. His word, however, is not enough. Rip's story is confirmed only when "an old woman, tottering out from among the crowd, put her hand to her brow, and peering under it in his face for a moment, exclaimed, 'Sure enough! It is Rip Van Winkle—it is himself! Welcome home again, old neighbor—Why where have you been these twenty long years?'"

Yet Rip is not really "home again." The town is equally transformed. In place of the ancient, sleepy village where every face was familiar, Rip finds himself in a town with different names and different faces. In the place of Nicholas Vedder's old village inn there now is the Union Hotel operated by a Jonathan Doolittle. People themselves are different. Not merely is their dress "of a different fashion. [...] The very character of the people seemed changed. There was a busy, bustling disputatious tone about it, instead of the accustomed phlegm and drowsy tranquility."⁵² Competitive individualism has reached the village, where it plays itself out on the levels of economics and, as well, politics. The new freedoms that are his as a result of the Revolution leave Rip unimpressed, much as "the changes of states and empires made but little impression on him." If the words and issues of the election he is thrown into "were a perfect babylonish jargon to the bewildered Van Winkle," he is much more pleased to be rid of the "one species of despotism under which he had long groaned and that was petticoat government. Happily that was at an end—he had got his neck out of the yoke of matrimony, and could go in and out whenever he pleased without dreading the tyranny of Dame Van Winkle." This, his deliverance, pleases him far more than his status as "a free citizen of the United States."

Still, following his return Rip is bereft of his subjectivity and thus must found a new identity or founder in the unsorted chaos of his reduced state. The basis of Rip's new identity is another story from him, the story about where he has been "these twenty long years," and it is this story, C. Michael Hurst argues, "that underwrites the terms of Rip's communal membership"—and with it, of his archetypal masculinity. Rip's new identity as a storyteller allows him to reinvent himself "as a town patriarch and a living cultural monument of the times before the war."⁵³ Indeed, Rip "takes his place once more on the bench at the inn door, and was reverenced as one of the patriarchs of the village, and a chronicle of the old times 'before the war.'"⁵⁴ Rip is not merely reintegrated within the community; through his role as a storyteller, he constitutes the very possibility *of* community by providing a basis for a common cultural heritage.⁵⁵ Rip, Crayon tells us, "used to tell his story to every stranger that arrived at Mr. Doolittle's hotel [...] It at last settled down to precisely the tale I have related, and not a man, woman or child in the neighbourhood, but knew it by heart."⁵⁶

It is, then, the store of cultural knowledge created and disseminated by Rip that binds the community within a framework of shared understanding. Rip's version of patriarchal masculinity altogether eschews the materialistic and competitive edge of capitalism in favor of nonmaterial, noncompetitive products of the imagination and, as well, products that are anchored in a common ancestry. Instead of the discontinuities that result from defining identity through the twin loci of the market and the frontier—the "Irvinian nightmare," in Hurst's apt phrase⁵⁷—there is the reassuring possibility of continuity throughout time. That possibility is reassuring precisely because Rip's role as "a chronicle of the old times 'before the war'" captures that time not through a factual exposition but through an act of storytelling, thus without provoking anxiety. By locating the tale in fantasy, Irving transforms the active content of genteel patriarchy—a verifiable

Three. Rip Van Winkle, Ichabod Crane, Other Masculinities

historical phenomenon and potentially lethal political force—into the passive content of reverie and daydream. Put differently, the "past that Rip captures cannot be a threat, because it cannot be true."[58] Moreover, Rip is an old man and so will be able to live out his final years in the past, without having to confront the future. His masculinity thus is the precise counterimage to that of Ichabod Crane, whose version of masculinity dissolves community in its bid to both the competitiveness and materialism of capitalism and the twin loci of market and the frontier as prime fields for iterating identity.

Though "Rip Van Winkle" purportedly is "a posthumous writing of Diedrich Knickerbocker," it is not a fantasy about America's transition from colony to independent republic. As a story written in 1818–1819, it registers the vast and rapid changes the country was going through thereafter—westward expansion, especially after the Louisiana Purchase of 1803, which fueled a new form of nationalism, and, on the economic side, a vastly accelerated economic growth that was fast leading into a deep crisis. Unlike Rip Van Winkle, however, Ichabod Crane looks upon the changes that were occurring as opportunities. Irving's anima-consciousness did not see it quite in this light: Ichabod is the very embodiment of the debt-based and frequently humiliated form of masculinity emerging out of the new economy. Ichabod, whose name means "inglorious" in Hebrew (אִיכָבוֹד),[59] reflects the ambivalent nature of manhood as it was evolving—both for Irving and for America more generally—under the sign of the unstable paper economy in and around 1819. Manhood then already was predicated upon individual achievement. The accident of birth, one's station, had become irrelevant, as had history or tradition, and men had to make something of themselves through competitiveness and selfishness. Failing to do so resulted in humiliation and dispossession. It was only natural, therefore, to enlist women in efforts to compensate for such risks. As David Leverenz remarks, "Male self-reliance and female domesticity became complementary tactics to preserve the family's class status."[60] Ichabod, who suffers all kinds of mortifications in what is ostensibly one "of the quietest places in the world,"[61] strives for just that—self-reliant manhood and female domesticity, the latter in the form of Katrina Van Tassel, the Dutch heiress.

Though "The Legend of Sleepy Hollow" should be read with the Panic of 1819 in mind, in early 1819 the story existed only in fragment form. Irving sent the manuscript to his brother Ebenezer with the sixth or next-to-last number, on December 29, 1819, though it was not published until March 15, 1820 (and in July 1820 by John Murray in England).[62] When we first meet the story's main character, Ichabod Crane, this itinerant schoolteacher travels "with all his worldly effects tied up in a cotton handkerchief."[63] At story's end, he "had changed his quarters to a different part of the country; had kept school and studied law at the same time, had been admitted to the bar, turned politician, electioneered, written for the newspapers, and finally had been made a justice of the Ten Pound Court." Ichabod thus figures as a prototype of the "self-made man," the more so since, as we learn from the Postscript, supposedly from a memorandum book by Diedrich Knickerbocker, he has been accepted into the inner circle of the government of New York, where he finds himself among the city's "sagest and most illustrious burghers." In this circle, we are led to presume, Ichabod witnesses the telling of his own story, and it is he who asks the intriguing crucial question, "what was the moral of the story, and what it went to prove."

The moral, the—unidentified—storyteller replies, is that "for a country schoolmaster to be refused the hand of a Dutch heiress, is a certain step to high preferment in the state."[64] Thus, there is a price for the self-made man who from the beginning expects soon to be able to "turn his back upon the old school-house; snap his fingers in the face of Hans Van Ripper [the farmer who lodges Ichabod Crane], and every other niggardly patron, and kick any itinerant pedagogue out-of-doors that should dare to call him comrade!"[65] Yet Ichabod not only loses a good match, which certainly emasculates or at least devalues him on the fluctuating but also competitive market of romantic exchange, but, more important from the perspective of his creator, a community to sustain him. The pumpkin that Brom Bones throws at him in wild pursuit is not an extension of the rural ideal that Sleepy Hollow represents so much as it signifies the community's forceful expulsion of the Yankee capitalist aggression that Ichabod represents.[66]

Through the community's successful resistance to capitalist acquisitiveness the tale's end reaffirms rural, precapitalistic values at the same time as it positions self-reliant masculinity in the new social regime of a market-based economy. Put another way, the possibility of masculine reinvention, imagined as Ichabod's new life in New York, is possible only at the expense of the communal stability that came with the old, landed social order. That order is paradigmatically enshrined in Sleepy Hollow itself, a small valley seemingly insulated against the advances of political and economic change. "[I]t is in such little retired Dutch valleys, found here and there embosomed in the great State of New York," Irving alias Diedrich Knickerbocker remarks on the metaphoric Eden, "that population, manners, and customs remain fixed; while the great torrent of migration and improvement, which is making such incessant changes in other parts of this restless country, sweeps by them unobserved."[67]

Irving would not be Irving if he had not represented Ichabod Crane as the "intrusive male" from Connecticut who, like the biblical serpent, threatens to destroy the animatic Garden of Eden of traditional, rural America with his acquisitiveness.[68] "From the moment Ichabod laid his eyes upon these regions of delight," Knickerbocker's account of Ichabod's first visit to the Van Tassel estate begins, "the peace of his mind was at an end, and his only study was how to gain the affections of the peerless daughter of Van Tassel."[69] While Ichabod is a laughable failure in his efforts to make Katrina his own, his form of masculine agency is nevertheless threatening. For, his romantic desire results from economic desire; it is only after cataloguing the worth of the Van Tassel property that his heart "yearns" for Katrina, and this yearning is driven by the fact that the young heiress represents access to the magnificent wealth that Ichabod imagines will be his once he gains her hand. As we are told, "his heart yearned after the damsel who was to inherit these domains, and his imagination expanded with the idea, how they might be readily turned into cash, and the money invested in immense tracts of wild land, and shingle palaces in the wilderness."[70]

Ichabod construes his relationship to Katrina primarily in present-day economic terms; for him, the Van Tassel property is merely a transferable asset, measurable in dollars and cents, that he could acquire and then sell in order to invest in speculative ventures on land in the western United States. Fancying "the blooming Katrina, with a whole family of children, mounted on the top of a waggon with household trumpery, with pots and kettles dangling beneath [...] he beheld himself bestriding a pacing mare, with a colt at her heels, setting out for Kentucky, Tennessee or the Lord knows where."[71] What Ichabod's fancy produces is, then, nothing less than a "peculiarly American narrative of Western capitalist desire [that] precludes American domesticity as a stable site of national identity."[72] But Ichabod not only unmoors domesticity from its very foundations. Seeing in Katrina merely the key to economic advancement, he becomes the perfect embodiment of the new "appetitive" economic man spawned by an ever-expanding capitalist marketplace that threatens to quite literally swallow peaceful enclosures such as that of Sleepy Hollow.

The analogy of the voracious, even cannibalistic nature of the new market economy to Ichabod's voracious appetite is vintage Washington Irving. Ichabod "was a huge feeder, and, though lank, had the dilating powers of an Anaconda," we read in one instance.[73] In another instance, we stare into Ichabod's "devouring mind's eye." That Irving intended to depict Ichabod as less than human is evident also from his cognomen, Crane, which suggests a predatory bird, a name that

> was not inapplicable to his person. He was tall, but exceedingly lank, with narrow shoulders, long arms and legs, hands that dangled a mile out of his sleeves, feet that might have served as shovels, and his whole frame most loosely hung together. His head was small, and flat at top, with huge ears, large green glassy eyes, and a long snipe nose, so that it looked like a weather-cock perched upon his spindle neck, to tell which way the wind blew.

In 1816, Irving himself had had no idea which way the wind blew. As he confessed to Henry Brevoort, "At present, I feel so tempest tossed and weather beaten that I shall be content to be quits with fortune for a very moderate portion and give up all my sober schemes as the dream of fairy-land."[74] The mood did not last. Though Irving went on to unsettle the values and understandings of middle-class masculinity, imprisoned as men were in their rivalries for money, dominance, property, and status, Ichabod Crane "also acts as a kind of double for Irving," a dysfunctional shadow insofar as "their shared fantasy life" can be understood "as linked to the seemingly fantastic world of economic success available in the new economy." Thus, the "vessel [...] suspended in the air" that Ichabod imagines reflects back on Irving himself. It cements the picture of Irving as an old-school Federalist and effeminate who was utterly unable or unwilling to take up a disciplined life of business or labor, at the same time as he felt uneasy about the world of the new economy even though as a man trying to make a living from writing he was part of that world.[75]

As a voracious consumer of fantastical narratives, Ichabod is easily duped by Brom Bones's hoax. The "apparition of a figure on horseback without a head," ostensibly the spirit that presides over Sleepy Hollow, also is a terrifying figure out of Ichabod's unconscious, and in more than one sense. On one hand the horseman, described as "hurrying along in the gloom of night, as if on the wings of the wind" and thus reflecting the same weightless quality attributed to the entire region, stands in as the embodiment of the period's speculative economy. On the other hand, the horseman, forever engaged in a "nightly quest of his head," is also a figure of castration.[76] Ichabod all but panics over Brom's threat to "'double the schoolmaster up, and lay him on a shelf of his own schoolhouse.'"[77] He really panics when he is actually assaulted by Brom, characteristically from the rear (Brom is "hard on his haunches"), which results in Ichabod's panicked sense that he will be split open ("would cleave him asunder").[78] It is through this central narrative circulating through Sleepy Hollow, then, that Irving brings together the period's "panic-prone, speculation-based economy and a castrated form of masculine identity," the "Impotent Lover" archetype.[79]

Not only is Ichabod a prototype of the new economic man, who admits only anger and ambition to public self-display; he also is a sexual failure, hence both "ineffectual" and "inadequate." In the nineteenth century, to be disempowered economically meant to be subject to an all but perpetual anxiety over humiliation at the levels of gender and of sexuality. Tellingly, it is the assault involving Brom's imposture as the Headless Horseman that moves Ichabod from persecuted to disempowered and humiliated. The terrifying horseman, David Anthony argues, embodies Ichabod's repressed knowledge that illusions of economic prosperity have been traded in for the hard fact of masculine humiliation. The headlessness itself suggests that something is missing, namely masculine wholeness and potency. In this regard, Ichabod is a kind of map for a new and identifiable "gothic" male subject emerging in early national America. Haunted by the apparitional nature of a paper economy that has made self-possession an increasingly elusive dream, but similarly haunted by anxieties at the level of gender and sexuality, Ichabod is in his various states of panic, hysteria, and ineffectualness "a figure for whom postures of terror and humiliation are becoming the norm."[80]

Altogether, "The Legend of Sleepy Hollow" is a story about the emasculating effects of the new economy and, as well, a story about the way in which manhood is being refashioned in order to adapt to the cultural given of financial instability and humiliation. Though repeatedly humiliated and "feminized," Ichabod Crane is quite capable of winning a place among other men, and so his humiliations and ineffectualness might be understood as a necessary step towards his later professional career as attorney, politician, and judge.[81] In this sense, Ichabod's is an emergent form of manhood in which submission and commerce intersect to form the nervous sensibility of middle-class manhood. This new gender formation is certainly vexed, but in an age when labor-based notions of masculine self-possession were rapidly giving way to models of male selfhood based on insubstantiality, gender panic and submission, this seems to have been an important and frequently deployed posture—one that reminds us that, in nineteenth-century America as much as today, the horrific extremes of the gothic are never far away from the everyday reality they seek to depict.

How was Irving to escape the haunting dilemma, the perpetual anxieties, and the lack of success in his own quest for achieved masculinity? A "realistic" solution seemed impossible. Though his financial difficulties (set in motion by the bankruptcy of P. & E. Irving in 1818/1819 and the ensuing Panic of 1819) largely had resolved themselves with the publication of the *Sketch Book*, the good times did not last. Following his German tour, financial worries again were piling up.[82] In March 1824 he finally tells John Howard Payne that he had to discontinue his theatrical projects as he needed a more reliable source of income; not much later, he writes Payne to remit a sum of money to him, "as it will assist me toward my travelling expenses, for my purse is running low."[83] Once again, Irving was rescued by engaging his fantasy life. On the surface, *Tales of a Traveller by Geoffrey Crayon, Gent.* has nothing much to do except pad itself out to the length of a book. Although Irving was made to substantially revise the manuscript for the first English edition, the finished product still resembled, in his own estimation, the "odds and ends" of miscellaneous material jumbled together "as the articles are apt to be in an ill packed travelling trunk."[84] Nevertheless, in a letter to his sister Catherine Paris, Irving boasts that *Tales of a Traveller* was both "in a *different mood* from my late works" and "touched off with *a freer spirit, and are more true to life*."[85] Irving repeats the sentiment in a letter to Brevoort of December 11, 1824, when he writes, "a great part of [*Tales of Traveller*] was written in a freer and happier vein than almost any of my former writings."[86]

In the collection itself, Crayon addresses the readers in a similar fashion. None of the pieces "carry their moral on the surface[....] On the contrary, I have often hid my moral from sight, and disguised it as much as possible by sweets and spices...."[87] The self-effacement that speaks from a "moral" hidden from sight or disguised is deceptive. It is, in itself, a call towards unveiling a hidden animus, digging, to use a metaphor Irving himself employed, for the stories' social symbolism. For instance, "Hellegat" or "Hell Gate," where the East River meets Long Island and which Knickerbocker remembers as "a place of great awe and perilous enterprise in my boyhood," quite literally becomes a gate to hell, foreshadowing Tom Walker's fate. In addition, the treacherous whirlpools of Hell Gate constitute an extended metaphor of the turbulent times and the "haphazard fellows" aka self-made men living therein, men who "live by their wits, and dislike the old fashioned restraint of law and gospel." Even more rewarding is a closer look at the final section, titled "The Money Diggers," which, incidentally, is the only part of *Tales of a Traveller* that critics did not altogether pan.[88]

The five sketches and legends of "The Money Diggers" all revolve around the drive to accumulate money, not through earning it but through finding buried treasure. Buried treasure is one of the most popular motives in literature.[89] In Irving's instance, the "buried money" references to Captain Kidd's long-rumored store, thus to an early moment of mercantile capitalism when, as Marx wrote in *Capital*, money was money and not yet capital. In this sense, treasure is an immediate form of value and stability, one that, by extension, is linked to a longed-for form of financially secure, self-possessed masculinity. In *Tales of a Traveller*, treasure is waiting to be discovered by "money diggers." A "money digger," the *Oxford English Dictionary* tells us, is an Americanism denoting "a treasure hunter, *especially* one who believes buried treasure can be located by divination or other mystical means."[90] Irving, of course, makes fun of the idea of locating treasure by such means. In doing so, he not only disabuses readers from the ruling passion among American males but also alerts us to the fact that "treasure" can as well be understood figuratively, referring to anything valued and preserved as precious—what Irving calls his "moral"—though whatever it is, it surely cannot be located by divination or other mystical means.

Two of the tales have as their hero Wolfert Webber. Yet Webber realizes his "golden dreams" not by divination or other mystical means but by becoming—serendipitously—a capitalist speculator, one who turns his land into capital. In other words, Wolfert, the wolf of Wall Street *avant la lettre*, becomes a self-made man, like Irving himself. Webber is a worthy burgher of Dutch descent, a family "patriarch" and "rural potentate,"[91] who is increasingly worried and embarrassed as his once isolated farm—his "paternal acres," a wished-for retreat from the forces of economic change and turmoil lurking in New York—is gradually becoming a victim of urban expansion. "The chief cause of anxiety to Wolfert [...] was the growing prosperity of the city," we are told at the beginning of the first tale. "[W]hile every one around him grew richer, Wolfert grew poorer, and he could not, for the life of him, perceive how the evil was to be remedied." In what follows, Webber consoles himself by visiting his local tavern, where he hears a series of tales about buried treasure in the area. The problem, however, is that regardless of who buried it, such treasure is as elusive as gold specie itself in America in the early 1800s.[92] Though Webber dreams nightly of immense treasures in his garden ("bags of money turned up their bellies, corpulent with pieces of eight, or venerable doubloons; and chests [...] yawned forth before his ravished eyes, and vomited forth their glittering contents"), his increasingly desperate efforts to find gold prove futile, despite the fact that he dreams the dream three times—so it must be true.

As Webber believes in the veracity of his dreams, he wrecks his fields in futile digging. As a result of his delusions, he morphs into another example of the disempowered and anxious male subject of the new economy, doomed to live in a world of "competitors" and "upstarts," including the presumed "pirate."[93] Webber soon panics, as "everybody avoided him." As if personal humiliation were not enough, Wolfert and his family soon face dissolution. Yet Irving or, rather Knickerbocker, who is nominally the author of "Money Diggers," is merciful. Wolfert Webber, after all, is a burgher of New York City, not a Connecticut Yankee. Thus, he eventually "woke from his dream of wealth." However, he is not quite off the hook, but finds himself in a kind of purgatory. By degrees a revulsion roots itself in his mind, "common to those whose golden dreams have been disturbed by pinching realities[....] Haggard care gathered about his brow; he went about with a money-seeking air, his eyes bent downward into the dust."

Webber's "purgatory" is represented as a kind of limbo, where time does not pass, and his fate is held in stasis. An interposed story at the beginning of "The Adventure of the Black Fisherman," the second of the two interlocked Webber stories, makes for additional suspense. The story hinges on the Black Fisherman's having stumbled across a gang of men burying their loot on a nearby island, and the appearance of a "mysterious stranger" carrying an even more mysterious sea chest. The stranger, presumably a pirate, drowns in a storm, and the chest likewise goes overboard.[94] Until now, Webber has been merely a comic figure, a cabbage-headed and greedy dreamer.[95] Now the narrative highlights his greed in a more serious way through an allusion to a tale from *The Arabian Nights Entertainment*. Webber's "infected fancy tinged every thing with gold. He felt like the greedy inhabitant of Bagdad, when his eyes had been greased with the magic ointment of the dervise [dervish], that gave him to see all the treasures of the earth." Webber's "brain fever" not only fuels the self-made man's ambitions but also causes a return of his "insanity." Moreover, the fever is contagious. Doctor Knipperhausen, instead of tending to Webber's health, himself "caught the malady from his patient," and instantly procures a divining rod and other necessary implements for the treasure hunt.

The worthy money diggers indeed find a chest, which Webber presumes is full of gold. Yet, "scarcely had he uttered the words when a sound from above caught his ear. He cast up his eyes, and lo! by the expiring light of the fire he beheld [...] what appeared to be the grim visage of the drowned buccaneer, grinning hideously down upon him."[96] Whether the visage really belongs to the old buccaneer, or to another money-digger, or to Webber's son-in-law and rescuer, or merely to a phantom of Webber's inflamed fancy, remains unexamined. The search for hidden treasure, the narrator interposes with tongue in cheek, is only for "such of my fellow citizens as are not engaged in any other speculations."[97] As readers, we are left to understand that, at least for the Irving of 1824, found gold, like successful speculation, is a mere illusion. Characters such as Wolfert Webber reflect a longing for an earlier, precapitalist period, even as Irving makes clear that such a period is forever closed. In this longing, the very concept of treasure signals a period that predates capitalism's "unceasing movement of profit-making."[98] Accordingly, Webber's "golden dreams" signify a kind of desperate desire to escape the very psychology of success and failure in antebellum America. Even an illusionary treasure is in this sense a reference to the earlier moment of mercantile capitalism. And even an illusionary treasure represents an immutable form of value and stability—one that, by extension, is linked to a longed-for form of fiscally secure, self-possessed masculinity.

Knickerbocker is fascinated with the popular response to rumors of buried treasure. Gone, however, is the distinction between money-grabbing Yankees and Dutchmen indifferent to gold that had pervaded *A History of New York*. Kidd's buried treasure "set the brains *of all the good people along the coast* in ferment."[99] But the most telling element here is that the Irving of *Tales of a Traveller* seems intent upon modifying the narrative of debtor masculinity he offered in "The Legend of Sleepy Hollow." A deluded victim to "conjecture" and "speculations" about buried treasure, Webber is lying on his deathbed when he learns that the property he is about to sign away to his daughter has become immeasurably valuable as real estate—yielding, not cabbages so much as "an abundant crop of rents [...] the golden produce of the soil."[100] The prospect instantly revitalizes him. Webber rises from his bed and resumes his life as a venerable patriarch of his native city. From hindsight, we might say that his fortunate alchemy performs a kind of "compromise work."[101]

Neither the diabolic dream product of speculative excess nor the hard work of his hands, nor the bounty of inheritance, the new value is happily mined from Webber's property simply through the passage of time. The passage of time transforms Webber into a modern-day landlord—a *rentier*—whose work consists of collecting cash from a series of temporary occupants inhabiting land much different from locales such as Squire Bracebridge's Hall or Baltus Van Tassel's paternal mansion. Wolfert Webber has become rich merely by holding on to his lands while Manhattan has grown up around them. He is one of those men "whose fortunes have been made, in a manner, in spite of themselves."[102] But neither Irving, whose fortune from writing likewise has been made in spite of himself, nor the narrator acknowledge that Webber has become wealthy by unintentionally profiting from what amounts to *de facto* land speculation. Apparently, for patriarchal masculinity to survive in the new economy, one must adapt to its demands. If, as Scott Sandage puts it, "the only identity deemed legitimate in America is a capitalist identity,"[103] Wolfert Webber allows readers to envision an imaginary resolution to the problem of masculine failure so pervasive under the sign of capitalist identity. In this imaginary realm, the "theft" of Webber's stable masculinity by modern capitalism and the new economy is reversed, if only momentarily.[104]

Like the Webber stories, "The Devil and Tom Walker" was not written until *after* Irving's German tour. "This morning," an entry in Irving's French journal for May 6, 1824, reads, "wrote story of the Devil & Tom Walker."[105] Similar entries are dated May 7 and May 8. On May 10, too, Irving "[w]rote a little at the story of Tom Walker, introducing dialogue between him & D[evil]—on subject of the bargain." Irving rewrote parts of the story on May 21, just before leaving for England on May 24, almost exactly nine years after he had left America.[106] "The Devil and Tom Walker" often has been seen as a poor copy of "The Legend of Sleepy Hollow," symptomatic of the decline of Irving's creative powers, if not of the haste in which he wrote it (the key entries in the journal for the story are all for May and June 1824). Although I do not believe that Irving's creative powers were in decline, then or later, his treatment of Tom Walker as an anxious or "nervous" male is considerably less vexed than that of Ichabod Crane. Irving is also more relaxed about the "speculating fever," which he treats almost as a natural event, said to "break out every now and then in the country" but which always is bound to "subside."[107] (Irving later took up the theme in his sketch "The Great Mississippi Bubble," a direct response to the panic of 1837, published in *Knickerbocker Magazine* of April 1840 and later reprinted in *The Crayon Papers*.)

Reference, in "The Devil and Tom Walker," to "speculating fever" is to the South Sea Bubble of 1720, a historic event which Irving turned into a timely moral fable of financial hubris. At the time the South Sea Bubble gave rise to popular pamphleteering and widespread political cartooning, much as it lay at the core of contemporary public discussions about paper money as "the devil in specie," a "nothing" pretending to be "something."[108] "It was a time of paper credit," Irving writes in "The Devil and Tom Walker":

> The country had been deluged with government bills; the famous Land Bank had been established; there had been a rage for speculating; the people had run mad with schemes for new settlements; for building cities in the wilderness; land jobbers went about with maps of grants, and townships, and Eldorados, lying nobody knew where, but which everybody was ready to purchase. In a word, the great speculating fever which breaks out now and then in the country, had raged to an alarming degree, and everybody was dreaming of making sudden fortunes from nothing. As usual the fever had subsided; the dream had gone off, and the imaginary fortunes with it; the patients were left in doleful plight, and the whole country resounded with the consequent cry of "hard times."[109]

The passage marks the story's "financial subplot," in Charles Zug's apt phraseology.[110] Radically different in its "realism" from the altogether nineteen different folk motifs Irving wove together from various sources, it speaks, not so much to the state of affairs in colonial Boston as to the present, to the speculative economy of the time. In the story we observe Tom Walker taking infinite pleasure in the abject postures of his many debtors. "In proportion to the distress of the applicant was the hardness of his terms," we learn.[111] This is a bizarre reversal of the Puritan notion of a covenant of grace, in which outpourings of wealth had found a ready place, as the Puritans saw in such outpourings the redemption of the debt of human sin through Christ's sacrificial death.[112] Tom, however, represents, not the Puritan elect but the class of "'corrupt' new men of paper." These men were, to borrow from Caroll Smith-Rosenberg, "the new capitalism's stockjobbers [who] lived in a passionate and venal world driven by fantasy and credit, obsessed with stocks, speculation, and debt."[113]

The financial instability of a speculative economy, we have seen, gave rise to panicky paper money men. In this regard, Tom Walker's dispossessed and anxious masculinity also displays the emasculating effects of the new economy. Tom's "precarious" form of male selfhood also is no longer centered around an interior form of self-possession but is contingent upon a commodified and "elusive" reputation. The banking business he enters upon epitomizes the period's paper money economy, while the "gothic" lens of the supernatural focuses on the buried treasure to be located by divination, as well as on a hypocritical religiosity, as when Tom becomes a "violent churchgoer," who, moreover, "always carried a small bible in his coat pocket."[114] Altogether, "The Devil and Tom Walker" is a fantastical narrative, a tale we might understand as a metaphoric nod to the many stories of speculative riches awaiting timely investors.

Irving's delineation of Tom's avarice and religious hypocrisy generates revulsion. Indeed, Tom Walker probably is Irving's least pleasant character. One might be inclined to overlook the bargain Tom makes with the devil in exchange for the location of Kidd's treasure as a fairy-tale element if not a direct allusion to Goethe's *Faust*. American writers during Romanticism often used the devil as a character.[115] In Irving's story, the one thing Tom Walker will not do to accommodate the devil is go slave trading, so there is at least a measure of decency left in him. (There is no record whether Irving, in naming his character, was aware of the notorious Thomas "Beau" Walker, who was the captain of, master of, or investor in slaving voyages to Sierra Leone in West Africa between 1784 and 1792. The fact in itself would not have raised eyebrows, as scores of European merchants and American plantation owners profited from the slave trade. But Captain Walker, who was British born, has been identified as a direct ancestor of two recent American presidents, George H.W. Bush and George W. Bush.[116])

It is also worth pointing out that Tom agrees both to the sale of his soul and to a new profession as a money lender because he is hounded by a greedy and miserly wife whom Irving depicts as far more castrating than the famously shrewish Dame Van Winkle. Yet in what manner is this bargain achieved! His appetite whetted by the prospect "of great sums of money buried by Kidd the pirate" and with "the black print of a finger burnt [...] into his forehead" as proof, Tom is quite willing to sell his soul in return for the devil's favor. Whereas a career as a slave dealer is a no-go for Tom, he is happy to "turn usurer," ready to lend money, not at two per cent a month, as suggested by the devil, but at four per cent. And when the devil promises that the "rhino" will be his "this very night," the two parties "shook hands and struck a bargain."[117] The exaggerated depiction of the bargain makes one suspect that Tom also figures as Irving's "distorted mirror image," his chthonic masculine shadow if you will, which Irving must somehow move beyond. As the editors of the *History of New York* for the *Complete Works* remarked, Irving "horse-traded like any of Diedrich Knickerbocker's damned Yankees to sell his wares for the best price."[118]

There are, of course, differences. Tom Walker, increasingly "anxious," becomes a "violent churchgoer," though neither his assumed religiosity nor his bible will save him. In the end he is carried off by a satanic figure dubbed "the black man."[119] In a scene that strongly echoes Ichabod Crane's persecution by the Headless Horseman, Tom is thrown "like a child into the saddle" and whisked away "on a horse that galloped like mad across the fields." More telling still, the "gold and silver" that once filled Tom Walker's war chest aka bank vault are transformed into "chips and shavings." The devil's money becoming ashes is a classical motif in folklore.[120] In the context of Irving's time, however, the paper money of America's new economy is itself a kind of bogeyman, one that vanishes with close scrutiny, leaving only masculine humiliation and panic in its wake.[121] By the same token, the "vast house" Tom had built for himself, "out of ostentation," though he "left the greater part of it unfinished and unfurnished out of parsimony," represents a corrupt and insubstantial form of value. It is a value based on the chimerical paper profits decried by bullionists, rather than the inherent value said to be contained in a monetary system based on the traditional gold standard. The latter is epitomized in Bracebridge Hall or the estate owned by Old Baltus Van Tassel, who is the perfect picture of dignified masculinity as a "thriving, contented, liberal-hearted farmer [...] satisfied with his wealth, but not proud of it," and concerned more with the "abundance" than with the "style" of his "paternal mansion."[122]

If "The Devil and Tom Walker" is a depiction of the debt-based and frequently humiliated forms of masculinity emerging out of the new economy, the story at one and the same time delineates the political mindset that was pivotal already in the elections of 1824, though effective only in 1828. In each instance, the electorate changed dramatically in both size (population growth) and composition (an unprecedented proportion of adult white males became first-time voters when property strictures were removed). Put differently, in "Tom Walker" Irving provides a narrative as much about money as about class. Already in "Rip Van Winkle," Irving lamented that serious political frictions divided traditional communities. Confronted by a local politician who wants to know whether he was a "Federal or Democrat," Rip is utterly confounded. In *Tales of a Traveller*, the discourse receives an additional twist. Irving responds to the expanding electorate with a decidedly anti-common man rhetoric, directed against the Jacksonian Democrats' political buzzword.

Tales of a Traveller was first published in August 1824. In November of that year, presidential elections were held, the first elections in U.S. history in which the popular vote really mattered—because of the expanding population of the country and, more importantly, because eighteen states chose their presidential electors by popular vote. Previous presidents either had been elected from a land-holding elite (Washington, Jefferson, Madison, and Monroe) or qualified as among the better-educated men of the nation (John Adams and John Quincy Adams). The elections of 1824 also were curious ones as there were only Democratic-Republican candidates, the old Federalist Party having dissolved following the disastrous loss of their candidate in the elections of 1816. The elections of 1824 pitched Andrew Jackson against John Quincy Adams.[123] As no candidate had a majority in the Electoral College, the decision was made in the House of Representatives. Jackson had the most votes in the College and the most popular votes, yet John Quincy Adams became president in 1825, thanks to a resolution in favor of Adams by the House.

The close contest and its resolution in favor of Adams resulted in any amount of bitterness, a bitterness that by 1828 crystallized into organized political parties which had their base in the unprecedented proportion of adult white males permitted to vote in a presidential election.[124] Neither genteel patriarchy nor elitist values fared any too well in the process of modernization America was going through in the first half of the nineteenth century. Washington Irving felt this acutely. Though he was in Europe at the time, news from home were important for him. Colonel Aspinwall, his close friend, not only provided him with the legend of Captain Kidd, the impetus to start "The Devil and Tom Walker," but also kept him informed about the state of affairs in America. Moreover, there are numerous entries about reading papers, such as one for December 8, 1825: "Read Am: newspapers."[125]

Mostly during his residence in Paris, Irving went to the brothers Galignani, book dealers and publishers whose shop he frequented. He would also talk to people who had just arrived from America, such as Samuel G. Ogden, a merchant of New York, whose shipping interests had brought him to France; or else, to a Mr. Wilkinson and a Mr. Richards, the former having been desired by Daniel D. Tompkins, James Monroe's Vice President from 1817 to 1825, to remember him to Irving, who had served under him in the War of 1812, when Tompkins was governor of New York and head of the militia.[126] On yet another occasion in February 1824, conversation at table turned on President Monroe's statement, in a message to Congress the previous December, of the Monroe Doctrine.[127] And there are more such informants, such as an "Eng Gent" Irving met at Dr. Mcloughlin's and who appeared to be "remarkably well informed about america—clear, distinct & precise in his information." Irving also mentions a "Mr Lee of N York who brings book and a letter from Miller [the London publisher of *The Sketch Book*]." Significantly, going to the Galignanis to read the papers often was a distraction when Irving was facing an impasse in writing: "After breakfast," he wrote in his French journal for December 13, 1823, "tried to summon up ideas to write but in vain—Went out & [...] read papers at Galignanis."¹²⁸

Friday, January 9, 1824, finds Irving at Madame De Quandt's Hotel Mirabeau, in the company of a "<little> German Lady [...] with tall thin dingy looking companion [...] a tall Frenchman with lively eye & much animation [and a] Dr Gall—middle sized old gent. with bald head."¹²⁹ At dinner the conversation "turned on misers." The passage is worth quoting at greater length. The "tall Frenchman" told

> how in consequence of his situation in a public office he had had frequent opportunities of witnessing <the> instances of extreme <miserlings> miserliness in beggars & others who died intestate & their property fell to the crown—one who lived in miserable lodgings, but ate [nothing but] turkey from the Kings poulterer—His bread must be from the Kings baker[....] He was a usurer, lent money on pledges—discovered money in marmites—covered with ordure[....] Mem of money-pledges &c but could find nothing of pledges—at length found a key—which suited a house in another street, where the found pledges treasured up far exceed the money lent.

The passage is followed by the story of the "Leipsick Miser," as told by Madame de Quandt herself. This miser had "purchased houses & chateaus" but "let them fall to ruin rather than repair them." And he was so miserly that when one of his own children died of scarlet fever, he kept the corpse until it was putrid, as "others might die & one funeral & coffin do for all."

Of the two miserly characters, the "beggars & others" and the gentlemanly "Leipsick Miser," Irving only used the "beggars & others" in his portrayal of Tom Walker as a "meager, miserly fellow."¹³⁰ It is not that Irving was without social conscience. He could tell—and sympathize with—misery when he saw it. "You have no idea of the distress and misery that prevails in this country," he wrote Brevoort from England in 1816. It "is beyond the power of description. In America you have financial difficulties, the embarrassments of trade & the distress of merchants [...] but here you have what is far worse, the distress of the poor [...] Hunger, nakedness, wretchedness of all kinds...."¹³¹ Irving's social conscience only went so far, though. For him, the social order was intact so long as people knew their places: "The cause of Liberty," he wrote in "Notes and Extracts, 1825," "is a cause of too much dignity, to be sullied by turbulence and tumult. It ought to be maintained in a manner suitable to her nature. Those who engage in it should breathe a sedate, yet fervent spirit, animating them to actions of prudence, justice, modesty, bravery, humanity & magnanimity." Another entry is even more direct: "Tyranny—the worst of all tyranny is that of the many. When the people take law <&> in their own hands. Every one who [blank]."¹³² Presumably, Irving planned to use these jottings for his contemplated series of essays on America.

None of these essays was ever published and Irving evidently destroyed the manuscript. Yet he began writing the essays in Paris in early 1825 and continued working on them at least through January 1826. They were, Henry Pochmann suggests, "probably critical and reflected [Irving's] disenchantment and uneasy thoughts in 1825."[133]

The Tom Walker story is set in the Boston area in the year 1727. Local legends of Kidd's buried treasure abound, and earthquakes are regarded as providence, sending "many tall sinners down upon their knees."[134] Even Tom's disappearance is readily accepted by "the good people of Boston [who] shook their heads and shrugged their shoulders, but had been so much accustomed to witches and goblins, and tricks of the devil, in all kinds of shapes [...] that they were not so horror-struck as might have been expected."[135] Irving's Boston is a place of isolation, parochialism, credulousness and superstitions, though Irving did not write a historical set piece. He found all this in his own time. As William Hedges argues, in "The Devil and Tom Walker" Irving brings into dramatic focus "Yankee shrewdness and puritan respectability,"[136] thus creating a genuinely American atmosphere, one that reflects the state of affairs in the 1820s. Tom may have sold his soul to the devil; he increases his wealth and thus seems to believe in the game enough to play it, yet he does not do anything with the money. Thus, he is a illustration of Tocqueville's description of the American man of the nineteenth century as "restless in the midst of abundance."[137]

For many people of the post-revolutionary generation, the "self-made man" was the "ideal character," unashamed of his obscure origins, and a strong believer in hard work and ingenuity. This model man "developed his inner resources, acted independently, lived virtuously, and bent his behavior to his personal goals."[138] Thus, the newly ambitious people valued work and not leisure. They also aspired to be property owners, but soon enough property no longer was the static land of the gentry or the yeoman farmer. For the risk-takers who were coming into their own in the 1820s, property was capital and capital was the fuel for dynamic, speculative investment. The model to release the ambitions of the risk-takers and to connect them to revolutionary ideals was, of course, Benjamin Franklin, who in his *Autobiography* (1771) presented his own life as an exemplary story of how to rise from artisan beginnings to patrician success and influence.

In Irving's eyes, Tom Walker is but a usurper. (And, from hindsight, an ancestor of the poor bootblack Ragged Dick, whose rise to middle class respectability in nineteenth-century New York City later was made immemorial by Horatio Alger.) Tom aspires to be a gentleman, though he lacks the requisite culture and civilization of his betters. The story thus hinges on the "real class animus" of early nineteenth-century America, which William Charvat described as a struggle between a "homogeneous patrician society and a rising materialistic middle class without education and tradition, who were winning cultural and economic power and changing the tone of American life."[139] Irving's disgust with and vilification of Tom Walker therefore can rightfully be understood as a conservative response to the Franklinesque model.[140] The author's rage fully comes to the fore in the story's conclusion. Using the voice of a sardonic "iron-faced Cape Cod Whaler," we are instructed thus: "Let all griping money brokers lay this story to heart."[141]

"The Devil and Tom Walker" was written at a time when the self-made man was still competing with earlier paradigms, the genteel patriarch and the heroic artisan. Soon, however, the patriarch would be displaced, and the artisan uprooted and brought into the new industrial marketplace. In the onslaught of the new times, the self-made man triumphed, though neither the patriarch nor the artisan disappeared overnight. Every new configuration contains masses of the old as residual elements. The new never marks a complete break with the past; rather, there is a reconfiguration of elements of the past with some elements that are new. Each time the past comes, it requires a change of perspective, even of paradigm. To the extent that the past keeps reappearing as the national present, the two spheres overlap and interpenetrate to reveal that colonial America and the fledgling United States were complementary. Things did not change quite so drastically as it first appears in the transition from colony to nation. Perhaps for that very reason, "The Devil and Tom Walker" is a deeply pessimistic tale.

In Irving's tale, not even the colonial elite holds up but is depicted as rotten to the core. Deacon Peabody, for instance, was "an eminent man, who had waxed wealthy by driving shrewd bargains with the Indians." And of the worthy Absalom Crowninshield (and one should note the quintessential Englishness in the name-giving), a newspaper piously announces upon his demise, "'A great man had fallen in Israel.'"[142] The fact that Crowninshield dies after the devil hews down the tree with the buccaneer's name on it only accentuates the lack of scruples and lust for money that lie behind the pious, dignified veneer of Yankeedom, despite (or because of) the puritan heritage. Crowninshield's (and, of course, Tom Walker's) fate is much more radical than Ichabod Crane's, who in the end is rumored to have gone on to a successful professional career. Altogether, "The Devil and Tom Walker" is a story about things coming apart, slipping out of control, or about sinister encroachments in our lives. As a story about a breaking down, it provides a glimpse, not of achieved masculinity but of the future of masculinity emerging under the sign of entrepreneurial capitalism, together with the psychological and human costs of an ideology centered on economic ambition as the hallmark of the good life.

"The Devil and Tom Walker" is not the only story in the "Money Diggers" section that is peopled with characters infatuated with becoming wealthy. While their addiction to wealth reveals them as dysfunctional shadows of the "Lover" archetype, the addiction is not the result of intrinsic flaws (human nature) so much as of the anxieties generated by the emerging capitalist order, together with its credit economy.[143] As regards Tom Walker, he too is but a player, focused on dreams of success, and plunging ahead, mobile, competitive, and aggressive in business, at the same time as he is temperamentally restless, chronically insecure, a sexual failure, and desperate to achieve a solid grounding for a masculine identity. Yet Tom's fate is decided by some kind of supernatural agency, as he is simply spirited away by one of Irving's theatrical sleight of hands, in contrast to Ichabod Crane, whom the community of Sleepy Hollow drives off the idyll. Moreover, Tom's story is told, not by Knickerbocker, but by an "iron-faced Cape Cod Whaler," who has no sympathy whatsoever for miserly Tom Walker, his equally miserly wife, or the greed of Tom's victims.

The whaler, an honest craftsman who probably has known what it is to be pinched with debt, represents the "Warrior" archetype, the energy of aggressive but nonviolent action, of courage, and the ability to bear pain. In sociological terms, he is the epitome of the "artisan paradigm" described by David Leverenz. Artisans formed a producing class, who defined manhood not in terms of "work and entrepreneurial competition" so much as in terms of "freedom, pride of craft and, to a lesser degree, citizenship, along with a good deal of ambivalence about patriarchal deference." Beyond that, their masculine identity was inseparable from the duties one owed to one's community.[144] The unnamed whaler defers to the patricians as a matter of course, in this instance to Knickerbocker's company of "worthy burghers,"[145] the Dutch aldermen and other worthies of post-revolutionary New York, all of whom embody the communal ideal. There is plenty of sociability, though no male rivalry. Finally, there is Geoffrey Crayon himself, the alleged "author," who, on the strength of his knowledgeable guidance stands in as the "Magician" archetype. These combined forces, of psychic energy as much as of the past—genteel patriarchs upholding the old-school Federalism—are arraigned against the new upstarts.

Irving may have had good reasons to describe the Cape Cod Whaler as "iron-faced," for by the 1820s artisans in general already were on the defensive. Artisanal production was on the point of becoming industrial production, which, in turn, would destroy work skills. As Adam Smith observed in 1776, the division of labor in a pin factory was doing wonders for productivity, at the same time as it was making workers as "stupid and ignorant as it is possible for a human creature to become."[146] Smith's observation does not apply just to the Whaler. Brom Bones, a "rustic" known for his "Herculean frame and great powers of limb,"[147] too is a laborer in a world in which labor-based forms of value are clearly in decline. Thus, he too is vulnerable to the long arm of the increasingly capricious economy. Though Sleepy Hollow is generally understood as a space insulated against the forces of the new economy, the strangely narcotic atmosphere that pervades the valley can be seen as a hint that the speculative economy has *already* made its way into Sleepy Hollow. As Knickerbocker expounds early on, "However wide awake [people] may have been before they entered that sleepy region, they are sure, in a little time, to inhale the witching influence of the air, and begin to grow imaginative—to dream dreams, and see apparitions."[148]

Brom Bones is all but entirely dependent upon Katrina Van Tassel's "vast expectations"[149] for his future support. Yet with the panic reaching to all corners of the United States in 1819, even the Van Tassel estate would be subject to possible ruin. One needs but turn to the frequent reports in both the Democratic-Republican and the Federalist press during the period of farmers who lost their property due to speculator schemes. The March 25, 1820, editorial in the *Independent American*, is a typical example, warning of those adventurers who will "impose on the credulity of the honest, industrious, unsuspecting part of the community [...] until their ruin is consummated."[150] The rivalry between Ichabod Crane and Brom Bones thus is one that pits two forms of unstable masculinity against one another, leaving them struggling for dominance over a fundamentally uncertain—and possibly bleak—future. Brom Bones, just like the Cape Cod Whaler, is cut off from the supposedly secure certainties of an economy where valuation is based on a gold standard.

Through the whaler, Irving also mimics an "oral" tradition of storytelling. Knickerbocker, out fishing on a boat with his buddies, claims to have learned the story from the whaler, who avers that he has given "the purport of the tale [...] as nearly as I can recollect."[151] The whaler himself sets up the story thus: "By the way, I recollect a story about a fellow who once dug up Kidd's buried money, which was written by a neighbour of mine, and which I learnt by heart. As the fish don't bite just now, I'll tell it to you, by way of passing away the time." Furthermore, phrases such as "some say," "the old stories add," "the most current and probable story," "according to the most authentic old story," "most authentic narrators," "the truth of these strange traditions," or "air of authenticity" are scattered throughout to reinforce the enactment of a traditional storyteller, whose purpose is to give a story an air of verisimilitude and whose originality lies in combining or recombining "already existing motifs."[152] We should also take note of the phrase "found among the papers of the late Diedrich Knickerbocker," with which the Money Diggers section is subtitled, as well as of the epigraph, an extract from Christopher Marlow's *Jew of Malta*:

> Now I remember these old women's words
> Who in my youth would tell me winter's tales;
> And speak of spirits and ghosts that glide by night
> About the place where treasure hath been hid.

All these instantiations of orality evoke nostalgia for the good old times of Irving's boyhood, the region of fable and romance, full of old women telling stories in which ghosts were still ghosts, not "horrid images of the spectral lord of the world," that is, of the real world of money and finance.[153] Knickerbocker's tales, revolving as they do around Kidd's treasure, seamen, pirates or not, a jolly gathering of worthy aldermen, ghosts and legends, clearly locate themselves within the realm of fantasy. Already with "Rip Van Winkle," storytelling, seen as evoking a common cultural heritage, constituted community, a framework both of cultural understanding and of continuity throughout time. In that project, time is captured not through factual exposition but through the act of storytelling. However, Irving depicts oral culture as a lived tradition at a time when it was being displaced by print, foreboding the beginning of a culture industry. The achievement of *Tales of a Traveller* and, in particular, *The Sketch Book* was to establish storytelling as a site in which, Michael Hurst remarks, "a new form of patriarchal control can flourish."[154]

The mode of oral storytelling by which Irving produced his tales cannot achieve complete stability. The vacillations of his stand-ins between recognitions of the legendary if not fantastic origin of a tale and denials of those origins (visible in the excessive use of authenticating formulae) leaves a lingering tension that threatens to subvert the stability of the imagined past it creates. This points to another deeply felt problem at Irving's time— the concern, even anxiety, that words do not mean what they say, that there is a dissociation of sign and thing, which in turn leads to a desperate desire for certainty. And there is another obstacle. The only way Irving can capture the tale "authentically" is to reproduce it as a written text, which leaves the story, and thus the stability it can provide, at the mercy of the market once again. From Irving's perspective, this is just as well. "The Money Diggers" stories pretend to have been "found" by Crayon in the papers of the late Knickerbocker, who had himself relied on other storytellers, such as the whaler, who is himself not the "originator" of the story about Tom Walker but had it from the writings of a neighbor. The credulity that this "nesting" of narrators requires thus serves to ease the tension produced by tales that self-consciously claim a double genesis in the realms of fantasy and fact. Put differently, there is always another story that can be told with similar effect, but only if one is willing to believe it.

With storytelling as a literary vocation, Irving had found a way to eschew commercial society, preserving his anima identity at the same time as he, authoring a successful book, succeeded as a man among men. This was certainly true of *The Sketch Book*, less so of *Bracebridge Hall*, and definitely not so with *Tales of a Traveller*, though Irving was convinced that the collection contained "some of the best things I have ever written."[155] Yet as soon as he received the first copies of the printed work, he was more anxious perhaps than ever. "An indifferent night," he wrote in his journal for November 7, 1824, "awoke very early: depressed, dubious of myself & public."[156] A fortnight later, he again woke up from a "restless night—broken sleep & uneasy thoughts—read much in the night."[157] Once reviews did come in, his worst fears were coming true. There is "nothing German" in the tales and sketches; at best, Irving "cribbed from the German books he has been dabbling in," he read in *Blackwood's Edinburgh Magazine*. The *Quarterly Review*, while conceding that the work had considerable merit, nevertheless observed that Irving "must in future [...] correct the habit of indolence which so considerable a part of 'Tales of a Traveller' evinces." American critics likewise panned both the book and its author. "The public have been led to expect better things as the result of [...] Irving's travels," wrote the *United States Literary Gazette* of November 15, 1824, while the *New-York Mirror and Ladies' Gazette* of September 25, 1824, pronounced Irving "overrated." And the critic for the *Metropolitan Literary Journal* wrote in the October 1824 issue, "let him shun tale-writing; it is not his forte."[158]

The lukewarm if not hostile reception of his collection put Irving into a most dejected mood. What probably hurt him the most were the doubts cast on his masculinity in the pages of the *New-York Mirror*: "It is suggested that Mr. Washington Irving's new work would sell more rapidly if the Booksellers would alter the Title, and call it 'STORIES FOR CHILDREN' by *a Baby Six Feet High*, instead of Tales of a Traveller."[159] Hurt by what he calls "ill-natured fling[s] at me," Irving wrote in his journal for April 29, 1825: "*It is hard to be stabbed in the back by ones own kin when attacked in front by strangers. No matter—my countrymen may regret some day or other that they turnd from me with such caprice, the moment foes abroad assailed me ....*"[160] He did not yet know that some who were not kin raved about the collection. *Tales of a Traveller* was instantly translated and serially published in the Dresden *Abendzeitung* as "Aus den Erzählungen eines Reisenden von Washington Irving, dem Verfasser des Skizzenbuches." Other translations followed, and no book of Irving's "has been more successful across the Rhine than *Erzählungen eines Reisenden*."[161] This side of the Rhine, however, Irving may himself have asked for criticism. In "To the Reader" he had declared, "I rummaged my portfolio, and cast about, in my recollection, for those floating materials which a man naturally collects in travelling; and here I have arranged them in this little work."[162]

In a letter to Henry Brevoort of December 11, 1824, Irving was even

Three. Rip Van Winkle, Ichabod Crane, Other Masculinities 103

more explicit; he summarized his method as obeying an *"artist touch,"* though he added that this is "not a thing to be appreciated by the many. I fancy that much of what I value myself upon in writing, escapes the observation of the great mass of my readers: who are *intent more upon the story than the way in which it is told.*"[163] And at the end of "Poor Devil Author," a sketch he included in *Tales of a Traveller*, Irving had written some truly prophetic words: "Take my word for it, the only happy author in this world is he who is below the care of reputation."[164] Irving was not, and so his disappointment spilled over into a letter to his young nephew, Pierre Paris Irving: "Many and many a times have I regretted that at my early outset in life I had not been imperiously bound down to some regular and useful mode of life, and been thoroughly inured to habits of business; and I have a thousand times regretted with bitterness that ever I was led away by my imagination."[165]

John Murray, when in 1822 he was offered *Bracebridge Hall*, already thought that Irving "had written himself out."[166] In actual fact, Irving "had written himself out" of his adulation for things English or, rather, for old England and its avatars, like Squire Bracebridge. Murray, who dropped hundreds of guineas for *Bracebridge Hall*, was right in his estimation. Irving, Stanley Williams writes, had "sucked England dry of the sentimental and the antiquarian."[167] Irving was, however, not through as a man of letters, though I sympathize with the impulse to make this argument. Irving indeed stopped writing fiction—"serious" literature—as it were.[168] Tellingly, he wrote to Murray, "I have nothing of my own in any state of forwardness; though my brain is teeming."[169] Another letter to Murray expresses the same predicament: "I have nothing ready for the press, nor do I know at present when I shall have, my mind having been rather diverted from composition of late, and occupied by a course of study."[170]

That there was a crisis is beyond dispute. However, I disagree with Henry Pochmann's verdict that "the Irving who lives and is vital is the young Irving, the Irving before 1832." Irving's histories, Pochmann continues, generally needed "little invention," as the subjects "were all ready to hand," while his biographies, including *Life of George Washington*, "lean toward compilation rather than original composition."[171] I am also somewhat puzzled by a much-quoted statement by William Hedges: "What [Irving] did desire to do is not easy to discover. To a large extent he may have been unconscious of his approach to history. And consciously he could not formulate his intentions except in stock phrases."[172] It is certainly true that Irving rarely if ever thought through exactly what he wanted to say and wait for it to mature clearly in his mind, before he wrote it down on paper. Rather, he trusted his general intentions and the wholeness his "speed-writing" would give. Put differently, for Irving the act of writing was not much different from the act of thinking—"thinking [...] with the pen," as he advised other writers.[173]

Needless to say, such a method was asking for laborious revisions. On the other hand, Irving's writings were framed by a single over-arching motive—to resolve the conflict between a dominant anima and a nagging, unloved, imperfectly realized masculinity. What neither Pochmann nor Hedges saw is that the histories and biographies came from a most productive second half of Irving's writing career, a period characterized by synthesizing, with renewed energy, passive conscious material and unconscious influences. Irving's drifting away from fictional stories and sketches towards history and travel writing, from fancy towards fact, should be seen as the continuation of his quest for achieved manhood. Reinventing himself as a writer, he found new ways of amplifying the archetypes, creating characters who in their dutiful masculinity were radically different both from the "gentle alternatives" he had invested in his "residuals" and from the "troubled" masculinities of Ichabod Crane and the "money diggers." In this regard, *Tales of a Traveller* is not the "second-hand miscellany" panned by Stanley Williams so much as it is a pivotal work in Irving's literary career. *Tales of a Traveller*, I find myself in agreement with the editor of the collection for the *Complete Works*, "ended the major phase of Irving's contribution to the short story, and almost four years were to elapse before the publication of his next substantial work, *The Life and Voyages of Columbus* (1828)."[174]

In January 1825, Irving's fellow-American John Neal tried to come to his rescue. "Go to work," he admonished Irving. "Lose no time."[175] Irving might have taken consolation from his own jottings. "Give me rugged toil, fierce disputation, wrangling controversy, harassing research, give me anything that calls forth the energies of the mind," he had pleaded years before.[176] A similar mood swing emerges from a sketch he had written in 1814: "Little minds are tamed and subdued by misfortune; but great minds rise above them."[177] Mood swings of this kind usually did not last. Before long, Irving would again be dissatisfied. On May 2, 1825, he scribbled in his notebook that he felt "extremely depressed—incapable of exertion—read fifty pages of Marshall's 'Life of Washington.'"[178] Irving's downheartedness continued. As he noted just over a fortnight later, "depression and incapacity to write—read Marshall's 'Life of Washington' till near two [p.m.]."[179] As I will show in greater detail in Chapter Six, in his final work Irving found the part of himself he had been seeking in the way he marveled at George Washington's masculine perfection. Immediately following *Tales of a Traveller*, however, Irving tried to find an unadulterated masculinity of responsible social maturity in Spain, or rather in Spain's past. Thus, it was not willpower so much as travel that once again sharpened Irving's dulled imagination; if it did not stimulate new ideas, at least it reawakened his romantic feelings, at the same time as, anticipating Thomas Carlyle's idea that heroic manhood was defined by commitment to an impersonal higher cause, it localized them.

Four

"Dear old romantic Spain"
Purloined Heroes

Washington Irving was not only devastated by the disappointing reception of *Tales of a Traveller*, but also the toilsome composition of it had bedeviled him. In order to escape the misery he was experiencing when his German tales project was leading nowhere he produced a number of short pieces that came to be known as "Sketches in Paris in 1825." Irving originally had intended them for a new *Sketch Book*, though the plan was abandoned, and they were first published in *Knickerbocker* for November–December 1840 and subsequently in *Wolfert's Roost*. One of the seven sketches that comprise this set is "The Field of Waterloo." The sketch begins as a melancholy reverie on Napoleon's last battle that took place there in 1815, but soon acquires luster from the story of "a French cavalier" who is about to dispatch a British officer when he realizes that the poor man has lost his sword-arm. The "generous warrior" (the expression is Irving's, though it carries an unmistakable overtone of a Jungian archetype) thereupon drops "the point of his sabre" and rides "courteously on." To these "desultory notes" Irving adds another story he purportedly picked up "in one of the French provinces." It's the story of a French aristocrat by the name of De Latour d'Auvergne, who rather than flee from the revolutionary turmoil joins the republican army, distinguishes himself yet refuses all rank above that of captain. Nor would he accept any recompense except a sword of honor and the title *Premier Grenadine de France*, bestowed by Napoleon himself. Killed in battle in Germany, the captain's place is retained in his regiment, and whenever the regiment is mustered, and his name is called out, "the reply was: 'Dead on the field of honor!'"[1]

The chivalry and archetypal manliness speaking from "The Field of Waterloo" is a lone exception in Irving's Paris years, during which he once confessed that he had absolutely "no disposition to write."[2] One wonders what course his literary career and, above all, his quest for his own imperfectly realized masculinity would have taken had it not been for an invitation from Alexander Everett, United States Ambassador to Madrid, to go to Spain. The two had met in Paris in July 1825, when Everett offered him the opportunity to accompany him to Madrid, though Irving then declined. However, in January 1826, he wrote to ask if the offer was still open. The invitation, which reached Irving in Bordeaux several weeks later, still stood. It was a true godsend, as it not only attached Irving to the Embassy in Madrid but also proposed that he translate the voyages of Columbus from Martín Fernández de Navarrete's collection of documents, *Colección de los viajes y descubrimientos*.[3] Irving instantly began making plans. He wrote to John Murray, his London publisher, about the compilation by Las Casas that he was going to use for his own book,[4] and soon after closed his trunks and in them shut that notebook of hypochondria, the French journal. If the invitation was an instance of good luck, Irving had not been totally inactive himself. During his residence in Paris, he had begun to seriously study Spanish, hiring a private teacher and purchasing dictionaries and grammar books; he also began to read widely in the history of the Arabs in Spain.[5] He had, however, no real purpose: "Studied Spanish to drive away unpleasant thoughts," he wrote in his journal on December 26, 1824.[6]

There was more. Irving considered the Spanish language as "full of power, magnificence and melody," mixing "Arabic fervor, magnificence & romance" with "old Castilian pride and punctilio."[7] No wonder, then, that things changed once he arrived in Spain. He found a new purpose in life and, equally important, a way out of the financial hardship he had been suffering from after the speculative failure of 1825. His destiny, Irving had come to believe, was to earn his living by writing. "When I once see a little capital of manuscripts growing under my hand," he wrote to Thomas Storrow, "I shall feel like another being and shall be relieved from a thousand cares and anxieties that have haunted my mind for a long time past."[8] In addition, writing proved to be therapeutic, as it lifted his mind "out of a kind of slough of apathy and almost melancholy into which it had sunk, and which, at times, made life a burden to me."[9] Both the financial embarrassment Irving found himself in and his need for self-therapy thus caused indirectly his *Life and Voyages of Christopher Columbus*, the first of his biohistories and the first book under his own name. More to the point, the exemplary manhood of Columbus served as a kind of halfway point in the arc that eventually led Irving back to George Washington.

Stanley Williams too saw the importance of the Spanish years. Spain, the biographer remarked, proved to be a "turning point" in Irving's life.[10] This was not so much because of Irving's work as cultural attaché, for, as James Perrin wrote, there is not "even one reference to [Irving's] ever having set foot in the U.S. Embassy."[11] Rather, Irving does research in Madrid,

Four. "Dear old romantic Spain" 107

travels through Andalusia, sojourns in the castle of the Alhambra, continues reading in Spanish literature and history, and imagining examples of archetypal masculinity. Phrased differently, the Spanish experience provided for Irving not only a field of presence in its own right, but also a field carrying discursive relations that speak to larger categories, such as ancient traditions, pre-modern customs and values, and, from and through these, achieved manhood.[12] Tapping into his unconscious, Irving unleashed projections onto just so many masculine heroes—Columbus, followed by Mahomet and his successors, Boabdil, the last of the Nasrid rulers, the residents, past and present, of the Alhambra, from Alhamar, the founder of the palace, to the beggars, vagrants, and idlers for whom the former palace has become a convenient "nestling-place," as well as the "proud, hardy, frugal and abstemious" Spanish peasants in general.[13]

In Spain, Irving was enormously productive. He published, in 1828, *A History of the Life and Voyages of Christopher Columbus*, which he regarded as "straight" history, even though it turned out to be much more. He followed *Columbus* up with the more literary *A Chronicle of the Conquest of Granada* (1829), purportedly by the monk Fray Antonio Agapida, *Voyages and Discoveries of the Companions of Columbus* (1831), and, in 1832, with a collection of romantic tales, *The Alhambra* (1832), featuring Geoffrey Crayon as "author." Irving also worked on *Legends of the Conquest of Spain* (1835), *Mahomet and His Successors* (1849), and, not to forget, the *Spanish Papers*, published posthumously by Pierre Munro Irving, from materials Irving had collected and drafted while at work on *Conquest of Granada*. Irving returned to America on May 21, 1832, after an absence of seventeen years.[14]

A History of the Life and Voyages of Christopher Columbus may have begun as a translation project but it soon took off in a completely different direction. Irving met Navarrete in Madrid and studied his work closely. He did not like what he saw. Translating Navarrete's collection of documents, he told Everett, went against his nature. Although he was to receive some fifteen hundred dollars for the translation, he would not submit himself to the limitations that this type of work made necessary. Moreover, he was convinced that Navarrete's was not a work for the general public. Irving's field was literature, and he wanted to write the story of Christopher Columbus by way of "combining all that had been related by different historians as well as the minor but very interesting facts existing in various documents recently discovered."[15] Irving was convinced that he was trying "an entirely new line."[16] The phrase is revealing. On one hand, "new line" reflects Irving's search for a satisfactory literary method for treating the non–American past. To write history in the form of literature, which people could read with pleasure, was a matter that "had occupied [Irving's] thoughts as early as 1823, when he determined to avoid in his future writings any imitation of Sir Walter Scott."[17] On the other hand, his Columbus developed into a site, even though on hindsight it was a provisional one, where Irving would find the part of himself he had been seeking. In this context, his optimistic boast that the biography would be "more advantageous for me than any work of mere imagination that I could have produced" takes on a meaning beyond the mere commercial.[18]

In Obadiah Rich's library of Americana in Madrid, Irving found Fray Bartolomé de Las Casas' *Historia de las Indias*, as well as several other unpublished histories. Yet his version of Columbus may well have been inspired by his childhood reading, such as Philip Frenau's poem "Columbus to Ferdinand" and a short biography of Columbus, both of which he had found in Noah Webster's *Lessons in Reading and Speaking* of 1790. The biography's author was no lesser writer than Joel Barlow, who in 1787 had come forth with "The Vision of Columbus," out of which grew a long epic poem, "The Columbiad" (1807). Immensely popular at the time, "The Columbiad" was unabashedly intended as a national epic for the United States, with Columbus delineated as a mythic hero.[19] Just as formative must have been the tercentenary of the discovery of America, celebrated in New York when Irving was nine years old. And long before Irving sat down to write his own version of Columbus, the name "Columbia" had come to replace Britannia, and Columbus and America's greatest hero, George Washington, were paired together through giving the name "Columbia" in 1791 to the federal district where the capital of the United States was going to be.[20]

Columbus also became a character in much romantic fiction. With the nascent literary nationalism, it was only logical that his "imagined virtues" were "indissolubly linked to the sympathetic purposes of the new American nation."[21] Like the writers of romantic fiction, Irving believed that history too was shaped by truly heroic characters, whose masculine achievements were to be commemorated and celebrated in what Nietzsche later called "monument history."[22] Irving at the time was convinced that there was no appropriate cultural landscape in America. Only Europe, he had written in the *Sketch Book*, "held forth the charms of storied and poetical association."[23] Accordingly, he chose Columbus, the Genoese in the service of the Spanish sovereigns, as his legendary hero-saint, the Warrior-Lover, to use the archetypal denominations. In this guise, Irving would offer his Columbus as a contribution to a genuinely *American* literature, "a more acceptable work to my country, than the translation I had contemplated."[24] Thus, Irving undertook to locate Columbus as a historical actor whose history, he wrote, was to instill patriotism in his readers—by "furnishing examples of what human genius and laudable enterprize may accomplish."[25] The phraseology—"human genius and laudable enterprize"—suggests Columbus'

Four. "Dear old romantic Spain" 109

nobility, an ideal that perfectly fit Irving's conception of achieved masculinity and that acquired even stronger contours through the stark contrast to Columbus' companions and, especially, his followers, "the dissolute rabble which he was doomed to command."[26]

Irving depicts the land that Columbus discovered as an earthly paradise, where the inhabitants seemed to be "existing in the state of primeval innocence of our first parents."[27] The "grasping avarice" of the "dissolute rabble," however, recklessly destroyed that paradise, making but "miserable victims" of the Indigenous population. "It seems almost incredible," Irving muses, "that so small a number of men [...] could in so short a space of time have produced such widespread miseries. But the principles of evil have a fatal activity."[28] The mythopoetic juxtaposition of good hero and evil antagonists perfectly fits Irving's quest for achieved masculinity. Historically, however, it is badly flawed. The principles of evil—call them civilization, capitalism, imperialism, or what not—did not come to the New World of themselves. Columbus was himself implicated in the evil, was its representative, an avatar of things to come. Yet Irving was no Cooper, who in his Leatherstocking cycle tirelessly explored the dilemma of Natty Bumppo as the unwitting vanguard of the eventual destruction of the American wilderness, the Indigenous population included. Irving, who needed a flawless hero, placed the responsibility for the consequences of civilization's destructive power not on the projector and policymaker of the voyages of discovery but on his followers. In doing so, he employed what John Hazlett has called "a very awkward double standard," blame for evil deeds on the followers, and ignoring "the obvious connection between Columbus' policies and the eventual destruction of the island paradise."[29]

The double standard had its price, as Irving had to suppress or at least palliate Columbus' complicity in the patriotic text. As a last resort, he praises Columbus, if not for bringing civilization, then at least for civilizing colonial conquest, exploitation, and enslavement. Columbus thus becomes dissociated from the "excesses of worthless and turbulent men," for, Irving claims, if his followers had not been so greedy, "a large revenue might have been collected, without any recourse to violence or oppression."[30] By elevating Columbus, Irving redirects blame from the Spanish empire (and, by implication, from western civilization) to later generations. The moral is quick to follow: If only Columbus' successors—villains like Roldán, Bobadilla, and Porras—had followed the explorer's "sound policy and liberal views," not only would Spain look different today; altogether, the Americas "would have been settled by pacific colonists, and civilized by enlightened legislators; instead of being overrun by desperate adventurers, and desolated by avaricious conquerors."[31] Here, then, is Geoffrey Crayon morphed into a moralizing historian, whose ideals of masculine perfection are in uncompromising opposition against the utilitarianism of the ambitious middle classes.

Columbus, Irving notes, was utterly unaware "that he had indeed discovered a new continent, equal to the whole of the old world in magnitude, and separated by two vast oceans from all the earth hitherto known by civilized man." If he had known, his "visions of glory" would have provided "the splendid empires which were to spread over the beautiful world he had discovered; and the nations, and tongues, and languages which were to fill its lands with his renown, and to revere and bless his name to the latest posterity!"[32] Whether knowingly or not, Irving here iterates the expansionist narrative that Thomas Jefferson had popularized, most famously in his first inaugural address of March 4, 1801. The fledgling United States, Jefferson wrote, was a "rising nation" with "destinies beyond the reach of mortal eye." The new nation, America, Jefferson said then, was special:

> Kindly separated by nature and a wide ocean from the exterminating havoc of one quarter of the globe; too high-minded to endure the degradations of the others; possessing a chosen country, with room enough for our descendants to the thousandth and thousandth generation; entertaining a due sense of our equal right to the use of our own faculties, to the acquisitions of our own industry, to honor and confidence from our fellow-citizens, resulting not from birth, but from our actions and their sense of them; enlightened by a benign religion, professed, indeed, and practiced in various forms, yet all of them inculcating honesty, truth, temperance, gratitude, and the love of man; acknowledging and adoring an overruling Providence, which by all its dispensations proves that it delights in the happiness of man here and his greater happiness hereafter—with all these blessings, what more is necessary to make us a happy and a prosperous people?[33]

There is a providential basis also in Irving's story of Columbus. Columbus, he writes in the very first chapter, always looked back upon his determination to go on in terms of "a secret impulse from the Deity."[34] Thus we are well prepared for the many symbolic coincidences Irving adapted from romances of his time. A swelling of the sea that unexpectedly interrupts a prolonged calm to Columbus seemed "providentially ordered to allay the rising clamors of his crew; like that which so miraculously aided Moses when conducting the children of Israel out of the captivity of Egypt."[35] Ultimately, however, such details are less important than "character" and the meaning of the voyages as a whole. For Irving, history was a drama of personalities, and if there are "poetic elements" of the seafarer's character, he deemed them essential for the depiction of a masculine archetype.[36] The book itself intentionally was an offering to his country, a conscious attempt to fulfill one of the essential goals of a genuinely "American" literature—the creation of an *American* hero. Imagined superiority—a model masculinity as it were—was sufficient for Irving to integrate a Catholic-Spanish *conquistador* into the family lineage of Anglo-Protestant America. Irving's Columbus is, then, a projection of his own deep-felt desire for achieved masculinity, a model for Spain, and a kind of Founding Father for the Americans and their errand into the wilderness.[37]

"The re-creation of national history," Hazlett notes, "was, to a large extent, a necessary extension of the individual's identity and history."[38] As regards Columbus, to be a kind of Founding Father for the Americans he had to suggest the idealized character of George Washington; he had to be a man of conviction. "When Columbus had formed his theory, it became fixed in his mind with singular firmness, and influenced his entire character and conduct. He never spoke in doubt or hesitation, but with as much certainty as if his eyes had beheld the promised land"—as they eventually would.[39] A measure of uneasiness remains, though. Columbus' ambition may have been "lofty and noble," yet he was not a pure saint. Irving shows him as deeply superstitious, as well as "naturally irritable and impetuous," though his soul, he quotes from a Spanish commentator, "'was superior to the age in which he lived.'"[40] "Distinguished men," Irving moralizes, and likely saw himself reflected in the description, "are composed of great and little qualities." If they are great, they are so mostly because they struggled against "the imperfections of their nature."[41]

In what anticipates the "self-cultivation" of his ultimate hero, George Washington, Irving credits Columbus with "restrain[ing] his valiant and indignant spirit." Thus, "praise is due to him for the firmness he displayed in managing himself."[42] The great store Irving laid by the idea of "self-cultivation" also speaks from his comment on Columbus' "vigilant self-command, for which he was afterwards remarkable."[43] As if this were not enough, Irving at the very end once again defends Columbus against the historical charge of excess ambition: "The manner in which his ardent imagination and mercurial nature was controlled by a powerful judgment, and directed by acute sagacity, is the most extraordinary feature in [Columbus'] character."[44] In order to create a genuinely *American* hero and, possibly, an imaginary portrait of how he himself wanted to be, Irving also dressed up his Columbus as a modern entrepreneur, one who is concerned that, "if there should arise no revenues, his labour and peril would produce no gain."[45] Yet if Columbus was a capitalist, he was a model capitalist, one who "contemplated works and achievements of benevolence and religion," such as relief for the poor, the foundation of churches, and, as well, "armies for the recovery of the holy sepulchre in Palestine," which he stipulated in his will.[46] Irving could not quite write out of the picture Columbus' religion. Columbus "was devoutly pious," Irving writes, though not in a fanatical way. His religion rather "diffused a sober dignity and a benign composure over his whole demeanour," even though it "was darkened by the bigotry of the age."[47] "Bigotry" often was accompanied by mercenary interests, as crusaders thought that their mission gave them "the right to invade, ravage, and seize upon the territories of all infidel nations, under the plea of defeating the enemies of Christ."[48] Not so Irving's Columbus, who comes to us as a "good Catholic" within what otherwise was inacceptable Catholicism. Irving could not, in good faith, credit the avowed religious motives of the crusaders, though in order to make Columbus palatable as a hero in an American origin story (and, for that matter, as his ideal self) he had to deny any mercenary interests on Columbus' part.[49]

As stated, Irving's Columbus served as a kind of halfway point in the arc that eventually led him back to George Washington. It is only logical, therefore, that *A History of the Life and Voyages of Christopher Columbus* is ambivalent about the character of its hero, much as there is uneasiness about the devastating imperialism that established the American colonies. In fact, there are two portraits of Columbus—oscillating between shining hero, "noble and lofty," the "patron and benefactor," and the much darker "conqueror" who ultimately is responsible for the fall of the new World.[50] Irving was aware that Columbus' character was "richly compounded of extraordinary and apparently contradictory elements."[51] However, he never explicitly developed the darker portrait, which would have stood in the way both of his personal quest and of his nationalist agenda. "The moral ambiguities of the internal conflict between different sides of Columbus' characters," John Hazlett wrote, are "subverted by the moral absolutes of literary nationalism's need for heroes."[52] And, we should add, by the moral absolutes of Irving's personal quest for achieved masculinity.

In the introduction to Book I, Irving cautiously hints that the "narrative of [Columbus'] *troubled life* is the link which connects the history of the old world with that of the new."[53] His contemporaries found this convincing enough. Asked by John Murray to read the manuscript, Robert Southey found it "remarkable" in its subject and gave it "unqualified" praise.[54] The published book also received unqualified praise. For Alexander Everett, writing in the *North American Review*, the biography was "the delight of readers [...] as nearly perfect in its kind, as any work can be." William Hickling Prescott, who in 1837 would publish his own Columbus biography, called it "the noblest monument."[55] Among the general public, who at the time readily embraced romantic valorization, much as they were receptive even to "Christian warfare," Irving's *Columbus* became spectacularly successful; it also became one of the most profitable books Irving ever wrote.[56]

With *Columbus* behind him, Irving for the first time in his career felt like a serious writer, one who could earn his living by his pen. However, work on the book had been purgatorial ("the hardest application and toil of the pen I have ever passed"),⁵⁷ and Irving more than once regretted that he had undertaken a task that required different talents from him as a serious historian. "Could I afford it," he confided to Henry Brevoort, "I should like to lay my writings aside when finished. There is an independent delight in study and in the creative exercise of the pen; we live in a world of dreams, but publication lets in the noisy rabble of the world and there is an end to our dreaming."⁵⁸ Given Irving's predilection for "a world of dreams," a world, that is, in which he could pursue his quest for his own masculinity, readers had to wait for a long time to see the published biography. This included Navarrete, who received the book as a gift from Irving in 1831 and praised it.⁵⁹ Publishers too had to learn to be patient. John Murray of London continued to press Irving to submit the manuscript. Irving agreed to set a date, February 27, 1827, for the first volume, even though a month earlier he had decided to completely revise the manuscript. Delays kept piling up. There were difficulties in researching, perhaps even some flaw in the book's perspective; possibly also, Irving found that there had been a weakness of style; on top of that, copywriters were hard to find and, once he had found one, work was dead slow.⁶⁰ It took until July 1827 that Murray received the manuscript for the first volume. The work appeared in four volumes in early 1828. An American edition was published by G. & C. Carvill in New York in three volumes, but from a different manuscript than for the English edition.

The English edition went through four different print runs; in addition, Murray published an abridged one-volume edition in 1829. And, shrewd publisher that he was, he also authorized Galignani and Baudry of Paris, as well as several other publishers to publish the book in France and Germany, to be used as a reader and textbook for students of English. None of these editions included Irving's revisions and corrections. The American reprint of 1831 did include some improvements, but Irving lacked the time and resources to read the proofs and would have to wait for Putnam's Author's Revised Edition of 1848 to find his revisions and corrections in print. Overall, new editions were published almost every year until 1850, then about every two or three years. Roughly told, there were about one hundred and seventy-five editions from 1828 until 1900, some of them expressly for the use as schoolbooks.⁶¹ And that is not counting the many translation—into Spanish, French, German, Dutch, Greek, Italian, Polish, Swedish, and Russian, all before Irving's death in 1859.

By the time *Columbus* was being prepared for Irving's Complete Works edition in 1980, it had seen almost 200 editions. "Few books in modern times," Andrew Burstein remarks, "have had such a reach, or such an impact."⁶² The work, especially Murray's one-volume abridgment, was the most popular biography of Columbus in the English language until the publication of Samuel Eliot Morison's *Admiral of the Ocean Sea* in 1942.[63] If Morison's biography won the Pulitzer Prize in 1943, Irving's effort also gained official recognition. In 1829 Irving was made a member of the Spanish Real Academia de la Historia, at the proposal of the eminent historian Martín Fernández de Navarrete. In 1830, the Royal Society of Literature in London awarded him a gold medal; Oxford University gave an honorary doctorate of civil law in 1831.[64] And, not to forget, *Columbus* left Irving financially in "a state of moderate hope as to the future."[65]

A History of the Life and Voyages of Christopher Columbus was eminently important to Irving in a personal way. Moreover, with the book Irving had come a long way from a satirist of the American present to a re-investor in national pride, offering a historical biography which actively narrates Columbus into an American cultural and historical teleology and its rhetoric of national identity.[66] As he wrote in the Preface, the subject of Columbus "was of so interesting and national a kind, that I could not willingly abandon it."[67] As a means to establish patriotism in his readers, Irving's Columbus was not so much a man of a remote past as a romantic hero and pioneer, one to help legitimate westward expansion, a harbinger of civilization, of modern times. A similar understanding can be found in two other major biographies and histories of Columbus published in the antebellum period, respectively by George Bancroft (1834), and by William Hickling Prescott (1837). The significance of Irving's *Columbus*, however, "lies not in its transformation of the ambiguous past into the moral absolutes of a national mythology [...] but in the complexities that developed out of the conflict between Irving's internalization of the national mythology and his obtrusive skepticism about America's past and his own role in society."[68]

If the version of the American past in *Columbus* was compromised by the genocidal and rapacious nature of European colonialism, we can see the same conflict and the ambivalence it engendered in *Astoria* (1836), Irving's history of the Northwest fur trade, in which John Jacob Astor appears as a kind of Columbian hero. The conflict also speaks from *A Tour on the Prairies* (1835), Irving's autobiographical travel narrative, in which he attempts to find his place within the national myth that the American wilderness would regenerate "effeminate" young Americans into heroic manly characters. In these writings, as in *Columbus*, the conflict between myth and reality is treated ambivalently rather than explicitly. Irving must have felt that there was something amiss in *Columbus*. As he later confided to Charles Lanman, when writing the book he had been "greatly perplexed to fix the boundary between the purely historical and the imaginative."[69] To unearth Columbus in Spanish archives was gratuitous, as Columbus already existed, in previous narratives by writers like Bartolomé de Las Casas and Andrés Bernáldez as well as in the imaginations of those who read them.[70] Irving's imagination only continued what had been done before and what he had read before. Reading the accounts of Columbus' voyages as a boy, Irving felt that they were "more delightful [...] than a fairy tale" and, moreover, became "indelibly stamped on [his] recollections."[71] Small wonder, then, that his Columbus was said to be the prototype of "the romantic hero of the nineteenth-century adventure-novel," with the biography itself resembling "a series of re-enactments of archetypal mythic dreams."[72]

With *Columbus*, Irving created "a history which finally manages to transform itself into fiction." For such an endeavor, the actual events are of minor importance, as are the details of Columbus' life. Irving dramatized and highlighted Columbus on his own terms—his imperfectly realized masculine ego—so that the romantic hero appears as an unmistakable expression of his own wished-for personality, a symbolic form of an *ideal* gender role. Irving, the historian Justin Winsor said towards the end of the nineteenth century, is "an amiable hero-worshipper." And on the occasion of the commemoration of the four-hundredth anniversary of Columbus's first voyage to America, the Spanish scholar Marcelino Menéndez Pelayo even wrote, "Today, unfortunately, books of this kind [meaning Irving's *Columbus*] are no longer being written, because the majority of those who are opposed to a dramatic and picturesque historiography are by their opposition making a tacit confession of their own inability to write in this way."[73]

Drama and picturesque description were anathema also to Irving's modern biographer, for whom *Columbus* is little more than a collection of "theatrical" characters, propped up by a variety of conventional stage devices. It is "a beautiful story, gracefully told," but the whole book, Stanley Williams says, is "an egregious legend [...] closer to literature than to history," with Columbus himself merely "the lineaments of a hero in the novels of Scott," an "idealization" that is hardly more real than Boabdil of Granada.[74] Irving's idealization of manhood, his habit of infusing into his characters emotions that more often than not were his own, may not resonate with modern critics. However, what Williams did not or did not want to see was that Irving's Columbus, as well as the later Mahomet, not to mention any number of minor characters, was yet another instance of Irving's self-analysis, a rehearsal of what he himself aspired to, achieved masculinity.[75]

Tellingly, in an early manuscript notebook, Irving had copied Friedrich Schiller's epigrammatic poem "Columbus" of 1795, in German: "Steure, muthiger Segler," which Walter Arndt rendered into English as "Sail on, captain courageous."[76] Irving's Columbus, too, displays the constants of hypermasculinity: he comes to us as "a man of great and inventive genius," full of "undaunted resolution" and with "glory" as "the great object of his ambition."[77] Given his "lofty and noble" ambition, Columbus was "anxious to distinguish himself by great achievements."[78] Nobility showed in his selflessness, as he wanted to vastly contribute to "the relief of the poor of his native city."[79] As befits a man who was "devoutly pious," whenever he made "any great discovery, he celebrated it by solemn thanks to God."[80] Of course, Columbus also envisioned new churches, "where masses should be said for the souls of the departed" and, not to forget, he envisioned "armies for the recovery of the holy sepulchre in Palestine."[81]

Columbus' conduct, Irving wrote, "was characterised by the grandeur of his views, and the magnanimity of his spirit." Thus, Columbus would travel through the newly discovered countries, not "like a grasping adventurer" but in order to "ascertain their soil and productions, their rivers and harbours." Like a true man of the Enlightenment, *avant la lettre* in this case, he "was desirous of colonising and cultivating [...] of conciliating and civilising the natives; of building cities, introducing the useful arts, subjecting every thing to the control of law, order, and religion; and thus of founding regular and prosperous empires."[82] Again like a man of the Enlightenment, with a pinch of Romanticism thrown into the bargain, Columbus also appears as a nature lover, proclaiming that "each new discovery is more beautiful than the last, and each the most beautiful in the world."[83] And if Columbus sought wealth, wealth was but "to arise from the territories he should discover." Thus, "he asked nothing of the Sovereigns but a command of the countries he hoped to give them, and a share of the profits to support the dignity of his command[....] What monarch would not rejoice to gain empire on such conditions."[84]

When Columbus arrives in Lisbon in 1477, he was an impressive physical specimen, "in the full vigour of manhood," an "engaging presence [...] tall, well formed, muscular, and of an elevated and dignified demeanour."[85] Whether this was true or not is impossible to know, though the characterization served Irving's purposes, for drama as much as for self-therapy. Columbus' "whole countenance had an air of authority," at the same time as he was "moderate and simple in diet and apparel, eloquent in discourse, engaging and affable with strangers, and of an amiableness and suavity in domestic life that strongly attached his household to his person."[86] Columbus formulates his theory and defends it with "dignity and loftiness," yet he has to wait for another eighteen years until his perseverance is crowned with success and he is ready to go on his first voyage, characterized by Irving as the "most momentous of all maritime enterprizes."[87] In the end, Columbus is allowed to return to the Spanish court in triumph, in what resembles "the progress of a sovereign."[88] A new coat of arms was then in order, and Columbus finds favor with the Spanish nobility.[89]

Columbus thus departs for his second voyage in "glory."[90] Soon, however, there is mutiny, horror, and genocide, and Columbus becomes a hero described by Irving as "consumed," "racked," "outraged in his dignity," "foiled in his plans," "endangered in his person," and "disordered."[91] Yet throughout all these travails, he "restrained his valiant and indignant spirit, and, by the strong powers of his mind," nobly bears all kinds of "despicable molestations […] griefs and vexations."[92] There is, however, no evidence in the ships' logs for the terror and attempted mutinies Irving describes. Nor were experienced sailors likely to be reduced to a hysterical, shivering, and sobbing mass at the sight of a meteor or the eruption of a volcano. Irving, the Spanish scholar Francisco Morales remarked, adds Gothic superstition and horror to the account in order to enhance the bravery of his hero, much as he merely indulges in fantasy when he has the crew conspire to throw their captain overboard.[93]

There is another aspect. Through exaggerating and inventing all kinds of horrors, Irving conveys the idea that those who aim high are bound to be disappointed and that for the righteous, afflictions are unending and inevitable. Indeed, his Columbus in many ways seems a tragic character, like Schiller's Wallenstein, whom Irving greatly admired. "The general truth" implicit in the book, William Hedges suggested, "that good men always suffer, seems to be our author's first law of history."[94] Indeed, not even with the help of his efficient and fearless brother Bartholomew is Columbus able to quell dissent and violence among the men, who would later blacken his name with the authorities in Spain.[95] As a result of this and other intrigues, we eventually see Columbus stripped of his command and in chains.[96] Despite the apparent note of gloom, however, Irving does not follow Las Casas, who summarizes Columbus' life as a prolonged martyrdom ("un luengo martirio").[97] Columbus may have become a bodily wreck, but he is still full of "spirit."[98] He has retained his "proud assurance," and, as "The Admiral," has been left with his "innate nobility" intact. Even on his deathbed, Irving remarks, did Columbus speak "with all the confidence of youthful hope."[99]

Columbus may have preserved his superiority in spirit, yet Irving, perhaps with a dose of self-irony, undermines his model masculinity by portraying the explorer as a "naturally irritable and impetuous" figure, who was prone to superstitions and delusions.[100] When a violent storm strikes at sea, for instance, the explorer instantly makes vows for a pilgrimage. Columbus certainly was deluded by not knowing what he had discovered, believing until the end that Cuba was the easternmost part of the Asian continent. He thus died "in ignorance of the real grandeur of his discovery," having miscued about the form of the earth, about certain legendary mines, and all in "a riot of the imagination."[101] "It is 'curious to observe,'"

Irving adds, "how ingeniously the imagination of Columbus deceived him at every step, and how he wove every thing into a uniform web of false conclusions" so that his voyages singularly were "a continual series of golden dreams, and all interpreted by the deluding volume of Marco Polo."[102]

Equally riotous were Columbus' "visionary meditations on mystic passages of the scriptures, and the shadowy portents of the prophecies."[103] And although at times he was quite capable of controlling his imagination by his "powerful judgment [and] acute sagacity," he was convinced that nations not acknowledging the Christian faith "were destitute of natural rights [and] that the sternest measures might be used for their conversion, and the severest punishments inflicted upon their obstinacy." Such convictions justified making captives of the Indigenous people, transporting them to Spain to have them converted to Christianity and, in the last instance, selling them into slavery. The oppression of the Indigenous population was soon exposed by Las Casas. Columbus, however, saw himself as "an instrument in the hands of providence." In endorsing and implementing such measures, he not only "sinned against the natural goodness of his character," but, Irving emphasizes, incurred an ineradicable "blot on his illustrious name."[104] It is not for nothing that Columbus at best was a kind of halfway point in the arc that eventually led Irving back to George Washington.

Another exemplar of the theme "how the mighty are fallen" is Boabdil el Chico, the last of the Moorish sovereigns of Granada, whose memory Crayon, Irving's author persona of *The Alhambra*, sets out to redeem. Boabdil, Crayon claims, has been "foully and unjustly slandered" in history books: "If ever [Boabdil] cherished the desire of leaving an honorable name on the historic page, how cruelly has he been defrauded of his hopes."[105] Boabdil had been reviled for the persecution of his wife, the murder of his sister and her two children, and the slaughter of the Abencerrages in the Alhambra's Court of Lions. Yet nowhere, Crayon writes, was there any authentication, neither in Spanish chronicles, nor in Arabic sources. And the main work on the chivalresque history of the civil wars in Granada, Ginés Pérez de Hita's *Historia de los bandos de zegríes y abencerrajes* (1595), is, in Crayon's words, "a mass of fiction, mingled with a few disfigured truths."[106] Clearly, Irving here sympathizes with Boabdil, much more so than in the more factual *Chronicle of the Conquest of Granada*, though he does not entirely gloss over the faults and limitations of his character. "He was personally brave, but wanted moral courage; and, in times of difficulty and perplexity, was wavering and irresolute." Regrettable as it may have been for Irving, there is no achieved masculinity here, for, "This feebleness of spirit hastened [Boabdil's] downfall, while it deprived him of that heroic grandeur which would have given grandeur and dignity to his fate, and rendered him worthy of closing the splendid drama of the Moslem domination in Spain."[107]

The story of Boabdil is another instance of Irving's readiness to identify with the defeated in history, and Irving makes sure his readers will find themselves in agreement with the story's conclusion that though Boabdil may have had some flaws, on the whole the historical "balance inclin[es] in his favor."[108] In his attempt to clear Boabdil's name Crayon creates a romance of his own making. Brushing aside Spanish historians,[109] together with all kinds of ballads, dramas, and romances—all of which had joined "to execrate the very name of Boabdil"[110]—, Crayon retraces Boabdil's exile from the Alhambra. Starting from the *Puerta de los Molinos* (the "Gate of the Mills"), he rides to the *Cuesta de las Lágrimas* (the "Hill of Tears") and, finally, to the summit of *el ultimo súspiro del Moro* ("the last Sigh of the Moor"). Through traveling in Boabdil's shoes, Crayon manipulates readers into empathizing with the last Nasrid king and viewing history from his, Crayon's, point of view. As Jeffrey Scraba notes, Crayon, by depicting Boabdil as an archetype of conquered and oppressed chivalry, "spatializes a process of sympathetic identification with Boabdil."[111]

In the winter of 1827, when *Columbus* was finished and in print, Irving had begun to take notes on the life of Muhammad, whom he always refers to as Mahomet. Inspiration possibly came from the Tripolitan Mustapha of *Salmagundi* (itself a vapid imitation of Goldsmith's Citizen of the World) and from his exposure, during his stay in Germany in the 1820s, to the rising Islamic and Koranic scholarship. Irving also read in the history of the Arabs and, during his stay in Spain, made tentative notes toward "The Legendary Life of Mahomet."[112] In 1831, he showed a preliminary version of *Mahomet* to Murray, who, seeing at once how specious Irving's pretensions to Oriental scholarship were (the manuscript was heavily documented), was not interested. Irving shelved the work, only to finish it off back in America almost twenty years later, from manuscripts in his traveling trunks. *The Legendary Life of Mahomet* was finally published as the first volume of *Mahomet and His Successors* by Putnam in 1849, a compact work that, like *Columbus*, weaves together facts and legends, the historical and the poetical. But more so than in *Columbus*, the part that Irving was most compassionate towards his subject is that of the prophet's being persecuted and outlawed in Mecca, leading up to the *hegira*, or flight from Mecca to Medina, which Mahomet entered, "more as a conqueror in triumph than as an exile seeking asylum."[113]

In the first volume of *Mahomet*, accounts of battles, comrades, as well as wives and concubines take a back seat, if they are not altogether suppressed. Irving here depersonalizes Mahomet's life, concentrating on the inspirational prophet and great man who has a mission to fulfill. In the concluding paragraph to Chapter I, for instance, he describes Mahomet as "the mighty genius" who should unite the "discordant tribes" and animate them "with his own enthusiastic and daring spirit, and lead them forth, a giant of the desert, to shake and overturn the empires of the earth."[114] In this climactic paragraph, Irving not only summarizes the meanings of Mahomet's life and career; he also recapitulates the attitude of his earlier *Columbus* and looks forward to the exemplary narrative of *Life of George Washington*, no longer that far off in the future. By depicting Mahomet in terms of representative manhood, moreover, Irving takes up Carlyle's generalization of Mahomet as the Great man and historical archetype, the "Hero-Prophet" sent down to the Arabs "with a word they could believe [...] as lightning out of heaven; the rest of the men waited for him like fuel, and then they too would flame."[115]

At the end of the first volume, Irving included a chapter titled "Person and Character of Mahomet; and Speculations on His Prophetic Career." In it, he compacts the prophet's exemplary manhood—unlike Columbus, Mahomet's destiny does not gain an added dimension of glory (or infamy) through the contrasted characters of enemies (or friends). Irving's Mahomet is *the* hero of Arabian history and culture, the personification of Arabia's latent energies and strengths, at the apex of her genius. Irving describes Mahomet's physical appearance as "square built and sinewy [...] uncommonly strong and vigorous [with] marked and expressive features, an aquiline nose, black eyes, arched eyebrows which nearly met, a mouth large and flexible, indicative of eloquence." His deportment, we learn, "was calm and equable [...] grave and dignified." As for his intellectual qualities, they were "of an extraordinary kind [...] a quick apprehension, a retentive memory, a vivid imagination, and an inventive genius." Beyond that, Mahomet was "sober and abstemious in his diet, and a rigorous observer of fasts. He indulged in no magnificence of apparel, the ostentation of a petty mind; neither was his simplicity affected; but the result of a real disregard to distinction from so trivial a source."[116]

Irving also emphasizes Mahomet's moderation (except for perfume and women), his justice, and his charity.[117] And while Irving does not believe in Mahomet as prophet, he in fine impartiality believes in Mahomet's belief that he was the prophet of God. "The truth is," Irving writes, "that the Koran as it now exists is not the same Koran delivered by Mahomet to his disciples, but has undergone many corruptions and interpolations [...] What he may have uttered as from his own will, may have been reported as if given as the will of God." Alternatively, Mahomet "may have considered his own impulses as divine intimations."[118] Likewise, it seems impossible to determine "what adequate object [Mahomet] had to gain by the impious and stupendous imposture with which he stands charged," be it wealth, distinction, power, or else, a genuine belief in "the reality of the dream or vision."[119] Yet there are cracks in the shining hero's façade. As Irving writes at the beginning of Chapter XVI, following Mahomet's arrival in Medina, the prophet "completely diverged from the celestial spirit of the Christian doctrines." Among the converts to his faith were numerous fugitives from Mecca, "proselytes from the tribes of the desert [...] men of resolute spirit, skilled in the use of arms, and fond of partisan warfare." Thus, "to his own surprise, [Mahomet] found an army at his command."[120]

The moment Mahomet "proclaimed the religion of the sword, and gave the predatory Arabs a taste of foreign plunder," Irving insists, "that moment he was launched in a career of conquest, which carried him forward with its own irresistible impetus."[121] Irving thus concludes that in the end Mahomet compromised his originally pure religious fervor with a perverted religion of the sword, himself morphing into a tyrant and sadist, the dysfunctional shadows respectively of the King and Warrior archetypes. To understand Islam as nothing but a religion of the sword surely is too simplistic, yet Irving proceeds to develop this interpretation in the *Successors* volume, also published by Putnam, in 1850. There the religion of the sword provides thematic coherence for the narrative of the twelve caliphs. The volume at first deploys an extended and continuous contrast between the stern and simple Arabs of the desert—models of achieved manhood as it were—and the luxurious and decadent Greeks, Persians, and other Eastern empires: "Even Abu Obeidah, in the humility of his spirit, contended himself with his primitive Arab tent of camel's hair; refusing the sumptuous tents of the Christian commanders, won in the recent battle. Such were the stern and simple-minded invaders of the effeminate and sensual nations of the East."[122]

Irving's celebration of true manliness does not last. Soon the Arabian conquerors lapse, in their turn, into the vices of the new subjects, much as Islam itself degenerates into factionalism, impiety, and effeminate luxury. The caliphate of Moawyah, the former Emir of Syria, we learn, "in the luxurious city of Damascus assumed more and more the state of the oriental sovereigns which it superseded. The frugal simplicity of the Arab and the stern virtues of the primitive disciples of Islam, were softening down and disappearing among the voluptuous delights of Syria."[123] Instead of "religious enthusiasm," there now was "the enervating luxury and soft voluptuousness of Syria and Persia sapping the rude but masculine simplicity of the Arabian desert." And so, "the single-mindedness of Mahomet and his two immediate successors is at an end."[124] Or was it really? Paradoxically, Irving does not explain the extraordinary triumphs of Moorish arms and art in that part of Europe he knew so well, the Spanish peninsula.[125]

Such deficiencies were not, however, in the way of the generally favorable reviews of *Mahomet and His Successors* and its popular success and esteem. "It is scarcely necessary to add," crooned the *United States Magazine and Democratic Review* in January 1850, "that the romantic story of the founders of the Moslem faith, is here told with a perspicuity and grace which has seldom been equalled." In a similar vein, the reviewer for the *Literary World* marveled at Irving's "genius" for making the book "interesting as a Fairy Tale." The *Successors* volume was received less rapturously, though *The Literary Gazette* found it "thoroughly redolent of the East" and considered that "For variety, adventure, and characteristic traits of a singular people, and the wonderful imposition of a strange religion upon the world, it is hardly possible to imagine a more stirring narrative. The essence of Romance pervades the solid structure of History."[126] Other reviewers were less generous. "We do not think [*Mahomet and His Successors*] contributes to throw any important new light upon the character either of Mahomet or his religion," griped *The Christian Observer* in June 1851. "Mr. Washington Irving is a pleasant writer, but not, we think, a very deep or acute thinker."[127]

Nonetheless, *Mahomet and His Successors* remained popular with the general public and was kept almost constantly in print throughout the nineteenth century. In fact, it was in press, in various formats and/or combinations of volumes, on the average of once or more every five years. It was also widely translated, into French, Polish, Russian, Spanish, Italian, Greek, Icelandic, and German, respectively as *Das Leben Mohammeds* and *Geschichte der Kalifen, vom Tode Mohammeds bis zum Einfall in Spanien.*[128] Modern criticism has been more discriminating. Especially the *Successors* volume came under fire when it became obvious that to a large extent it depends on a mere three sources, from which Irving did not bother even to paraphrase but simply copied them out. Irving's claim, in the preface, that he was "much indebted" to his sources, thus is a colossal understatement, to say the least.[129] For the most part, *Successors* is at once a chronological history of the separate caliphates and an account of the expansion of Islam from the death of Mahomet in 632 to the invasion of Spain in 710. The haste in which it was written cannot be overlooked, nor can Irving's "downright unfamiliarity with his sources."[130] Small wonder, then, that Stanley Williams altogether dismissed the two volumes as "nondescript compilations."[131]

But are there really no redeeming features about *Mahomet and His Successors*? After all, Mahomet was the founder of the Islamic faith, and Irving was especially fair-minded on the religions of the East and Mahomet's reformative fervor. Is it, moreover, too far-fetched to see parallels between Mahomet's foundation and that of the Mormon faith? Mary Bowden, for instance, makes a strong case that the first volume was actually written in defense of Joseph Smith and his followers.[132] If this seems somewhat improbable, what about Mahomet as the founder of a powerful nation, whose people—men especially—lived simply and frugally, and thus might form a valuable lesson to the U.S.? As does, and even more so, the continuation of the story in the *Successors* volume. There is an almost despairing tone in the second half of that volume, so that it seems safe to assume that the book was affected by Irving's personal state of mind, weighed down by the accelerating sectionalism. Irving, Mary Bowden maintains, "was writing this volume in the years when the South, fearful that the admission of California as a free state would upset the balance of power, was again suggesting secession, at a time when Calhoun was proposing a dual executive, each having veto power, at a time when civil war once more seemed imminent."[133]

The auras with which Irving surrounded his Spanish and Moorish heroes are all mythological. *Mahomet and His Successors* is, after all, another romantic history, described by Irving himself as a factual chronicle based, not on modern source material but on old historians and, as he wrote to Alexander Everett, "colored and tinted by the imagination so as to have a romantic air."[134] This was, of course, a necessary element in Irving's personal quest for masculine perfection, but it is not appreciated today, when Irving's exaggerations of heroic masculinities are seen with suspicion, though at the time they served the troubled nation. Irving in practically all of his Spanish writings created legends that bloomed in their own time and that hardened over the next decades or so, giving us, in *Columbus*, a saintly and heroic explorer betrayed by his underlings and, in other writings, valiant Moorish leaders, the one crushed and exiled, the other the founder of a powerful nation. Importantly also, by writing *Columbus*, *Mahomet*, and other books of its kind, Irving had not turned his back on his country, as many of his detractors accused him of after almost two decades spent abroad.

"As far as my precarious and imperfect abilities enable me," Irving wrote to Henry Brevoort in 1821, just two years after the publication of *The Sketch Book*, "I am endeavouring to serve my country—Whatever I have written has been with the feelings and published as the writing of an American—Is that renouncing my Country?"[135] At the same time, Irving rejected his friend's suggestion to return to America. "How else am I to serve my country? By coming home and begging an office of it; which I should not have the kind of talent or the business habits requisite to fill? *If I can do any good in this world it is with my pen.*"[136] To the extent that Irving's avowed intention with *Columbus* and, as well, with *Mahomet*, was thoroughly nationalist, he would continue to live by this maxim, not just with his *Life of George Washington*, but also with his Western writings. More to the point, *Columbus, Mahomet and His Successors*, and other Spanish writings, the

Western writings, even *Goldsmith*, are way stations on an arc of imagined masculinities that leads back to Washington. These writings were, Henry A. Pochmann and E.N. Feltskog have argued, albeit from a different angle, "a crucial preparation for the *Life of George Washington*, the introductory statement of Irving's major theme, the Great Man as molder and model of history as romantic art."[137]

Irving left Madrid on March 1, 1828, and stayed in Andalusia until the end of July 1829, when he left Spain to take up the post of secretary in the American embassy in London. He had been appointed to the post by Martin Van Buren, then Secretary of State in the cabinet of Andrew Jackson, of whose "*hickory* characteristics" Irving tried to convince himself.[138] Irving's friends and family were pleased with the appointment and, for the most part, Irving, always eager to please friends and family rather than take a stand, was too. "I accepted this appointment," he wrote to his brother Peter, "because it would gratify my friends, and would link me with my country."[139] Away from his immediate circle, however, his enthusiasm was lukewarm at best: "I only regret," he wrote from the Alhambra, "that I had not been left entirely alone, and to dream away life in my own way."[140] For Irving, Jenifer S. Banks noted, the Alhambra was "a paradise with virtually no women, certainly none making any demands on him."[141] Dreaming away his life in his own way therefore would have meant, firstly, to indulge in his anima-ego and, secondly, to dream up images of achieved manhood.

As for the latter, traveling from Seville to Granada, Irving (or, rather, Crayon, the original "author" of *The Alhambra*) meets a perfect model of an "Andalusian Majo," a "tall, vigorous, and well-formed [young man], with a clear olive complexion, a dark beaming eye, and curling chestnut whiskers that met under his chin. He was gallantly dressed in a short green velvet jacket, fitted to his shape, profusely decorated with silver buttons, with a white handkerchief in each pocket."[142] By the same token, the "frank, manly, and courteous" muleteer stands in as the embodiment of the Andalusian countryside. Irving may have felt a bit uneasy about such descriptions, and so he slyly hints that Crayon, indulging in romantic reverie over the past, merely reproduces the typical stereotypes of "the proud, frugal and abstemious Spaniard, his manly defiance of hardships, and contempt of effeminate indulgences," along with the "sublimity" of the "sternly simple features of the Spanish landscape."[143]

It is a moot point to speculate what Irving would have looked like in the garb of a "proud, frugal and abstemious Spaniard." Yet excepting an oil painting and a drawing David Wilkie made in Seville in 1828, when Irving was forty-five years old, no pictorial record of Irving's understanding of Spanish masculinity exists. The painting, now titled "Washington Irving in the Archives of Seville," shows Irving "seated in a dusky chamber at a

Four. *"Dear old romantic Spain"* 125

table looking over a folio volume which a monk who was standing by my side had just handed down to me. Wilkie thought the whole had a Rembrandt effect." The drawing, in contrast, focuses on Irving's face, "indolent, yet intellectual," looking out "on these carefree days in old Seville."[144] While the painting, thanks to its localization, does convey an atmosphere of Spanishness and so has a certain romantic glow, it is not nearly as glaringly and heroically romantic as Thomas Phillips' 1813 portrait of Byron, which shows the poet wearing the Albanian costume which he had bought four years earlier.[145]

Byron too visited Spain, in August 1809, on his way to the eastern Mediterranean. In *Childe Harold's Pilgrimage*, begun during the tour but not published until 1812, Byron briefly refers to a Spanish myth from the origins of the *reconquista* and the subsequent expulsion of the Moors. Significantly, the stanza that deals with Spain begins with a kind of invocation, of "Lovely Spain, renown'd, romantic land!"[146] After that, Byron becomes harshly ironical when he develops his references to the Spain he saw. Irving, whose approach likewise can be ironic, asking readers to question received notions of Spain, never met Lord Byron, but he admired his works, reviewed them in 1814, and reportedly read Byron's memoirs before they were destroyed after the poet's death.[147] Irving also was pleased to learn that Byron liked his writings and had pronounced to John Murray that Crayon was "very good."[148] In 1831, Irving visited Byron's former home, Newstead Abbey, where he made voluminous notes, which he included in the essay he later published in *Crayon Miscellany*. At work on the essay, Irving had before him Byron's poetry and Thomas Moore's *Life of Byron*. Irving omitted all dates, though, focusing on his emotional response to Byron.[149]

In the absence of a pictorial record of Irving in Spanish garb, we may speculate that perhaps he found the part of himself he had been seeking in the Spaniard he chanced upon while traveling from Seville to Granada in the spring of 1829. Offering wine and bread to what he thought was "a solitary beggar," Irving, in the guise of Crayon, is quite astonished at the grateful man's response: "'It is many years [...] since I have tasted such wine. It is a cordial to an old man's heart.' Then, looking at the beautiful wheaten loaf, '*bendito sea tal pan!*' '*blessed be such bread!*'" Crayon, when he realizes that, on account of the man's "manly demeanor," he had mistakenly identified an unemployed and destitute shepherd as "some broken-down cavalier," professes to be deeply impressed with "the innate courtesy of a Spaniard, and the poetical turn of thought and language often to be found in the lowest classes of this clear-witted people."[150] Altogether, *The Alhambra* is replete with fond memories, of true gentlemen (and, as well gentlewomen), and of likable folks represented as Rouseauvian *hommes naturels*. Such as, for instance, the thirty-five-year-old Mateo Ximenes (or Jiménez), whom Irving met at the Alhambra and who inspired him to write *Tales from the Alhambra*, as it came to be called.

Irving had caught his first glimpse of Granada on March 9, 1828. "It is a most picturesque and beautiful city, situated in one of the loveliest landscapes that I have ever seen," he gushed. The city then was in a much-depleted state, its population down to about five percent from what it was in the fifteenth century, when it was the capital of the Moorish kingdom. Nevertheless, for Irving it still was "*bellissima* Granada!"[151] It was with some regret that he left Granada to continue his tour of Andalusia, settling in Seville in mid–April. Irving needed access to the Archives of the Indies for his corrections to *Columbus*. He also wanted to write a continuation. Traveling from Seville to Palos and La Rábida, he collected material and, important for him at the time, visited the scenes where the famed events had taken place. Although he made notes and even sent an article to the London *Quarterly Review* in September, *Voyages and Discoveries of the Companions of Columbus* did not appear in print until 1831.[152] Irving's mind was with a book on Granada. By early May 1828, he was constantly at work on it, finishing the first part of *A Chronicle of the Conquest of Granada* in late August. In May 1829, he was back in Granada, crooning over it, in a letter to Henry Brevoort, as

> one of the most remarkable, romantic, and delicious spots in the world. […] when I am not occupied with my pen, I lounge with my book about these oriental apartments, or stroll about the courts, and gardens, and arcades, by day or night, *with no one to interrupt me*. It absolutely appears to me like a dream; or as if I am spell bound in some fairy palace.[153]

This is an understatement, as Irving's "imagination" always "continued busy" while he was staying in Granada, which ten years later he fervently describes as "Lovely Granada! City of delights!"[154] In *The Alhambra*, Irving and Geoffrey Crayon, his alter ego and product of his anima consciousness, merge into what might be called the archetypal romantic tourist, who makes his journey meaningful through memory, imagination, stories and legends listened to, as well as the books he has read. Tellingly, the guide from Seville to Granada is made to play "the renowned Sancho" to his own Don Quixote. The guide, "el pobre Sancho," accepts his role with gusto; in his company the whole country becomes "dear old romantic Spain," and even humble inns are magically transformed into enchanted castles.[155] Reading reality through Cervantes' great novel, Crayon remembers a rough wedding serenade, writing, "I was aroused by a horrid din and uproar, that might have confounded the hero of La Mancha himself whose experience of Spanish inns was a continual uproar. It seemed for a moment as if the Moors were once more breaking into the town."[156] Indeed, whenever

Crayon describes people and places, his mind is carried back "to the chivalric days of Christian and Moslem warfare, and to the romantic struggle of the conquest of Granada."[157]

"There is a romance about all the recollections of the Peninsula dear to the imagination," Irving has Crayon, old-fashioned gentleman of letters and new romantic artist in search of the charms of storied and poetical association, exclaim at one point.[158] The farewell to the city that "has ever been the subject of my waking dreams,"[159] is, then, a most sorrowful parting. Appropriately, Irving allows Crayon a final glimpse of Boabdil's hill of tears, "*La cuesta de las lagrimas* ... noted for the 'last sigh of the Moor.'" After that, it's all over, in a scene suggestive of the expulsion from Eden: "A little further and Granada, the Vega, and the Alhambra, were shut from my view; and thus ended one of the pleasantest dreams of a life, which the reader perhaps may think has been too much made up of dreams."[160] Irving's personal farewell was much more down-to-earth, and though he does employ a metaphor (and a skewed one, for that matter, as Irving went overland through southern France), there is no suggestion of a lost Eden: "When I took my last look at the Alhambra from the mountain road of Granada," he wrote to Brevoort from Valencia, "I felt like a sailor who had just left a tranquil port to launch upon a stormy sea."[161] Given this difference in affect, whatever memories, including memories of model masculinities, there are in *The Alhambra*, they result from Crayon's animatic reading of and hearing about Andalusia, much as Don Quixote had read Castile-La Mancha through chivalric romances. Put in more general terms, any experience of unknown places is always necessarily mediated through the stories about them we have read, or have been told, as Crayon absorbs and transmits local legends and anecdotes told by the inhabitants of the Alhambra.

In *A Chronicle of the Conquest of Granada*, published just a month before the events described by Crayon in "The Journey,"[162] the stories, legends, and anecdotes from "the chivalric contests between Moor and Christian," the Reconquista, mostly are those of the zealously pious and xenophobic monk Fray Antonio Agapida, Irving's fictitious author-persona. Irving's own appearance was that of an unnamed editor-narrator who claims that he has pieced together "disjointed fragments" of Agapida's manuscripts, which have been discovered in convents and monasteries throughout Spain.[163] Irving knew what he was doing, writing to Thomas Aspinwall that the *Chronicle* was to be "something of an experiment [...] between a history and a romance."[164] Irving had added Agapida's manuscripts in order to embellish the dry records he had found in Spanish archives and communicating an appropriate point of view, thus throwing "over the whole a colouring that may give it some thing of the effect of a work of the imagination."[165] The intention to use the Agapida pseudonym as author, which established a balance between "truth" and "colouring," was however, thwarted by Irving's London publisher, John Murray, who instead used Irving's full name as author. Irving was piqued, because he was afraid readers might mistake the opinions expressed, which are those of a "Detached Manipulator," the Magician archetype's dysfunctional shadow, as his own. He later explained that the friar was "manifestly a mere fiction—a stalking horse, from behind which the author launches his satire at the errors, the inconsistencies, and the self-delusions of the singularly medly [sic] warriors, saints, politicians, and adventurers engaged in that holy war."[166] Nevertheless, he abandoned the Agapida ruse with Putnam's "Author's Revised Edition" of his works.

Conquest of Granada tells the story of the downfall of the Nasrid kingdom at the hands of Ferdinand and Isabella, the Catholic kings, *los reyes católicos*. Relying on a number of sixteenth- and seventeenth-century histories, chiefly de Hita's *Historia de los bandos de zegríes y abencerrajes* of 1595, Irving depicts "a stern, iron conflict, more marked by bigotry than courtesy."[167] There is "blind violence and rage"[168] galore, and whatever chivalry there may have been, it is drowned out by Agapida's blatantly Catholic perspective. For the worthy friar, the decade-long war was "a holy crusade ... undertaken for the advancement of the faith, and the glory of the church."[169] From this perspective, the perspective of the victors, who understood the Reconquista as a manifestation of God punishing the infidels, Moorish resistance is but a "heathenish and diabolical obstinacy to the holy inroads of the cross and the sword."[170]

Irving was not one to celebrate the victors uncritically. To provide a corrective to Agapida's fanatical biases, Irving added the voice of the French ambassador, who professes to have been "filled with wonder at the prowess, the dexterity and daring of the Moslems."[171] The alternatives were truly bleak. As the veteran warrior Muza Ben Abil Gazan pronounces just before the surrender of Granada, in store were "the plundering and ransacking of our city; the profanation of our mosques, the ruin of our homes, the violation of our wives and daughters—cruel oppression, bigoted intolerance, whips and chains; the dungeon, the faggot and the stake...."[172] The valiant Muza is prepared to fight to the last; if he had been king, Irving might have told a story of masculine perfection. With the wavering and irresolute Boabdil, however, we get a story of failed manhood embodied in the passive "Weakling" archetype, the "King's" dysfunctional shadow. "It is a feeble mind," Boabdil's mother exclaims scornfully, "that waits for the turn of fortune's wheel; the brave mind seizes upon it and turns it to its purpose."[173] Reviled by a veteran warrior as "an apostate, a traytor, a deserter from his throne, a fugitive among the enemies of his nation," Boabdil is further upbraided by his mother, Ayxa la Horra, after surrendering Granada without a fight: "'You do well,' said she, 'to weep like a woman, for what you failed to defend like a man!'"[174] It was not until the appearance of *The Alhambra*, in 1832, that we get a more sympathetic account of the last Nasrid King, when Crayon retraces Boabdil's exile from the palace to the viewpoint known by the name of *el ultimo súspiro del Moro* ("the last Sigh of the Moor").

Though Stanley Williams dismisses Fray Antonio Agapida as "Diedrich Knickerbocker in a Spanish cowl,"[175] there is, once again, a deeper meaning, namely that all narratives about the past are biased, partial and incomplete, their "substance" consisting of layers of romance. Irving wanted his readers to realize that all the sources are unreliable, as the histories too read the conquest of Granada as a sort of romantic pageant that includes ancient fortresses, awe-inspiring mountain sceneries, dark scenes of revenge, and, not to forget, the fate of the "unlucky" Boabdil.[176] For Irving, then, history is textual, whether the sources are fictional or authentic. Thus, the Crayon of *The Alhambra* sees the places just made historically and romantically resonant by *A Chronicle of the Conquest of Granada* and, to an extent, by *Columbus*, which had opened the doors to the Alhambra for the book's creator in the first place. Once there, Crayon takes into his heart Mateo Ximenes (or Jiménez), who introduced himself as "a son of the Alhambra." Ximenes, though still young, serves as guide, thus impersonating the "Magician" archetype and for that very reason representative of the Spaniards' native nobility.[177]

Mateo Ximenes is the provider of valuable local knowledge and marvelous stories "not to be found in books."[178] To the youth's oral treasures, Crayon adds legends of his own, borrowed from the pages of de Hita's history or from having "trod in fancy the romantic halls of the Alhambra."[179] Once again, there is a considerable irony, which forces readers to question received notions of Spain. For, whatever local knowledge and marvelous stories Ximenes provides, and whatever Crayon has gleaned from de Hita and other Spanish texts or fantasized during his residence, already they have been "diligently wrought into shape and form."[180] They are, therefore, but illusions of past glories and legendary associations behind which lurked the naked reality of the present crumbling Alhambra. But that is just the "power" of "this old dreamy place," Crayon remarks in the opening pages of "The Court of Lions," "clothing naked realities with the illusions of the memory and the imagination."[181] These illusions acquired a life of their own thanks to the distance Irving's anima consciousness had put between the actual stay and the place of final composition, London. The tension is most palpable in a passage from "Spanish Romance," which ruefully laments "the present day [...] when the universal pursuit of gain is trampling down the early growth of poetic feeling, and wearing out the verdure of the soul."[182]

The historical revisionism and, to an extent, self-therapy Irving undertakes in *The Alhambra* only added to his celebrity status. It already had got him access to the Alhambra, and permission to live in the former palace, in the governor's own apartments. What he wrote reflects real intimacy with the charming scenes described in *The Alhambra*. "I never had such a delicious abode," he confided to his friend, Prince Dolgorouki in 1829.[183] For Irving, the Alhambra proved an imaginative paradise. As he ecstatically wrote, "It is a singular good fortune to be thrown into this most romantic and historical place, which has such a sway over the imaginations of readers in all parts of the world."[184] Listening to Ximenes' chatter and scrambling about the palace, Irving filled his notebooks with descriptions and observations. Though he was determined to write a book about it, he still felt that his writing could not do the palace justice. "How unworthy is my scribbling of the place," he communicated to Antoinette Bolviller.[185] But not only did the Alhambra, or Spain in general, impact on Irving. His writings on Spain also impacted on Spanish critics and readers, and they are enduringly popular.[186] In and around Granada, tourist-oriented bookstores prominently feature *The Alhambra* translated into just so many languages, much as *A Chronicle of the Conquest of Granada* is marketed to the unwary visitor as an authoritative history. In addition, the former Governor's quarters have been renamed the "Washington Irving Apartments" and are now (or were until the Covid-19 pandemic struck) open to visitors. *The Alhambra* not only became wildly successful in inspiring—particularly American—tourists to visit the castle; the book, which according to a Spanish literary historian captured the "soul of Granada" more than any other writing, also contributed to the Spanish government's decision to restore the monument.[187]

If Irving's image has been permanently established in the fortress, *El legado Andalusí* (The Legacy of Andalusia), an organization dedicated to promoting knowledge of Andalusia's Moorish past, is offering a tour that retraces Irving's 1829 journey from Seville to Granada, described in the opening pages of *The Alhambra*.[188] Eventually, "*bellissima* Granada" paid back to its adopted son in kind. On the occasion of the sesquicentennial of Irving's death in 2009, Granada's Alhambra Foundation staged an elaborate exhibition, accompanied by a lavish catalog offering scholarly essays and any number of illustrations.[189] The exhibition opened in October. In the final days of December, a bronze statue of Washington Irving was revealed. The statue, by the Spanish sculptor Julio López Hernández,[190] recreates the "romantic traveler" in realistic style, complete with notebook (in his left hand) and his pen (in his right hand). Behind him is his traveler's bag, seemingly being kicked by his left leg; his right leg leans against a symbolic pedestal with an inverted Nasrid capital, as if to draw creative energy from it.[191] Ironically, however, Irving did not even write *The Alhambra* while he stayed in the palace. He fused personal reminiscences with the legends he compiled later, finishing the original 1832 edition while he was living in London. Irving habitually made older works spring up under new forms. "What was formerly a ponderous history," he had written in the *Sketch Book*, "revives in the shape of a romance—an old legend changes into a modern play—and a sober philosophical treatise furnishes the body for a whole series of bouncing and sparkling essays."[192]

In the magic space of the Alhambra, Irving found inspiration enough, once again bringing to the fore his anima-ego. Perhaps for that very reason Irving, who was always afraid lest he appear as too "effeminate," decided, in *The Alhambra*, to hide behind the antics of his easygoing man of feeling, Geoffrey Crayon and, in *A Chronicle of the Conquest of Granada*, to employ as author-persona a fanatical Catholic, the sixteenth-century monk Fray Antonio Agapida. Through the duality of writer/persona Irving distances himself from romantic sentimentalizations, contradicting both the charge of naive nostalgia and his own animatic enthusiasms. But as much as both works are chockfull of examples of achieved manhood, there was a caveat already in *Columbus*. In "Observations on the Character of Columbus," which Irving added to the main text, we learn that his purpose had been not to paint "a great man merely in great and heroic traits." Rather, Irving had wanted to mix great and heroic traits with Columbus' "little qualities" in order to achieve "a faithful portrait."[193]

The same can be said about *The Alhambra*. Irving's intention, we learn from the preface to the revised edition of 1851, had been to "revive the traces of grace and beauty fast fading away from its walls; to record the regal and chivalrous traditions concerning those who once trod its courts; and the whimsical and superstitious legends of the motley race now burrowing among its ruins."[194] The phrase "the motley race now burrowing among its ruins" is telling. It is one thing to glorify and sentimentalize common folk, but it is quite a different matter to let them have the vote, acknowledging the democratic right of all to participate in political decision-making processes. So much to Irving's political convictions. One may take issue with these, as long as one acknowledges that *The Alhambra* is a triumph of the imagination, a literary space where reality and romance become indistinguishable.[195] Even Stanley Williams, Irving's severest critic, concedes that *The Alhambra* in some respects excels all other writings of Irving, especially in its "brilliance of coloring and warmth of tone."[196] Spanish literature, Williams later wrote, for Irving provided "an enchanted garden for the antiquarian lover of legends, for the dreamer destined to find it more beautiful than his dreams—and for a writer in search of fresh material. [...] Here might be unearthed something for an American public a little tired of Geoffrey Crayon."[197]

A little tired of Geoffrey Crayon the American public may have been, yet *The Alhambra* of 1832 was still authored by "Geoffrey Crayon," hence rightfully referred to as Irving's "Spanish *Sketch Book*."[198] None of the other Spanish works is as nearly as elaborate, though like his romantic histories, Irving wrote it in obedience to the maxim, from his Spanish friend, Fernán Caballero, "*poetizar la realidad sin alterarla.*"[199] "Poetizar" for Irving meant framing the prison house of middle-class manhood with what at first sight looks like a clear allegiance to patrician values. Take Crayon, who in *The Alhambra* is positioned both as a tourist of the sites he visits and describes, and as an antiquarian of the stories and legends he relates. While he takes possession of them, Irving's ironic self-consciousness as author lets us see that Crayon's indulgence in romantic reverie is but an enabling fiction.[200] Nowhere is this more obvious than in Crayon's marveling about the Alhambra being "as much an object of devotion [to the romantic traveler] as is the Caaba to all true Moslems," at the same time as Irving discloses that at the time of his visit the castle was grossly neglected and that he (and, for a time) his friend Prince Dmitri Dolgorouki were the only foreign visitors during the entire four-month stay.[201]

However self-reflexively the Alhambra is produced as a romantic site, however much Crayon himself produces the authentic experiences and picturesque scenes he is in search of, for Irving places are constituted by the stories told about them—and so are people. In each instance, historical, literary, and legendary associations accrue. Even the lack of infrastructure and the constant presence of *ladrones*, *bandoleros*, and *contrabandistas* that made traveling difficult in the early nineteenth century, are constituted by stories, songs and ballads, and so are not a real threat but rather have "a most picturesque effect."[202] A little further on his journey, Crayon encounters a scene that "was a study for the painter: the picturesque group of dancers, the troopers in their half military dress, the peasantry wrapped in their brown cloaks [and, not to forget] the old meagre Alguazil, in a short black cloak, who [...] might have figured in the days of Don Quixote."[203] The picturesque, derived as it is from landscape painting, is a function of an ideal form of nature, and the discovery of ideal scenes in existence had been Irving's forte from early on. Traveling in Europe in 1805, Irving admitted to his journal, "I look chiefly with an eye to the picturesque."[204]

Looking "with an eye to the picturesque" is not without its pitfalls. For one thing, it cements Irving's self-image of an observer. There is a most telling scene in *The Alhambra*, in which we find Irving/Crayon seated on a balcony, looking down into the city of Granada.

> [A]s the astronomer has his grand telescope with which to sweep the skies ... so I had a smaller one, of pocket size, for the use of my observatory, with which I could sweep the regions below, and bring the countenances of the motley

groups so close as almost, at time, to make me think I could divine their conversation by the play and expression of their features. I was thus, in a manner, an invisible observer, and, without quitting my solitude, could throw myself in an instant into the midst of society,—a rare advantage to one of somewhat shy and quiet habits, and fond, like myself, of observing the drama of life without becoming an actor in the scene.[205]

Irving from early on had adopted the role of a considerate, timid, and polite observer, not a participant, a "mere spectator of other men's fortunes and adventures," as he wrote in *The Sketch Book*. In Granada, too, he stuck to the role of a genteel observer, a self-conscious, quasi-aristocratic gentleman who is keenly conscious of his superiority, a role he would also bring to bear on the people he met on the prairies of his native America.[206]

Leaving aside personal features like shyness and timidity, the picturesque, Ann Bermingham has shown, is profoundly ideological. While it compensates for all kinds of present evils, real or imagined, it inscribes the very loss it seeks to recover.[207] Irving in his Spanish writings grafted the picturesque onto the Romantic enthusiasm for primitivism. Under this banner, *The Alhambra* preserves memories of past glory in tales of old Moorish Spain. Through them, Irving reinvents an ideal masculinity glorified in the Spanish past. In *Columbus*, Irving had bemoaned "the bigotry of the age."[208] He had been especially harsh on the crusaders' conviction that, being Christians, all was fair in their conquests, though Columbus was allowed to shine as a "good Catholic" within an otherwise inacceptable Catholicism. There is a similar double standard in "The Legend of Don Munio Sancho de Hinojosa," which Irving collected for *The Alhambra*. In "The Legend," the charms of storied and poetical association lead Irving or, rather, Crayon, back to the days of the wars between Catholics and Arabs. Don Munio comes to us as "a noble Castilian cavalier," the "lord of a border castle," and a "hardy and adventurous knight," who is constantly engaged in some kind of border warfare.[209] One day, Don Munio surprises a Moorish cavalcade headed by "a youthful cavalier, superior to the rest in dignity and loftiness of demeanor, and in splendor of attire," and accompanied by his beautiful bride. When the gallant captive informs his captor that they are on their way to getting married, the noble Don Munio makes them his guests, stages their nuptials at his own castle, makes them magnificent presents, and finally escorts them into safety. "Such," Irving wrote, "in old times, were the courtesy and generosity of a Spanish cavalier." Several years later, this very same Moorish cavalier unknowingly kills Don Munio in battle. When he recognizes whom he has slain, "he smote his breast. 'Woe is me! [...] I have slain my benefactor! the flower of knightly virtue! the most magnanimous of cavaliers!'" The noble cavalier in his grief escorts the bier to Don Munio's castle, throws himself at the feet of the freshly widowed Doña Maria, and, at his expense, has a sepulcher erected in a convent to Don Munio's memory. As if this were not enough, unbeknownst to the mourners, on the day the Castilian cavalier was killed a train of Christian knights reportedly approached Jerusalem, led by no other than Don Munio, who had "come to fulfill their vow of a pilgrimage to the Holy Sepulchre." "Such," we read in conclusion, "was the Castilian faith in the olden time, which kept its word even beyond the grave."

In "The Legend of Don Munio" as well as elsewhere in *The Alhambra*, dissatisfaction with "modern" civilization and culture, embodied by Crayon, finds compensation in a more "primitive" culture of tradition, legend, and simple but noble values. At the very outset of *The Alhambra*, therefore, Irving contradicts the common image of Andalucía as "a soft southern region, decked out with the luxuriant charms of voluptuous Italy." Rather, southern Spain is "a stern, melancholy country, with rugged mountains, and long sweeping plains, destitute of trees, and indescribably silent and lonesome, partaking of the savage and solitary character of Africa." The entire landscape "impresses on the soul a feeling of sublimity [...] immense plains [possessing a] solemn grandeur [...] these boundless wastes [on which the eye catches] a single horseman, armed with blunderbuss and stiletto [all having] something of the Arabian character."[210]

In *The Alhambra*, Irving wrote the persona of Geoffrey Crayon into the scenes he describes, there partly in an effort to create an ironic distance. Yet much as he wanted his readers to question received understandings of Spain, Irving himself romanticized the land and people of Southern Spain, even after his return to the United States. In June 1839, "Recollections of the Alhambra" appeared in *Knickerbocker Magazine*. "In the silent and deserted halls of the Alhambra; surrounded with the insignia of regal sway, and the still vivid, though dilapidated traces of oriental voluptuousness," Irving recalls,

> I was in the strong-hold of Moorish story, and every thing spoke and breathed of the glorious days of Granada, when under the dominion of the crescent. When I sat in the hall of the Abencerrages, I suffered my mind to conjure up all that I had read of that illustrious line. In the proudest days of Moslem domination, the Abencerrages were the soul of every thing noble and chivalrous.[211]

This is as good an example of Irving's "Spanish orientalism"[212] as any. Yet there is more, in terms of a harsh cultural critique. Already the Geoffrey Crayon of the *Sketch Book* was a "romantic" traveler, a "gentleman," who as an amateur belongs to a different world from that of entrepreneurial capitalism and rugged individualism; equally from a different world are the Crayon from *The Alhambra* and, especially, the Irving from "Recollections of the Alhambra." As Irving writes in the prologue to "Recollections,"

Four. "Dear old romantic Spain" 135

> For my part, I gave myself up, during my sojourn in the Alhambra, to all the romantic and fabulous traditions connected with the pile. I lived in the midst of an Arabian tale, and shut my eyes, as much as possible, to every thing that called me back to every-day life; and if there is any country in Europe where one can do so, it is in *poor, wild, legendary, proud-spirited, romantic Spain; where the old magnificent barbaric spirit still contends against the utilitarianism of modern civilization.*[213]

Irving deleted this passage in 1855, when he revised the proof sheets for the *Knickerbocker*. As the editors for *Wolfert's Roost* in the Complete Works have shown, "the differences between the periodical and the 1855 version are numerous."[214] The text of Irving's "Recollections of the Alhambra" in *Complete Works* is from the 1855 edition of *Wolfert's Roost* by Putnam, the First American edition, marked as 1A. There, the passage reads as follows:

> It was a dreamy sojourn, during which I lived, as it were, in midst of an Arabian tale, and shut my eyes as much as possible to every thing that should call me back to every-day life. If there is any country in Europe where one can do so, it is among these magnificent ruins of poor, wild, legendary, romantic Spain. In the silent and deserted halls of the Alhambra, surrounded with the insignia of regal sway, and the vivid, though dilapidated traces of Oriental luxury, I was in the stronghold of Moorish story, where everything spoke of the palmy days of Granada when under the dominion of the crescent.[215]

There has been a noticeable toning-down. In the original version, the juxtaposition of the "old magnificent barbaric spirit" against the "utilitarianism of modern civilization" was the expression of writerly rage. Irving turns upside down the traditional valuation imposed on the opposition of "civilization" versus "barbarism." Within that valuation, a characteristic of colonial discourse since the age of discovery, the god-term clearly had been "civilization"; for the Irving of the "Recollections" of 1839, it is "magnificent barbarism." (Elsewhere, as in Irving's writings on England, or in writings which deal with the old Dutch, the old colonial spirit, or the "Creole Village," Irving invests in the much weaker opposition "modern" versus "traditional," which also includes Indigenous people, from Philip of Pokanoket to the Osages of *Tour of the Prairies*.) In 1839, Irving may well have gotten a bit tired of Crayon's anima-identity, remembering what he had resolved to acquire some twenty years earlier—"manliness and independence of character."[216] By 1855, Irving seems to have mellowed and softened considerably. He was older then and his nostalgia for Spain had lessened in proportion to his becoming, in Stanley Williams's words, "a citizen of the republic."[217] If America's ideals became Irving's own, he would place his talents at the service of the nation's aspirations for a genuinely national literature. He had already done just that in his revision of *A History of New York*. With the first volumes of *Life of George Washington* published by 1855, what would be more inappropriate than pitting an "old magnificent barbaric spirit" against "the utilitarianism of modern civilization," which had reached its most advanced expression in the United States?

By 1855, Crayon was once again a safe bet for reminiscing about Spain to a genteel audience. It no longer mattered that Crayon, in his "unsettled condition as bachelor, traveler, and antiquarian" could be seen as "a trope for failed and ineffectual masculinity," thus constituting a nagging reminder of Irving's own precarious gender identity, his imperfectly realized masculinity.[218] Crayon had stood in as the "author" for the first editions of *The Alhambra* in 1832, though hints to him were abandoned for the "Author's Revised Edition" in 1851, as well as in all subsequent editions. Spain itself did not go away, though. Irving had written a great deal while in Spain. Digging into his trunks after his return to the United States, he would find a manuscript he had left unfinished since 1829 when he left Granada. Others had been left sketchy, but it took little effort to prepare them for publication.

While at work on *Columbus*, researching in various libraries and reading from a number of Spanish writers, Irving had made copious notes for *The Conquest of Granada*, which came out in 1829, as well as for other Moorish chronicles.[219] His greatest effort by far went into "The Legend of Don Roderick," which he had left unfinished in 1829, publishing it in *The Crayon Miscellany* in 1835, as part of the "Spanish legends."[220] Given the vast material Irving had accumulated in Spain, it is quite possible that he had in mind other volumes that might have appeared later, except that *Astoria* and *Bonneville* took up too much of his time then.[221] Some of the Spanish chronicles—characterized by Irving himself as "lightminded and chivalrous and quaint and picturesque and adventurous, and at times comic"[222]—finally appeared in the *Spanish Papers*, which his nephew published posthumously in 1866.

Legends of the Conquest of Spain was completed in June 1835. The published work was immediately successful.[223] Irving had hit the right tone for his readers, stating, in his Preface, that "Spain is virtually a land of poetry and romance, where every-day life partakes of adventure [...] enterprize and daring exploit."[224] There is plenty of adventure, enterprise, and daring exploit—hence hypermasculinity—in "The Legend of Don Roderick." Enter, then, Don Roderick, the gothic king resident in Toledo, whose "soul was bold and daring and elevated by lofty desires. He had a sagacity that penetrated the thoughts of men and a magnificent spirit that won all hearts."[225] When Don Roderick goes to battle, "arrayed in robes of gold brocade [...] a sceptre in his hand [and wearing] a regal crown, resplendent with inestimable jewels," it is "as if the sun were emerging in the dazzling

Four. "Dear old romantic Spain" 137

chariot of the day from amidst the glorious clouds of morning." Yet Don Roderick is not exempt from hubris. He has opened, against the advice of his counselors, the portal to a haunted tower. There he finds a mysterious casket which, upon being opened, predicts the conquest of his kingdom by foreign invaders. Who are soon to appear, in the shape of Arab troops under General Taric ben Zeyad or, in Spanish, Taric el Tuerto, Taric, the one-eyed. The decisive battle is lost, despite "the valour of the christian cavaliers," with the brave Don Roderick among the last to be slain. Or maybe he was not slain at all, as some legends tell that he mysteriously disappeared, to return once more.

In *Legends of the Conquest of Spain*, Irving also reached a new pitch of masculine achievement:

> The Spaniards, in all ages, have been of swelling and braggart spirit, soaring in thought, pompous in word and valiant, though vain glorious, in deed. Their heroic aims have transcended the cooler conceptions of their neighbors, and their reckless daring has borne them on to achievements which prudent enterprize could never have accomplished. Since the time too of the conquest and occupation of their country by the Arabs, a strong infusion of Oriental magnificence has entered into the national character, and rendered the Spanish distinct from every other nation in Europe.[226]

It is easy to dismiss such words as the product of a romantic's imagination pandering to rugged individualists in Jackson's America. Yet Irving on more than one occasion had found his own feelings about the past confirmed. "The Spaniards are all Kings—independent in their feelings," the Duke of Gor, a cultured young Spaniard, declaimed in his Granada palacio—to Washington Irving.[227] *Legends of the Conquest of Spain* followed the publication of *A Tour on the Prairies*. When we look at the exaggerated valor and nobility of the Spaniards, Irving must have realized that manhood in America was not nearly as noble and glorious as he might have imagined it, the Osage warriors with their "Roman countenances" excepted.

FIVE

On the Prairies and in the West

Manhood Wrapped in the Nation's Flag

BY THE 1830S, THE CULTURAL TIDE with regard to manliness had changed dramatically. Manhood now was defined in terms of republican simplicity, manly resolve, and rugged individualism. In contrast, "aristocratic" and, more generally, genteel conceptions of manhood—allegedly the trademarks of wealthy Easterners and the decadent Europeanized landed gentry—bore the opprobrium of effeminacy. One laudatory biography of Andrew Jackson from 1820, for instance, began with an alarmed outcry against the "voluptuousness and effeminacy" that came in the wake of the sudden rise of new wealth in America, characteristics that were "rapidly diminishing that exalted sense of national glory."[1] Jackson then was the prototype of the American male, the paradigm of rugged individualism. His political followers, in turn, in 1828 used the issue effectively against John Quincy Adams, whom they charged with bringing effeminate luxuries and amusements into the White House, substituting, they said, "for republican simplicity and economical habit a sickly appetite for effeminate indulgence."[2] In the campaign of 1840, the Whig opposition seized upon the very sentiments that the Jacksonians had unleashed. The rhetoric of that campaign, which pitted William Henry Harrison, the hero of Tippecanoe and former governor of Indiana, against Martin Van Buren, was a political masterpiece of gendered speech. Harrison was the "Cincinnatus of the West," whose manly virtues and log cabin origin were contrasted with Van Buren's ruffled shirts and his cabinet composed of "Eastern officeholder pimps."[3]

Irving at last saw through the shabby strategy of using manhood as political currency. Yet he had to tread cautiously in his depictions of masculine heroes. This had not been too difficult with Columbus or Mahomet, who were heroes from a remote past. George Washington would be more of a problem, since the factual aristocracy of the Virginian patrician class he had married into could not be overlooked or ignored. In *Life of George*

Washington, we'll see, Irving had to prove that, firstly, patriarchal masculinity was *not* inherently evil and, secondly, that America, too, had its robust "natural aristocracy." However, the proposition implied quite a bit of Englishness below the surface of American life. Terence Martin captures the conundrum in his argument that in Irving's time America "was a new nation which saw itself, fresh and innocent, as emancipated from history."[4] Any notion of "Englishness" therefore posed a threat to "national memory as a mode of productive forgetting."[5]

Washington's putative "Englishness" would have disturbed the process of forgetting necessary for the production of an American identity that denies its colonial origins. In contrast, an "un–English" Washington, framed in terms of stability and community, would have permitted American readers to reimagine the Revolution and its aftermath as without relations to England. Irving reconciled the two mutually excluding ideals of aristocracy and republican simplicity, of Englishness and American exceptionalism, by emphasizing that Washington actually worked, felicitously combining "industry and temperance" with "riches," without producing "luxury" and, consequently, "effeminacy, intoxication, extravagance, vice and folly."[6] And, Irving adds, Washington may have been home-sick for Mount Vernon, yet he sacrificed his personal yearnings for civic duties. Irving himself, who was so fond of his Sunnyside home, also dutifully followed the summons to the post of minister to Spain.

This chapter deals with Irving's quest for his own imperfectly realized masculinity in the arena of his native country. No longer an expat, Irving was convinced that he could easily find the part of himself he had been seeking on the prairies and in the West. "I am extremely excited and interested by this wild country and the wild scenes and people by which I am surrounded," he wrote to his sister Catherine Paris in October 1832, adding that he was "completely launched in savage life."[7] Though he had always admired the glories of Europe's past, he now eschewed the "effeminate calling" of European travel. Had Irving really changed, or did he assert his nationalism mainly because he was thought by some of his countrymen to have imbibed too much of Europe? This is a question I will come back to later. Suffice it to say, at this point, that in *Tour on the Prairies* he would celebrate and relish the "simple" camp life on the western frontier as a curative, a means for men to re-masculinize themselves:

> I can conceive nothing more likely to set the youthful blood into a flow than a wild wood life of the kind and the range of a magnificent wilderness abounding with game and fruitful of adventure. We send our youth abroad to grow luxurious and effeminate in Europe; it appears to me that a previous tour on the prairies would be more likely to produce that manliness, simplicity and self-dependence most in unison with our political institutions.[8]

Notice the phrase "youthful blood." When Irving wrote this, his "blood" was anything but "youthful." He was beyond fifty, and repeating a sentiment he had articulated in 1825, at age 42.[9] Irving was residing in Paris then, preparing a series of essays on America. Both statements echo the mythical Jacksonian qualities of rugged individualism and egotistical ruthlessness that characterized the cult of masculinity of the time. Yet as I will show, the masculinity Irving celebrated and relished in his Western writings is more complex. Of course, there is the personal sense of physical bravery in the face of danger, as Irving romantically embraced the concept of the natural man, whether as a hardy trapper, fur-trader, ranger, or proud Native warrior. However, Irving also felt that too much nature could make men primitive and savage. Searching for a balance between civilization and nature, he suggested spending time in nature and then returning to civilization, to "our political institutions." As for those men who lived in the wilderness permanently, Irving's ideal was a fairly androgynous conception of manhood, in which rugged individualism and bravado, wilderness ethos and savagery were refined by the sentimental capacities of the affections. In framing masculinity in terms of androgyny, a composite of animus and anima traits, Irving at one and the same time preserved his woman within and attenuated the masculine type of gendered rage which in antebellum America was directed against the effeminate luxury of the upper classes in the East, the emasculation of those working for wages, and the reforming efforts, by women and the clergy, which pressured men to adopt manners suitable to family life.[10]

Gendered rage transformed Andrew Jackson into "a pupil of the wilderness" (George Bancroft), a man "of violent character" (Alexis de Tocqueville).[11] Gendered rage likewise informed the rewriting of the biographies of Daniel Boone and David Crockett as primitivist narratives of innate, instinctual manhood—of manhood in constant retreat from advancing civilization, conceived of in terms of feminizing luxury, sensuous pleasure, and weakness in general.[12] Irving, though he too would shun the feminizing impulses that were at the core of his anima personality, nevertheless clung to the ideal of a sentimental traveler in search of picturesque scenes but always ready to return to civilization. Let's take a look at the brief sketch of Daniel Boone in Irving's Notebook of 1818, which he kept in England.[13] Irving had read avidly about Boone and his adventures. He apparently knew John Filson's *The Discovery, Purchase and Settlement of Kentucke* (1784), which contains Boone's account as an appendix, titled "The Adventures of Col. Daniel Boone." From this, as well as from other books about travel in America available to him, mostly in the British Museum, Irving copied extensively.[14]

For us, the most interesting passages are about the time Boone spent in the wilderness alone, in 1770, where at one point he found himself "surrounded with plenty in the midst of want. I was happy in the midst of dangers & inconveniences. In such a diversity it was impossible I should be disposed to melancholy. No populous city, with all the varieties of commerce & stately structures could afford so much pleasure to my mind as the beauties of nature I found here." It is quite unusual to say this in the midst of frontier warfare, by a Daniel Boone whose "footsteps have often been marked with blood."[15] In 1770, Boone had one companion killed by Native Americans, while the other two, including his brother, returned home. Altogether, Boone lost a brother and two of his sons in the wars against the Indigenous population. An additional note on Boone later in Irving's Notebook clearly anticipates the picturesque rhetoric of *A Tour of the Prairies*: "Boones [sic] first view of Kentucky from the Cumberland Hills—noble forests with buffalos Clover underneath like park lands."[16]

Irving had returned to America on May 21, 1832, after an absence of seventeen years. In a way, he must have felt like Rip Van Winkle. Since his departure for Europe, New York City had nearly doubled the number of inhabitants, from some 110,000 to over 205,000. The influence of the mother country, waning, though still strong when he left, had disappeared entirely. Now he faced a thriving metropolis full of money-grabbing, political-minded, ambitious people, together with immigrants from all over. New York welcomed its native son, staging a public dinner in his honor.[17] Visits to, *inter alia*, Washington, DC, and Boston followed. Irving was, at least temporarily, at peace with his native country. As William Dunlap, a writer Irving knew from his youth in New York, noted in his diary:

> Irving professes himself convinced that Democracy is the only true system and expresses his astonishment after seventeen years' residence in various parts of Europe to see the superiority in our state of society. I told him I had always been a Democrat and saw in the system not the bringing down of the few but the exaltation of the many. He said he was convinced of it. That his feelings and political creed were changed. He stated the contrast between the misery of some parts of Europe and the discontents and anxieties of all, with the general admiration, cheerful pressing on to something better ahead and enjoyment of the present which appeared everywhere in this country was amazing to himself and kept him in a fever of excitement and exultation.[18]

We should not take the political views expressed here at their face value. Irving was a literary personality, and the purported "fever of excitement and exultation" spilled over into his determination to write an American work, if only to get back to those critics who griped that he had been throwing away his talents on English and Spanish themes.[19] Writing from Granada in 1829, Irving had hinted at the "importance [...] and I may say duty of producing some writings relating to our own country which would be of a decidedly national character." Irving, who at the time was feeding his romantic imagination in Southern Spain, added that not only were "writings relating to our own country" wanted by his friends in America but also would be gratifying to his "feelings and advantageous to my literary character at home."[20] Of course, Irving needed inspiration to write, and the best place to find such inspiration, he decided, was out on the prairies. In August 1832 he embarked on a trip to the Oklahoma Territory. Three years later, *A Tour of the Prairies* was published by John Murray of London, to be followed by the American edition from Philadelphia's Carey, Lea & Blanchard, a French edition with Galignani in Paris, as well as a Dutch translation. A German translation was published by J.G. Cotta of Stuttgart, titled *Ausflug auf die Prairien zwischen dem Arkansas und Red River*.

"*A Tour of the Prairies*," a reviewer wrote, "is a sort of sentimental journey, a romantic excursion, in which nearly all the elements of several kinds of writing are beautifully and gayly blended into a production almost *sui generis*."[21] A century later, critics were much less enthusiastic, if not condescending, in their dismissal of the book as "tales of the West designed for readers enamored of idealized scenes whose realities horrified them."[22] Irving, we learn from Stanley Williams's biography, had discovered "that a romantic might feed his emotions even in this America."[23] The discovery was, however, accidental, as Irving had rather stumbled into the role of a "frontiersman" in the summer of 1832, when he was traveling across Lake Erie, on board the steamboat *Niagara*. There he struck up a conversation with Henry Ellsworth, the lead member of President Jackson's Indian Commission. The commission had been appointed, *inter alia*, to "visit and examine the country set apart for the emigrating Indians, west of the Mississippi." In addition, they were to acquaint themselves with Native American claims, settle difficulties between tribes, report on places for the location of "tribes yet to emigrate," and to make necessary treaties.[24]

To modern ears, "country set apart for the emigrating Indians" sounds like a cynical euphemism for what in fact were the territories earmarked for tribal relocation under the terms of the inauspicious Indian Removal Act of 1830.[25] Irving may not have been fully aware of the hollowness of such rhetoric, and he likely did not think there was anything amiss in "tribes yet to emigrate." Although the link is made clear right at the beginning of *Tour on the Prairies*, when Irving mentions that the party was headed by one of the Commissioners, he never openly admitted his complicity (as a tourist-traveler) in Indian Removal; rather, it is up to the reader to link the violence of the U.S. Rangers with the image of "bands of buccaneers penetrating the wilds of South America on their plundering expeditions against the Spanish settlements."[26] What Irving did choose to tell is that when Ellsworth invited him to come along, this was an offer "too tempting to be resisted."

It gave him a chance to see, as he wistfully writes in a letter to his brother Peter, "the remnants of those great Indian tribes, which are now about to *disappear as independent nations*, or to be amalgamated under some new form of government."[27]

Irving hoped to catch more than a romantic view of "savages." It was the real, not the stock, Native Americans that he wished to encounter, and he later felt that he had accomplished this. "In fact, the Indians that I have had an opportunity of seeing in real life, are quite different from those described in poetry."[28] And, Irving might have added, they are different from the Indigenous people described in the "ponderous tomes" of natural history he had lampooned in *The History of New York*.[29] Altogether, in the printed version of his tour, Irving offers to correct the stereotypical image of Native Americans as "stoics [...] taciturn, unbending, without a tear or smile." They may well be like that, he adds, when they encounter white people whom they distrust. Yet when they are among themselves, "there cannot be greater gossips. Half their time is taken up in talking over their adventures in war and hunting, and in telling whimsical stories. They are great mimics and buffoons, also, and entertain themselves excessively at the expense of the whites."[30]

Irving arrived in St. Louis in mid–September. Once there, he immediately called on William Clark—"The Governor," as he was still called—who had explored the American West with Meriwether Lewis and the Corps of Discovery in 1804–1806. Irving described Clark as a "fine healthy robust man," "frank and intelligent," with long, flowing hair. At the time of Irving's visit, Clark was Superintendent of Indian Affairs and had been involved in the uprising led by the Sauk chief Black Hawk in protest of treaty violations. Militia butchered the protesters and Black Hawk surrendered to the authorities, a mere two weeks before Irving's arrival. Irving was determined to meet the captive, only to find him, as he reported to Catherine Paris, "an old man [...] emaciated & enfeebled by the sufferings he has experienced and by a touch of cholera." Irving had a hard time believing that this was the man who allegedly had committed countless atrocities and professed that he also found it impossible "to get at the right story of these feuds between the White & the red man," adding that "my sympathies go strongly with the latter."[31]

In his journals, Irving goes well beyond expressions of sympathy, assessing Black Hawk as an anthropological specimen. Listening to a doctor who was "given to craniology," he interprets the Chief's "aquiline nose" as an unmistakable signifier of the Native American's "benevolence."[32] This was meant as living proof of Indigenous otherness. The classification is also evident from a letter to his brother Peter, in which Irving describes the prisoner as "a meager old man upwards of seventy [yet with] a fine head, a *Roman style of face*, and a prepossessing countenance."[33] Genuine manhood, Irving apparently believed, does not wash off so easily. The disposition continues once his group was on the way to the western border of the state of Missouri, angling toward Fort Gibson in what is now eastern Oklahoma. There Irving's search for masculine archetypes is successful as he encounters the Osage warriors' "*Roman countenances*" and "*noble bronze figures.*"[34]

In the Osages' "Roman countenances" we can see Irving reaching out for what would be taken as anthropological correctness.[35] But the nobility Irving marveled at in the Osages of the prairies also provided him with the part of himself he had been seeking. They are noble (that is, in an aboriginal state) because they had not "yielded sufficiently, as yet, to the influence of civilization."[36] Importantly, the Osages were what Irving called "friendly Indians"—that is, one of the tribes "with which the United States have Treaties."[37] Indeed, it is only "friendly Indians" that Irving writes admiringly about, both in his journals and letters, and in print. In contrast, the very word "Pawnee" seems to have been enough to make Irving shudder, not at first sight, as he never saw any of them, but at a signifier that had proven useful in Jackson's Indian policy.[38] Irving had failed in the primary object of his tour—to see "the Pawnees, the Comanches, and other fierce and as yet independent tribes" that roamed the prairies in the western stretches of the territory, where "Mouldering skulls and skeletons bleaching in some dark ravine" bore witness to the dangers awaiting the unwary traveler.[39] The failure to encounter the Pawnees left Irving with the Osages, whom he singles out as "the finest looking Indians I have ever seen in the West." Their "noble bronze figures" distinguish them as the most aboriginal Native Americans, proof that America had its own wilderness, not just the equal of Europe's but superior to it.

Irving's raving about "figures of monumental bronze," "model[s] for statuary," or "studies for a painter or a statuary" speaks both to his personal quest for achieved masculinity and to his deep admiration of Indigenous people.[40] Yet their magnificence belongs to another world. These Native Americans recall the great civilizations of antiquity. By comparing them to Romans, Irving consigns them to the past, transforming them into objects to be looked and marveled at. Irving's "Indians" thus fade into representative males or females, arranged in rather static tableaus. This was the trademark of picturesque description, that is, of the "habit of viewing and criticizing nature as if it were an infinite series of more or less well composed subjects for painting."[41] The picturesque is a function of an ideal form of nature, derived from landscape painting. The key for picturesque compositions was variety. The discovery of picturesque scenes had been Irving's goal from early on.[42] In *A Tour on the Prairies* Irving elevated the picturesque to descriptions of the native population, grafting frontier skills—manly rites of passage—onto his portraits. As he had done in Southern Spain in the late 1820s, he links the picturesque to the Romantic enthusiasm for primitivism.[43] Thus one can understand why even in the printed book Irving admits that he found his "ravenous and sanguinary propensities daily growing stronger upon the prairies." The party's encampment too "had a savage appearance; with its rude tents of skins and blankets; and its columns of blue smoke rising among the trees."[44] Years later, Irving still praised Charles Lanman's book *Adventures in the Wilds of America* as a "*vade mecum* to the American lover of the picturesque and romantic."[45]

Irving never lost sight of his quest for his own imperfectly realized masculinity. In his encounters with Indigenous people there is, then, almost always fascination with physical manhood and manly characteristics. "Such is the glorious independence of man in a savage state," he writes about a young Osage.

> This youth with his rifle, his blanket and his horse, was ready at a moment's warning to rove the world, he carries all his worldly effects with him; and in the absence of artificial wants, possessed the great secret of personal freedom. We of society are slaves not so much to others, as to ourselves; our superfluities are the chains that bind us, impeding every movement of our bodies and thwarting every impulse of our souls.[46]

This is as good an example of Irving's predicament and of the romantic tendency to juxtapose "nature" against "civilization" as any to be found in *A Tour on the Prairies*. Irving not only felt that he needed to remedy his own deficient masculinity. His travelling companions too seemingly would benefit from a stay in the wilderness. Of Henry Ellsworth, the federal official, he wrote that "the greater part of his days had been passed in the bosom of his family, and the society of deacons, elders, and select men, on the peaceful banks of the Connecticut." Of Charles Latrobe, referred to in print as "Mr. L.," Irving says that the life of luxury he had lived in England had made him "soft." Only the nineteen-year-old Swiss count, Albert de Pourtalès, seemed ready to prove his masculinity, anticipating a part in the Indigenous people's "hardy adventures."[47]

As for Irving himself, he imagined masculinity in the form of the romantically heightened natural man at the same time as he preserved and expanded his own patrician manhood. He was, as Richard Cracroft noted, "ever the genteel observer [...] a self-conscious, aristocratic gentleman, keenly conscious of his civilization."[48] When Irving looked at a Native American, therefore, he saw a proud barbarian ready to be transformed into a civilized citizen of the United States. (Conversely, when he looked at an African American, he saw something less than human, something just above an animal. Never in his life did Irving imagine the possibility of blacks becoming full citizens.[49]) Irving strongly believed that Native Americans were educable, and he was genuinely interested in their customs, beliefs, and superstitions. Moreover, faithfully adopting the rhetoric of American cultural nationalism, he even acknowledges Indigenous people as, in his words, "*our* aboriginal tribes."[50]

At first sight, the passages about the Osages strike one as an advertisement for the wilderness as national training grounds for the male body and mind, later to be represented as masculine archetypes. Yet Irving's position, as indicated, was contradictory. Clearly his "Indian rhetoric" follows the "noble savage" parable, if not the "fetishization" of Native Americans that goes by the name of the "sublime," mining the sentimental drama in the Indigenous people's last stand.[51] There is, however, never a call to convert completely to the native experience. Rather, it is the land that is to be converted by preserving and appreciating the native heritage. Irving's appraisal of the frontier therefore does not fundamentally challenge his anxiety and apprehension about the prevailing cult of masculinity; instead, it implies that an American identity is best formed, not by the Jacksonian persuasion but by social and political institutions originating from western civilization in unison with the benefits of a tour to the margins of that civilization and beyond. Or, as Edward Everett remarked in reviewing *Tour on the Prairies*, by "turning these poor barbarian steppes into *classical land*."[52]

Irving's transformation or, put less benignly, reification of the Indigenous population into so many splendid figures became possible only as the West was won. By the 1830s, Native Americans had disappeared from the lives of most white Americans, except in the West and in the countryside. For the majority of white Americans, they were mere objects to be looked at, like specimens of natural history. Representations of them as vanishing Americans abounded in this period. Native Americans appeared on paintings and prints, on notes issued by private commercial banks, in Cooper's Leatherstocking novels—and in the writings of Washington Irving. The method, Laura J. Murray argues, transformed the Indigenous population into passive victims, denying them history and positioning them in the realm of romance.[53] Irving, Murray points out, expressly lamented the lack of historic record. "[T]hey have left scarcely any authentic traces on the page of history," Irving had written in "Philip of Pokanoket," yet for him this lack became an artistic opportunity. Stalking like "gigantic shadows in the dim twilight of tradition," Native Americans for that very reason are worthy of "an age of poetry, and fit subjects for local story and romantic fiction."[54] Irving thus seems to dismiss history altogether, replacing it with "the dim twilight of tradition," all in generous admiration of Indigenous nobility and, by extension, of their achieved masculinity with which he could identify.[55]

"Philip of Pokanoket" was originally printed in *Analectic Magazine* of June 1814, following "Traits of Indian Character," which had appeared in the February issue.[56] In each sketch there is a profound regret, not simply for the extinction of the Indigenous population but for the impact of that extinction upon American society. Phrased differently, each sketch reflects Irving's concern about the progress of American civilization and the costs of that progress. It is entirely consistent, therefore, that the Indian sketches were republished in *The Sketch Book*. As Donald A. Ringe pointed out, it was more than a vague sense of the past that had attracted Irving to Europe. Rather, many of the sketches in the collection demonstrate that change and progress result in the destruction of order and stability and "that important values are lost when men prefer change to stability."[57] As Irving explains in "The Author's Account of Himself," he had gone to Europe to escape "from the commonplace realities of the present, and lose myself among the shadowy grandeurs of the past."[58]

In his western writings, Irving wrote as an insider, an inhabitant of the land he describes, together with the people therein. American society, he wrote, was so "full of youthful promise" that its "shadowy grandeurs of the past" could be found only among the aboriginal cultures. These cultures were independent and entirely devoid of "the restraints and refinements of polished life" and they had given rise to a nobility "of sterling coinage."[59] Irving saw not only America's aboriginal societies as societies with a past, with a cultural heritage, and a potential for achieved masculinity; he identified a similar heritage in the Dutch communities of New York, the German communities of New Jersey and Pennsylvania, or the Creole villages of the lower Mississippi valley. Much as he deplored the obliteration of these heritages by the onslaught of the (in his words, now trite) "Almighty dollar," he also deplored the obliteration of America's past—including the Indigenous population—in the process. The theme of the obliteration of the past, Daniel Littlefield has shown, can be found in Irving's works from early on, and his later works dealing with Native Americans merely are more detailed illustrations of his belief that the Indigenous population was doomed.[60]

Littlefield does not mention this, but it is worth pointing out that Irving was a contemporary of the brothers Jacob and Wilhelm Grimm, whose wild collecting of folk tales likewise was driven by fear of loss. Their word of admonition too was "still!" Thus, the Grimms manically transferred into print folk traditions and popular legends that, they felt, soon would be swallowed by the maelstrom of time. Irving's feelings were similar. As he ominously predicted, it was not just Native Americans who "will vanish like a vapour from the face of the earth."[61] The Dutch communities of New York, the German communities of New Jersey and Pennsylvania, the French Creole villages of the lower Mississippi valley, and—for Europe—the villages of rural England or the peasant communities of Southern Spain likewise were on their way out. But they all—and there are more in Irving's writings—held a cultural heritage that Irving, literary archaeologist that he was, felt was worth preserving. Irving had realized from early on that the exclusive focus on progress—read, individual advancement, profit, and greed—eclipsed all concerns for the preservation and salvaging of present existence, hence of responsibility for future generations. If he fought to salvage (if only through writing down) the "remnants [...] about to disappear," his motivation is perhaps best rendered in the words of Robert Musil's "man without qualities," for whom "the right thing to do would be / To rescue something from [what is coming to an end]."[62]

In the United States, what was coming to an end was, *inter alia*, Native American nationhood. By the time Irving went on his tour, the Indian Removal Act had become law, Jackson's policy was well under way, and the writer had a hard time seeing Native Americans in their closest approximation of an aboriginal state. This is particularly noticeable in Irving's rough notes, which, John McDermott claims, are "remarkably factual and reliable. Here Irving did not bother with fancies."[63] Although Irving did not meet a great many Indigenous people, he honestly wrestles with the phonetic features of Indigenous names, some of which appear in altogether different spellings. And he marvels at first sights—at a "Group of Osages [...] blankets—leather leggings & moccasins—hair cropped except bunch at top—Bust bare or wrapped in blanket." On the same occasion, he observes some Creek people, one "with turban [...] like an Arab [another] with scarlet turban and plume of black feathers like a cock tail, one with white turban & red feathers—Oriental look—like Sultans on the Stage. [...] They look like fine birds of the Prairie."[64]

When Irving observes the "noble attitudes" of the Osage warriors, elevating them to the status of masculine archetypes in classical splendor, this is somewhat at odds with the information that they "will steal horses & then bring them home pretending to have found them and claiming a reward."[65] Later in his journal, he once again complies with anthropological correctness in describing the Osages as "true Indians—Hunters—full of ceremonies & superstitions." Yet he also records their self-image as "poor people [...] we cannot farm & our hunting is failing us—The pride of the Osages is broken." Hence, there is little for them to do except "steal horses."[66] Also throughout the journals, Irving's point of view shifts considerably, depending on whom he was traveling or talking with at the time of his jottings. When at missions, the emphasis is on civilizing the Indigenous population; at agencies or with Governor Clark, it is on tribal and religious customs, occasionally, on sentiment; and, not to forget, Irving is at pains to distinguish between "friendly Indians" and "the terror of the frontier."⁶⁷ Altogether, the journals are much more spontaneous than the literary version. Whereas the published *Tour* concentrates, much more so than the chronicles by other members of the four-week expedition, on rhetoric, romanticism and, if you like, self-therapy, the journals may be said to show Irving "*without his mask*."⁶⁸

Importantly, the hypermasculine warriors of the printed *Tour* are not "real" people but composites, with little in the rough journals to justify the portraits. For instance, an entry from October 12, 1832—"figure of Indian—naked bust—blanket [...] wild eyes"—reappears in print as an "Osage on horseback issuing out of a skirt of wood [...] about nineteen or twenty years of age [...] with the fine Roman countenance common to his tribe [...] his naked bust would have furnished a model for a statuary."⁶⁹ Elsewhere, a few phrases served as the foundation for the considerable fabric about the lawlessness and depravity of the frontiersmen as opposed to the "glorious independence" of the Osage people in their "savage state."⁷⁰ In his journal entry for October 11, 1832, Irving reports meeting "a tall red haired lank lanthern-jawd faced settler with one eye habitually closed when he winks—Says some of the Osages are near. They had stolen one of his horses—says they will steal horses & then bring them home, pretending to have found them and claiming a reward." Later on the same day Irving noted that the "old lanthern jwd man [...] Had just met with Osage leading him [the horse] back—who said he had wandered to their camp. Lanthern jawd man was for tying him up & giving him a swing with rushes, but we interfered."⁷¹

In the published book, Irving embellished the "fabric" of his notes by what he termed his "filigree work."⁷² He thus transformed the "old lanthern jwd man" into "a white settler or squatter, a tall raw boned old fellow, with red hair, a lank lanthorn visage, and an inveterate habit of winking with one eye, as if everything he said was of knowing import." This very man now

> declared that the Indians had carried off his horse in the night, with the intention of bringing him home in the morning, and claiming a reward for finding him; a common practice, as he affirmed, among the Indians. He was, therefore, for tying the young Indian to a tree and giving him a sound lashing; and was quite surprized at the burst of indignation which this novel mode of requiting a service drew from us.⁷³

Irving would not be Irving if he had not stitched on a general moral to the episode:

> Such, however, is too often the administration of law on the frontier, "Lynch's law," as it is technically termed, in which the plaintiff is apt to be witness, jury, judge and executioner, and the defendant to be convicted and punished on mere presumption: and in this way I am convinced, are occasioned many of those

heartburnings and resentments among the Indians, which lead to retaliation, and end in Indian wars."

Following this, Irving juxtaposes the lawlessness of the frontier against Indigenous nobility, a contrast that is all too visible in physical appearances: "When I compared the open, noble countenance and frank demeanour of the young Osage, with the sinister visage and high handed conduct of the frontiers-man, I felt little doubt upon whose back a lash would be most meritoriously bestowed."[74]

In a later chapter, Irving again deplores "the capricious and overbearing conduct of the white men; who, as I have witnessed in my own short experience, are prone to treat the poor Indians as little better than brute animals."[75] Passages of this kind are important on two counts: First, the frontier of 1832 that Irving saw was a place where customs, beliefs, and languages were merging as whites, blacks, and Native Americans came together in new and unexpected ways. For Irving, this spelt social chaos, if not nature let loose, and he was deeply ambivalent about all this. For example, one member of the Ellsworth party, Antoine Deshetres, called Tonish, who was of French, English, and Osage descent, is introduced as a "little vagabond," another one of "these half breeds" and entirely "without morals."[76] As for Irving himself, he clearly did not think that Tonish's was the kind of masculinity American men, let alone he himself, should aspire to. Always keenly aware both of his "feminine" personality and of his self-image as a genteel observer, Irving never got carried away by the new and typical phenomena, never fully immersed himself in the culture of the frontier.

As they traveled, Irving came to admire the masculine camaraderie of the rangers, who were mostly young men "in high health and vigor, and buoyant with anticipations," especially of fighting Native Americans. He even participated in camp activities, such as shooting at a mark, leaping, wrestling, and "playing at prison bars."[77] But the rangers were "true" white men, not "half breeds," not corrupted by nature, and they were to soon return to the East. By and large, however, Irving never was at ease under the casual familiarity of the woodsmen, and on occasion was outspokenly antagonistic to these frontier types. Though he was sensitive to the growing importance of the West in the national psyche, he remained the cultured cosmopolitan, the gentleman tourist, whose anima identity required "loyalty to civilization."[78] His view of the West and its inhabitants as novelties of romance, together with his ambivalence towards westward expansion resulted in considerable tensions in the published *Tour*—between the emotional and cultural realities of the frontier, between loyalty to traditional values, heritage and his inner self, and the nationalistic rhetoric.[79]

If only there had not been the Pawnees—"the terror of the frontier; a race who scour the Prairies on fleet horses, and are like the Tartars or roving Arabs."[80] Irving's fear, if real fear it was, soon gave way to excited anticipation, as he knew that this also was buffalo country. Eventually Irving had his kill; yet having to finish off the bison at close range, he was through with being a sportsman. He also had had enough of life as a frontiersman. The "excitement was over," "the novelty and excitement of the expedition were at an end," and our hardy frontiersman was "weary and exhausted."[81] His journals were crammed with more than enough notes for a book, and he wanted to return to New York to start writing.[82] Irving completed the manuscript for *Tour on the Prairies* in November 1834, though he was reluctant to publish it. "So much has been said in the papers about my tour to the West, and the work I was preparing on the subject," he confided to his brother Peter, "that I dread the expectations formed, especially as what I have written is extremely simple, and by no means striking in its details."[83]

The anti-climactic evaluation of his own work notwithstanding, in January 1835 Irving resolved "to break the ice, and begin to publish" his manuscript.[84] The book debuted in London in March 1835; the American edition was published a month later, on April 11. It was Irving's long-awaited American book, and to many American readers, the wait was worth it. "Irving among the [...] Osages of the frontier!" bubbled an effusive reviewer. By November, Irving's "sentimental journey," his "romantic excursion" had sold more than 8,000 copies, and sales in England were just as encouraging.[85] It is entirely fitting to see *Tour on the Prairies* as a *literary* effort, the product, not of a practitioner of natural history or ethnography so much as of a "feminine" literary personality who was quite capable to work in the mode of the western adventure narrative, a popular genre of the period and of nineteenth-century American literature more generally.[86]

Irving kept up the western adventure narrative in his books about the Northwest, *Astoria, or Anecdotes of an Enterprise Beyond the Rocky Mountains* (1836) and *The Adventures of Captain Bonneville* (1837). Both books were popular at the time, though modern scholars have frequently reproached Irving for depicting Astor as a benign, patriarchal figure, and for uncritically praising the "courage, fortitude, and perseverance" of the early fur traders and trappers, while at the same time completely (or, rather, almost completely) avoiding pro–Native American passages in them.[87] Did Irving not know that the broad foundation of his friend John Jacob Astor rested on suffering and debauchery? Did he really so calmly take for granted that eventually the fur-bearing animals were going to be exterminated in a cruel sacrifice to the Almighty Dollar? And did he really believe that the "scenes of wild life among trappers, traders and Indian banditti" were mere entertaining stories of "adventure, description, and stirring incident; with occasional passages of humor"?[88]

Yet it will not do to make Irving blinder than he was. The trappers, fur traders, and "the grand enterprizes of the great fur companies" may have fired his imagination as a youth when he met many of them during a trip to Montreal in the summer of 1803, and they continued to be one of the most romantic themes for him. Irving in his relentless search for models of masculinity also had fallen for the romantic appeal of a new breed of westerners, the mountain men, who led a "wild, Robin Hood kind of life" and altogether were "hardy, lithe, vigorous, and active; extravagant in word, in thought, and deed; heedless of hardship; daring of danger; prodigal of the present; and thoughtless of the future."[89] Privately, Irving, always searching for a place as a man among other men, was quite prepared, in the late 1830s, to look upon "the excessive expansions of commerce, and the extravagant land speculations [...] as incident to that spirit of enterprise natural to a young country in a state of rapid and prosperous development."[90] His nostalgia for Europe had lessened, and, despite reservations, he had become "a citizen of the republic," letting America draw him to herself. America paid back in kind, perpetually identifying his talents with the ubiquitous aspirations for a genuinely national literature. "Imperceptibly," Stanley Williams wrote, America's "ideals became his own."[91]

In the process of telling the story of Astor's fur-trading empire, however, Irving was far from convinced that what was going on in the West would "give solidity and strength to our great confederacy [...] our immense empire."[92] Instead, he described how the adventurers' "conduct and example gradually corrupted the natives," and he continued to denounce white atrocities against Native Americans, with the whites, not the Native Americans, as the aggressors. "We kill white men," Irving quotes one of the tribal chiefs, "because white men kill us."[93] Similarly, in *Bonneville*, the Blackfeet are said to cherish a "lurking hostility to the whites" ever since one of their tribe had been killed by Meriwether Lewis of the Lewis and Clark expedition. By way of contrast, Irving records Captain Bonneville's opinion that the Nez Percés, in spite of the unfavorable reports of others, are "one of the purest-hearted people on the face of the earth."[94] Again in *Astoria*, Irving mentions an Indigenous woman who "displayed a force of character that won the respect and applause of the white man."[95]

Significantly, all these voices belong to the "remains of broken and almost extinguished tribes [...] expatriated beings, wrongfully exiled from their hereditary homes, and the sepulchres of their fathers." In this context, Irving's remark that there was "a tendency to extinction among all the savage nations"[96] repeats the theme of cultural discontinuity, mutability, and loss that is noticeable already in his earliest writings. Small wonder, then, that a reviewer found, "The arrangement has all the art of a fiction."[97] One might find it difficult to reconcile the obvious romantic appeal of the "hardy fur traders [...] who had wonders to recount of their wide and wild peregrinations"[98] with the theme of the disappearance of the Indigenous population. Yet Irving also realized that like so much of America's past, the Indigenous population included, the great fur businesses, too, were passing, and he felt compelled, therefore, "to fix these few memorials of a transient state of things fast passing into oblivion."[99] Nor should we forget that from start to finish, *Astoria* is the story, not of the success of Astor's enterprise but of its failure, not because of a lack of business acumen on Astor's part but because the U.S. government failed to protect Astoria once the War of 1812 had begun, and, after the war, failed to remove from the region the agents of the rival British fur trading companies. "[W]e regret the failure of this enterprise in a national point of view," Irving wrote. Thus *Astoria* (as well as *Bonneville*) stands "not as an endorsement of the fur industry but as an indictment of American foreign policy."[100]

Astor's enterprise also failed because of human insufficiency. The loss of the trading vessel *Tonquin*, off Vancouver Island, is Irving's case in point. Neglecting Astor's injunctions to be cautious, the captain, "brave but headstrong," carelessly allows too many Native Americans on board ship, where they start to trade for knives. As soon as the ship is to be cleared, the warriors, now well armed, begin to attack the crew, soon killing most of the men. The few survivors are later captured and tortured. Another survivor, the ship's clerk, who has been left for dead below deck, finally blows up the fated ship, taking with him any number of natives. The captain's "harshness and imprudence" and "proud contempt of danger" speak to a masculinity of sorts, of manly resolve perhaps, certainly of single-minded bravado—life on board a trading vessel hardly offered luxury leading to effeminacy, not even for a captain. And industrious the good Captain Thorn may have been, yet he obviously lacked the sentimental capacities of the affections. After all, his insult to a Native American chief was the cause of the attack on the *Tonquin*. Nor, of course, does the savageness of the Native Americans, whose "friendship," it turned out, was merely "apparent," square with Irving's ideas of achieved manhood.[101]

In *Bonneville*, Irving is even more outspoken in his conviction that the Indigenous population was passing and that the fur trade too had outlived its time. "[T]his singular state of things is full of mutation, and must soon undergo great changes, if not entirely pass away. The fur trade, itself, which has given life to all this portraiture, is essentially evanescent." Irving firmly predicts that some "new system of things [...] will succeed." The dispossessed tribes will amalgamate; they will take in renegade white people from every nation and become "predatory and warlike" bands. These "modifications" will make necessary the establishment of military posts to protect Americans in the West.[102] Irving's conclusion may sound accommodating, imagining the U.S. government as an honest broker, yet it should not be interpreted as a softening of his former pro–Native American stand and an uncritical embrace of the idea of America's manifest destiny. To be sure, Irving was still fascinated by the notion of a man's winning manhood on the frontier. He admires the manliness of the trappers, who seemed "midway between the savage state and civilization" and, above all, of Captain Bonneville, whom he depicts as truly heroic and by no means hamstrung by the commercial interest of recapturing the fur trade lost when Astoria collapsed. On the contrary, Bonneville is a picture of manliness who had "engrafted the trapper and hunter upon the soldier."[103] What also stimulated Irving's account were tales he remembered of the "vast and magnificent regions" of the West.[104] By and large, though, Irving records, not a civilizing process so much as the accompanying violence of westward expansion, which threatened to "un-civilize" the entire nation.[105] These records helped mute, perhaps unwittingly, whatever "imperialist intentions" Irving may have had.[106] And if he saw the establishment of military posts as necessary it was because the West, its aboriginal inhabitants included, was being despoiled as a result of unbridled westward expansion and commercial imperialism.

Clearly, this estimation is at odds with the suggestion, put forth by Andrew Burstein, that *Astoria* shows Irving's moving away from glorification of Indigenous people, towards celebrating an empire of business. Worse, *Bonneville*, for its part, was nothing but a celebration of expansionism in terms of a modern romance of legitimate conquest. In these two works, Burstein contends, Irving "stopped mourning the Indian's sacrifice to America's destiny," putting in its stead his defense of U.S. Indian policies, including removal.[107] There are, perhaps, good reasons to see *Astoria* as a cautious endorsement of entrepreneurial capitalism. Not, however, in the sense that Irving had modeled Astor after Ichabod Crane, his early allegorization of a Yankee exploiter ready to turn everything into cash. Herman Melville may have come to write, in "Bartleby the Scrivener," that Astor's name "rings like unto bullion."[108] Irving, in contrast, felt quite at home with Astor, that "high-minded gentleman," as Poe had written in his review of Irving's book.[109] Astor, Irving wrote, "was not actuated by mere motives of profit," but by the desire for fame achieved by men who through their enterprises "have enriched nations, peopled wildernesses, and extended the bounds of empire."[110] Peter Antelyes has written, correctly I think, that Irving depicted Astor as a "dreamer of empire [...] a daring and constructive thinker." In this regard, Astor was more a "discoverer," an "American Columbus" capable of beating market panics rather than a mere "merchant seeking his own profit."[111]

Irving himself may have had good reasons to portray Astor as an "aristocratic capitalist."[112] He was, after all, always in search of achieved masculinity, on aristocratic terms, and may already have been thinking about George Washington, on whose biography he would seriously be at work in due time. Hence Astor's was "an aspiring spirit that always looked upward, a genius bold, fertile and expansive, a sagacity quick to grasp and convert every circumstance to its advantage, and a singular and never wavering confidence of signal success."[113] Yet unlike Washington, Astor remains a problematic man, of narcissistic complacency and wavering between patrician sophistication and entrepreneurial ruthlessness, based on the kind of "go-ahead" attitude that went with the capitalist ethos.[114] As for *Bonneville*, Irving clearly wanted to expose the more "sanguinary" side of the fur trade. Irving may have described the trappers as the "cavaliers of the mountains," but they are by no means exemplars of achieved masculinity; rather, they are incarnations of American rugged individualism, self-interested savages like Cooper's "lawless whites of the frontiers," whose "heartless longing for profit" Natty Bumppo deplores in *The Deerslayer* (1841).[115]

Astoria and *Bonneville*, like the other bio-histories, are largely compilations, heavily based on secondary sources. This time, however, Irving used material provided by their subjects. Still at work on *Tour on the Prairies*, Irving had been approached by John Jacob Astor about a work on the settlement of Astoria. Irving was a longtime friend of the millionaire, and Astor left his journals, letters, articles, and other documents pertaining to his northwest exploits in the fur trade and the establishment of the Pacific Fur Company at the mouth of the Columbia River entirely at the writer's disposal, together with the promise to pay "liberally" for the project. Irving had no mind to plough through Astor's voluminous papers and proposed that Astor hire his nephew, Pierre Munro Irving, as researcher and assistant.[116] Uncle and the nephew, who at the time was grieving over the untimely death of his wife, got their deal and Washington Irving sat down to write, an "entertaining and instructive" work that was, "not merely a history of the great colonial and commercial enterprise, and the fortunes of [Astor's] colony, but a body of information concerning the whole region beyond the Rocky Mountains."[117]

Irving had decided to work on *Astoria* at the millionaire's home in Hell Gate. It was there that he met one of Astor's acquaintances from the fur trade, a French-born army captain by the name of Benjamin Louis Eulalie du Bonneville. Irving instantly pressed him for tales of his adventures. "There was something in the whole appearance of the captain that prepossessed me in his favor," he later wrote.[118] Fortunately for Irving, Bonneville also had written a book about his time in the West. Unable to find a publisher, Bonneville asked Irving if the materials might be useful to him. After glancing over the papers, Irving decided to purchase the manuscript for $1,000.[119] Eventually, Irving became genuinely excited about his book on Bonneville. "It is *all true*," he wrote to his London agent in the spring of 1837. "It is full of adventure, description, and Stirring incident; with occasional passages of humour."[120] American readers and reviewers also saw it in this way. The *New York Review* hailed Irving as "a man of genius" for his ability to elevate "common subjects" to new heights and, not to forget, to give full vent to American nationalism.[121] To Irving's great disappointment, however, *Bonneville* was not well received in England. Not only did British reviewers criticize the book as an expression of American vulgarity and acquisitiveness. The book, the *Literary Gazette* sniffed, was "more prolific of extraordinary heroism in females, than we were prepared to expect among these savages."[122] Yet this was precisely what Irving had intended to convey.

The theme of Native American dispossession, together with a sense of loss and regret continues in a number of minor writings from Irving's later career. For instance, in an 1839 essay titled "National Nomenclature" Irving, who at the time was most anxious about how the United States would be perceived in the world at large, suggests restoring Indigenous names to locations "of sublimity and beauty." New York, he wrote, should become the "City of Manhattan" and the United States of America the "United States of Alleghenia" or "Appalachia."[123] In "Wolfert's Roost," likewise published in 1839, Irving traces the Indigenous legends surrounding Wolfert's Roost in New York and tells how the Roost and all its domains came into possession of the Dutch.[124] Irving tells a similar story of the "invasions and encroachments of white men" in "The Seminoles," published a year later, in this instance from the time of the early Spanish explorers to the time of the Treaty of Moultrie Creek of 1823.[125] It is significant that Irving's last work on Native Americans is a sympathetic account of their resistance to white encroachment and to the government's removal policy, for it contradicts claims by scholars that Irving softened his pro–Native American views and uncritically embraced Manifest Destiny with all its dire consequences for the Indigenous population. It may be regretted that Irving did not openly condemn those facts of national life, but as Daniel Littlefield succinctly put it, "to stand against American expansion would have been like standing against a tidal wave."[126]

Irving's attitude toward the West may have been ambiguous, yet he never failed to open up to the Indigenous population. His receptivity, so typical of an anima persona, made it easy for him to be genuinely interested in the customs and beliefs of different nations and tribes, and he consistently did his best not to perceive Indigenous people through a veil of prejudices. This estimation should be seen as a compliment, and more than one critic has recognized Irving's responsibility in his ethnological descriptions.[127] As early as 1814, Irving had offered to "speak in behalf of a race of beings, whose very existence has been pronounced detrimental to public security." In determined opposition to the "popular feeling" hardened by Jackson's early Indian policy that had culminated in the Creek War, Irving stated: "[I]t is good at all times to raise the voice of truth, however feeble."[128] In this context, it should be pointed out that Irving always resisted the idea of a "natural nation" of white Americans. Instead, he saw Native American cultures as part of the nation's heritage, deploring their demise, much as he deplored the demise of other "pasts," from the Dutch settlers of New York to the villagers of rural England. Irving's views about the devastating effects of "progress" and, in America, of Manifest Destiny, no doubt impacted on his ambivalence toward the West.

Irving had come by his interest in Native Americans "honestly, for it was shared by his brother William and his great friend Henry Brevoort, both of whom had Indian trading interests."[129] Trading interests had led to Irving's first encounter with Indigenous people in the summer of 1803, during an excursion to upstate New York. The twenty year old does not appear to have been greatly impressed by the Native Americans he encountered, but not even the incident in which a woman's "much flattering attention" provokes her irate—and drunken—husband to calling him a "damned Yankee" and leveling him to the floor with a blow, turned him against the Indigenous population. Instead, Irving seems to have fondly remembered another incident from the tour—a mock ceremony in which an honorary name was awarded to him—"*Vomonte*," which, he was told, translated as "*Good to Everybody*."[130] The naming ceremony is a marvelous example of recognizing Irving's "feminine" personality, yet it would be his last interaction with Indigenous people for almost thirty years. In his published writings, however, they make an appearance much earlier.

In the satirical *Salmagundi*, the "erudite" Linkum Fidelius applies his acumen also to the original settlers of America. About them he purportedly wrote "two folio volumes to prove that America was first of all peopled either by the antipodians, or the cornish miners, who he maintains, might easily have made a subterranean passage to this country, particularly the antipodians, who, he asserts, can get along under ground, as fast as moles."[131] By now, the reader has been warned. The "Chronicles of the Renowned and Antient [sic] City of Gotham," from which this is taken, is but a burlesque of pedantry and a facetious display of gratuitous antiquarian knowledge. Diedrich Knickerbocker's *History of New York* is, in a sense, a new version of Linkum's "Chronicles." The larger canvas of the book that made Irving a celebrity in 1809 also made it possible for him to launch a much fuller attack on all kinds of myths about the formation of the Union, especially those that rationalized the conquest of Native American lands. Revolted by the arrogance of power at a time when that kind of protest was not yet sounded in America, Irving mocks the "heroic" efforts of the first white settlers, who rather than find the Eden they had been expecting were confronting a "howling wilderness" with "forests to cut down, underwood to grub up, marshes to drain, and savages to exterminate."[132] Irving fills almost the entire first book with satirical attacks against the rapacity and false logic of white settlers. America, we are told, has been built solely on the unwarranted seizure of Indigenous land in a history of murder, theft, and fraud legitimized by legal authority.[133]

Irving did not invent colonial history out of thin air. When the early colonists spoke of reclaiming North America from the wilderness, they did not see their taking of the land as robbery. In 1609, for instance, the preacher Robert Gray in a tract published in London to promote colonization in Virginia declared that "the greater part" of the earth was "possessed and wrongfully usurped by wild beasts [...] or by brutish savages." A Virginia pamphlet claimed that it was "not unlawful" for the English to possess "part" of Native American lands.[134] Of course, the English soon wanted more than just a "part" of Native American territory, not least for the cultivation of tobacco as an export crop. Tobacco and, later, cotton stimulated not only territorial expansion but also immigration. About two centuries after the first English settlements the jurist James Kent argued that the entire American continent was "fitted and intended by Providence to be subdued and cultivated, and to become the residence of civilized nations."[135] Kent's treatise on Native American rights and titles was first published in the late 1820s, with a second edition following in 1832. Thus, his disquisition may be seen as both a counternarrative to Irving and a preview of the racialized views of savagery that, after its first peak especially in seventeenth-century New England, again were coming into prominence as Manifest Destiny was taking hold.[136]

When compared to Kent's rationalizations and the racism behind Manifest Destiny, Irving's views must be called truly progressive and humanitarian. The fairness and generosity that speak from them were reinforced by observations Henry Brevoort made on the western frontier in 1811. Brevoort's observations, together with the views Irving himself articulated in *A History of New York*, reappear or are reflected in Irving's Indian sketches, first published in the *Analectic Magazine* in 1814, when Irving was its editor, and later republished in *The Sketch Book* in 1820. Irving's express purpose in these essays had been to correct the image of Indigenous people, who he said had been wantonly dispossessed from the early years of colonization, and later grossly misrepresented through "vulgar prejudice and passionate exaggeration." Native Americans, he wrote, "cannot but be sensible that the white men are the usurpers of their ancient dominion, the cause of their degradation, and the gradual destroyers of their race."[137] The gratuitous violence and dishonesty of the first settlers compares most unfavorably to the mature masculinity of King Philip aka Metacom, who is portrayed as one of a "band of native untaught heroes; who made the most generous struggle of which human nature is capable; fighting to the last gasp in the cause of their country, without a hope of victory or a thought of renown [...] a patriot attached to his native soil."[138]

Irving's revisionist strategy in the Indian sketches is two-fold. First, he emphasizes that to call Indigenous people "savages" should not be taken to mean that they were devoid or incapable of civilization. On the contrary, Native Americans were "formed for the wilderness" as the Arabs were "formed for the desert."[139] What he admires in Native Americans he would come to admire in the Moors of Spain—their attachment to community and nation, as well as to family, tribe, and the land. And there was Irving's yearned-for true masculinity, fearlessness and decision: "No hero of ancient or modern days can surpass the Indian in his lofty contempt of death, and the fortitude with which he sustains its cruelest infliction. Indeed we here behold him superior to the white man, in consequence of his peculiar education."[140] If Native Americans, Native American males, that is, are held up as archetypes of achieved manhood, white civilization, by implication, is condemned for its cruelty and injustice, which are but manifestations of immature masculinity, dysfunctional shadows. By analogy, if Native Americans were "uncivilized," they were so only because their values, customs, and institutions differed from those of Europeans.[141] Second, Irving claims that the deplorable condition of present-day Indigenous people—"drunken, indolent, feeble, thievish, and pusillanimous"[142]—was by no means their "natural" state but rather the result of cultural discontinuity and dispossession at the hands of European imperialists, which reduced them to "mere wrecks and remnants of once powerful tribes." Worse, the Eastern tribes had already disappeared, and the same fate awaited the tribes and nations that skirted the frontier as well as those lingering in areas that were still unexplored. They all, Irving ominously predicts, "will vanish like a vapour from the face of the earth."[143]

What Irving presents in general terms in "Traits of Indian Character," he dramatizes in "Philip of Pokanoket," the result of his reading the racialized accounts of seventeenth-century historians. Their writings, Irving saw, merely demonstrated the extent to which "the footsteps of civilization may be traced in the blood of the aborigines."[144] As in the earlier sketch, Irving traces the causes of King Philip's War of 1675 to the early colonists' disregard of and contempt for the Native Americans' cultural heritage. It was the "diseased state of the public mind," not the bloody deeds of Native

American warriors, that resulted in a policy that aimed at forcing the Indigenous population into submission, "dependent and despised in the ease and luxury of the settlements."[145] Altogether, Philip's story provides an historical basis for Irving's prediction that American society would destroy the Indigenous population, seeing the natives merely as the people in the way, for that was precisely what they were for many white people.

In the original version of "Traits of Indian Character" Irving also observed that the "popular feeling [against the Indigenous population] is gradually hardened by war." Thus, he felt compelled to "speak in behalf of a race of beings, whose very existence has been pronounced detrimental to public security."[146] The "war" was the War of 1812, which wreaked slaughter on a number of tribes as a result of their involvement. As to "detrimental to public security," the phrase is an oblique reference to Jackson's early Indian policy, most notably his brutal handling of the Native American uprising in Florida, which provides a kind of frame. "Traits of Indian Character" thus was most topical in 1814, and the three or so pages of criticism of the behavior of the U.S. military in the Creek War then were entirely appropriate. By 1820, with publication of the *Sketch Book* pending, the criticism was no longer topical.[147] Irving deleted the passage, making the tone uniformly nostalgic to fit in with the other sketches.[148] This is obvious also from the order in which the sketches are arranged. The two Indian sketches are placed between "Stratford-upon-Avon" and "John Bull," which seems strategic: The *Sketch Book* was to please American readers fond of "olde England" as well as English readers interested in things exotic. Surely English readers wept over Irving's pessimistic remark that Indigenous people "will vanish like a vapour from the face of the earth." At least some readers—English and American alike—might have sympathized with King Philip and his "band of native untaught heroes."[149]

"Untaught" King Philip and his followers may have been, and thus seemingly lacking anything English settlers at the time identified as civilized—Christianity, agriculture, cities, letters, clothing, and sophisticated weaponry. Yet in calling Philip a "patriot," Irving again challenges earlier testimonies in which Native Americans personified mere savagery. These were racialized interpretations, an ideology built around the idea that savagery for the Native Americans was inherent. Hence they invariably were seen as "cruel, barbarous and most treacherous" (William Bradford), a "wild and savage people" living "like herds of deer in a forest" (Richard Johnson), "run[ning] over the grass" like the "foxes and wild beasts" (William Wood), and, worst of all, utterly unable "to make use of [...] the Land," without "any settled places, as Towns to dwell in, nor any ground as they challenge for their own possession" (Francis Higginson).[150] To all these accounts, Irving's cultural relativism is in diametrical opposition. But there is more. Philip of Pokanoket is held up as a model of hypermasculinity for his "military genius and daring prowess [and for] displaying a vigorous mind; a fertility in expedients; a contempt of suffering and hardship; and an unconquerable resolution; that command our sympathy and applause."[151] But it is by depicting King Philip as a "patriot" that Irving raises Native Americans to the level of the American revolutionaries who, as patriots, had resisted and eventually separated from the English, thus proving their achieved manhood consistent with classical masculine republicanism.

King Philip or Metacom, to use his Indigenous name, was not only "proud of heart," with a pronounced "love of liberty" and a "haughty spirit." Irving is also intent on "feminizing" him, portraying him as quite capable of "the softer feelings of connubial love and paternal tenderness, and [...] the generous sentiment of friendship."[152] In this way, King Philip is a composite of sorts, a synthesis of masculinity and femininity, animus and anima characteristics. Irving had delineated many of his masculine archetypes in a similarly androgynous fashion, regardless of the ensuing contradictions. In Metacom's "love of liberty," Irving once again recycled the cant of old-school Federalism in order to codify an exclusively male conception of civic virtue. In the chief's "softer feelings," however, Irving validated the very sentimentalization of manhood that classical masculine republicanism negated.[153] The depiction of King Philip and his followers in terms of classical masculine republicanism at least in part was spawned by and pandering to anti–British sentiments fired by the War of 1812.[154] The androgynous synthesis, however, owes much to Irving's inner life of "sensibility"[155] as well as to his respectfulness for America's Indigenous population and his sympathy for their plight. This attitude is consistent with the testimony of other works, including *The Life and Voyages of Columbus*, first published in 1828. Columbus' first impression of the Indigenous population, Irving tells us, was of the natives' sweetness and gentleness. "So loving, so tractable, so peaceable are these people," Irving quotes from the seafarer's journal. "They love their neighbors as themselves, and their discourse is ever sweet and gentle, and accompanied with a smile; and though it is true that they are naked, yet their manners are decorous and praiseworthy."[156]

To return to Irving's western writings. On the prairies, Irving loved riding on horseback; he enjoyed scouting for prairie hens, hunting wolves, and trading with the Osage people. In the evenings he would jot down various stories he had gleaned from the wandering tribes—such as the Delawares' belief that a feather dropped from heaven was a token of satisfaction from their guardian spirit, as well as the Osages' belief that the soul of a deceased person carries with it all bodily tastes and habits. These stories so fascinated Irving that he included them in the printed book.[157] He was likewise fascinated by burial customs. An Osage chief who had died lately was buried in a "mound on a hill surrounded by [...] three poles with flags—trophies—a scalp—scalping knife," he recorded one evening. Another night, he wrote of a little girl buried with her "play things" and "favorite little horse"—just the sort of weepy tale that resonated with the author of the *Sketch Book* and that thus found its way into the printed *Tour on the Prairies*.[158]

Only an anima-consciousness seems capable of such lines, one who despises the "commonplaceness" of the self-made men as well as the "coarseness and vulgarity" of the frontier people. Such a consciousness also is utterly averse to public life. In April 1838 Martin Van Buren, eighth President of the United States, offered Irving a position in his cabinet as Secretary of the Navy. While anyone else would have snapped up this opportunity, Irving declined the appointment. In a letter to the president he wrote, *inter alia*, that he was "too sensitive to endure the bitter personal hostility, and the slanders and misrepresentations of the press, which beset high station in this country." He added that he had to confess to "a weakness of spirit and a want of true philosophy" and would rather remain in the path of his "habits of quiet, and a love of peace of mind."[159] The discrepancy between Irving's purported "female defects" and the role model American society then provided for men to be accepted as men could hardly be greater. By the time Irving wrote to Van Buren, he already had imagined just so many masculine archetypes, Columbus, Mahomet, Boabdil, various Spanish peasants and, not to forget, the splendid warriors on the prairies. But their struggle for dominance had only been an exotic adventure, not a realistic, if displaced, account of what men now had to do to survive and prosper in the real world. As I suggested in Chapter One, the real world was grossly alien to Irving. Irving always retained his feminized masculinity, remaining out of touch with his masculine strength because he was dominated by the anima (or rather, his imperfectly realized masculine ego).

There exist, George Santayana wrote in 1911, men and women "not occupied intensely in practical affairs ... in invention and industry and social organization." The latter is "the sphere of the American man ... all aggressive," the former that of, metaphorically and literally, "the American woman."[160] The two spheres are at odds also in a sketch titled "The Creole Village," which originated from Irving's frontier notebooks, begun in 1833.[161] Traveling by steamboat down the Mississippi, that river of "ancient Louisiana," it occurs to Irving "that many things lost in the old world are treasured up in the new."[162] Reminiscing upon his travels through Europe, Irving muses upon "the little, poverty-stricken villages of Spanish and French origin," whose inhabitants retained "their old habits of passive obedience to the decrees of government [and] dwell in the houses built by their forefathers, without thinking of enlarging or modernizing them." With memories of his European years in his baggage, Irving also finds suitable masculinities, though not in Santayana's mold.[163] One is the "great man, or Grand Signior of the village," who rules, not by law but by "custom and convention," retaining "the true Gallic feature and deportment" to be met with "in the remote parts of France." Another village worthy, "Compere Martin," is singled out because he "could sing, dance, and, above all, play on the fiddle, an invaluable accomplishment in an old French creole village."

Irving was only too happy to find an alternative lifestyle in Jackson's America. Thus, the contrast to the lifestyle of the newcomers, Irving's fellow Americans, with their "eagerness for gain, and rage for improvement," could not be more pronounced.[164] Juxtaposing "modern" versus "traditional," there is no question which side Irving stands on. He glorifies the colonial European communities which seemingly preserve diverse and regional cultures, even though their disappearance seems inevitable. Irving's nostalgia for a past about to be lost brought forth one of the most memorable passages in the sketch: "In a word, *the almighty dollar*, that great object of universal devotion throughout our land, seems to have no genuine devotees in these peculiar villages."[165] As Irving travels on, however, he looks wistfully back upon "the moss-green roofs and ancient elms of the village," full of dire forebodings that the inhabitants' "happy ignorance" will soon be replaced by the "bustling and prosperous existence" of an American town, with its town lots, courthouses, jails, banks, "rival hotels, rival churches, and rival newspapers; together with the usual number of judges and generals and governors; not to speak of doctors by the dozen, and lawyers by the score."

By Irving's standards, judges, generals, and the like are all self-made men, failed and misguided masculinities, mere dysfunctional shadows— like a James Barnard Blake, who wrote in his diary of April 13, 1851, that "it is not in man's nature to be idle, to do nothing at all." Or else, like a New York college student, who wrote to his fiancée in 1844, "It is so unmanly so unnatural to spend a lifetime in the pursuit of nothing."[166] The doleful jeremiad of "The Creole Village" not only exposes the tensions between the prevailing national rhetoric of entrepreneurialism and competition, and the emotional and cultural realities with their profound anxieties. It also is proof that soon after his return home, Irving's "Americanization" began to sour and that the ties with his native country were beginning to weaken. Yet unlike the bellicose Cooper, Irving never publicly denounced the crass materialism, the vulgarity, and the corrupt and divisive politics. He saved his disgust and culture shock for his private letters.

Writing to his niece, Mrs. Thomas Wentworth Storrow in Paris, Irving articulates his dislike of "the all pervading commonplace which is the curse of our country. It is like the sands of the desert [*sic!*], which are continually stealing over the land of Egypt and gradually effacing every trace of grandeur and beauty and swallowing up every green thing."[167] Once again, these are outpourings of an anima-ego, and in their exaggeration typical of expat psychology. It was doubtless in order to escape this "commonplace civilization" full of "vulgarity," that Irving in 1835 bought twenty-four acres on the Hudson River near Tarrytown, New York, and gradually remodeled the small cottage he found there into Sunnyside, a fine house of romantic architecture. Except for a four-year absence while United States Minister to Spain (1842–1846), Irving lived there from 1836 until his death in 1859.

Two years after the purchase of the Tarrytown cottage the nation was hit by an economic panic, brought on by a wave of rampant and uncontrolled speculation. Irving, who already during his time in Paris had remarked that "The world is usurped by the plodder & moneymaker," responded to the panic of 1837 with "'A Time of Unexampled Prosperity.' The Great Mississippi Bubble." The piece was published in *Knickerbocker Magazine* of April 1840 and later reprinted in *The Crayon Papers*.[168] Set in France during John Law's paper money scheme of the 1720s, Irving's moral fable of financial hubris is a wonderful send-up of America's new venture capitalists and their speculative enterprises, his own included. Though he was a self-made man himself, Irving nevertheless had a keen eye for the dangers of an unfettered capitalism.[169] "Promissory notes, interchanged between scheming individuals," Irving wrote, "are liberally discounted at the banks, which became so many mints to coin words into cash; and as the supply of words is inexhaustible, it may readily be supposed what a vast amount of promissory capital is soon in circulation."[170] The historic event ushered in the downfall of the father of modern paper money and in 1727 led to the prohibition of paper money as legal tender by the British government.[171]

In the "prelude" to the sketch, Irving compares what the business world calls "'times of unexampled prosperity'" to the delusive calms before a storm at sea:

> Every now and then the world is visited by one of these delusive seasons, when "the credit system," as it is called, expands to full luxuriance, everybody trusts everybody[....] Now is the time for speculative and dreaming or designing men. [...] Speculation is the romance of trade, and casts contempt upon all its sober realities. [...] Could this delusion last, the life of a merchant would indeed be a golden dream; but it is as short as it is brilliant. Let but a doubt enter, and the "season of unexampled prosperity" is at end. The coinage of words is suddenly curtailed; the promissory capital begins to vanish into smoke; a panic succeeds, and the whole superstructure, built upon credit and reared by speculation, crumbles to the ground, leaving scarce a wreck behind.[172]

Historians generally agree that the panic of 1837 resulted mainly from an overexpansion of business, combined with the extension of loans to

Five. On the Prairies and in the West 165

many persons who could not pay them. In the East, a housing bubble drove up real-estate values by a hundred and fifty percent; in the West, there was over-speculation in public lands, intensified by railroad building. The depression was made worse by the over-issue of worthless bills from commercial banks, which drove up inflation, and, not to forget, by the unfortunate policies of the nation's chief executives—Jackson's war on the Second Bank of the United States, which triggered the rapid proliferation of commercial banks that began issuing increasingly worthless notes; Van Buren's inability to cope with the depression; and John Tyler's vetoes of congressional bills that called for the re-establishment of a national bank of issue.[173]

When Van Buren became president, the dire consequences of Jackson's financial policies hit the country with full force. In March, stock prices on Wall Street fell across the board. By May, there had been about a hundred bank failures in New York alone, causing a loss of about $15 million. By the end of the year, across the nation over six hundred banks had closed their doors forever. With no credit available, new businesses could not be created, bankruptcies were recorded by the tens of thousands, and business losses—compounded by Britain's stoppage to cotton imports—were registered at $741 million (about $10 billion today). Almost ninety percent of the factories in the East shut down, resulting in mass unemployment. Cargo ships were idled, almshouses were filled beyond capacity as the prices for bread, meat, fuel, and rents skyrocketed, and countless families went hungry and froze in the winter of 1837–1838. In New York's Chatham Square riots erupted as the swelling ranks of the city's poor broke into a warehouse storing flour. The crisis also affected Washington Irving, whose family suffered considerably from Van Buren's disastrous presidency. It also must have brought back memories of 1819, the year when the Irving clan was hit by another financial crisis—and the year the word "panic" as it pertained to money and finance entered the language.[174]

Irving's western writings brought a world of ambition and freewheeling enterprise into parlors back east, not just as an exotic adventure but as a realistic, if displaced account of what constituted a "Jacksonian religion" that could be felt "more starkly on the frontier than anywhere else."[175] Irving himself would have none of such grossness. He would rather have joined in former Yale president Timothy Dwight's regret that as the pioneer pushed further and further into the wilderness, he became "less and less a civilized man." Or, he would have sympathized with Crèvecoeur's lament that on the frontier, men "degenerated altogether into the hunting state" and became, ultimately, "no better than carnivorous animals of a superior rank."[176] Irving certainly had hoped he could find pure masculinity in the hardy trappers and fur traders of the West, as well as in Indigenous warriors, yet unlike later writers, he never believed in regeneration through violence, neither to animals, nor to other people, nor to himself. In contrast, Francis Parkman, Jr., in *The Oregon Trail* (1847) as well as in his later *Discovery of the Great West* (1870), created narratives of just such "masculine salvation."[177]

Irving also had felt the years in Europe had not brought him the masculine perfection he had set out to find. Out west, he therefore tried to showcase his manhood as a buffalo hunter, but there's no feeling of triumph. On the contrary, the episode ends in a forceful reappearance of the anima-ego. Chasing buffalo on horseback, he repeatedly fails to get a good shot on target (at one point his pistols miss fire), until finally, borrowing a gun, he brings a buffalo down. But once the excitement is over, Irving contends with his conscience. "I could not but look with commiseration upon the poor animal that lay struggling and bleeding at my feet. His very size and importance, which had before inspired me with eagerness, now increased my compunction." A pistol shot finally puts the animal out of its misery. For Irving's anima-ego, "to inflict a wound thus in cold blood [proved] a totally different thing from firing in the heat of the chase." At the end of the episode, we find him "meditating and moralizing over the wreck I had so wantonly produced."[178] The buffalo's tongue, which an aide carves out for him, must have felt a bitter trophy to bear back to camp. One is left to wonder if rhetoric of this kind provoked Ralph Waldo Emerson to remark, in his journal of September 28, 1836, that Irving's writings were "all feminine."[179]

Altogether in his western writings, Irving displayed a profound ambivalence about the course of American history and the constituent elements of an American identity, his own included. Of one thing he seemed sure, though—his fellow Americans of the frontier were unsuitable as archetypes of achieved masculinity. Irving already had scoured the pasts of England and Spain, reinventing a form of aristocratic patriarchy, so now it was time for him to again look towards the past, and likewise from an aristocratic point of view. He would, finally, set his sights on George Washington. Through relocating English and Spanish patriarchy to an American setting, Irving set the stage for an authentic American national culture to emerge from the authentic American myth he created. With *Life of George Washington*, the result of "a liberal infusion of *stronger* material," Irving could convince himself that America had sounder roots, not just the "commonplaceness" of the self-made men or the "coarseness and vulgarity" of the frontier people, and he was bent on recovering these roots for the benefit of his fellow Americans as well as himself. Irving's "Washington," Stanley Williams found, was intended to "glitter," like its creator, on the "dull soil" of America.[180]

Six

Life of George Washington
Manly Perfection in the Father of His Country

IRVING'S *LIFE OF GEORGE WASHINGTON* was published in five volumes between 1856 and 1859. The product of his final years, it remains his most personal work, a "cherished purpose of his heart" and a labor of love.¹ It shows the depth to which Irving was able to reach into the archetypal structures of the unconscious which, by definition, are unrepresentable in and of themselves. In its appearance, *Washington* is a drama of the present, not of a remote past. Politically, it speaks to the nostalgia of old-school Federalism. George Washington, much more so than other pets of Irving's creative imagination—the country squires, adventurers, and other heroes of lost causes—upholds the old Federalist hope of civilized urbanity and "statesmanship of the highest order" in the midst of democratic leveling and vulgarity.² From the way Irving marvels at Washington's hypermasculine attributes, I will demonstrate in this chapter, we sense that he has finally found the part of himself he had been seeking. The product of an elaborate amplification of the archetypes, America's first president stands out as a benefactor, a father who benevolently rules over his family, both of kin and of nation. Morally self-sufficient, this "George Washington" not only compensates for Irving's own imperfectly realized masculinity; he also is offered to readers as an exemplar, a man whose authority is that of character rather than of position. At the same time, Washington represents the patriotic iconography of generations of symbolically fatherless sons, the generations of American men born after the Revolution. From the undisguised valuation of a vanished culture emerges a pattern of dutiful masculinity that could hardly be more different from the ideology of the self-made man prevalent in Irving's own days. In this very regard, the larger-than-life image of the man who "has attended" Irving "through life," also speaks to the crisis of masculinity that can be traced principally to the growing power of entrepreneurial capitalism.³

"[A]ny intensified ideology of manhood," David Leverenz contends, "is a compensatory response to fears of humiliation." Thus, "manhood becomes a way not of dominating, but of minimizing maximum loss."[4] In the following, I'll extend Leverenz's insight to show how *Life of George Washington* is one of the key sites within which compensation is offered to men who, threatened by social anarchy, no longer had a secure sense of themselves as men. By the time of Irving's *Life*, the firmness of patriarchal lineage had dissolved; in the newly formed world without birthrights, no one knew their place. Yet Irving came to George Washington only via a detour that took him back to good old England and his own feminized male ego. In 1840, Harper of New York published *Life of Oliver Goldsmith*, followed by another edition in 1847. A revised and enlarged edition came out in 1849, this time published by Putnam as part of the Author's Revised Edition of Irving's works. In the Preface to that edition, now titled *Oliver Goldsmith: A Biography*, Irving describes the book as a "labor of love [...] a tribute of gratitude to the memory of an author whose writings were the delight of my childhood, and have been a source of enjoyment to me throughout life."[5] "[L]abor of love" seems a bit disingenuous, as Irving had taken on the biography primarily to pay his mounting bills. He didn't need to start writing from scratch, though, but could draw on an essay he had worked on from late December of 1823 until June 1824, then a welcome break from the tedium and hassle of finishing *Tales of a Traveller*.[6]

Oliver Goldsmith is not a life and times biography but quite a conventional one, with its focus almost exclusively on the private affairs of its subject. The book met with almost universal applause. As the reviewer for *Graham's Magazine* wrote in November 1849, Irving's intention had been to convey "to the reader a living expression of Goldsmith's character and life; and of depositing his image softly in the mind."[7] One English reviewer praised "the ease and gracefulness with which the narrative is composed."[8] Most telling, however, is the kudos in the *Christian Review*, with its focus on the qualities of the book's author: "None but a man of genial nature should ever attempt to write the Life of Goldsmith: one who knows how much wisdom can be extracted from folly; how much better for the heart it is to trust than to doubt; how much nobler is a generous impulse than a cautious reserve; how much truer a wisdom there is in benevolence, than in all the shrewd devices of worldly craft."[9] What the reviewer is saying here is that, paraphrasing Jung's disciple James Hillman, *Oliver Goldsmith* testifies to Irving's special way of being in the world and giving back soul to the world, in short, to his anima consciousness.[10] Irving deeply admired Goldsmith, he repeatedly acknowledged him as his favorite writer, and he claimed to have adopted Goldsmith's mild irony for himself.[11] Indeed, in no other work did Irving inject so much of himself, his "feminine" literary personality as it were, as if the innermost selves of both men were woven into the biography. Goldsmith's writings, we learn from the first chapter, "mingle with our minds, sweeten our tempers, and harmonize our thoughts; they put us in good humor with ourselves and with the world, and in so doing they make us happier and better men."[12]

Reading Goldsmith, Irving wrote in the 1825 essay, "we think of him in every page; we grow intimate with him as a man, and learn to love him as we read."[13] Irving adopted the passage almost verbatim for the 1849 edition of the full biography, together with other characterizations, such as "artless benevolence," "amiable views of human life and human nature," "good feeling," but also "pleasing melancholy."[14] The biography, John McWilliams suggested, "casts Goldsmith very much in Geoffrey Crayon's image."[15] If Crayon, the man of feeling, was Irving's alter ego, it is no surprise that there are unmistakable parallels between Irving's animatic character and that of his Goldsmith. Goldsmith is completely averse to serious study; he is equally whimsical, unsuited to any "regular pursuit," utterly heedless in "pecuniary matters," peevish and petulant, especially when travelling, and overly sensitive to criticism. At the same time, he has "that bonhommie which won the hearts of all who knew him." Irving, it seems, loved Goldsmith as a brother, though he is also aware of the differences between them, one of which he singles out: Goldsmith, Irving writes, grew up under the "gentle, benevolent ... spirit of his father [which] walked with him through life."[16] What a contrast to Irving's own father, the stern, Presbyterian deacon, who, had he prevailed in shaping the boy's male gender identity, would have left us with a Washington Irving whose human feelings of vulnerability had been suppressed and whose emotional connection and gentleness had been denied!

Irving's *Goldsmith* became tremendously successful. Already the 1840 edition, which Harper published as part of their Family Library, sold well, though Putnam's 1849 edition did even better. It was followed by any number of new editions and was constantly republished. There also was an English edition, as well as translations into German, French, and, incredibly, Welsh.[17] And yet, Irving himself was not entirely happy with the biography, complaining that he had had no time to finish it off as he wished.[18] The year 1849 no doubt had been stressful. Irving was revising his works for the Putnam edition, he was working on *Mahomet*, he was busy organizing Astor's estate and library, and he was haunted by the life of George Washington, his pet project for many years. There may have been something else, though. Irving's Goldsmith certainly answered to the sentimental and evangelical expectations of the time. Yet as charming and delightful as this Goldsmith is, he had been preceded by Columbus, Mahomet, and other masculine archetypes, and was to be followed by George Washington. Possibly, therefore, Irving's dissatisfaction stemmed from the dearth of masculine features in his subject. Was Goldsmith, then, the anima-ego's last sigh? I do not pretend to definitively answer this question here. Clearly, Irving's imagination was not always "active" in the way C.G. Jung spelled it out.[19] As Irving told Theodore Tilton, an editor of the *New York Independent*, following the publication of the last volume of *Life of George Washington*, "An author's right time to work is when his mind is aglow—when his imagination is kindled. These are his precious moments. Let him wait until they come; but, when they have come, let him make the most of them."[20]

There are, surprisingly perhaps, certain parallels between *Life of Oliver Goldsmith* and *Life of George Washington*. An observation by Irving's nephew, that the "character of Washington grew upon [Irving] constantly,"[21] as easily applies to Goldsmith. The most obvious parallel, however, is the genesis of these two works. If *Goldsmith* goes back a long way, Irving also had planned to write a Washington biography for many years. Offers to write one were made in the 1820s. They prompted him to collect materials, and by 1829 he had definite plans for the work that would be his "crowning labor," about the man for whom he was named.[22] Even so, the first volume of *Washington* did not appear until 1855, the fifth and last only in 1859, the year of Irving's death. As Sue Fields Ross, the editor of the *Journals and Notebooks* volumes of Irving's *Complete Works*, noted, "From letters, journal entries, and biographical data, we may infer that Washington Irving's most intense periods of work [on *Life of George Washington*] were in 1825 (when in eighteen May entries in his journal, he mentioned reading John Marshall's biography), 1828, late 1829, 1841, 1843, 1847, 1849, and practically 1851 until the end of his life."[23]

Are we surprised that Irving throughout his life felt under obligation to pay homage to his namesake? As he told Charles Lanman in 1857, he "loved the subject" and thought first of writing a biography "twenty years ago." This would have set the beginning of the project at about 1837, around the time George Bancroft published his *History of the United States*. Irving also told Lanman that he "had the work all written, in chapters, to the inauguration of Washington as President," some ten years ago, that is, in or about 1847. If he had, he did not like it and had been tempted to put it into the fire. Really, Irving continued, he ought to have "commenced it forty years ago."[24] This takes us back to 1817, when John Marshall's tomes commanded the image the American public formed of the nation's first president. There is, indeed, a significant entry, perhaps the earliest reference to Irving's serious interest in Washington, in the journal he kept in England in 1818: "We cannot vie with aristocratic Europe we ought not to want it. Away then with false parade—false taste and to be [*half line erased*] about the—Washington—his character a natural property—his example as valuable as

Six. Life of George Washington

his services [*five lines erased and illegible*]."25 Additionally, some pages on, we find an isolated entry, "Character of Washington."26

Three years later, in the "Haddon Hall Notebook" of 1821 (composed mostly from excursions to Birmingham and into Derbyshire with his painter friend Charles R. Leslie in September 1821), Irving copied from a collection of anecdotes he had found in London's *Monthly Magazine*: "Col. Wakefield says that the Washington family emigrated from Thorn, in the neighbourhood of Doncaster—Yorkshire & I understand that traces of them are preserved in the churchyd. in ye monumental form."27 July 1825 finds Irving in Paris. *Tales of a Traveller* had just been published and Irving was deep into Marshall's five-volume *The Life of Washington*, when Archibald Constable, an Edinburgh publisher he had met in September 1817, making some arrangements in respect to books, directly approached him about a Washington biography.28 Irving instantly made some notes, yet he declined the offer, concluding, "I feel myself incapable of executing my idea of the task. It is one that I dare not attempt lightly. *I stand in too great awe of it.*"29 The letter *from* Constable "has not been located," though the request from this publisher "probably provided the initial impetus" for Irving's later biography.30 Additional impetus came from Irving's reading of Marshall's *Life*, which was based on records and papers provided to him by the late president's family. Reading five volumes of Marshall's biography of Irving's boyhood hero was not an easy feat and must have been even more unpalatable since the tomes, which were published within eight years after Washington's death in 1799, were hastily written and noticeably dull. They certainly did little or nothing to relieve Irving from feeling depressed and downhearted after the hostile reception of *Tales of a Traveller*.31

The idea of a book on Washington was with Irving again in Spain. At work on his biography of Columbus, in 1826, Irving was shown letters of Washington and, again, takes up Marshall's *Life*.32 Three years later, Irving attended a dinner "in memory of Gen[eral] Washington."33 The year before had seen the publication of *The Life and Voyages of Columbus*. Irving continued studying Spanish history and legend, working on *Chronicle of the Conquest of Granada, Companions of Columbus, Legends of the Conquest of Spain, The Alhambra,* and *Mahomet*. It was not until the fall of 1841 that Irving gathered material and began to work with determination on a life of George Washington. By that time, his political leanings had taken a decisive turn. Irving had been on good terms with Andrew Jackson. He had stood outside of the United States at Jackson's victory in the campaign of 1828; he had been ignorant of the mob scene at the White House on inauguration day, and of the scandals of the first term. Irving, it seems, took to Jackson not because of Jacksonian politics so much as because of some form of masculine attachment. Jackson in the 1820s was the paradigm of rugged individualism, the prototype of the American male.³⁴ Irving too was convinced that "the old general [...] has good stuff in him," he professed to admire Jackson's "*hickory* characteristics," and he was quite prepared to grant him "some degree of *rough chivalry*."³⁵

Irving had been on good terms also with Martin Van Buren, who, as Jackson's Secretary of State, appointed him Secretary of Legation to London in 1829. There was much personal regard and sympathy, though as of 1838, political differences grew, not least over Nullification and Van Buren's independent treasury scheme.³⁶ Moreover, Van Buren's disastrous presidency hurt the entire Irving clan. Thus, when in 1840 Van Buren failed to respond to Irving's letter in which he attempted to have his brother Ebenezer appointed to the new subtreasury in New York, Irving, always the political chameleon, at once supported the Whig slate of William Henry Harrison and John Tyler in the presidential election. Upon the suggestion of Daniel Webster, John Tyler, Harrison's successor after a month as president, suggested Irving to the Senate as United States Minister to Spain. The nomination sailed through on February 10, 1842.³⁷ Although Irving's personal sympathy for and friendship with Van Buren eventually was restored,³⁸ his *Life of George Washington* was to have a Federalist-Whig bias, as if to remind his fellow Americans of their debt to a dignified Federalism.

Collecting material on Washington continued through the spring of 1842, when William Hickling Prescott apparently furnished material (or at least much advice for Irving's incipient life).³⁹ In return, Prescott had Irving's promise for doing research in Madrid on behalf of his projected history of the conquest of Mexico—a project that Irving had started on but had renounced to Prescott in 1838.⁴⁰ In April 1842 Irving left for England and, eventually, for Spain. The appointment to the ambassadorship was prestigious, but it meant one more interruption to the work on George Washington. Irving took his notes with him but, Stanley Williams remarks, "his literary passion had atrophied." On occasion, he revised fussily his notes, but he wrote under difficulty, and only when tormented by the specter of poverty. Faced with heavy losses through his investment in Astor's land, he decided, in 1845, "to write on until the pen drops from my hand."⁴¹

While the decision seemingly supports Stanley Williams's conviction that Irving's career as a writer was little more than that of a mere "prospector on the trail of literary gold,"⁴² we should not forget that Irving's literary personality was decidedly "feminine." Thus, to "write on" also meant to continue the quest for his own imperfectly realized masculinity. Irving returned to America in December 1846, having resigned from his appointment in Spain. With encouragement from George Putnam, in September 1847 he began to work on Washington with renewed energy. "If I can only live to finish it," he wrote to Pierre Munro Irving, "I would be willing to die the next moment. [...] If I had only ten more years of life!"[43] Irving worked assiduously throughout 1848, mostly in New York, where he had moved in December 1847. Once again, other projects intervened, including the revised edition of his works, another edition of *Goldsmith*, a Knickerbocker miscellany, and the second volume of *Mahomet and His Successors*. While Stanley Williams dismisses all of these writings as a mere "concession to the practical purposes of the hack writer," for Irving, in search of a vital part of himself, it was hard work. "Altogether," he wrote to Sarah Storrow, "I have had more toil of head and fagging of the pen for the last eighteen months, than in any other period of my life."[44]

In 1851, Irving was seriously at work again, using "25 years of notes and Jared Sparks's earlier 12-volume edition of Washington's writings."[45] He also followed, wittingly or unwittingly, Sparks's definition of a "historical biography" as one that "admits of copious selections from letters and other original papers."[46] Even so, "Irving's heavier debt was not to Jared, but to George, whom he often let speak for himself."[47] When Irving could, he simply bypassed Sparks to return to originals, for example documents that turned up in Washington, DC, on his research trips. In early 1853, for instance, we find him doing research in various archives and on a visit to Mount Vernon, then still in the family possession. Irving wrote back to his nieces at Sunnyside from the nation's capital on February 6, 1853: "I cannot say that I find much that is new among the manuscripts of Washington, [Jared] Sparks having published the most interesting; but it is important to get facts from the fountain head, not at second hand through his publications."[48] By letting Washington speak for himself, Irving created what he called the biography's "flexible texture of narrative," with Washington as the "principal actor" in the "great drama" of American nationhood.[49] In the end, the two, actor and drama, become indistinguishable as Washington permitted Irving, not only the commemoration and celebration of significant masculine achievement but also vicarious participation in "that manliness and independence of character which it has ever been [his] ambition to acquire."[50]

In March of 1853 Irving had Pierre Munro Irving read the *Washington* manuscript, and the ailing, distracted author was greatly heartened when the nephew praised it. Work continued, and Irving traveled to Virginia to read some Washington manuscripts and to examine some sites. He also checked the Philip Schuyler papers, still in family hands, and the Horatio Gates papers at the New-York Historical Society, then on Washington Square.[51] In February 1855, Putnam published *Wolfert's Roost*, a miscellany from the *Knickerbocker* magazine, which was well received by the reading public. In May of the same year, the first volume of *Life of George Washington* was published, also by Putnam. Just before its publication, Irving had been in bed for a few days after being thrown off his horse "Gentleman Dick."⁵² When the second volume of the *Life* followed in December, readers got to know George Washington as a "gentleman."

Following the publication of the second volume, Irving hired Pierre Munro as his literary assistant, to compile material and draft preliminary chapters for subsequent volumes (he formally authorized the nephew's salary of $135 a month in February 1856).⁵³ Irving, who was often ill and seldom left Sunnyside, his "empire," as he proudly called it, continued work on *Life of George Washington* with his nephew's help.⁵⁴ The third volume was published in July 1856, and the fourth in May 1857. By that time, yet another financial panic had hit the nation, and Irving, now comfortable financially, bought the plates for the entire edition from Putnam, who needed cash because of the national economic crisis. There was only one more volume to go now, but Irving worked on it only intermittently, as his health deteriorated. He felt greatly relieved when his nephew and his wife, Helen, moved to Sunnyside to stay. Irving finished the fifth and final volume of *Washington* on March 15, 1859. "Ah," he cried after the last chapter was finished, "I have got to the dregs and must take them." He was done. His nephew made some final revisions and saw the book through the press. Putnam published it in April. In November, Irving admitted, in an interview with journalist Theodore Tilton, to a "great fatigue of mind, throughout the whole task, [which] had resulted from the care and pains required in the construction and arrangement of materials, and not in the mere literary composition of the successive chapters."⁵⁵ Death came to Washington Irving on November 28, 1859.

I have not yet addressed the question what drove Irving to give himself, late in his life, so wholeheartedly to the life of George Washington. He already was a very tired man, confessing, over and over again, that all writing was bothersome. "Nothing but sheer necessity," he confided to Sarah Storrow, "will ever drive me again to full literary application."⁵⁶ This was before the revised edition of his works, another edition of *Life of Oliver Goldsmith*, a Knickerbocker miscellany, and the second volume of *Mahomet and His Successors* relieved him of financial worries. And with all these writings behind him, his reputation also was secure, much as his financial worries had dissolved. What, then, brought him back to produce his longest book ever? Was it vanity, the realization how impressive a full-length portrait of his hero might be as a conclusion to his career? Stanley Williams thinks so, and he tirelessly tears to shreds *Life of George Washington* as built entirely "with borrowed bricks," only "adorning it [...] with incident and anecdote drawn from out-of-the-way places."⁵⁷ This most cruel verdict will not be allowed to stand as is.

By the time Irving finished *Life of George Washington*, any number of

Washington biographies had been published. Between 1800 and 1860 alone, at least four hundred books, essays, short sketches, and character studies appeared; some, including John Bell's of 1775 and James Hardie's of 1795, were published already during Washington's lifetime.[58] All these efforts contributed to consolidating Washington's god-like status, though none as fully as Mason Locke Weems's. Begun before Washington's death and published as a 90-page pamphlet in 1800, Weems's biography became the most widely circulated life of Washington through the Civil War. His argument that Washington's status was due to "his Great Virtues" tapped into the sentimental and evangelical mentality of the time. Schoolbook writers repeated and disseminated the "Parson's" anecdotes, however apocryphal (the cherry-tree story was added only in 1806), far beyond their original publication.[59] In contrast, Marshall's reverential *Life of Washington* was not well received. Historians often praised its accuracy and well-reasoned judgments, while also noting his frequent paraphrases of published sources such as William Gordon's 1801 history of the Revolution or the British *Annual Register*. Marshall's Federalist bias also was not always appreciated, nor was his heavy style. What likewise spoke against Marshall was that the biography had too much of background and of the facts of Washington's public career and achievements, while it was almost completely silent on personal traits and circumstances, including his marriage to Martha Washington. As John Adams quipped, Marshall's *Life* "is a Mausoleum, 100 feet square at the base, and 200 feet high."[60]

Biographies published in the centennial year, 1832, with a belated one by Jared Sparks in 1839, offered more details of Washington's private character, though they retained the tendency, characteristic of earlier biographies, to keep Washington at arm's length. The idea seemed to have been that to place Washington in a more prosaic or pedestrian story might deflate the flawless hero or cut him down to size. Sparks's *Life*, which essentially was the same work as the first volume of *The Writings of George Washington* (1834), created a Washington that is as perfect as could be, blending the Jovian Washington of neoclassicism with Weems's priggishness, and continuing the theme of the persecution of the saint that had been popularized by Marshall. Today, Sparks's work is remembered for the author's tampering with Washington's language, cavalierly omitting passages, and adding some of his own.[61]

In contrast to his predecessors, Irving worked hard to present a living man rather than a marble statue, using simple language and avoiding any pompousness and grandiose style. And in contrast to the "Life and Letters" biographies, so popular in the nineteenth century, *Life of George Washington* is a thoroughgoing narrative history. Still, it is a matter of debate whether Irving was successful in this, in particular since he—like his predecessors—fabricated speeches, conversations, and thoughts that he either had no way of knowing about or were based on dubious childhood memories. Moreover, Irving could not rid himself of his dream of achieved manhood, which brought him partially beyond his class to search for a more forceful elite. And, like Sparks and other predecessors, Irving was writing what Bernard Bailyn has called "heroic history," which commemorates and celebrates significant masculine achievements.[62] Characteristically, Irving's Washington appears hypermasculine already as a youth, when he undertook "rugged and toilsome expeditions in the mountains among rude scenes and rough people," expeditions that "inured him to hardships and made him apt at expedients."[63] Hardships and expedients for instance came when Virginia Governor Robert Dinwiddie was looking for a suitable man to lead an expedition against the French and their Native American allies in the Ohio country. Such a man, we are told, required "physical strength and moral energy," together with "courage" and "sagacity."[64]

All these manly virtues flowed into what Max Weber—inspired by Theodore Roosevelt's boisterous campaigning style, which he observed traveling in the United States in the election year of 1904—termed "charismatic authority." Weber applied the—originally religious—concept of charisma to "a certain quality of an individual personality, by virtue of which he is set apart from ordinary men." The manifestation of a charismatic leader's exceptional personal qualities or the demonstration of extraordinary insights and accomplishments inspire loyalty and obedience from followers. In contrast to the current popular use of the term charismatic leader (and, as well, Irving's understanding of it), Weber defined charismatic authority not so much in terms of character traits as in terms of a relationship between leader and followers. The validity of charisma thus is founded on its "recognition" by the leader's followers (or "adepts"—what Weber called "*Anhänger*").[65]

Washington's charisma served him well during the Revolutionary War. The commander in chief, Irving writes, "remained firm and undaunted" even after the disastrous loss of New York and the forced retreat across the Delaware in December 1776.[66] Depictions of the "heroic" reach a crescendo towards the end of the final volume. Washington, Irving writes, possessed "fewer inequalities and a rarer union of virtues than perhaps ever fell to the lot of one man. Prudence, firmness, sagacity, moderation, and overruling judgment, an immovable justice, courage that never faltered, patience that never wearied, truth that disdained all artifice, magnanimity without alloy."[67] "Heroic history," needless to say, has been disparaged by modern critics such as William Hedges, who complains that what we look for in vain in Irving's *Washington* is "penetrating interpretation," for instance of decisive battles or other momentous events. "Character," that is, achieved manhood, makes interpretation as superfluous here as in Irving's *Columbus* or any other of his bio-histories.[68]

Life of George Washington was the first biography to include a chapter on the Washington family in England. The Washingtons are "of ancient English stock," the book begins, "the genealogy of which has been traced up to the century immediately succeeding the Conquest."[69] Irving also included in his biography a chapter on the "aristocratical days of Virginia," some fifteen pages in length, in which he raves about the "*beau ideal*" of Washington's existence.[70] When Irving wrote this, the squirearchy of Washington's time was as remote from many Americans in the 1850s as it is today. It did persist in the South, though, in somewhat attenuated form, until the Civil War when it, too, expired, resurrected off and on in fiction and film. Though Irving also injected a goodly dose of republicanism into the Virginia gentleman, the British tradition is unmistakably there.[71] This must have been difficult to swallow for Americans holding fast to Adamic myths. But Irving insisted that only if one accepted Washington's Englishness can he truly fulfill his role as one of the giants upon whose shoulders the founder's children and grandchildren stand. Irving also had to be mindful of the growing sectionalism in his country, and thus was extremely careful to create a Washington that would offend neither Northern nor Southern sentiments. Although he never mentions the word "sectionalism," he made sure to include, in his text, "every letter, every conversation of Washington's that reprobated sectional antagonism."[72] In this way, Irving left an eighteenth-century story to speak for itself to the onrushing nineteenth century. So strong was Irving's desire for a picture of developing national unity that he even pocketed the animus he once displayed toward Yankees, from *The History of New York* to the likes of Ichabod Crane and Tom Walker.[73]

Altogether, Irving's *Life of George Washington* weaves together romance and anecdote to accentuate a national tradition. It is the story of "divers rugged individuals" finding ways to put selfish interests behind them and to commit themselves to an impersonal common cause. In this story, Irving emphasizes, it was not the "self-made man" but an idea that constituted a higher case—"hardwon union, in war and peace, not sorry division, union—and therefore strength."[74] A good example of the importance Irving saw in "hardwon union" is the triumphal march of the victorious General and his troops into New York City on November 25, 1783, on the heels of Guy Carleton's British troops. In this highly effective scene, the British troops are depicted as all "show," whereas the American troops had "done and suffered for us," that is, for *all* Americans. They are, therefore, "*our* troops." Mere appearance is juxtaposed to true, authentic being. The "weather beaten and forlorn" look of the American troops speaks of true manhood, ready for sacrifice, serving the public good, the common weal or cause.[75] This is brought into sharper focus through perspective, which is that of a woman.[76] As for Washington, he remains the true gentleman in the British tradition, thus offering a common heritage to both sides. Nor would any side have objected to seeing Washington as a Cincinnatus who, "gladly, when he had won the cause, hung up his sword never again to take it down."[77]

Building his argument carefully, Irving writes that George Washington was "like a parent" to his adopted children, while in a later volume he emphasizes the "paternal spirit with which [Washington] watched over the army."[78] Volume three has Irving comment on the dissensions and feuds in the early Congress, which he deplores as "the dawning of sectional spirit."[79] Then in the final volume, published only two years before the beginning of the Civil War, Irving writes that the Father of His Country "knew no divided fidelity, no separate obligation; his most sacred duty to himself was his highest duty to his country and his God."[80] *Life of George Washington* could not have been timelier. In the 1850s, regional tensions were heating up fast. Especially the slavery crises (the Fugitive Slave Act had been passed in 1850, establishing a shaky compromise) stirred up any amount of distrust, invective, and sheer hatred in political debates as well as in the public at large.

Literary historian Andrew Delbanco recently showed how the basic values of civility, a decent respect for the humanity of one's political opponents, and a willingness to accept policy defeat collapsed towards the end of the decade, precipitating the nation's descent into Civil War.[81] In this regard, *Life of George Washington* provided a counternarrative to the nastiness Irving observed around him. Drawing on the remarks made by the Marquis de Chastellux following a visit, in late November 1780, to the Continental Army's camp at Morristown, Irving characterizes Washington in the following terms: "Brave without temerity; *laborious without ambition*; generous without prodigality; noble without pride; virtuous without severity; he seems always to stop short of that limit where the virtues, assuming colors more vivid but more changeable and dubious, might be taken for defects."[82] Characterizations like this constitute Irving's *Washington* as a monument to the honor of the victorious general who was to become the nation's first President.

The characterization of Washington as a man "laborious without ambition" warrants closer scrutiny. For the founders, ambition had not exclusively been a pejorative term, suggesting neither personal gain nor an unbridled lust for power, from Cato and Brutus through Machiavelli and Montaigne. Men like Washington understood their ambition—which at first was an ambition for land, to be followed by ambition for political independence—as a decent and civilizing virtue; at the same time, they wanted to acknowledge the desire for greatness connected with an undertaking that, later, became graced by God's approval—enshrined in the motto *annuit coeptis*.[83] As for personal ambitions, Irving quotes from a letter Washington wrote to his brother John Augustine in June 1775, in which the newly-appointed commander in chief of the Continental Army declares that the command was an honor he had "neither sought after, nor desired."[84]

If George Washington was ambitious, he had worked on harnessing his ambitions from early on. The best example no doubt is the "code of morals and manners" he compiled for himself in 1747 from a guidebook titled "Rules of Civility & Decent Behaviour in Company and Conversation." The book served the young man to subject himself to a rigid regime of propriety and self-control.[85] It was followed by *A Course of Gallantries*, a translation of a French book of manners Washington acquired in 1785, together with a copy of Chesterfield's *Letters to His Son*, which was immensely popular at the time. By the time Irving was at work on his biography, however, ambition in America no longer was offset by attempts at self-mastery. Instead, it had become central to a middle-class ideology of ruthlessly competing individuals. When Irving presents Washington as a man "laborious without ambition," therefore, he uses "ambition" in the sense the word had acquired by mid-century, that is, together with its acquired toxins.[86]

Emphasis on character must have been essential, given Irving's peculiar approach to Washington's Virginia, read Southern, heritage. Insistence on manners or, rather, gentlemanly deportment, an acute attention to social rank and to one's own place within that ranking, speak to the ethical and behavioral concerns of an honor-based culture. In this culture, one's personal identity was inseparable from one's public reputation.[87] For the most part, antebellum historians and biographers had dealt with Washington's Southern background only in passing, if at all. In Irving's *Washington*, however, it is an essential ingredient in the shaping of Washington's exemplary character. What is even more astonishing is that Irving, on the brink of the Civil War and after decades of abolitionist activity, manages to romanticize and rationalize Washington's stance on slavery, by delving into internal struggles his hero may have entertained. In this way, Irving depicts Washington's slaveholding as something that shaped his character in a positive way.

According to Irving, the wealthy Virginian landowners, Washington included, had all the "independence of men living apart in patriarchal style on their own rural domains; surrounded by their families, dependants and slaves, among whom their will was law,—and there was the individuality in character and action of men prone to nurture peculiar notions and habits of thinking, in the thoughtful solitariness of country life."[88] Human nature, about which not even Irving had any illusions, here is held in check by a hierarchical society in which everyone has his or her place. Such a view, together with the underlying nostalgia, is unacceptable in the twenty-first century. From a modern perspective, therefore, it is as if for Irving slavery was morally acceptable as long as the system was run by virtuous people. Such as George Washington, for whom, Irving writes, "glory was a secondary consideration [and] formed no part of his aspirations."[89]

Irving's biography appeared at a propitious time. While interest in Washington had always been high, in the antebellum period his image was celebrated in histories, biographies, belles lettres, drama, and the arts. In October 1851, for instance, Emanuel Gottlieb Leutze's monumental painting *Washington Crossing the Delaware*, a thoroughly romantic view of Washington as the heroic savior of his country, went on exhibit in New York.[90] In 1854 *Graham's Magazine* began with the serial publication of Joel Headley's biography, which immediately boosted new subscriptions. Two years later, some seven thousand people waited inside New York's Academy of Music to listen to one of Edward Everett's speeches on "The Character of Washington."[91] With reverence for Washington's memory reaching a peak in the 1850s, it was only logical that George P. Putnam went out of his way to make publication of Irving's *Life* an event in the nation's cultural history. It was a shrewd move. The book was tremendously successful, a "perfect triumph" of literature.[92] Putnam published it in six varying formats—a Popular Edition, an octavo or Subscribers' Edition, an ambitious "Illustrated Edition" in 68 folio parts, a large Paper or Quarto edition, a Sunnyside Edition, and a Mount Vernon edition.

The success of *Life of George Washington* cannot be separated from the fascination with history in antebellum America. Between 1800 and 1860, Ann Douglas noted, over one-fourth of the best-sellers were either histories or books on historical topics. Moreover, by 1860 there were over one hundred active historical societies in the United States, and history had been taught at elementary-school level since 1840. Historians themselves were deliberately "literary," seeing themselves as practitioners of belles lettres.[93] Irving, unlike Sparks, Bancroft, or Preston, had no formal training as a historian. He knew how to write, though, and his historical biography of Washington had a tremendous appeal to educated middle-class readers and advanced students, for whom it became standard. It was even considered for schoolchildren, by John Fiske in 1887.[94] Yet for Americans who with elders and children would gather at the fireside for a winter's evening tale, Weems's book remained more appealing.[95] So did lighter and more popular biographies by, *inter alia*, James Kirke Paulding (1835) or Caroline Matilda Kirkland (1857). Paulding's two-volume *Life of Washington* was written for use in schools and expressly dedicated to the "pious, retired, domestic Mothers" of America. Although Paulding points his moral at least as obviously as Weems, the book, which Irving also read and quoted from in his own work, received much praise from Edgar Allan Poe in the *Southern Literary Messenger*.[96]

Irving purposely cast his multi-volume history of the Father of His Country and the nation's first president in the form of a dramatic narrative in the American romantic tradition. That tradition, unlike its European counterparts, including the British, did not stand in opposition to society so much as it was predicated on the grandeur of the American nation, yet to be built. As Irving explains in the preface, Washington's life had to be part of "the great drama in which he was the principal actor."[97] By this means, biography became history, and history was essentially myth, the sacred story of the divine hero, the archetypal warrior who, together with equally heroic comrades, devoted himself to a higher purpose and thus accomplished the foundation of the new nation. In this drama of cinematic breadth, there was no space for the analysis of ideas. In the midst of constant movement and action, ideas can be tedious, almost intangible. The evolution of Washington's political ideas is almost entirely absent, though they greatly affected the future United States.[98] With the scholarly romance constituting the most "masculine" narrative form, Irving had found the perfect medium to delineate Washington as the ideal vision of achieved manhood, the ultimate archetypal masculinity in the realm of truth and unswerving principles.

The great American historians of the antebellum period—Sparks, Bancroft, Prescott—persistently thematized not politics so much as struggle, conquest, expansion, and discovery. Their work is, in the broadest sense, military history.[99] Irving's Washington too has a "soldier's eye," together with a "passion for arms" that displayed "the old chivalrous spirit of the De Wessyngtons," his English ancestors.[100] Irving's vision anticipates by a century and a half Stephen Brumwell's estimation that Washington's "colossal status rested upon the twin pillars of his character, the gentleman and the warrior."[101] Irving had originally planned *Washington* for three volumes, ending with the inauguration. He feared that the history of Washington's administration might yield too little in terms of "personal or picturesque detail,"[102] perhaps also of the kind of manly perfection he was seeking for himself. With the success of the first volume, however, he determined that he wouldn't just write part of Washington's life; he would write *all* of it, ending his career on the most distinguished topic, the nation's foremost Founding Father.

Although at one point "the magnitude of the theme" threatened to overwhelm him, the five volumes provided Irving with the grandest stage for his visions of achieved masculinity.[103] There was ample space for depicting Washington's heroic stand against an unjust colonial regime and, just as heroically, against plotters and schemers of the likes of Thomas Conway and Horatio Gates, or incompetent and self-serving politicians. There also are accounts of Washington dealing heroically with Shays' rebellion, his handling, with aplomb, of the Whiskey Rebellion, his effective dealing with public credit and the banking system, and his care of revenue for the federal government. Moreover, we learn about Washington's resolute opposition to monarchical tendencies, his struggle against political adversaries who attempted to blacken his wartime reputation, and his brave attempts to settle the political feuds in his cabinet. And we learn that he consented to a second term in office, against all his inclinations. Small wonder that in Irving's eyes, Washington represented the apex of manliness, "the last stage of perfection to which human nature is capable of attaining."[104]

Irving never was deeply involved in the study of violence and often downplays the warrior part of George Washington. Even as commander in chief, his Washington was not a "professional soldier" for whom war was "a career." On the contrary, war for Washington was "a painful remedy, hateful in itself, but adopted for a grand national good."[105] In contrast, as early as 1807 a biographer had described Washington as the paradigmatic soldier, "full of correct and *manly* ideas." At about the same time, Marshall had depicted him as *General* Washington. Paulding's Washington of 1835 likewise is preeminently a soldier, whose manliness is the epitome of a "battlefield code." At a critical moment during the battle of Princeton, Paulding writes, Washington "snatched a standard, and calling on his soldiers to come to the rescue of their country, dashed into the midst of the enemy." Even in Caroline Kirkland's biography, written, the authoress emphasized, for the instruction and edification of the young, Washington's dominant character trait is his "military turn."[106] There also had been a long tradition of painting and printmaking to show the steely resolution and fiery spirit of Washington the "gentleman warrior" (the term is Stephen Brumwell's). Perhaps the best examples, in the arts, of this tradition are John Trumbull's *The Death of General Mercer at the Battle of Princeton, January 3, 1777* (ca. 1789–ca. 1831), now in the Yale University Art Gallery, as well as his *General George Washington at Trenton* (ca. 1792–94), now at the Metropolitan Museum in New York.[107] And almost contemporaneously with Irving's description of the Virginia gentleman and the nation's first soldier a lithograph by Nathaniel Currier appeared.[108]

As for Washington the gentleman, Irving writes that he had benefited from the "mental and moral culture at home from an excellent father," as well as from the influence of his brother Lawrence, described as "a well-educated and accomplished youth." Fourteen years older than George, Lawrence became George's protector, at the same time as the younger brother, then about seven or eight years old, "looked up to his manly and cultivated brother as a model in mind and manners." The elder brother's manliness and accomplishments, together with the brotherly affection between the two, Irving emphasizes, was to have a decisive "influence [...] on all the future career of the subject of this memoir."[109] As indeed it did. As early as 1776 George Washington defined the true criteria for an office (in the military) in terms of "a just pretension to the character of a Gentleman, a proper Sense of Honor, & some Reputation to lose." In other words, men like Washington himself, "the Virginia planter who felt little in common with the scruffy plebeians around him."[110] And Irving? His comment on Washington's resignation from military command to civilian life is telling: "It was truly edifying to behold how easily and contentedly he subsided from the authoritative commander-in-chief of armies, into the quiet country gentleman. There was nothing awkward or violent in the transition. He seemed to be in his natural element."[111]

A somewhat different image of a gentleman emerges from the first volume, in which we are invited to savor the description a contemporary chronicler gave of Washington's arrival in Boston in early July of 1775: "His excellency was on horseback, in company with several military gentlemen. It was not difficult to distinguish him from all others. He is tall and well-proportioned, *and his personal appearance truly noble and majestic*."[112] Earlier in that volume, readers are asked to consider the awe-inspiring effect produced by "Washington's noble person and demeanor, his consummate horsemanship, the admirable horses he was accustomed to ride, and the aristocratical style of his equipments."[113] With passages of this kind Irving was in good company. In James Fenimore Cooper's 1821 novel *The Spy*, Washington—appearing until near the end as Mr. Harper—is likewise cast as an impeccable gentleman radiating stability and calm:

> [Washington's] countenance evinced a settled composure and dignity; his nose was straight and Grecian; his eye, of a gray color, was quiet, thoughtful, and rather melancholy; the mouth and lower part of his face being expressive of decision and much character. His dress [...] was rather heightened by his erect and conspicuously graceful carriage. His whole appearance was so impressive and decidedly that of a gentleman, that [...] the ladies arose from their seats....[114]

It is worth comparing these descriptions to what the *Oxford English Dictionary* defines as the criteria for a gentleman: "A man of gentle birth, or having the same heraldic status as those of gentle birth; properly, one who is entitled to bear arms, though not ranking among the nobility, but also applied to a person of distinction without precise definition of rank [...] A man in whom gentle birth is accompanied by appropriate qualities and behaviour; hence, in general, a man of chivalrous instincts and fine feelings."[115] The dictionary's definition certainly befits descriptions of George Washington as a man of good, courteous conduct, a man of decency, obligation, and personal responsibility, with a firm sense of propriety, amiable and constant, willing to sacrifice for others, and able to discriminate between good and bad, between the noble and the ignoble, between virtue and vice. Altogether, the image of Washington as a gentleman comprises many values—from behavior and morals to education, social background, the correct attire and table manners, much as it draws on such ambiguous concepts as class, culture, and, not to forget, Englishness.

Irving never tires of expounding Washington's affinities with Englishness. When in 1766 Britain imposed the Stamp Act on the American colonies, there was much unrest, especially in Boston. Yet according to Irving, a single word in a letter from Washington to George Mason "evinces the chord which still vibrated in the American bosom." Washington not only carefully read the *Country Magazine*, from which he learned to present himself in a most elegant way, basing his deportment and style of life on the model of the English country gentleman. Above all, "he incidentally speaks of England as *home*." "It was the familiar term," Irving continues, "with which she was usually indicated by those of English descent; and the writer of these pages remembers when the endearing phrase still lingered on Anglo-American lips even after the Revolution."[116] The passage not only demonstrates the extent to which Irving himself always felt "English" (for which he was regularly chastised), but also that there really never was any easy *cultural* severance between Britain and the United Colonies in the Revolutionary era, accompanying separation. Indeed, Americans often conceived of themselves as the true guardians of English values and traditions and thus readily embraced and tried to preserve the culture of their forebears. Thus, the United States of the early republic truly was a "culture of diaspora" in which both pre- and post-Revolutionary culture were understood as the perfection of English values, consciously reproducing those values in a new, American, context.[117]

And yet, a year and a half into Washington's presidency, the British historian and statesman Edmund Burke, horrified by the events in revolutionary France, bitterly lamented that "[t]he age of chivalry is gone." For Burke, the future boded ill, in the form of a society governed by self-interest and force.[118] But what was the "age of chivalry" like that Burke had professed to admire so much? In America, the colonial elite of merchants, lawyers, and landed gentry depended, not merely on slave labor and the exclusion of women from public life but also on a much larger class of artisanal producers, whose key values were personal independence, pride in their craft, and a measure of republican civic virtue. These values did not always square with the patricians' demand for respect and deference, but by and large this

Six. Life of George Washington

did not put too much strain on social harmony. Only with the rise of the professional, bureaucratic, and commercial middle classes did serious conflicts emerge. For, the middle classes or, rather, middle-class men, increasingly defined personality in terms of providing for oneself, the acquisition of money, and relentless work. To be sure, this meant fewer privileges, as relations between humans became more egalitarian. However, with money the only criterion to establish difference, these relations were neutralized, so that individuals became, as Tocqueville wrote, "strangers one to the other."[119]

There were many attempts, in antebellum America, to channel competitive impulses, much as dominating impulses were increasingly criticized. The "mania for self-control" is evident from a host of advice manuals for young men—among them William Ellery Channing's book *Self-Culture* of 1838, which originated as part of the Franklin Lectures, towards working classes, purportedly Channing's "fellow citizens [...] who are occupied by manual labor." Self-culture for Channing meant "the control of the animal appetites," that is, the bringing under control of unwieldy human nature in the interest of culture.[120] In other words, the purpose of self-culture was the development of a specific habitus or second nature, of certain psychic structures shaped by social attitudes. Irving appears to have adopted the rhetoric, as when he emphasizes "that rigid propriety and self-control to which [Washington] subjected himself and by which he brought all the impulses of a somewhat ardent temper under conscientious government."[121]

If Irving had no illusions about human nature, neither did George Washington. "We have errors [...] to correct," Irving quotes from Washington writing to John Jay during the political crisis preceding the adoption of the federal Constitution. "We have probably had too good an opinion of human nature in forming our confederation." Washington therefore propounded the use of some form of "coercive power," adding that, "We must take human nature as we find it. Perfection falls not to the share of mortals."[122] Washington himself was aware of his own shortcomings, his "high temper and a spirit of command" as well as, presumably, the "lion part of his nature."[123] For Americans in the antebellum period, resurrecting and romanticizing the chivalric avatars of bygone eras was rather a way to civilize personal ambition and the acquisition of money, as if symbolically quarantining them.[124] Yet chivalry had no base in antebellum America, except perhaps in the South. Nevertheless, it lived on as an ideal, a model, a guide that would prevent the masculine tone of the gentleman from passing out of the world, leaving the field to his dysfunctional shadow.

Long before writing *Life of George Washington* Irving had created old Squire Bracebridge who, according to his son, "took honest Peacham for his text book, instead of Chesterfield."[125] Lest readers of *The Sketch Book* missed the point, Irving in a footnote explains that "honest Peacham" refers to *Peacham's Compleat Gentleman* (1622), an outline of the qualities a man of the early seventeenth century, that is, a Cavalier, needed to be considered a gentleman. The book's author, Henry Peacham (1578–1644), was a courtier at the royal court in London. He was well connected and cultivated relationships with both Catholic and Protestant circles. Peacham suffered considerably during the reign of James I, when freedom of thought and speech were repressed. *The Compleat Gentleman* is dedicated to William Howard, the youngest son of the Earl of Arundel, though Peacham's political sympathies were closer to protestant factions, like those of the founder of Bracebridge Hall, said to have come back with Charles II.[126]

Idealizations of the age of chivalry abound in *Life of George Washington*. Thus, we are told that in 1657, during the English Civil War, John and Andrew Washington came to Virginia, which then was "a favorite resort of the Cavaliers."[127] George Washington's values too are securely anchored within the Anglo-Virginia gentry, whose "rising hope" he was.[128] Moreover, the social order in Washington's colonial Virginia appears as a veritable haven of patriarchal manhood. "There was no turbulent factious opposition to government in Virginia; no 'fierce democracy,' the rank growth of crowded cities, and a fermenting populace."[129] What Thomas Jefferson would celebrate as "natural aristocracy" had not yet given way to "artificial aristocracy," founded on urban industrialism, commercialization, and personal ambition, and, as antebellum America saw it, tainted by effeminate luxuries bringing with them weariness, exhaustion, and fatigue.[130] Virginia's "natural aristocracy" could pride itself on a social harmony that was still intact, with the blessed patriarchs living apart on their own rural domains.

In antebellum America, the South became the last stand of the genteel patriarch, soon to be recast as a Confederate cavalier, which Southerners pitted against the North's self-made Yankees. Never mind that the outcome of the Civil War signaled the triumph of the urban industrial entrepreneur over the genteel southern patrician. Contemporaries saw northerners and southerners as distinctly different species, different expressions of manhood. Georgia-born William Lowndes Yancey, a fire-eating secessionist, pontificated in 1855 that "The Creator [...] has made the North and the South [...] Those who occupy the one are cool, calculating, enterprising, selfish, and grasping; the inhabitants of the other are ardent, brave, and magnanimous, more disposed to give than to accumulate, to enjoy ease rather than to labor."[131] Irving was not a Southerner and, not to forget, he wrote for the masses. If on occasion he slyly hints at the genteel patriarch and cavalier, he generally downplays Washington's Southernness. Telling the story of how Washington became commander-on-chief of

Six. Life of George Washington

the Continental Army, Irving emphasizes that even John Adams, a staunch New Englander, found "something charming" in "the conduct of Washington, a gentleman of one of the first fortunes upon the continent," and graced by the most "noble and disinterested" views.[132] In addition, Irving insists that Washington, unlike most Virginia planters, who "were prone to leave the care of their estates too much to their overseers and to think personal labor a degradation," actually worked. Washington's "letter-books," Irving writes, "are monuments to his business habits."[133]

Irving may have had good literary reasons for making Washington appear larger than life. The antebellum period in general was a time of intensive cultural production during which a genuinely American historical and cultural memory came into being. In this process of culturally constituting the United States, the American Revolution was the "natural" starting point. Biographies as well as history books abounded. Representations of revolutionary figures and events in paintings, lithographs, pictorial histories, and illustrated magazines from the 1830s to the 1850s likewise contributed to an archive that was seminal in the formation of a usable past. As sites of memory, all these representations helped to define the nation. While on occasion they contested historical and cultural memories, more often than not they stabilized larger narratives. The apotheosis of George Washington in particular was almost a national compulsion in Irving's own time. Yet even while alive, Washington was the object of a cult. In March 1791, the *Pennsylvania Gazette* wrote that Washington was only the last in a long list of "heroes" from Solon to Caesar to Alexander to Frederick of Prussia to General Wolfe—all "the boast of their countries"—and now America also had its "genius," George Washington, "the true model for emulation, and a just example of future heroes."[134]

"Until Lincoln appeared as challenger for the title of foremost American hero," literary historian William A. Bryan reminds us, "George Washington had no rival for that title."[135] Irving's *Washington* too represents and speaks to patriotic sentiments. It was written to maintain a form of communal trance and participation in the national mythology. There was no space in it for readers' self-awareness, for establishing a personal contact with the deeper strata of experience. Washington was quite literally "usable." "With us," Irving writes on the final page of the bio-history, Washington's memory "remains *a national property*, where all sympathies throughout our widely-extended and diversified empire meet in unison. Under all dissensions and amid all the storms of party, his precepts and example speak to us from the grave with *a paternal appeal*; and his name—by all revered—forms a universal tie of brotherhood—*a watchword of our Union*."[136] If Americans only heeded Washington's "precepts and example," Irving admonishes his readers, Americans can yet regain the "universal tie of brotherhood."[137] It is no exaggeration to say, as Mary Bowden did, that Irving's *Life of George Washington* was "a five-volume plea that the Union be preserved."[138]

For Irving, Washington's memory not only was "a national property" in the sense that Mount Vernon had been turned into a true *lieu de mémoire* by the Mount Vernon Ladies' Association of the Union.[139] The very words and phrases that Irving used in his final portrayal of America's revolutionary hero and first president—"a rarer union of virtues," "example," "paternal appeal"—reveal the underlying principle of his own political vision. "I must deal cautiously with the party questions," he remarked to his nephew in the summer of 1858. "I wish to stand in my history where Washington stood, who was *of no party*."[140] Irving's remark echoes a letter Washington wrote to Henry Knox, the Secretary of War, speaking of the "difficulty to one, who is *of no party*."[141] It is tempting to see in these parallels the—quintessentially American—dream of politics without partisan conflict, and of politics without political parties. That dream, Sean Wilentz wrote, ran deep in American political culture of the revolutionary era and the early republic.[142] Washington in his Farewell Address of 1796 had given expression to the classical formulation of American anti-party thought. Parties, the outgoing president wrote, were not "natural" but "artificial" and intolerable—"of fatal tendency," and he duly warned of their "dangers" and of the "fury of party spirit."[143] The professed neutrality of political ideas then served a strategic point *within* the larger political process: Washington could play the critical role of embodiment of the Constitution only by being nonpartisan.

Irving too was profoundly distrustful of the partisan politics. In a letter to his friend Gouverneur Kemble he speaks with disgust about "political councils that are accompanied by acrimonious and disparaging attacks upon any great class of our fellow citizens."[144] Irving had introduced his remark by a disclosure of sorts of his political views: "I am thoroughly a republican, and attached, from complete conviction, to the institutions of my country; but [...] I have no relish for puritans either in religion or politics, who are for pushing principles to an extreme, and for overturning everything that stands in the way of their own zealous career."[145] What this shows is not so much Irving's republicanism than the power emotional impulses had over his political preferences. Irving fell for the admiration and sympathy a political leader would awake in him. His admiration, during the 1820s, of Andrew Jackson has been mentioned. In 1850, Irving spoke equally admiringly of Zachary Taylor, Old Rough and Ready, calling him "a really good man and an honest man, uniting the bravery of the soldier with the simplicity of the quiet citizen."[146] The citations could be repeated almost endlessly. They all show that Irving's politics should be seen in terms of masculine attachments rather than in terms of a temperamental reluctance to risk his reputation espousing controversial political

Six. Life of George Washington

views. It is not that Irving's opinions always remained his own. Irving was attracted to politics largely by the drama in it, and especially at a time when most politicians were actors. A characteristic remark by Irving would run thus: "The grand debate in the Senate occupied my mind as intensely for three weeks, as did ever a dramatic representation."[147]

Irving did not lack political interest or convictions. References to them in his writings are frequent enough and clear enough, showing that he knew what was going on about him and that he was quite capable of participating in the life of the body politic he belonged to. Yet he was a political pragmatist, who believed that extremists, no matter which side of an issue they were on, were bad for politics and for people. In an early letter to Henry Brevoort, he characteristically expressed his delight that there were "worthy and intelligent men" in both parties, "with honest hearts, enlightened minds, generous feelings, and bitter prejudices."[148] More than half a century later, his nephew rendered Irving's "political faith" thus: "...though always keenly alive to everything that affected the interest or honour of his country, *he had no party prejudices or strongly marked political opinions.*"[149] Critics rarely took this at face value, possibly because it would make Irving appear as a political chameleon, and so Irving's political faith has been the subject of lively debates.[150]

Vernon Lee Parrington saw Irving's political style as nonconfrontational, suggesting that it was based on a "philosophy of compromise."[151] In a similar vein, Brian Jay Jones, Irving's popular biographer, found that Irving

> was more loyal to conviction than party. His own politics were, by today's standards, progressively conservative, favoring business, nonregulation, and individual rights, while valuing older traditions—all convictions that appealed to a proper gentleman. If his political party drifted too far from his core values, Irving simply abandoned the party. He didn't lack for conviction, merely the stomach for the fight. His own political style was decidedly nonconfrontational, a trait that served him well.[152]

That Irving, dominated as he was by his anima-ego, didn't have the stomach for fight is evident from a decision he made in the spring of 1838 when some Tammany Hall Democrats wanted him as a candidate to run for Mayor of New York against incumbent Aaron Vail, a defiantly anti–Jacksonian Whig. Irving declined as a matter of course. "Nothing could induce me to undertake an office for which I find myself so little fitted." Months later, he beat back similar demands to run for Congress. "I must run mad first," he said.[153]

Though Irving eventually turned his back on politics, his emotional impulses and, concomitantly, his readiness for masculine attachments, remained intact. In the spring of 1853, he was in Washington to see Franklin Pierce, a staunch Jacksonian and brigadier general in the Mexican war, sworn in as the fourteenth president. Irving was struck by the symbolic elegance of the ceremony. "It was admirable to see the quiet and courtesy with which this great transition of power and rule from one party to another took place," he wrote to Sarah Storrow. "I [...] have seen the two presidents [Pierce and his predecessor, Millard Fillmore] arm in arm, as if the sway of an immense empire was not passing from one to the other." He also met Pierce briefly and appears to have liked him. "He is a quiet, gentleman like man in appearance and manner."[154] Irving's George Washington, too, was a gentleman, and so it is no surprise that in 1857, in the midst of finishing his biography, Irving had the following to say to Charles Lanman: "Every American should be proud of the memory of Washington, and should make his example and his wonderful character a continual study."[155] And when a friend told him that he had read the work to his children, Irving was overjoyed. "That's it," he allegedly exclaimed, "that is what I write it for. I want it so clear that anybody can understand it. I want the action to shine through the style."[156]

As with *The Life and Voyages of Christopher Columbus*, Irving is again using history to teach, about the nation's founding as much as about masculinity realized to archetypal perfection. George Washington Greene, a contemporary reviewer, felt that Irving had drawn his hero "in all the majesty of his greatness," and he rightfully characterized *Life of George Washington* as "a work which fathers would transmit to their children as a precious legacy." Greene goes on to praise the author as "the great teacher of the nation," one who leaves his readers' hearts "glowing with fervent gratitude and generous patriotism." The conclusion oozes with sentiment: "How meet was it that, while [George Washington's] ashes repose beside the waters of the Potomac, his life should have been written on the banks of the Hudson!"[157] Indeed, Irving uses the life of the nation's founder and the transformation he effected of the United Colonies into the United States to show that regional and sectional differences can be overcome, and that all parts of the country were dependent on one another. Hence, he emphasizes Washington's "precepts and example."[158] For, if all else fails, Washington's memory must serve to bind the states together. And when Irving capitalizes the "U" in Union, this only shows how conscious he was of the tense ring of that word in the partisan rhetoric of his own time.

"Union" had been a topic already in Washington's "Farewell Address" of 1796, in which he hoped for his fellow citizens that "your Union and brotherly affection may be perpetual [and that] the free constitution, which is the work of your hands, may be sacredly maintained."[159] The sentiment continued to occupy the attention of later leaders. Daniel Webster, for instance, at the centennial celebration of Washington's birthday in 1832 told Americans that Washington's policy had reached its apex "in the avowed objects of the Constitution itself" and that "the Union was the great object of his thoughts."¹⁶⁰ In 1825, at the laying of the cornerstone of the Bunker Hill Monument, Webster had said that the Founders' actions urged contemporaries to always be mindful of "OUR COUNTRY, OUR WHOLE COUNTRY, AND NOTHING BUT OUR COUNTRY." Webster spoke again at the monument's completion in 1843, this time with a warning: "Woe betide the man who brings to this day's worship feeling less than wholly American!"¹⁶¹ Less than a decade later, Webster struck the same chord at a Fourth of July ceremony, only with even more urgency. He begins with the reminder that the Declaration of Independence, "sealed in blood," had now "stood for seventy-five years" and still stood. He then goes on to conjure forth the "venerable form" of the Father of His Country, "dignified and grave," but with "concern and anxiety" for the country's future. In a climactic moment, Webster addresses Washington's legacy thus: "We cannot, we dare not, we will not, betray our sacred trust." Thus, "so long as our lives may last, no ruthless hand shall undermine that bright arch of Union and Liberty which spans the continent from Washington to California."¹⁶²

In contrast to Webster's ceremonial words, Irving's dream of reforming "our Union"¹⁶³ also speaks to an intensified ideology of manhood, one that is conscious of a masculinity not to be found in industry, commerce, and politics, nor in moral zeal. George Washington, Irving writes in concluding the fourth volume,

> fought for a cause, but not for personal renown. Gladly, when he had won the cause, he hung up his sword, never again to take it down. Glory, that blatant word, which haunts some military minds like the bray of the trumpet, formed no part of his aspirations. To act justly was his instinct, to promote the public weal, his constant effort, to deserve the "affections of good men" his ambition. With such qualifications for the pure exercise of sound judgment and comprehensive wisdom, he ascended the presidential chair.¹⁶⁴

Words like these establish Washington's archetypal masculinity on Carlylean terms. In this regard, Washington's responsible social maturity provided genteel readers with moral simplicities to steer their lives by, if not to save the entire nation. By the same token, the hero's nobility formed, not a Hegelian progression in the consciousness of liberty, but, because of his exceptional character, a compensatory response to perceived threats of dispossession, loss, defeat, and humiliation. "No one could share the sunlight with this Washington," Andrew Burstein remarked, "but could stand only in his shadow."¹⁶⁵ This includes Washington Irving himself, whose undoing the writing of the five-volume biography undoubtedly was.¹⁶⁶ When *Life of George Washington* appeared, Irving's replication of genteel paternal values, of nostalgia for what came to be called the "republic of virtue," gained him both the respect (to a degree) and the affection of the American middle-class reading public.¹⁶⁷ Washington is "a living personality, not […]

a political or military automaton," an anonymous reviewer enthusiastically wrote in *Knickerbocker* magazine of July 1855.[168] Just as adulatory and reverential was George Washington Greene's review of the first four volumes in the *North American Review* of April 1858. And thanks to Irving's high reputation in Germany, Washington was instantly reviewed there as well.[169]

On hindsight, it is safe to say that Irving (and his contemporaries) finds himself reflected in a fantasy space in which outmoded models of manhood are staged and negotiated. Compensatory in nature, these models have no place for intangible factors such as emotion and race, looking instead to visions of a financially secure, self-possessed masculinity and property as markers of stable selfhood. Irving's attempt to forge a secure sense of masculinity makes sense in light of his personal quest for masculine perfection, as well as in an age of intense uncertainty, an age in which that manhood was no longer in effect.[170] At the same time, the nostalgia contributed to Irving's downfall, if not neglect, especially when compared to classics like Melville or Hawthorne, who directly challenged their readers and had to wait for the transformation of American higher education before, thanks largely to the efforts of professors of English, their writings became canonized, gaining the respect if not the affection of readers.[171]

Irving's "first law of history," William Hedges observed, was that "good men always suffer."[172] Hedges here has in mind Irving's Columbus, who in many ways seems a tragic character, whose "ambition" may have been "lofty and noble," yet who was forced to bear all kinds of "despicable molestations [...] griefs and vexations."[173] There is a sense of tragedy also in *Life of George Washington*. Washington too appears as a maligned martyr whose misfortunes were those alien forces that constituted him as a suffering servant or an innocent man in the midst of cabal and corruption. At the end of operations for 1777, in an atmosphere of plots, intrigues, and conspiracies, Washington was "painfully aware" of the "machinations" against him. "Yet," Irving writes, Washington "rose above the tauntings of the press, the sneerings of the cabal, the murmurs of the public, the suggestions of some of his friends, and the throbbing impulses of his own courageous heart," thus evincing once more "that magnanimity which was his grand characteristic."[174] Endurance cemented Washington as a model of wounded innocence for the nation.

In the concluding remarks to the fourth volume of his biography, Irving pleads for his readers' understanding for having spent so much space on the Revolutionary campaigns. Yet knowledge of the "moral grandeur" of this momentous event, he writes, is essential in order to "appreciate the sagacity, forecast, enduring fortitude, and comprehensive wisdom with which [Washington] conducted it."[175] The extreme paucity of resources, neglects, miseries of all kinds, including the desolate winter camps—all these ills Washington sustained thanks to his "patience and fortitude." Irving also seeks to justify his quoting at length from Washington's copious correspondence, which he claims was a "truthful mirror of his heart and mind [and a] thorough exponent of his conduct." Letters, especially official ones, are anything but a "truthful mirror," yet for Irving, Washington's character is to be found in them "in all its majestic simplicity, its massive grandeur, and quiet, colossal strength."

"In the innocence of the father," Catherine Albanese wrote, commenting on the Revolutionary era, "Americans recognized their own innocence."[176] A half-century on, the father's innocence came to be questioned, and Americans would recognize many traits, though innocence was rarely among them. Moreover, many Americans were painfully aware of the fact that the age of great men was long gone, and that any attempt to resurrect the charismatic leaders of the distant past would spawn only demagogues, not genuine masculine heroes. This did not yet detract readers of Irving's *Washington*. As William H. Prescott, one of the nineteenth-century's premier historians, wrote to Irving on August 7, 1857, with the second volume just out: "I have never before fully comprehended the character of Washington; nor did I know what capabilities it would afford his biographer."[177] In a similar vein, George Bancroft wrote to Irving about volume four, calling it "the most vivid and truest" portrait of Washington that had "ever been written."[178] The estimation lasted for almost a century. Writing in 1917, George Haven Putnam found words of praise for Irving's "strain of romance" and "the power of [his] imagination," as they had enabled him to picture to himself and to make vivid, not only memorable scenes but, above all, "the nature, the purpose, and the manner of thought" of his hero.[179] A generation later, Dixon Wecter concluded that, "as literature," Irving's *Washington* "is still the best book about Washington."[180]

Modern historians have been less enthusiastic by far, as history has become more technical, scientific, less synthesized in form. Daniel Boorstin, surveying early lives of George Washington, wrote that Irving's five volumes certainly were the best, though he "too was afflicted by the contagion of dullness." Thus, these volumes were "more widely bought than read."[181] James T. Flexner, another historian and author of a four-volume Washington biography, altogether dismisses Irving's *Washington* as "one of the author's least effective works," though, he adds, "it adheres to the record."[182] And in 1974, Ralph Ketcham disparages *Washington* for finding its hero marble and leaving him marble.[183] Almost alone among modern historians is Douglas Southall Freeman, whose seven-volume biography draws on Rupert Hughes's biography from the early twentieth century, on Marshall's *Life*—and on Irving's *Life of George Washington*. "One can hardly ask for a better modern recommendation of the Irving work than this," a recent commentator found.[184]

As for students of literature, they mostly appear to have deferred to historians, as such, and merely borrowed their denigrating remarks or simply damned with faint praise. A lone exception is Andrew Myers who, writing at the time of the Bicentennial of the American Revolution, waxes especially appreciative of Irving's depiction of George Washington as "a believable patriot and hero." With a good deal of self-irony, Myers dubs himself a "lonely long-distance reader," albeit one who in the process of laboring through the 2,500-some pages of what more often than not serves as "furniture" rather than as "bedside reading," nevertheless gained "a new, but not uncritical, respect, for both the man and the artist." Thus, Myers finds it saddening that "very little has been written of late about this extensive biography [...] Indeed there has been a famine of close comment in dissertations, or scholarly articles, or in chapters of appropriate full-length books—at any time in this century."[185]

At the time, the time of the nation's bicentennial, Myers could cite a mere two articles that he deemed representative of an interest in Irving's *Washington*. One is by George S. Hellman, which only touches on some bibliographical aspects, concerning an account by Tobias Lear, Washington's secretary of many years; the other is by Elsie Lee West, who discusses Irving's works on Columbus, Goldsmith, and George Washington as fine biographies that belie the notion that Irving's writing was really over by 1830.[186] Five years after Myers's article, Mary Bowden published the Washington Irving volume for Twayne's United States Authors Series. "Today," she wrote, "the virtue of Irving's *Washington* is that it is magnificently readable." In fact, "all Irving's books are readable today, [...] many are worth reading, and [...] a few demand reading and rereading." Such as *Life of George Washington*, which is "history to teach." Especially Irving's focus on the importance of "Union" makes it "magnificently readable," even though the work is "uneven and incomplete" as a "life." There is little of the private man, Bowden notes, perhaps because Irving saw George Washington as "eminently a public character," and because he wanted to evoke "a glorious past."[187] And, one might add, because Irving, stuck in his conflict between a dominant anima and a suppressed masculinity, wanted to evoke what he saw as manly perfection.

Overall, then, Irving's *Washington* is truly "reverent." Is this really so bad? In this regard, I concur with University of Georgia sociologist Barry Schwartz, who argues that "the Washington myth" only veils a baser conception of America's founder and first president, one that is the truer one. But a baser conception is itself to invoke a fabrication, the product, according to Schwartz, "of a cynical rather than a suspicious age, an age whose basic assumptions induce many to deny the social value of heroic actions by reducing them to ignoble motives."[188] Art historian Mark Thistlethwaite

Six. Life of George Washington

has a similar view: "Washington was the great *exemplum virtutis* for America, and any work of art in which he figured [...] possessed a morally didactic possibility."[189] Either way, Washington always has been a "projection surface" with regard to the times' cultural values. For this very reason, Irving's "Washington" has as much to do with the historic person as with the biographical persona of its author, his emotional deficits, his cultural values, as we well as those of the time. Any reading of *Life of George Washington* thus reveals as much about its author and the time in which it was produced as about its subject and the time of its subject.

Biographies of Washington Irving always include one of the earliest major events in the writer's life—the young boy being presented to George Washington when the president was settling into the capital of New York City. Stanley Williams explains how well-known the story was to the American people: "The incident of Washington Irving's meeting with the President has been repeated in story and sketch until it has the aroma of fable. The day and month are unknown, but the fact is demonstrable."[190] A meeting of this kind would not have been unusual. Washington's step-grandson, George Washington Parke Custis told how, on city streets, as the president walked along, "often would mothers bring their children to look on the paternal chief."[191] Pierre Munro Irving, his uncle's chief biographer and assistant, gives an account of the meeting,[192] and so does Charles Lanman, following Irving's visit to the State Department, to examine the Washington Papers held there. Lanman, an employee, was detached to accompany him. On this occasion, Irving told him the story of his actually meeting the president:

> "My nurse," continued Mr. Irving, "a good old Scotchwoman, was very anxious for me to see him, and held me up in her arms as he rode past. This, however, did not satisfy her; so the next day, when walking with me in Broadway, she espied him in a shop; she seized my hand, and darting in exclaimed in her bland Scotch. 'Please, your excellency, here's a bairn that's called after ye!' Gen. Washington then turned his benevolent face full upon me, smiled, laid his hand upon my head, and gave me his blessing, which," added Mr. Irving earnestly, "I have reason to believe has attended me through life. I was but five years old, yet I can feel that hand upon my head even now!"[193]

Stanley Williams adds the information, reported in the *New York Herald* of February 1, 1853, that Irving "remembered Gen. Washington perfectly."[194] "Perhaps," the biographer proceeds, "the sentiment of this conjunction, occurring in an age uncritical of Washington, found reëxpression in the idealized portrait of the general in the biography [...] At least it is certain that to write of George Washington became from earliest youth a dream of Irving's."[195] The incident itself must have led to a kind of identification from the beginning. One doesn't need to be a psychologist to see in the president's patting on the head of young Irving a form of manipulative baptism, as well as a compensation for the absence of love or affection from his own father, the Scotch Presbyterian deacon, stern and severe, and quite incapable of that kind of love. George Washington, whose "paternal appeal" Irving showcases at the close of his biography,[196] thus is the perfect image of the ideal benevolent father and model of achieved masculinity that Irving never had.

When Irving speaks about Washington, he often, unconsciously, also speaks about himself, about his deep need to integrate into himself the masculine attributes he marveled at in his hero. Irving indeed had a "deep-seated love for his subject," which resulted in an "imperative need" to write his hero's life.[197] He was determined that the biography, even before he was actually at work on it, become his "great and crowning labor."[198] George Bancroft hit the nail on its head when he wrote to Irving that the "throbbings of your heart" are but too "marked and perceptible along the pages" to be missed.[199] Bancroft then had no way of telling how broad Irving's research was.[200] His estimation, however, fully supports the notion that *Life of George Washington* functions as a kind of national park for Irving, giving him a wish-fulfilling excursion from his middle-class self into vicarious identification with a national hero, on whom he projects an ideal or complete version of masculine perfection. In the fifth volume Irving quoted Thomas Jefferson's remarks that Washington's "integrity was most pure; his justice the most inflexible I have ever known; no motive of interest or consanguinity, of friendship or hatred, being able to bias his decision. He was, indeed, in every sense of the words, a wise, a good, and a great man."[201]

With *Life of George Washington*, then, Irving created a space where patriarchal control flourishes, safe from the encroachments of the market economy. Irving, who has shed the mask of Crayon, himself now assumed the patriarchal control that he had established within storytelling from a fictional persona to himself. The effects were well received, even to the point of ecstasy. "One could scarcely wish for our most eminent American author a more triumphant 'crowning glory' to a career of the highest literary renown," the reviewer for the *Knickerbocker* gushed,

> than that he should become the historian of the "Saviour of his country," as he had been before of its great Discoverer. The LIFE OF WASHINGTON by WASHINGTON IRVING! The combination will carry with it, and create, a permanent popularity; such as has not been accorded to any other book within the last century; and from this time forward, to the remotest years of our country's history, WASHINGTON and WASHINGTON IRVING will walk down the corridors of time together.[202]

One could think of a more tempered and nuanced comment, but Irving did earn himself the title "patriarch of American letters,"[203] and he did create the ultimate animus image, the perfect masculine archetype.

Epilogue

I BEGAN THIS BOOK BY ADVANCING Washington Irving's anima persona, a persona that seemed unable to identify with his own masculinity. The ensuing conflict, essentially one between purportedly "female" defects such as shyness and uncertainty, and the confident public image Irving habitually projected or felt he had to project, became visible throughout his life and writings, together with attempts to resolve the conflict. In his relentless quest for his own imperfectly realized masculinity Irving gave life to a plethora of male voices and images. These voices and images would belong to narrator personae like Jonathan Oldstyle and Lancelot Langstaff, Diedrich Knickerbocker, Geoffrey Crayon, and Fray Antonio Agapida. They also would belong to fictional protagonists like Rip Van Winkle, Ichabod Crane, Tom Walker, and Wolfert Webber. And they would, finally, belong to historic figures like Christopher Columbus, Boabdil, J.J. Astor, Captain Bonneville, Oliver Goldsmith and, finally, to George Washington. With *Life of George Washington*, Irving for the first time felt he had "come of age—of full age."[1] Irving playfully wrote this in anticipation of his seventieth birthday, though we might as well see this as an inkling of his having resolved the conflict between his anima-consciousness and his imperfectly realized masculinity. Irving's aim, Stanley Williams noted, was, "with limitations, psychological," though not just in terms of "a sense of completeness, of closing the windows."[2] In George Washington, Irving in a way recreated his own father, the bearer of the animus image he had been unable to identify with. In Washington, Irving transformed the figure of his own desires into an avatar of masculine perfection. His Washington is confident and purposeful, courageous and full of valor, he remains calm even in turmoil, knows his limitations, has an overarching perspective, lives with integrity, honors others, acts with honesty, takes responsibility for his actions, and protects his "kingdom." As commander in chief and, later, as president, he also provides order, not as a mythic lawgiver but as a metaphorical father and mentor, speaking to his "children" through his various addresses. And he leaves a legacy—as the "Father of His Country."[3]

In some fashion that Irving never fully grasped, Washington had been with him all his life, a shadow-self he had glimpsed from time to time from the corner of his eye but had the courage to fully confront, amplify, or expand only in his final years. Until then, Irving refashioned himself beyond the ugly manhood he perceived around him in at least four ways, and most always disguised as someone else. First, Irving turned feelings of depression, alienation, and fear into irreverent satire, mixed with hilarity and irresponsible humor that made light of nearly everything. As Jonathan Oldstyle, he lampooned the vile and unpolished manners of middle-class New Yorkers; as Diedrich Knickerbocker, he derided his political nemesis, Thomas Jefferson, as well as the ungainly manners and odious practices of money-grubbing Yankees and, in somewhat extenuated form, the sluggish, graceless, and unaspiring Dutch New Yorkers. Second, Irving linked himself to all things English, assuming the pose of the curious stranger sent, in the aftermath of the War of 1812, to observe the English, their country, their traditions and practices. Through Geoffrey Crayon, the man of feeling reminiscent of Henry Mackenzie's Harley, Irving gave a sympathetic description of what was attractive in England—London antiquities, literary sites, and the country estates of the gentry, together with their customs and traditions. These attractions made his readers forget that the days of England's glory, if glory it had been, were irretrievably gone.

Irving eventually exchanged the sentimentality of English romanticism for the heroic of Spanish romanticism. He gladly linked himself to the Spanish past, which he found rich in loyalty, solidity, human worth, and exemplary manhood, a manhood that also affected Geoffrey Crayon, whose boastful male vanity happily mimics the machismo bravado of Southern Spain. Warming his soul on "illustrious instances of high-wrought courtesy, romantic generosity, lofty disinterestedness, and punctilious honor," Irving, this "master of the obsolete in times and substance," once again resurrected the myths of a lost culture, churning out massive records "of prouder times and loftier modes of thinking."[4] Following his Spanish period, Irving became an observer of his own nation, finding romance in its westward turn. In the country west of the Mississippi he also hoped to find the part of himself he was seeking, feeding his imagination with trappers, mountain men, fur traders, and noble as well as ignoble Indigenous people. Nevertheless, Irving was profoundly ambivalent about the course of American history and the constituent elements of an American identity predicated on the Jacksonian creed of westward expansion and rugged individualism. But he not only found that his fellow Americans of the frontier were utterly unfitting as archetypes of achieved masculinity. He also realized that the masculinities he had hitherto imagined had been a way of avoiding the story that revealed itself to him in the mirror every day. That story was rooted in the nation's past, which in *Life of George Washington* he transformed into a truly mythic past, in which its dignified hero became the fullest and nearly perfect expression of the "King" archetype, the one to bind the nation together in a harmonious, unchanging whole.[5]

Stanley Williams, who devoted ten years to his definitive biography, concluded that as a writer, Irving was gifted but unoriginal and, above all, had "no principles, but only tastes to lead him wither they might."[6] Upon its appearance, the two-volume biography received glowing reviews. In one instance, a reviewer noted that Irving was "not troubled by any impulse to unravel the universe."[7] It is easy to take exception to such pronouncements. Irving did have an artistic vision, which he had articulated at age twenty-one—"forming that manliness and independence of character which it has ever been my ambition to acquire."[8] If that vision had little to do with unraveling the universe, it had everything to do with Irving's conflict between a dominant anima and a nagging, unloved masculinity. The vision manifested itself in the cast of his male characters which it was the purpose of this book to examine. Although fantasies, these figures were real psychic processes that were happening to Irving personally. "Shadows have proved my substance," he wrote to his niece Sarah Storrow, "from them I have derived my most exquisite enjoyments."[9] Irving of course is different from his personae, yet he nevertheless was an agent in whatever drama of masculinity was unfolding, "just as if [he] were one of the fantasy figures."[10] The various instantiations of archetypal masculinity thus were adumbrations, not of Irving himself but of how he did not want to be or—especially with George Washington—of what he wanted to be, of his ideal self, as a "hero."

Irving's writings in many ways are roadmaps to models of achieved manhood. From hindsight, these models often jar with one another, with one set validating sentimentality, and another set engaging in its very opposite, a rhetoric of tough masculinity devoid of feminizing impulses. Yet of all the masculine archetypes Irving imagined, George Washington is the only "King" archetype, the only one to incorporate the archetypes of Lover, Magician, and Warrior. The last one to see the light of day, Washington had sprung "from seeds planted years before." He is the result both of Irving's traumatic experience of a dysfunctional father and, by way of compensation, of his life-long hero-worship of the victorious general whom he had seen with his own eyes walk down Broadway in the New York of 1789. Irving, Williams notes, wrote of Washington "as he had long known him in imagination."[11] In a wider context, Washington is also the ultimate masculine model, the exemplary hero, whose moral purity and responsible social maturity served to stave off prevailing anxieties in antebellum America and, with the Civil War pending, to alleviate the disquieting threat of political disunion and carnage. And yet, the weary tone of *Life of George Washington* speaks, for one thing, to Irving's waning strength at an age when "memory comes in the place of imagination."[12] For another thing, it speaks to Irving's disillusionment with any prospects for categories that resisted the values of exchange or negotiation, and the period's instabilities. *Life of George Washington*, perhaps especially so, displays Irving's tragic conservatism, tragic insofar as Irving wanted to preserve, not what existed but what had been lost or was on the way out. Americans at mid-century no longer had any real use for Washington—awesome, remote, and largely unreal—as a symbol of nationality or national unity. Instead, images of Abraham Lincoln began to occupy a larger space in the American psyche.

Reverence for Lincoln set in during the presidential campaign, when he was hailed as "our Prairie King." The title "King" would have been impossible for Washington, the icon of classical republicanism, but for Lincoln it spelt natural nobility and leadership. Lincoln was seen as a man of the people, "No gentleman, like Washington," as the poet Richard Henry Stoddard would later write.[13] Following Lincoln's assassination, there was a resurgence of tradition, with the martyred president explicitly understood as a "A second Washington! / So great in every virtuous plan."[14] Elevated to the role of Savior of His Country, Lincoln was also expected to "affirm and reassert the principles of Washington." Praise of the Father of His Country was somewhat disingenuous, as it effectively broke Washington's unique hold on the nation's affections. "Mt. Vernon and Springfield will henceforth be kindred shrines," one eulogist declaimed.[15] Washington Irving died in 1859 and so could not witness the North's ascendancy. Thus, one is left to wonder how he would have depicted the younger one of "Columbia's noblest sons."[16] Would he have been able to also project onto Lincoln an instantiation of exemplary manhood? Or would he, like Herman Melville's young woman astronomer, Urania, have his prayers to be made "self-reliant, strong and free" remain unanswered, much as his own prayers for "manliness and independence of character" had remained unanswered?[17]

Several scholars have read Irving's career in terms of a "quest" or "pilgrimage" of some kind.[18] This pilgrimage or premier motive, I have argued throughout, was a quest for the half Irving had lost, for his imperfectly realized or "softened" masculinity. Dominated as he was by the anima (his feminine personality components), the purpose of his quest was to compensate for his "sensibility," an emotional response to loss, deprivation, and mourning. That quest was far from easy. Underlying the smooth surfaces of Irving's writings are self-doubt, guilt, fear of being coopted by the social imperative of competitive manliness, and strategic evasiveness. "I am always at a loss to know how much to believe of my own stories," he wrote in the introduction to *Tales of a Traveller*.[19] This is intrinsically baffling, a challenge to the critic's sense of interpretive authority and control over the reading experience. It does, however, make sense in light of Irving's "creative sorrow,"[20] his life-long search for an adequate form of manhood as part of himself. If that search made him turn to the past, his reverence for the past too was "an expression of his sadness."[21]

"More than any other writer except Henry Adams," Michael Warner found, "Washington Irving was fascinated with history, and especially with political history. From *The History of New York* at the beginning of his career to the *Life of George Washington* at its very end, historical writing dominates his output. Even his most belletristic works lean heavily on the vogue for historical fiction." There is a caveat. Irving writes history, Warner continues, "as though his aim were to have historical consciousness without inhabiting time."[22] We need not share Warner's belief that Irving merely produced "nostalgic time."[23] There is no doubt that Irving's past is never the past as actually experienced; it is the past as imagined, as idealized through memory and desire, and utterly devoid of any sense of historical progression, with or without the workings of a Hegelian "*Weltgeist*." But the importance of Irving's literary productions lies, not in a resulting "atemporal stasis" but—on the strength of working with his unconscious—in his peopling the various pasts with a multiplicity of archetypal masculinities. In other words, Irving captured the past not through factual exposition but through acts of storytelling, filling the contents of reverie and daydream with so many "shapes" from "airy nothing."[24]

Irving had to try hard to find his way in the world, making the most of his limited talents, moderate ambition, and "feminine" personality. That he succeeded beyond his expectations—and those of others—delighted him. But Irving had never set out to write for posterity, as Longfellow might have assumed when he called him "an honorable name and position in the history of letters," or when he bestowed on him the honorary title of "patriarch of American letters."[25] Irving, the middle-class son of a New York merchant, wrote both for a life, his own, that is, and for a living. He churned out books, reviews, and articles for close to six decades, at times working with such regularity that he was even accused of "bookmaking." Like many of today's best-selling authors, who publish books readers love but critics loathe, Irving wrote for the masses—and for profit. Already contemporary critics were scandalized by this: "[H]e who writes for the sole purpose of obtaining money," a reviewer griped in 1824, "is entitled to no praise, because he selects topics that will excite the popular passions." Such topics would include ghosts, as the same critic noted with indignation. Irving "knew *Ghost merchandise* would sell to the best advantage."[26]

Catering to popular tastes, writing not for the sake of literature but for profit, follows an honorable tradition. "Irving, like Shakespeare, wrote for the masses."[27] His mode of writing was, in Robyn Warhol's useful terminology, "conventionally engaging"—in contrast to the "conventionally distancing" modes of writing cultivated by the great writers of the American Renaissance, who instead articulated an alienated and intellectualized self-consciousness of deviance.[28] In itself, the two modes are simply two modes of writing. Yet the distinction can easily become a mode of social control, not least with critics of an anti-mimetic bias, who put complexity and alienation, thus the conventionally distancing, over pleasure and geniality or, in Irving's instance, the "sweet and wholesome" influence of his writings appreciated by genteel readers through the nineteenth century.[29]

Irving may have become a "classic American,"[30] yet his writings were losing their power in the years following the Civil War and, especially, in the new century. Modern readers and critics were increasingly uncomfortable with the value of Irving's writings, which cannot in good conscience be said to jibe with the elitist tradition of alienated mind play. Vernon Parrington, for instance, found Irving disappointingly conservative, if not apolitical, and incurably romantic. Parrington all but writes off a half century of creative effort when he dismisses Irving as an "incorrigible *flâneur*, [whose] business in life was to loaf and invite the picturesque," as he found the "immediate and the actual [...] an unsatisfying diet for his dreams."[31] In a similarly modernist vein, Carl van Doren in 1932 wrote that in the American popular imagination Irving, like other past masters, had "shrunk and faded."[32] Especially punitive was Irving's most dedicated biographer, who slashed the author's purported readiness to turn even the dregs of his trunks into cash.[33]

In the eyes of these critics, critical analysis was the be-all and end-all of literature, apart from, perhaps, intellectual verbal play. Irving, they would agree, was utterly incapable of any of these. Nor would they see anything truly original in the writings, least of all Irving's romances of achieved manhood. At best, they would concede that Irving had the merit and ability to refashion materials he took from folklore and (German, later Spanish) romanticism in an American cloak, making them his own. Since, the critical tide has changed, and there has been considerable re-evaluation as well as a renewed curiosity about Irving's methods and, per Andrew Burstein's magisterial biography of 2007, of Irving's life. William Hedges' article on Irving's *Columbus* (1956) may mark the beginning of the resurgence of Irving studies, together with Edward Wagenknecht's monograph of 1962. Other fine monographs followed, by Mary Bowden (1981) and Jeffrey Rubin-Dorsky (1988). Also forthcoming were collections of critical essays, respectively edited by Andrew Myers (1976) and Ralph Aderman (1990). The number of scholarly articles that have been published since the 1990s is, simply, awesome, as is the range of topics.[34] And there is even a vibrant

"Washington Irving Society," resurrected from a defunct one during the 2009 American Literature Association conference in Boston.[35]

When Vernon Parrington, Carl van Doren, Stanley Williams and others were heaping scorn on Irving's artistry, they neglected to mention that the texts they nobilitated as classics had been rather unpopular in the nineteenth century. Even Hawthorne's *The Scarlet Letter*, easily the most popular of the books now hailed an American classic, sold only 10,000 copies in its first five years. Melville's *Moby Dick* sold only 2,500 copies in its first five years, and only 450 more in its first twenty.[36] "Dollars damn me," Melville wrote to Hawthorne, "What I feel most moved to write, that is banned,—it will not pay. Yet, altogether, write the *other* way I cannot."[37] The quotations could be multiplied a hundredfold. They all reveal the self-consciousness of American Renaissance writers of their deviancy from prevailing social norms and gender formations. To them, "conventional American manhood seemed blithely inhospitable to any kind of literary spirit."[38] Irving would have sympathized. But writers like Melville and Hawthorne found a way out of the impasse only by making "a potentially hostile or indifferent audience, men preoccupied with competing for money and property, part of their rhetorical strategies."[39] They knew, or thought they knew, that men preoccupied with competing for money and property didn't read—at least not for pleasure.[40] The "literary spirit" David Leverenz cites is the property of writers who at their time considered themselves deviants, alienated from mainstream society, whose sniffy transcendence of "the mediocre & the dull" resembles the pervasive tendency of patrician men of affairs to invoke the fall of the Roman Empire in response to Jacksonian democracy. Moreover, these writers' rhetorical quarrels stemmed from their self-conscious resistance toward the rising middle-class and female market for fiction and to an authorship that increasingly became a feminized profession.[41]

In contrast to writers like Melville and Hawthorne, Irving preserved his "conventionally engaging" mode of writing. "I am for curing the world by gentle alternatives," he, hiding behind Geoffrey Crayon, wrote in the Introduction to *Tales of a Traveller*, "not by violent doses; indeed, the patient should never be conscious that he is taking a dose."[42] This may have been a literary pose, to placate or even deceive genteel readers. For, the apparent self-effacement often veiled a hidden animus that found expression, especially in the earlier writings, in a good deal of "violent doses." Still, one will be hard pressed to find instances where Irving attempted to liberate his voice from his class background and "polite" English conventions of taste, wit, and polish. And while from his Spanish period onward he linked himself to images of masculinity that the purveyors of sentimental manhood would have abhorred, Irving never developed what would have amounted to a premodernist style to explore and exalt a sense of deviance from conventional social norms. There is, for example, no "inadequate" reader in Irving's writings, that rhetorical device discovered by Renaissance writers in their attempt to liberate themselves from upper-class conventions without feeling fettered to "middle-class" values. On the contrary, Irving habitually encouraged a relatively gentle, "feminine" reader by crafting his moral dramas from within a background of gentility and from "polite" models; moreover, he offered these dramas as alternatives to an ideology of manhood constructed in terms of competition, materialism, and hard work.

When, as we have seen, Irving wrote to his friend Henry Brevoort that he had attempted "no lofty theme," preferring instead to address himself "to the feeling and fancy of the reader more than to his judgment" and to willingly risk that his writings "may appear light and trifling in our country of philosophers and politicians,"[43] his attitude of evasiveness nonetheless delighted contemporary readers, especially those who wanted sentimental simplicities to make their lives more bearable. The rhetoric of geniality and gentility, consonant with Irving's "softened masculinity,"[44] was there from the beginning. *Salmagundi*, Irving's first literary effort, was authored "by an American Gentleman." Other pseudonyms, like Jonathan Oldstyle, Anthony Evergreen, and Launcelot Langstaff, also were all "Gent." A "Gentleman of New York" signed as the author of an early biographical sketch of Thomas Campbell. Geoffrey Crayon, of course, likewise appears as "Gent." Even Diedrich Knickerbocker, the heirless remnant of bygone Dutch ancestors, must be considered a "gentleman." The accessibility of the rhetoric of geniality and gentility not only reflects the pervasiveness of the patrician paradigm and aspirations toward gentility among Irving's readership. The word "gentleman" also was most to Irving's own liking. A gentleman, Henry Seidel Canby wrote, "changes very little from youth to age, varies scarcely at all in works of very different character," and, as the perfect instrument for Irving's "feminine" literary personality, "became, as a style should, the very accent of the man."[45]

It is an often-quoted story that in 1850 Irving provided John Murray III with a detailed family genealogy to help the publisher make his case in a copyright suit in court. From it we learn that the Irvings came from a notable family from the Orkney Islands, which traced its descent from William de Irwyn, the armor-bearer of Robert Bruce.[46] Though Irving had no wish to appear as an Englishman, this rare gem of personal vanity perfectly matches his romances of achieved manhood. In these writings, Irving found a way to focus his personal as well as his writerly fears of not somehow being able to win a place among other men, his rage against his own "female" defects, against the United States and against the American social structure. Though a participant himself, Irving was deeply suspicious of the marketplace where the Irving family business had failed and where he himself had almost failed as a writer (or had in fact, as he purportedly had "written himself out" by the early 1820s). He also was uneasy about the forced compromises and self-diminishments of middle-class life, and, especially, he was disgusted by "the all pervading commonplace" that not long after his return home in 1832 he denounced as his country's "curse."[47]

Irving often described himself as a Federalist, though it is difficult to say what kind of Federalist he was. Less difficult to say is that his concerns often reflect the old-school Federalist cause for the dominance of reasonable patricians. Yet this cause had been lost from the start, because the rhetoric of achieved masculinity aimed to bring back an elite to cultural dominance at just the moment that the elite was being displaced from social and cultural leadership. By mid-century, institutionalized social structures such as class and patriarchy had ceased to be the basis of masculine self-esteem. In their stead had come materialism, competition, and the power dynamics in the workplace. Irving's description of merchants as belonging to an elite class only deepens the sense of a lost cause. "In our country, too, a commercial life does not imply the abandonment of other paths off honorable ambition," he wrote to his nephew Pierre Paris Irving, adding his hope that America's merchants would "become like the merchants of the old commercial republics of Europe—men fit to entertain and to confer with princes."[48]

Irving, that moderate Federalist who was comfortable with moderate Republicans, was patrician in his self-expectation, if not in his social background, and so was both fascinated and repulsed by the aggressive materialism and drive for dominance he witnessed in many of his fellow men. Indeed, his best work takes fire from profound fears of loss and humiliation as well as from complex feelings about male rivalry for dominance. This is not to blot out the strategies he used to transcend economic, social and personal conflicts. One may justifiably feel impatient with Irving's evasiveness, not to mention his defensive strategies when he is at his most conventionally sentimental, portraying, in a compensatory response that all but buries fears about male rivalry, mature masculinity in terms of genteel patriarchy. Nonetheless, to be a man of culture had become an effeminating, even hateful oxymoron in America well before the Civil War. An American man was made for action; he was expected to rise to wealth and power, to get on in the world. His life had little substance or meaning when he lacked work; worst, it would leave him "like a woman."[49]

Irving must have intuited these changes from early on. He no doubt knew that the very profession he had chosen for himself, writing, was often seen as a manipulative manifestation of effeminacy. Perhaps for this very reason he, like Howells and Henry James after him, adopted the role of a considerate, timid, and polite observer, not a participant. And, again like Howells and James, Irving often articulated a wish to be a practical man rather than a writer struggling to live by his craft.[50] The most telling manifestation of such a desire is in a letter Irving wrote to his niece Helen about her husband, Pierre Munro Irving, his first biographer: "Tell him I promise not to bore him about literary matters when he comes up. I have as great a contempt for these things as anybody, though I have to stoop to them occasionally for the sake of a livelihood—but I want to have a little talk with him about stocks, railroads and some more of screwing and jewing the world out of more interest than my money is entitled to."[51] Of course one can see a certain playful exaggeration in the tone of this letter, rather than a settled conviction on the subject of literature. At the same time, the letter shows Irving's painful awareness of the difficulties of a writer's life—and of the difficulties of proving one's manhood through writing.

It does not come as a surprise, then, that in an earlier letter Irving expressed his pleasure that the nephew was "really becoming a thorough and efficient man of business." This is followed by a note of encouragement: "*Buckle to your business like a man.* Turn your mind and your pride into it for a time, and you may become the founder of the fortunes of your family."[52] In an even earlier letter to another nephew Irving articulated his regret that he had not "been imperiously bound down to some regular and useful mode of life [and] the habits of business."[53] Irving adds his hope that the nephew will never "follow my footsteps, and wander into the seductive but treacherous paths of literature. There is no life more precarious in its profits and fallacious in its enjoyments than that of an author."[54] A few months later, Irving appears only too happy that the nephew had decided to enter his father's counting house, where he could be sure to have "a certain and prosperous path in life marked out."[55] These letters not only reflect Irving's personal difficulties in trying to make a living from writing. They also register the psychological costs of the freewheeling capitalism that was turning America into "a money-mad nation without value, without principles," to use William Charvat's apt words.[56] Moreover, it makes us aware that Irving's writings too should be seen as symptoms of a larger cultural malaise. They are records of plight, much as they are key sites within which compensation is offered. Their rhetorical surfaces, heroic or unheroic, reveal a social reality that is much darker and far more distressing than Irving, who has been described as all "moderation," would openly admit.[57]

Throughout his life, Irving—like Hawthorne, whom he admired—tried to succeed both as a writer and as a man among "real" men. There was in him a concealed rebelliousness, together with a profound self-distrust about his deviance from middle-class norms of manhood. More than once, Irving baffled his family by staying away from home. If this helped him firm up his self-control, his art gave partial voice to profound fears. Searching for self-empowerment, he ultimately resolved his feelings of manly inferiority through patriarchal and patrician reidentification, which come to us as so many avatars of responsible social maturity, of dutiful masculinity. Irving was seventy-five years old when in a letter to a young relative he described the personal qualities he most admired:

> I have always valued in you what I considered to be an honorable nature; a conscientiousness in regard to duties; an open truthfulness; an absence of all low propensities and sensual indulgencies; a reverence for sacred things; a respect for others; a freedom from selfishness, and a prompt decision to oblige; and, with all these, a gayety of spirit, flowing, I believe, from an uncorrupted heart, that gladdens everything around you.[58]

The description at the same time is a pretty good self-portrait, and Irving certainly possessed all these qualities to varying degrees.

Emily Fuller, née Foster, to whom Irving may have proposed marriage in 1824, after his death remembered him as "thoroughly a gentleman, not merely externally in manners and look, but to the innermost fibers and core of his heart. Sweet-tempered, gentle, fastidious, sensitive, and gifted with the warmest affections...."[59] On another occasion, she writes that years later, Irving "was still the same.... All gentle and tender affections, Nature in her sweetest or grandest moods, pervaded his whole imagination, and left no place for low or evil thoughts."[60] Characterizations of this kind show that, socially acceptable male gender stereotypes notwithstanding, Irving was able to retain "feminine" feelings of vulnerability, emotional connection, and gentleness. It does not therefore come as a surprise that friends and acquaintances would gather around Irving at his home.[61] Irving had bought twenty-four acres on the Hudson River near Tarrytown, New York, in 1835. Taking inspiration from Wolfert's Roost, Wolfert Acker's seventeenth-century dwelling, he gradually remodeled the small cottage he found there into Sunnyside, a fine house of romantic architecture.[62]

Except for the four-year absence while United States Minister to Spain, Irving lived at Sunnyside from 1836 until his death in 1859. He loved the place, confiding to his nephew that he "would not exchange the cottage for any chateau in Christendom."[63] Over the years, Sunnyside also became a veritable family nest, which housed brothers, nephews, other dependents—and his nieces, who tended and nursed him in his old age. Irving finally was able to warm himself at a family hearth, "surrounded by affectionate beings who cherished" him, and proud to have become the *"pere de famille."*[64] According to Michael Warner, Irving maintained himself as a "patriarch to his nieces, his bachelor brother, miscellaneous dependents, and American letters in general." Irving's conception of patriarchy was essentially benignant, a kind of benevolent paternalism," yet he consistently made the picture of himself "to be felt as archaic," more like the kindly patriarch of an eighteenth-century sentimental novel. Hence Irving was not a genuine patriarch so much as a "surrogate" one.[65]

A daguerreotype of Irving taken at Matthew M. Brady's studio about 1855 beautifully captures the patriarch image, whether genuine or surrogate.[66] The head and shoulders portrait shows a portly elderly gentleman, of fairly stout stature, with a full face, characteristic of his age (Irving was 72 then), slightly balding but made up for by a skillfully made wig, and elegantly but conservatively dressed. Was this, one wonders, the image of "healthful manliness" that *Harper's New Monthly Magazine* presented to worshippers in December 1856?[67] Irving's contemporaries, used to drawing conclusions about a person's character from outward appearances, would rather have seen the kind of gentleman one would expect to find hobnobbing with politicians, lawyers, or the newly moneyed urban entrepreneurs, bankers included.[68] This was a change that those who recollected his early days in his patrician merchant family could not fail to notice, sometimes unkindly. George P. Putnam, his American publisher, saw a different Irving, of manly sincerity, earnestness, and restraint. "I had always too much earnest *respect* for Mr. Irving ever to claim familiar intimacy with him. He was a man who would unconsciously and quietly command deferential regard and consideration; for in all his ways and words there was the atmosphere of refinement. He was emphatically a gentleman, in the best sense of that word."[69]

"Respect" and being a "gentleman" is, of course, all very fine and good, but as the venerable Francis Grund, journalist and author of *The Americans in Their Moral, Social, and Political Relations*, observed in 1839, "There is nothing our women dislike so much as corpulency."[70] In this regard, Brady's daguerreotype surely does not convey the lineaments of accepted or acceptable manhood. For this, we have to turn to Irving's Columbus, who comes to us in "the full vigour of manhood," an "engaging presence [...] tall, well formed, muscular, and of an elevated and dignified demeanour."[71] This Columbus is the product of an artist, whose author, when writing the historical biography, had been "greatly perplexed to fix the boundary between the purely historical and the imaginative."[72] Irving, we have seen, let his own imperfectly realized masculinity live in projections onto masculine heroes rather than within himself. As for the biographical person, friends and acquaintances would emphasize Irving's "genial humor" and "kindly nature," a *"bonhomie"* that made him truly lovable.[73]

Being a good man in some abstract moral sense is not nearly enough in any society. What matters is being good at being a man, at playing a socially ascribed role in full public view. As a successful writer-entrepreneur, Irving certainly proved his manhood. He was taking chances with his pen, and he showed an attitude. "There was something audacious about Washington Irving that too few have given him credit for."[74] Irving's audacity was not confined to his writing. There were moments when his courage showed up, perhaps none more so than in a letter to his brother Ebenezer, in which he boldly declared that he was "determined not to return home until I have sent some writing before me that shall, if they have merit, make me return to smiles, rather than skulk back to the pity of my friends."[75] It likewise took plenty of courage to buckle down to some cheerless drudgery to save his family from financial ruin, or, when failure was unavoidable, to rely on nothing but his "inner strength."[76]

Yet as Francis Grund's words reveal only too clearly, the physical appearance of a man counts, too. Shortly after Irving's return from Spain, Fredrika Bremer, an authoress who had read him in Sweden, drew him aside at a fashionable dinner in New York. After, she described him as a "man of about sixty, with large, beautiful eyes, a large well-formed nose, a countenance still handsome, in which youthful little dimples and smiles bear witness to a youthfully fresh and humorous disposition and soul."[77] There is no mention of height or bigness, the measure of a man not merely in the United States, let alone of muscularity, athletic prowess, and a radiating self-assurance. Of course, these are only necessary, not sufficient criteria for validating manhood. Nevertheless, they are criteria, all too visible in the clean-cut Englishman or the all-American boy, and, separated by a world of difference, they have their dark side in various destructive and murderous "male fantasies." Such fantasies, the German cultural analyst Klaus Theweleit has shown, are essential to the formation and nature of the fascist psyche. Swayed by its toxicity, men are utterly incapable of relating to other humans. Instead, they live inside their iron-hard shells as the only means of reigning in their anxieties and fears. Without a stable ego-identity, such men rely on physical "self-improvement," on steeling their male bodies, and they depend on the strictest hierarchies to provide at least a semblance of structure, while their gendered rage makes them feel nothing but contempt for weakness, feminizing luxury, or sensuous pleasure.[78]

Irving often enough reflected upon his own manliness, or rather, his deficiency thereof, yet he never indulged in such male fantasies, no matter how attractive they might have been (and still are) for some people.[79] Contrary to nineteenth-century gender norms, he retained his "femininity," holding on to his anima-ego, his most precious gift. The "feminine" components of his personality may well have helped him see through conventional manliness as social role-playing, a deeply conflicted, pressured, and forced pose, a mask worn on the outside. Hence his relentless search for what he would have considered achieved manhood. Looking back on his earlier masculine archetypes, however, it is almost as if Irving (or we, as readers) hadn't known them very well. He only gradually understood (as we, as readers, must understand) that they were all precursors to "George Washington," all shadows in his life as George Washington was a shadow, a person not known but loved and revered from a distance. Or maybe Washington was a dream. Maybe he was a character in a vast romance. Maybe he was a projection of Irving's unconscious, a projection that, if amplified, promised the integration of personality Irving could only hope for. Be that as it may, male archetypes assumed a more important role than Irving had originally envisaged for them, as if his imperfectly realized masculinity had moved to center stage and taken command of a larger narrative of identification, of making them part of himself. In this regard, Irving's masculine archetypes became symbols of transformation, guides or torchbearers to point or lead the way out of a precarious form of male selfhood, of purportedly "female" defects, of shyness and uncertainty, which were in perpetual conflict with what he believed or believed society believed to be masculine perfection. Irving himself was unable or unwilling to follow these guides to the end, to permit them to really become part of himself. No matter where he found it, in "distant Europe" or among the scenes of his "native country," he could let masculine perfection live only in projections.[80] Perhaps for that very reason, Irving never had to say to himself, bitterly, there goes my miracle.

Chapter Notes

ABBREVIATIONS

BTA—Washington Irving. *Bracebridge Hall, Tales of a Traveller, The Alhambra.* New York: Library of America, 1991.

CW-Astoria—*The Complete Works of Washington Irving: Astoria, or Anecdotes of an Enterprize beyond the Rocky Mountains.* Ed. Richard Dilworth Rust. Boston: Twayne, 1976.

CW-BH—*The Complete Works of Washington Irving: Bracebridge Hall or The Humourists. A Medley by Geoffrey Crayon, Gent.* Ed. Herbert F. Smith. Boston: Twayne, 1977.

CW-Bonneville—*The Complete Works of Washington Irving: The Adventures of Captain Bonneville.* Ed. Robert A. Rees and Alan Sandy. Boston: Twayne, 1977.

CW-CM—*The Complete Works of Washington Irving: Crayon Miscellany.* Ed. Dahlia Kirby Terrell. Boston: Twayne, 1979.

CW-Columbus—*The Complete Works of Washington Irving: The Life and Voyages of Christopher Columbus.* Ed. John Harmon McElroy. Boston: Twayne, 1981.

CW-Conquest—*The Complete Works of Washington Irving: A Chronicle of the Conquest of Granada.* Ed. Miriam J. Shillingsburg. Boston: Twayne, 1988.

CW-Goldsmith—*The Complete Works of Washington Irving: Oliver Goldsmith: A Biography / Biography of the Late Margaret Miller Davidson.* Ed. Elsie Lee West. Boston: Twayne, 1978.

CW-History—*The Complete Works of Washington Irving: A History of New York.* Ed. Michael L. Black and Nancy B. Black. Boston: Twayne, 1984.

CW-Journals—*The Complete Works of Washington Irving: Journals and Notebooks.* Ed. Nathalia Wright et al. 5 vols. Madison and Boston: University of Wisconsin Press and Twayne Publishers, 1969–1981.

CW-Letters—*The Complete Works of Washington Irving: Letters.* Ed. Ralph M. Aderman, Herbert L. Kleinfield, and Jenifer S. Banks. 4 vols. Boston: Twayne, 1978–1982.

CW-Mahomet—*The Complete Works of Washington Irving: Mahomet and His Successors.* Ed. Henry A. Pochmann and E.N. Feltskog. Madison: University of Wisconsin Press, 1970.

CW-Misc.—*The Complete Works of Washington Irving: Miscellaneous Writings.* Ed. Wayne R. Kime. 2 vols. Boston: Twayne, 1981.

CW-SB—*The Complete Works of Washington Irving: The Sketch Book of Geoffrey Crayon, Gent.* Ed. Haskell Springer. Boston: Twayne, 1978.

CW-Traveller—*The Complete Works of Washington Irving: Tales of a Traveller by Geoffrey Crayon, Gent.* Ed. Judith Giblin Haig. Boston: Twayne, 1987.

CW-Washington—*The Complete Works of Washington Irving: Life of George Washington.* Ed. Allen Guttmann and James A. Sappenfield. 3 vols. Boston: Twayne, 1982.

CW-WR—*The Complete Works of Washington Irving: Wolfert's Roost.* Ed. Roberta Rosenberg. Boston: Twayne, 1979.

HTS—Washington Irving. *History, Tales and Sketches.* New York: Library of America, 1983.

JCW—C. G. Jung. *The Collected Works of C.G. Jung.* Trans. R.F.C. Hull. 20 vols. Bollingen Series XX. Princeton, NJ: Princeton University Press, 1953–1979.

PMI—Pierre M. Irving. *The Life and Letters of Washington Irving.* 4 vols. New York: G.P. Putnam, 1862–1864.

STW—Stanley T. Williams. *The Life of Washington Irving.* 2 vols. New York: Oxford University Press, 1935.

Washington—Washington Irving. *Life of George Washington.* 5 vols. New York: G.P. Putnam, 1855–1859.

Prologue

1. *Washington*, V:iii.

2. "Universal History, the history of what man has accomplished in this world," Carlyle wrote, "is at bottom the History of the Great Men who have worked here." *On Heroes, Hero-Worship and the Heroic in History* (New York: Frederick A. Stokes, 1893), 223.

3. See PMI, respectively 1:106; 149; 198–203; 332; and 2:369. For Napoleon as a "noble fellow," see Irving to Henry Brevoort, July 16 (?), 1815, *CW-Letters*, 1:401. For Irving's admiration for Espartero, see his letter to Helen Irving, wife of his nephew, Pierre Munro Irving, September 1842, PMI, 3:231; for Narváez, see his letter to Catherine Paris, Madrid, February 19, 1845, *CW-Letters*, 3:889–90. As for William the Conqueror, Irving began a project on him in Paris in 1824, though he never completed it. A manuscript fragment was discovered and published by Stanley T. Williams as "Anecdotes of William the Conqueror" at the end of his *Journal of Washington Irving (1823–1824)* (Cambridge, MA: Harvard University Press, 1931), 245–56.

4. The sketches all appeared in *Analectic Magazine*, for which Irving served as editor 1813–1814. See Elsie Lee West, "Washington Irving, Biographer," *Washington Irving Reconsidered: A Symposium*, ed. Ralph M. Aderman (Hartford, CT: Transcendental Books, 1969), 48–49. On Irving's admiration of Decatur, see STW, 1:135–36, 144.

5. James Hillman, *anima, an anatomy of a personified notion* (Putnam, CT: Spring Publications, 1985), 23–25, quotation 23.

6. Richard Powers, *The Overstory* (New York-London: W. W. Norton, 2018), 3.

7. To get a first impression, go to https://www.anima-garden.com/experience/, accessed October 13, 2018. André Heller's *Anima* (Wien: Brandstätter Verlag, 2018) is an opulent picture book, with photographs by Albina Bauer and texts by Andrea Schurian. Heller's novel, *Das Buch vom Süden* (Wien: Paul Zsolnay Verlag, 2016), may serve as a literary how-to manual for the Anima garden.

8. From Garrison Keillor, "The Writer's Almanac," October 21, 2020, https://www.garrisonkeillor.com/radio/twa-the-writers-almanac-for-october-21-2020/, retrieved December 17, 2020. I have not been able to verify Coleridge's authorship. There is, however, a somewhat similar reference in Thomas Wolfe's 1930 novel *Look Homeward, Angel* (London: Four Square Books, 1960), 307: "For if a man should dream of heaven and, waking, find within his hand a flower as token that he had really been there—what then, what then?"

9. Irving to Peter Irving, Alhambra, June 13, 1829, *CW-Letters*, 2:436.

10. *JCW*, 5: §678. For psychological functions, see *JCW*, 7: §339.

11. From a card accompanying Heller's *Anima* book, translation mine.

12. Washington Irving, "Review of *The*

Works of Robert Treat Paine," *Analectic Magazine*, 1 (1813), 252, qtd. in William L. Hedges, *Washington Irving: An American Study, 1802-1832* (Baltimore: Johns Hopkins University Press, 1965; repr. Westport, CT: Greenwood Press, 1980), 14.

13. Donald G. Mitchell, "Preface of 1863," qtd. in Andrew Burstein, *The Original Knickerbocker: The Life of Washington Irving* (New York: Basic Books, 2007), 318, emphasis in original. Mitchell was an essayist with whom Irving struck up an acquaintance in the 1850s. In an address on the occasion of Irving's one-hundredth birthday, Mitchell spoke lovingly of the man's "kindness" and "goodheartedness." "Address," in Andrew B. Myers, ed., *A Century of Commentary on the Works of Washington Irving* (Tarrytown, NY: Sleepy Hollow Restorations, 1976), 54-61, quot. 61. For "sensibility," see STW, 1:294.

14. Henry Wadsworth Longfellow, "In the Churchyard at Tarrytown [1876]," in *A Century of Commentary on the Works of Washington Irving*, ed. Andrew B. Myers (Tarrytown, NY: Sleepy Hollow Restorations, 1976), 39. Longfellow was twenty-four years younger than Irving, though the two had much in common. Not only did young Longfellow write an Irving-derived sketchbook, *Outre-Mer: A Pilgrimage Beyond the Sea* (1833); he was just as averse to the crass materialism and money-grabbing in America as Irving. And like Irving, his anger always remained gentle. Also like Irving, Longfellow, when asked to run for Congress, professed to have no interest in going into politics. Last but not least, the two men shared certain indolent habits as well as an almost morbid sensitiveness and bouts of depression. For more on Irving's counterpart, see Nicholas A. Basbanes, *Cross of Snow: A Life of Henry Wadsworth Longfellow* (New York: Knopf, 2020).

15. Charles Dudley Warner, *Washington Irving* (Boston-New York: Houghton Mifflin, 1881), 303. For more, see George Sanderlin, *Washington Irving: As Others Saw Him* (New York: Coward, McCann & Geoghegan, 1975).

16. "To the Reader," in *CW-Traveller*, 4.

17. Each idea, William James wrote in an 1880 article, emerges from "random images, fancies, accidental out-births of spontaneous variation in the functional activity of the excessively instable human brain ..." James, "Great Men, Great Thoughts and the Environment," *Atlantic Monthly*, October 1880, 441-59, here 456, qtd. in Henry M. Cowles, *The Scientific Method: An Evolution of Thinking from Darwin to Dewey* (Cambridge, MA: Harvard University Press, 2020), 178.

18. Hillman, *anima*, 23; on "receptivity" as the premier attitude of an anima persona, see Emma Jung, *Animus and Anima*, 55.

19. Irving, "The Wife" and "The Widow and her Son," *The Sketch Book of Geoffrey Crayon*, in *HTS*, respectively 764, 839.

20. STW, 2:110.

21. STW, 1:294-95. (The opposition of "fair sex" and "noble sex" originated with Immanuel Kant.) For criticisms of Irving's gender bias, see, for instance, Michael Warner, "Irving's Posterity," *ELH* (*English Literary History*) 67:3 (2000), 776.

22. See Hugh J. Dawson, "Recovering 'Rip Van Winkle': A Corrective Reading," *ESQ: A Journal of the American Renaissance* 40:3 (1994), 251-73, esp. 269, and C. Michael Hurst, "Reinventing Patriarchy: Washington Irving and the Autoerotics of the American Imaginary," *Early American Literature* 47:3 (2012), especially 657-59 and 662-64. For "tea and sympathy," see Ann Douglas, *The Feminization of American Culture* (1977; New York: Doubleday, 1988), 102.

23. *The Alhambra*, in *BTA*, 726.

24. On the hero as a representation of the animus archetype, see Hillman, *anima*, 61, based on Jung's thesis that animus and anima are quasi-personal archetypes (see *JCW*, 5: §388). For Irving's characterization of Columbus, see *CW-Columbus*, 31; for his characterization of Washington, see *Washington*, V:320.

25. The human mind, William James wrote, "is always interested more in one part of its object than in another, and welcomes and rejects, or chooses, all the while it thinks." James, *The Principles of Psychology*, vol. 1 (New York: Henry Holt, 1890), 284, qtd. in Cowles, *The Scientific Method*, 182.

26. On the distinction between "anima as experience" and "anima as notion" see Hillman, *anima*, 99.

27. Hillman, *anima*, 5-13.

28. *JCW*, 9, part I: §§290-297 and *JCW*, 14, passim.

29. *JCW*, 9, part I: §§5–7, 53–67, and *JCW*, 6: §807.

30. Moreover, the idea that there are feminine and masculine aspects in men is fundamental also to modern psychoanalysis. See Gerald I. Fogel, "Being a Man," *The Psychology of Men: New Psychoanalytical Perspectives*, ed. the same et al. (New York: Basic Books, 1986), 3–22.

31. Isaiah Berlin, "Historical Inevitability," in *The Proper Study of Mankind: An Anthology of Essays*, ed. Roger Hausheer (New York: Farrar, Straus and Giroux, 1997), 119–90, here 131.

32. For "enigmatic quality of Irving's real self" see Austin McC. Fox's introduction to *The Legend of Sleepy Hollow and Other Selections from Washington Irving* (New York: Washington Square Press, 1962), viii.

33. "The Works of Robert Treat Paine," *Analectic Review* 1 (1813), 252. For "all pervading commonplace" see Irving to his niece Sarah, now Mrs. Storrow, Honesdale, July 31, 1841, *CW-Letters*, 3:145.

34. Hurst, "Reinventing Patriarchy," 659.

35. *Washington*, V:320.

36. For "bullyboys," see David Leverenz, *Manhood and the American Renaissance* (Ithaca, NY: Cornell University Press, 1989), 87.

37. Heinz Kohut, "Beyond the Bounds of the Basic Rule: Some Recent Contributions to Applied Psychoanalysis," *Journal of the American Psychoanalytical Association* 8 (1960), 567–86, here 584. Kohut is at great pains to set off Jungian "deep biography," which explores the connections between, in this instance, the writings and the subject's inner world (the creative imagination, but also dreams, visions, daydreams, remembrances, hallucinations), against Freudian "pathography," which starts from the apriority of the pathological. For examples of the latter, see the contributions to *Psycho-Pathographien des Alltags: Schriftsteller und Psychoanalyse*, ed. with an Introduction by Alexander Mitscherlich (Frankfurt am Main: Suhrkamp, 1982).

38. Irving to his niece Sarah, Honesdale, July 31, 1841, *CW-Letters*, 3:145. On the notion that Irving had "written himself out," see STW, 1:207 and 2:21.

Chapter One

1. Ann Douglas, *The Feminization of American Culture* (1977; New York: Doubleday, 1988), 19. It was in response to this situation, Douglas explains, that educated women and liberal, literate clergymen and popular writers banded together to have a profound effect on the only areas that an increasingly aggressive capitalist system left open to their influence—literature and the arts. In these fields they were able to promote values that were not only deeply conservative but also had the sanction of sentimentality, and they played an important part in the creation and character of nineteenth-century culture—while the avantgarde was being ignored. See *ibid.*, 6–10 and passim, and see David Anthony, "'Gone Distracted': 'Sleepy Hollow,' Gothic Masculinity, and the Panic of 1819," *Early American Literature* 40:1 (2005), 115. For "labour of headwork," see *CW-SB*, 276.

2. Irving to Henry Brevoort, New York, May 15, 1811, *CW-Letters*, 1:316. Irving wrote this when his services were urgently required at his brothers Ebenezer and Peter's business. The business was in the line of the importation and sale of hardware and cutlery.

3. *Ibid.*, emphases added.

4. *JCW*, 5: §678.

5. *Ibid.*, §388.

6. *JCW*, 8: §§270–81, 435, 439, and 573.

7. *JCW*, 9, part I: §146. Emma Jung, too, records a case of a writer's unique relation to the anima. William Sharp, an English author of the late nineteenth century, first studied law, then worked at a banking house before he turned to literature and the arts, eventually publishing under the pseudonym of Fiona Macleod—to the unreserved praise of no lesser person than William Butler Yeats. See *Animus and Anima*, 84–85.

8. Catherine Jones, "Romantic Opera in Translation: Carl Maria von Weber and Washington Irving," *Translation & Literature* 20:1 (2011), 29–47.

9. STW, 2:99, 2:357n41, and passim. For Irving's "European Journal, 1804–1806," see *CW-Journals*, 1:284. On his Western tour, in 1832, Irving cast himself as "the old actor on a different stage" (*CW-Journals*, 2:37). On the Paris experiments, see *CW-Journals* 3:262–65, and 280, and Judith Giblin Haig, "Washington Irving and the Romance of Travel: Is there an Itinerary in Tales of a Traveller?" in *The Old and New World Romanticism of Washington Irving*, ed.

Stanley Brodwin (Westport, CT: Greenwood Press, 1986), 61–68; also of interest are Walter A. Reichart, "The Aspiring Dramatist," in *Washington Irving and Germany* (Ann Arbor: University of Michigan Press, 1957), 121–36, and "Washington Irving and the Theatre," *Maske und Kothurn* 14 (1968), 341–50, reprinted in *Critical Essays on Washington Irving*, ed. Ralph M. Aderman, Critical Essays on American Literature (Boston, MA: G. K. Hall, 1990), 166–78.

10. STW, 1:446n111.

11. James Hillman, *anima, an anatomy of a personified notion* (Putnam, CT: Spring Publications, 1985), 23.

12. Erika Freeman, "Unglücklich zu sein macht dich auch nicht schlauer [Being unhappy doesn't make you any smarter]," ZEIT Magazin, no.21 (Hamburg, May 14, 2020), 14–24, here 21.

13. Hillman, *anima*, 23. Had the focus of the present study been exclusively on Irving's observable behavior, use of the Jungian categories of "introvert" and "extrovert" might have been fruitful. On the two psychological types, see *JCW*, 6: §§621-25, 931-50, and 8: §§81-84.

14. *JCW*, 10: §220.

15. Citing Coleridge, Virginia Woolf argued that genius is androgynous, fusing male and female traits. "[O]ne must be woman-manly or man-womanly," she wrote, adding that in the androgynous mind "some marriage of opposites has to be consummated." Virginia Woolf, *A Room of One's Own* (London: Hogarth press, 1935), 157, qtd. in Alex Ross, *Wagnerism: Art and Politics in the Shadow of Music* (New York: Farrar, Straus and Giroux, 2020), 504. The preferred term of the Jungian faithful is "hermaphrodite." A "hermaphroditic consciousness," James Hillman argues, is capable of holding anima and animus in abeyance. See *anima*, 177, and *JCW*, 9, part I: §512, and §678. Jung elsewhere referred to an ancient alchemical treatise concerning the "*homo Adamicus*" who, "although he appears in masculine form, nevertheless carries about with him Eve, or his feminine part, hidden in his body." *JCW*, 11: §47. The idea of the androgynous inner man and, *horribile dictu*, of God as an androgynous being, is also at least hinted at in the Bible. The fifth chapter of Genesis, for instance, begins, "In the day that God created man, in the likeness of God made he him; Male and female created he them, and called their name Adam, in the day when they were created." (Gen. 5:1–2). Cf. a. Gen 1:27: "So God created man in his own image, in the image of God created he him; male and female created he them." Both qtd. from KJV. For more, see John A. Sanford, *The Invisible Partners: How the Male and Female in Each of Us Affects Our Relationships* (New York-Mahwah, NJ: Paulist Press, 1980), 3–6.

16. PMI, 1:229. Elsewhere, Pierre Munro Irving talks about "the portrait with the fur collar" (4:315). Andrew Burstein considers Jarvis's portrait as "notable for the dark, sensitive eyes—for a face that bespeaks a quiet intensity". Andrew Burstein, *The Original Knickerbocker: The Life of Washington Irving* (New York: Basic Books, 2007), 70. The portrait, used as frontispiece to *The Original Knickerbocker*, is now owned by Historic Hudson Valley. See https://hudsonvalley.org/.

17. For green as anima color, see *JCW*, 5: §678. The portrait features as frontispiece to vol. I of Stanley Williams's biography. A full-color reproduction of the portrait is on the cover of *150 W.I.: Washington Irving and the Alhambra*, Temporary Exhibition, Granada, Chapel and Crypt of the Palace of Charles V, Alhambra and Generalife Historical Monument, October 2009—February 2010, ed. Carmen Yusty Pérez, October 2009-February 2010 (Granada: Patronato de la Alhambra y Generalife / Tf Editores [Madrid], 2009). A mezzotint engraving of the Newton portrait by Charles Turner (1824) is in the Yale University Art Gallery, New Haven, Connecticut, Mabel Brady Garvan Collection, https://artgallery.yale.edu/collections/objects/45678.

18. Irving to Ebenezer Irving, March 3, 1819, PMI, 1:412.

19. See Van Wyck Brooks, *The World of Washington Irving* (1944; New York: Dutton—London: Dent, 1950), 174, and Edward Wagenknecht, *Washington Irving: Moderation Displayed* (New York: Oxford University Press, 1962), 45–47.

20. On Leslie's portrait, see PMI, 2:28–29. On Irving's admiration of Newton's "eye for coloring," see his letter to the painter and historian William Dunlap of March 9, 1834, CW-Letters, 2:788–89.

21. *JCW*, 9, part I: §142, emphases in original.

22. *JCW*, 9, part II: §41n5, and *JCW*, 16: §469.

23. *CW* 9, part I: §57, emphases in original.

24. Henry Wadsworth Longfellow, "Address on the Death of Washington Irving," in *Poems and Other Writings* (New York: Library of America, 2000), 800.

25. *The Journal of Emily Foster*, qtd. in Burstein, *The Original Knickerbocker*, 172, and PMI, 4:353.

26. Burstein, *The Original Knickerbocker*, 154; for "softened masculinity," see *ibid.*. Dolph Heyliger is a character from *Bracebridge Hall* and, as Burstein argues (*ibid.*, 165–66), another one of Irving's alter egos.

27. *JCW*, 9, part I: §§59, 62–64.

28. *JCW*, 10: §220; *JCW*, 9, part I: §146, and Sanford, *The Invisible Partners*, 13, 95–99.

29. See, for instance, Michael Warner, "Irving's Posterity," *ELH* (*English Literary History*) 67:3 (2000), 773–99, Bryce Traister, "The Wandering Bachelor: Irving, Masculinity, and Authorship," *American Literature* 74:1 (2002), 114–15, 122, and, for a quite different view, drawing on scientific studies that link homosexuality in men to the number of older brothers they have, Burstein, *The Original Knickerbocker*, 333–35.

30. *CW-Journals*, 3:281; the manuscript fragment is printed in full in STW, 2:255–62; for other echoes of Matilda's death, see *CW-Journals*, 2:186n44 and 195n71. See a. Stanley Williams, "Washington Irving, Matilda Hoffman, and Emily Foster," *Modern Language Notes* 48 (March 1933), 182–86.

31. PMI, 1:229.

32. Brian Jay Jones, *Washington Irving: An American Original* (New York: Arcade Publishing, 2008), 88.

33. Irving, the historian Andrew Burstein argues, "treated his male friends as wife substitutes. *This had to do with intimacy, not sex as we understand it*." Burstein, *The Original Knickerbocker*, 118, emphases added. F. O. C. Darley and Christian Schussele captured a men's gathering in an 1863 painting, *Washington Irving and His Literary Friends at Sunnyside*. For a reproduction of the painting, see the exhibition catalog *150 W.I.: Washington Irving and the Alhambra*, 58. On nineteenth-century male intimacy, see also E. Anthony Rotundo, *American Manhood: Transformations in Masculinity from the Revolution to the Modern Era* (New York: Basic Books, 1993), 82–87, and chap. 4, 75–91.

34. For discussions of Irving's relationships with women, see Henry August Pochmann, *Washington Irving: Representative Selections* (New York: American Book Company, 1934), xxiii–xxiv; Wagenknecht, *Moderation Displayed*, 126–54, and Jenifer S. Banks, "Washington Irving, the Nineteenth-Century Bachelor," in *Critical Essays on Washington Irving*, ed. Ralph M. Aderman, 253–65.

35. Burstein, *The Original Knickerbocker*, 305.

36. In this connection, see Jenifer Banks: "In his fiction as in his life, [Irving] reduced women to two basic and essentially adolescent classes: his positive category included figures of nurturing, sustaining supporters of men or figures of passive innocence and virtue; his negative category included the aggressor, the seductress and the albatross threatening or draining men." "Washington Irving, the Nineteenth-Century Bachelor," 258.

37. Madrid, December 12, 1842, in *CW-Letters*, 3:437; on Irving's lack of resources, see PMI, 1:221–22. Burstein, *The Original Knickerbocker*, 110–12, endorses this view of Irving's bachelorhood.

38. Traister, "The Wandering Bachelor," 114–15, 122. For a similar position, see Vincent J. Bertolini, "Fireside Chastity: The Erotics of Sentimental Bachelorhood in the 1850s," in *Sentimental Men: Masculinity and the Politics of Affect in American Culture*, ed. Mary Chapman and Glenn Hendler (Berkeley: University of California Press, 1999), 19–42.

39. HTS, 931; reference is to Master Simon, the wit of the Bracebridge family and Irving's double in more than one sense. For, in "A Bachelor's Confessions," this Master Simon confesses to keeping a lock of a woman's hair, a painful reminder of an unhappy romance and the kind of confession Irving would make in a long letter to Mrs. Foster in Dresden in 1823. On Irving's "bachelor aesthetic," see Traister, "The Wandering Bachelor," 112–13, 130–31.

40. Bertolini, "Fireside Chastity," 21. For "an absolute old Bachelor," see Irving's letter to Henry Brevoort, May 23, 1829, *CW-Letters*, 2:425.

41. HTS, 51.
42. Irving to William Irving, Jr., August 1, 1804, CW-Letters, 1:44.
43. During the three weeks or so in May and June 1805 that he kept a diary record, Irving went to the theater some seventeen times. See "European Journal," CW-Journals, 1:284-88.
44. PMI, 1:140. For "botany, chemistry," etc., see ibid.
45. I am following here David D. Gilmore, *Manhood in the Making: Cultural Concepts of Masculinity* (New Haven-London: Yale University Press, 1990), 1-3, 21-23.
46. JCW, 9, part II: §41; cf. a. §§25-42 and JCW, 9, part I: §§120, 134. With considerably less pathos, see Emma Jung, *Animus and Anima*, 11: " ... the anima and animus mutually constellate each other ... since an anima manifestation calls forth the animus, and vice versa ..."
47. Irving to Antoinette Bolviller, May 28, 1828, PMI, 2:320; the line is from *Hamlet*, V, ii, 10.
48. JCW, 6: §870.
49. JCW, 7: §§202-319, 8: §191 and 266ff., and 14, *Mysterium Coniunctionis*.
50. JCW, 9, part I: §178.
51. JCW, 14: §522n400 and §131n68.
52. JCW, 14: §749. The most comprehensive description of the active imagination is in Jung's essay "The Transcendent Function," in JCW, 8, 67-91. See also JCW, 7: §§366-404, and 9, part I: §61.
53. JCW, 8: §403. See a. Jung's essay of 1936, "Dream Symbols of the Individuation Process," in JCW, vol. 12, and, as a separate publication based on Jung's seminars and published by Princeton University Press in 2019 under the editorship of Suzanne Gieser.
54. JCW, 9, part I: §§206-207. Elsewhere, Jung writes that active imagination "to some extent takes the place of dreams" (JCW, 8: §403). Robert L. Moore and Douglas Gillette identify a separate technique, "focused imaging," which is related to prayer, hence called "invocation." *King, Warrior, Magician, Lover: Rediscovering the Archetypes of the Mature Masculine* (New York: HarperCollins, 1991), 151-53; on "active imagination" as such, see ibid., 145-51.
55. Moore and Gillette, *King, Warrior, Magician, Lover*, 153-54.
56. Ibid., 154-55.

57. The term "psychological faith" belongs to Robert Grinnell, "Reflections on the Archetypes of Consciousness: Personality and Psychological Faith," *Spring* (1973), 32-45, as qtd. in Hillman, *anima*, 111.
58. STW, 1:26. For "spontaneous amplification of the archetypes," se JCW, 8: §403.
59. "Legend of Prince Ahmed Al Kamel," BTA, 893. Elsewhere, Irving mused about "the picturings of [my] fancy." Qtd. in Wagenknecht, *Moderation Displayed*, 75.
60. Irving to Peter Irving, Seville, March 3, 1829, PMI, 2:372.
61. "The Mutability of Literature," HTS, 854.
62. Ibid.
63. For "self-hypnosis," see STW, 1:223.
64. On this subject, see Antonio R. Damasio, *The Feeling of What Happens: Body and Emotion in the Making of Consciousness* (New York: Harcourt Brace, 1999).
65. The animus, like the anima, in itself is but a (largely unconscious) psychological function, though it has "a personal nature," JCW, 13: §62; see a. JCW, 7: §339 and §388 ("personal agencies").
66. Irving to his sister Catherine Paris, May 17, 1842, PMI, 3:198.
67. JCW, 18: §238.
68. Irving to his niece Helen, wife of his nephew Pierre Munro Irving, Sunnyside, June 26, 1859, qtd. in Wayne R. Kime, *Pierre M. Irving and Washington Irving: A Collaboration in Life and Letters* (Waterloo, Ontario: Wilfrid Laurier University Press, 1977), 210.
69. William Shakespeare, *A Midsummer Night's Dream*, V, i, ll.12-17, *The Yale Shakespeare*, ed. Wilbur L. Cross and Tucker Brooke (New York: Barnes & Noble, 1993), 125-51, here 145.
70. Ibid., ll.7-8.
71. "The Author," in BTA, 11.
72. See Henri F. Ellenberger, *The Discovery of the Unconscious: The History and Evolution of Dynamic Psychiatry* (New York: Basic Books, 1970), 706.
73. "Notes while preparing Sketch Book," 1817, 73, qtd. in STW, 1:153.
74. JCW, 14: §753.
75. Irving to Brevoort, Paris, December 11, 1824, CW-Letters, 2:90. For a similar outpouring, see Irving to Brevoort, Madrid, April 4, 1827, ibid., 2:226.
76. Mitchell, "Address," in Andrew B.

Myers, ed., *A Century of Commentary on the Works of Washington Irving* (Tarrytown, NY: Sleepy Hollow Restorations, 1976), 54–61, quot. 57. George S. Hellman was the first biographer to offer a more balanced account, in *Washington Irving, Esquire: Ambassador at Large from the New World to the Old* (New York: Knopf, 1925).

77. PMI, 2:414.

78. For "enigmatic quality of Irving's real self," see Austin McC. Fox's introduction to *The Legend of Sleepy Hollow and Other Selections from Washington Irving* (New York: Washington Square Press, 1962), viii.

79. See Michael Balint, *The Basic Fault: Therapeutic Aspects of Regression* (London; Tavistock, 1968), 28.

80. Irving liked his joining the militia, in which he was granted the rank of Lieutenant Colonel, though the hoped-for military excitement and glory never came. See STW, 1:142–53, and Burstein, *The Original Knickerbocker*, 99–101.

81. JCW, 7: §§303–304. Cf. a. JCW, 6: §806: "Everything that should normally be in the outer attitude, but is conspicuously absent, will invariably be found in the inner attitude."

82. On the link between compensation and psychological self-guidance, see JCW, 8: §988. For "symbols of transformation," see JCW, 5.

83. In *Knowing Woman* (New York: Putnam, 1973), Irene de Castillejo explicitly refers to the animus as "torchbearer" (76).

84. STW, 1:156; and see 180, 217, 223, 225, 360, and passim.

85. Jeffrey Rubin-Dorsky, *Adrift in the Old World: The Psychological Pilgrimage of Washington Irving* (Chicago: University of Chicago Press, 1988). Cf. a. Joy S. Kasson, *Artistic Voyagers: Europe and the American Imagination in the Works of Irving, Allston, Cole, Cooper, and Hawthorne* (Westport, CT: Greenwood Press, 1982).

86. Rubin-Dorsky, *Adrift in the Old World*, xiv–xvi. On Irving's anxiety occasioned by the ruin of the family business, see *ibid.*, 34–36.

87. Irving was not alone in disclaiming professional status and motivation, much as there were other writers of the time who discovered their calling in travel. See Ann Douglas, *The Feminization of American Culture*, 236–37.

88. Rubin-Dorsky, *Adrift in the Old World*, xiv–xvi. In a similar vein, David Anthony has understood Irving's *The Sketch Book* as "reflecting a nostalgic longing for a period predating the modern period of commerce and credit, one that found an anxious Irving financially embarrassed and decidedly out of place." Anthony, "'Gone Distracted,'" 42.

89. Irving to Emily Foster, Paris, August 23, 1825, *CW-Letters*, 2:129.

90. PMI, 1:25.

91. STW, 1:5.

92. Irving, "Christmas Eve," HTS, 926. On Bracebridge and the yeoman ideal, see Rubin-Dorsky, *Adrift in the Old World*, ch.4, esp. 147ff.

93. Burstein, *The Original Knickerbocker*, 7–8; STW, 1:5–7, 101, 405n165; PMI, 1:208. Young Irving was by no means the only child suffering from his father's lack of affection. Almost every classic American writer, Quentin Anderson has shown, had an absent or weak or otherwise problematic father in his childhood. See *The Imperial Self: An Essay in American Literary and Cultural History* (New York: Vintage, 1971).

94. Years later, when Ebenezer came to live at Sunnyside, Irving said about him, "He has all father's devotion and zeal, without his strictness." Irving to his sister Sarah, now Mrs. Van Wart, 1840, PMI, 3:156. On fathers tending to enforce gender stereotypes more than mothers, especially in sons, see Michele Adams and Scott Coltrane, "Boys and Men in Families: The Domestic Production of Gender, Power, and Privilege," in *Handbook of Studies on Men and Masculinities*, ed. Michael S. Kimmel, Jeff Hearn, and R. W. Connell (Thousand Oaks, CA: SAGE, 2009), 230–48, here 234.

95. See Burstein, *The Original Knickerbocker*, 7; STW, 1:4–5; and PMI, 1:24–25, 365.

96. PMI, 1:25. Pierre Munro was a son of Irving's eldest brother William.

97. See Sanford, *The Invisible Partners*, 96–97.

98. BTA, 500; further references to "Buckthorne, or the Young Man of Great Expectations" are to *ibid.*, 523 and 565, emphases added.

99. For "the woman within," see Rotundo, *American Manhood*, 274. Jenifer S. Banks, too, engages in the subject of Irving and

women, though she exteriorizes the conflict, presenting Irving as "a prototype of the American male struggling to reconcile the conflict between freedom and adult responsibility, independence and social obligation, fantasy and reality." Thus, "Rip Van Winkle" is the perfect "image of the oppressive power of women and man's flight from them." See "Washington Irving, the Nineteenth-Century Bachelor," 254.

100. STW, 1:294. In a letter to Mrs. Foster from April or May 1823, Irving laments his "morbid sensitiveness" (*CW-Letters*, 1:737–55), and in a manuscript fragment, which probably dates from May or June 1823, he speaks twice of a "morbid sensitiveness" and of the "dark shadows that obtrude themselves upon my brightest moments" (qtd. in STW, 2:255, 261; and see 1:238–54). Irving's "sensibility" also made him temperamentally unable to take his stand—thus, he accepts an appointment, in 1829, to the American legation in London, though his heart was in the Alhambra. Had he stayed, Williams suggests (STW, 1:369), *The Alhambra* might even have surpassed *The Sketch Book*.

101. "The soul of sensibility," Irving quotes from the *Bibliothèque universelle des romans*, "cannot be distracted from the examination of itself. Its qualities, its vows, its wants, its destiny absorb all its thoughts. Always returning to this state of meditation, of privation, of secret fermentation, ... to question and to know itself, to correct its faults, enjoy its dispositions, such is its sole care and sole pleasure." Qtd. in STW, 1:464–655n112.

102. None of all this, Andrew Burstein points out, equals a sustained or clinical depression but rather sounds what we might call "artistic temperament." *The Original Knickerbocker*, 115 and 366n13.

103. Irving, "The Author's Account of Himself," *HTS*, 735, 743. Irving is even more open to Mrs. Foster, writing about his habit of "contemplating" people and things "from a distance, and my imagination lending [them] tints." Prague, June 1, 1823, PMI, 2:157.

104. STW, 1:294.

105. *Ibid.*, 2:158–59; and see 1:205, 214, 221, and *HTS*, 1116. Walter A. Reichart, editor of Irving's journals and notebooks, remarks that physicians diagnose this painful inflammation as *"erythema multiforme,"* a somewhat uncommon affliction, which usually affects nervous or neurotic individuals. One of the suspected etiological factors reported to cause *erythema multiforme* is a virus of the *Herpes simplex* types. The virus lives in the human body, where it is dormant but becomes active in periods of stress and worry, when the body's immune system is weakened or disabled. See *CW-Journals*, 3:221n187.

106. STW, 2:398n3.

107. *CW-Journals*, 3:15.

108. Irving to Henry Brevoort, May 19, 1818, *CW-Letters*, 1:526.

109. See *CW-Journals*, 3:3–91, and 261.

110. *Ibid.*, 3:209.

111. *Ibid.*, 3:258; the entry is dated December 17, 1823.

112. *CW-Letters*, 2:41.

113. *CW-Journals*, 3:337.

114. See STW, 2:54–57.

115. Irving's funds then were running so low that in a letter to John Howard Payne he writes: "I am now practicing the most rigid economy to make that pittance hold out until I can either get at my resources in America (which are likewise locked up as it were by the embarrassments of the times) or can raise ways & means by dint of pen." Irving to Payne, December 22, 1825, *CW-Letters*, 2:454.

116. *CW-Journals*, 3:743; the note is undated, though it is followed by a description of the wines of the Médoc region, which Irving visited in October 1825.

117. Clinical psychoanalysts thus speak of "depersonalization disorder (DPD)." See Philip M. Coons, "Depersonalization and Derealization," in *Handbook of Dissociation*, ed. Larry K. Michelson and William J. Ray (Boston, MA: Springer, 1996), 291–305. Henri F. Ellenberger uses the concept of "creative illness" for a similar condition, which usually occurs after a long period of intense intellectual labor. See *The Discovery of the Unconscious*, 672.

118. STW, 1:236–54. It is worth noting, however, that there is no hint of a proposal, its rejection, or subsequent depression in Irving's journals or surviving letters. Moreover, Pierre Munro Irving, Irving's nephew, even claims that his uncle never thought of marrying Emily. While it may have been "'a hopeless and consuming attachment,'" on Emily's part it was returned by "'the warmest friendship only.'" PMI, 4:215–16;

quotations are from the journal of Emily's sister, Flora Dawson, née Foster. Yet the overprotective nephew probably withheld material pertaining to Irving's love affair. Drawing on George Hellman's biography of 1925, as well as on Emily Foster's journal, recently discovered, Stanley Williams writes that a proposal was "extremely probable." Ultimately, however, Williams deems the questions of proposal and rejection as irrelevant. Unlike Matilda Hoffman, Emily Foster left no mark in Irving's writings, published or unpublished. STW, 1:407n185 and, for a full discussion, Chap. 10.

119. *JCW*, 11: §534.

120. Irving to Pierre Paris Irving, Paris, December 7, 1824, *CW-Letters*, 2:85.

121. Irving to Pierre Paris Irving, Paris, March 29, 1825, *ibid.*, 2:107.

122. *CW-Journals*, 3:506; see a. PMI, 2:238, and STW, 1:283.

123. Irving to Constable, August 19, 1825, *CW-Letters*, 2:126–27, emphases added.

124. As Irving set down in his journal on January 30, 1826 (*CW-Journals*, 3:563): "Recd. letter from Mr Everett, attaching me to Embassy at Madrid. Inclosing passport and proposing <the> my translating voyage of Columbus." "Mr Everett" was Alexander H. Everett, who had just been appointed United States Ambassador to Madrid by President John Quincy Adams.

125. STW, 1:297.

126. *The Alhambra*, BTA, 726.

127. Andrew Myers, "The New York Years in Irving's *Life of George Washington*," *Early American Literature* 11 (1976), 68. For "my history," see Irving's letter to his brother Ebenezer, December 21, 1842, PMI, 3:274. For "happy magic," see Bancroft's letter to Irving, May 30, 1855, PMI, 4:194. For a picture of Irving's Sunnyside, see *150 W.I.: Washington Irving and the Alhambra*, 93.

128. Richard Henry Stoddard, *The Crayon Papers, preceded by the Life of Washington Irving* (New York: John Alden, 1883), 9.

129. Barrett Wendell, *A Literary History of America* (London: T. F. Unwin, 1901), 179.

130. Hart Crane, qtd. in Burstein, *The Original Knickerbocker*, 130.

131. *JCW*, 7: §332.

132. *JCW*, 13, §60; for "not so much a unity as a plurality," see *JCW*, 10: §181. The plurality of animus figures corresponds to a plurality of anima figures, especially in literature. As Graham Hough found, "we are faced with an *embarras de richesse*. [...] Are all the heroines of romantic and idealized fiction anima figures? Yes. Are they equally anima figures regardless of the quality of the fictions in which they appear? I am afraid, yes. ... From Dante's Beatrice and Petrarch's Laura to the vulgarest heroines of soap-operas and girlie magazines, all are recognizable as anima images." Hough, "Poetry and the Anima," *Spring* (1973), 93, qtd. in Hillman, *anima*, 155.

133. Emma Jung, *Animus and Anima*, 11.

134. Moore and Gillette, *King, Warrior, Magician, Lover*, 49–141. The book has found a rich following, as see Brett, "The Four Archetypes of the Mature Masculine," art of manliness.com, July 31, 2011, last updated March 29, 2020, https://www.artofmanliness.com/articles/king-warrior-magician-lover-introduction/, retrieved April 7, 2020.

135. The King archetype's shadows, for instance, would be the "Tyrant" (active) and the "Weakling" (passive). By the same token, the Warrior archetype's shadows are, respectively, the "Sadist" and the "Masochist." The Magician, in turn, is shadowed by the "Detached Manipulator" and the "Denying 'Innocent' One," and the Lover, finally, by the "Addicted" and "Impotent" lovers. See *King, Warrior, Magician, Lover*, 63–70 (for the Shadow King), 88–94 (for the Shadow Warrior), 111–16 (for the Shadow Magician), and 131–40 (for the Shadow Lover).

136. Immature "boyhood" archetypes are the Divine Child, the Hero, the Precocious Child, and the Oedipal Child. Their respective shadows are the "High Chair Tyrant" and the "Weakling Prince," the "Know-it-all Trickster" and the "Dummy," the "Grandstander Bully" and the "Coward," and, finally, the "Momma's Boy" and the "Dreamer." *Ibid.*, 16–17 and, for the full discussion of "Boy Psychology," 13–42.

137. Joseph Campbell, *The Hero with a Thousand Faces* (1949; second edn. Princeton, NJ: Princeton University Press, 1968), especially Part II, Chapter iii, "Transformations of the Hero." On the hero as a representation of the animus archetype, see Hillman, *anima*, 61.

138. Moore and Gillette, *King, Warrior, Magician, Lover*, xvii, xviii.

139. For the former argument, see Philip Young, "Fallen from Time: The Mythic Rip Van Winkle," *Kenyon Review* 22:4 (Autumn 1960), 547–73, quotations 570, 568; for the latter, see Terence Martin, "Rip, Ichabod, and the American Imagination," *American Literature* 31 (1959), 137–49, quotation 148.

140. Irving to John Murray, May 9, 1829, *CW-Letters*, 2:414–15.

141. Irving to Alexander Everett, Puerto Santa Maria, October 21, 1828, PMI, 2:348.

142. Irving to Peter Irving, Alhambra, June 13, 1829, *CW-Letters*, 2:436. On Irving's penchant for "enchantment," "magic," and the like, see Antonio Rodriguez Almodóvar, "The Fairytale Factor in the *Tales of the Alhambra*," 150 *W.I.: Washington Irving and the Alhambra*, 78–87.

143. Irving to Brevoort, Alhambra, May 28, 1829, *CW-Letters*, 2:424.

144. Notebook of 1810, *CW-Journals*, 2:36.

145. Irving to Brevoort, July 16, 1816, *CW-Letters*, 1:450.

146. "The Mutability of Literature," HTS, 854.

147. "The Author's Account of Himself," *ibid.*, 743.

148. "The Voyage," *ibid.*, 747.

149. Cf. JCW, 14: §736: The anima is the "quintessence of fantasy-images." Jung was not the only one to see fantasy-images under an animatic phenomenology. The French philosopher Gaston Bachelard associated the anima with reverie, while for Henry Corbin, another French philosopher and theologian, the anima was tantamount to the imagination. See Bachelard, *The Poetics of Reverie: Childhood, Language, and the Cosmos* (Boston: Beacon Press, 1971), chap. 2, "Animus and Anima"; and Corbin, "Mundus Imaginalis," *Spring 1972*, 1–19, here 6–7.

150. Equally familiar with the writings of many of the Romantics was C. G. Jung. As the Canadian psychiatrist and medical historian Henri F. Ellenberger has shown in his encyclopedic study of the history of dynamic psychiatry, Jung's system is deeply rooted in European romanticism, drawing on the writings of Friedrich Wilhelm Schelling, Johann Gottlieb Fichte, E. T. A. Hoffmann, as well as on any number of romantic novels and poems. It is not too far-fetched to say, therefore, that Irving's writings and Jung's theories circulate inseparably, as documents of a given historical discourse. They are texts relating to other texts within, to use Foucault's term, specific structures of thought. Ellenberger, *The Discovery of the Unconscious*, Chapter 4, 199–201, Chapter 5, 292–94, and Chapter 9, 727–31; for "individuation, see *ibid.*, 204; for more on Jung's theories, see *ibid.*, Chapter 9, 657–748, especially 671–73, 705–13. Michel Foucault, *The Order of Things: An Archaeology of Knowledge* (New York: Pantheon, 1970), 168. See also D. G. Myers, "The New Historicism in Literary Studies," *Academic Questions* 2 (1989), 27–36, https://doi.org/10.1007/BF02682779.

151. See, for instance, STW, 1:225; Walter A. Reichart, *Washington Irving and Germany* (Ann Arbor: University of Michigan Press, 1957), 156; Sara Puryear Rodes, "Washington Irving's Use of Traditional Folklore," *Southern Folklore Quarterly* 20 (1956), 143–53; and Charles G. Zug III, "The Construction of 'The Devil and Tom Walker': A Study of Irving's Later Use of Folklore," *New York Folklore Quarterly* 24 (1968), 243–60.

152. Pere Gifra-Adroher, *Between History and Romance: Travel Writing on Spain in the Early Nineteenth-Century United States* (Madison, NJ: Fairleigh Dickinson University Press, 2000), 134, 123.

153. On Byron as well as on ethical concerns as a criterion for radical romanticism, see Ann Douglas, *The Feminization of American Culture*, 255–56.

154. Irving, "The Legend of Sleepy Hollow," HTS, 1071.

155. Michael S. Kimmel, *Manhood in America: A Cultural History* (1996; 3rd edn. New York: Oxford University Press, 2012), 37.

156. Irving, "The Wife," HTS, 762.

157. See Erich Neumann, *The Great Mother: An Analysis of the Archetype*, trans. Ralph Mannheim, Bollingen Series (Princeton, NJ: Princeton University Press, 1955); orig. published in 1951 as *Die große Mutter. Der Archetyp des großen Weiblichen* (Zurich: Rhein-Verlag).

158. Ann Douglas, in her pioneering study of the feminization of American culture, offers a convincing example in the form of a letter Sylvester Judd, a divinity student at Harvard, wrote in 1839: "There is but little of the genuine emotion in our [sex]. The habits of men are too commercial

and restrained, too bustling and noisy, too ambitious and repellent. ... Women are the bonds of society. ... Men are like mountains, bold, icy, moveless, that woo the winds and worship the stars, but frown an eternal defiance at each other." *The Feminization of American Culture*, 102. For "piety, purity, submissiveness, and domesticity," see Barbara Welter, "The Cult of True Womanhood: 1820–1860," *American Quarterly* 18:2 (1966), 151–74, here 152.

159. "The Wife" was among the manuscripts that Irving's brother Ebenezer read aloud to friends in New York and, "when they applauded, he broke down and wept with joy." STW, 1:173.

160. See Michael Davitt Bell, *Development of American Romance: The Sacrifice of Relation* (Chicago: University of Chicago Press, 1980), 148, 35, 29–36.

161. Irving's admiration was not only for Scott the writer. For him, Scott, who was twelve years his senior, also was a model of masculinity, "tall, and of a large and powerful frame ... moving rapidly and with vigor," as he described him after his first visit to Abbotsford in 1817. See "Abbotsford," *CW-CM*, 126.

162. Henry A. Pochmann and E. N. Feltskog, for instance, are quite explicit on the Great Man as molder and model of history as Irving's major theme: "Historical Note," *CW-Mahomet*, 559. Additionally, see Emma Marras, "Writing on the Boundary between History and Romance: Washington Irving's Treatment of Columbus' Experience," in *Visions in History. Visions of the Other*, ed. Gerald Gillespie and Margaret R. Higonnet, Proceedings of the 1991 Congress of the International Comparative Literature Association, volume 2 (Tokyo: Congress Headquarters, 1995).

163. BTA, 817.

164. See Adams and Coltrane, "Boys and Men in Families," 234–35.

165. Gilmore, *Manhood in the Making*, 224.

166. The best historical monograph on the subject of manhood and masculinity remains Rotundo, *American Manhood*. Most useful also are David Leverenz, *Manhood and the American Renaissance* (Ithaca, NY: Cornell University Press, 1989); Kimmel, *Manhood in America*; and David Anthony, *Paper Money Men: Commerce, Manhood, and the Sensational Public Sphere in Antebellum America* (Columbus: Ohio State University Press, 2009). On the longing for and emergence of charismatic leaders as intrinsic to the modern world, see David A. Bell, *Men on Horseback: The Power of Charisma in the Age of Revolution* (New York: Farrar, Straus and Giroux, 2020).

167. On America's conversion to acquisitiveness, see Gordon S. Wood, "Ideology and the Origins of Liberal America," *William and Mary Quarterly* 44:3 (July 1987) 628–40, and *Empire of Liberty: A History of the Early Republic*, Oxford History of the United States, vol. 4 (Oxford-New York: Oxford University Press, 2009), 22–31, 218–22.

168. The term "self-made man" came into use in the 1830s, probably coined by Henry Clay. See *The Life and Speeches of the Honorable Henry Clay*, ed. Daniel Mallory (New York: Amringe and Bixby, 1844), 2:31. Together with "middle class," "self-made man" soon replaced the "middling sort" or the "middling orders." I am here following Rotundo, *American Manhood*, 7–8 and 18–20; Leverenz, *Manhood and the American Renaissance*, 3–4, and Chapter 3; and Kimmel, *Manhood in America*, 11–57.

169. On these collective fictions or "paradigms" of manhood, see Leverenz, *Manhood and the American Renaissance*, 74. In contrast, E. Anthony Rotundo conflates the "patrician" and the "artisan" paradigms into what he calls "communal manhood," by which he means that a man's identity was inseparable from the duties he owed to his community (*American Manhood*, 2–3, 11–18). Michael S. Kimmel (*Manhood in America*, 20–25) offers a typology of American manhood or masculine archetypes that is similar to Leverenz's. Taking his cue from Royall Tyler's five-act comedy *The Contrast*, which premiered in New York on April 16, 1787, Kimmel distinguishes the "Genteel Patriarch," the "Heroic Artisan," and the "Self-Made Man."

170. On the emergence of the term "middle-class," see Karen Halttunen, *Confidence Man and Painted Women: A Study of Middle-Class Culture in America, 1830–1870* (New Haven, CT: Yale University Press, 1982), 29.

171. *CW-Journals*, 3:676. "Beatus ille, que procul negotiis ...," *Epodes* II, ll.1–4.

172. David Graeber, *Bullshit Jobs. A Theory* (New York: Simon & Schuster, 2018).

173. Alexis de Tocqueville, *Democracy*

in America, 1835–1840, ed. Thomas Bender (New York: Modern Library, 1981), vol.2, 2nd Book, Chapter XIII, 464.

174. PMI, 2: 282. Irving had written to Brevoort in a similar vein about his ambition for "acquiring real reputation" on an earlier occasion. London, July 10, 1819, *CW-Letters*, 1:550.

175. Irving to Henry Brevoort, Alhambra, May 23, 1829, PMI, 2:388.

176. Irving to Ebenezer Irving, London, March 3, 1819, *ibid.*, 1:412.

177. Jones, *Washington Irving*, ix.

178. *Harper's New Monthly Magazine*, April 1851, as qtd. in Burstein, *The Original Knickerbocker*, 315.

179. Longfellow, "Address on the Death of Washington Irving," 802.

180. For "sordid dusty, and soul-killing" see Irving to Henry Brevoort, New York, May 15, 1811, *CW-Letters* 1:316.

181. On Irving as a professional writer under a capitalist mode of production, see R. Jackson Wilson, *Figures of Speech: American Writers and the Literary Marketplace. From Benjamin Franklin to Emily Dickinson* (New York: Knopf, 1989; repr. Baltimore, MD: Johns Hopkins University Press, 1990). On the transition from socially embedded exchange (patronage, charity, gift exchange, competition, family wealth, personal estate) to impersonally conducted business see Leon Jackson, *The Business of Letters: Authorial Economics in Antebellum America* (Stanford, CA: Stanford University Press, 2008). See a. William Charvat, *Literary Publishing in America, 1790–1850* (Philadelphia: University of Pennsylvania Press, 1959), esp. chap. 2, and *The Profession of Authorship in America, 1800–1870*, ed. Matthew J. Bruccoli (New York: Columbia University Press, 1992), esp. 49–67.

182. John McWilliams, "'The Almighty [Unmentionable] Dollar': Washington Irving and Money," *Literature in the Early American Republic: Annual Studies on Cooper and His Contemporaries* 2 (2010), 220. For "literary reputation" and "for profit," see Irving's letter to Moses Thomas of March 3, 1818: "I notice what you say on the subject of getting up an original work; but I am very squeamish on that point. Whatever my literary reputation may be worth, it is very dear to me, and I cannot bring myself to risk it by making up books for profit." *CW-Letters*, 1:520.

183. See Peter Bürger, "The Institution of 'Art' as a Category in the Sociology of Literature," *Cultural Critique* 2 (Winter 1985), 5–33, here 21. For an analysis of print culture and its economic implications, see Rosalind Remer's *Printers and Men of Capital: Philadelphia Book Publishers in the New Republic* (Philadelphia: University of Pennsylvania Press, 1996).

184. STW, 1:80–82.

185. Pierre M. Irving provides tables of the sums Washington Irving realized in England and the United States. PMI, 4:410–11.

186. *CW-Letters*, 3:36.

187. The legislation did not pass, though, and the issue was not resolved until 1891, when an international copyright law finally was adopted. For an understanding of the copyright issue see James J. Barnes, *Authors, Publishers, and Politicians: The Quest for an Anglo-American Copyright Agreement, 1815–1854* (Columbus: Ohio State University Press, 1974).

188. *HTS*, 1116–1117. For the full story, see STW, 1:108–14.

189. Irving to Brevoort, London, August 12, 1819, *CW-Letters*, 1:554.

190. Irving to Colonel Thomas Aspinwall, December (?) 1828, as qtd. in Wagenknecht, *Moderation Displayed*, 181.

191. Henry C. Carey, *Letters on International Copyright*, 2nd edn. (New York, 1868), 63, as qtd. in STW, 2:395n129.

192. PMI, 4:410–11. To this should be added the more than £12,000 realized for copyrights in England, which brings the whole amount realized on Irving's works during his lifetime to some $205,000—about $8 million today according to Samuel H. Williamson's online device at MeasuringWorth, http://www.measuringworth.com/uscompare/. On Irving's industrious cultivation of literary capital, see Ben Harris McClary, *Washington Irving and the House of Murray* (Knoxville: University of Tennessee Press, 1969).

193. PMI, 4:121.

194. "The Author's Account of Himself," *HTS*, 744.

195. "Westminster Abbey," *ibid.*, 894.

196. Hillman, *anima*, 23.

197. Irving, Biographical fragment, *CW-Letters*, 1:743–44.

198. Irving to Mary Fairlie, May 2, 1807, *CW-Letters*, 1:232.

199. *Washington*, 1:36; *CW-Journals*, 3:670; and *Salmagundi*, No. VII, in *HTS*, 143, emphasis in original. On Irving's Hamiltonian fear of the mob achieving political victory when it was but ill-equipped to govern, see Donna Hagensick, "Irving: A Littérateur in Politics," *Critical Essays on Washington Irving*, ed. Ralph M. Aderman (Boston, MA: G.K. Hall, 1990), 181–83. The essay was reprinted from *Washington Irving Reconsidered: A Symposium*, ed. Ralph M. Aderman (Hartford, CT: Transcendental Books, 1969), 53–60.

200. On upper-class fantasies, see Daniel Walker Howe, *The Political Culture of the American Whigs* (Chicago: University of Chicago Press, 1979), 25–32.

201. James Fenimore Cooper, *Home as Found* (1838), ed. with an introduction by Lewis Leary (New York: Capricorn Books, 1961), 7–8; for a similar sentiment, see Cooper, *The American Democrat* (1838), ed. with an introduction by George Dekker and Larry Johnston (Harmondsworth: Penguin, 1969), 152.

Chapter Two

1. See Andrew Burstein, *The Original Knickerbocker: The Life of Washington Irving* (New York: Basic Books, 2007), 16–20.
2. STW, 1:39.
3. Brian Jay Jones, *Washington Irving: An American Original* (New York: Arcade Pub., 2008), 20.
4. Washington Irving, "Letters of Jonathan Oldstyle, Gent.," *HTS*, 23.
5. James W. Tuttleton, who wrote the notes and selected the texts for the Library of America edition of *History, Tales and Sketches*, argues that "Oldstyle" also suggests the Old Style or Julian calendar that was replaced by the New Style or Gregorian calendar in 1752. *HTS*, 1127.
6. *Ibid.*, 6.
7. *CW-Journals* 3:658; Chesterfield's letter is dated November 3, 1749, here quoted from *The Works of Lord Chesterfield; including his letters to his son* (New York: Harper & Brothers, 1838), 289, 288. See a. *Lord Chesterfield's Letters*, ed. David Roberts, Oxford World's Classics (New York: Oxford University Press, 1992, reissued 2008). Chesterfield also looms large in *Bracebridge Hall*, in the sketch titled "Gentility" (*BTA*, 110–113).

8. "Gentleman." *Merriam-Webster.com Dictionary*, Merriam-Webster, https://www.merriam-webster.com/dictionary/gentleman, accessed March 25, 2020.
9. *HTS*, 23.
10. *Ibid.*, 6.
11. *Ibid.*, 24–25.
12. *Ibid.*, 37–38; further references in this paragraph are to *ibid.*, 26, 25.
13. Teresa Goddu, *Gothic America: Narrative, History, and Nation* (New York: Columbia University Press, 1997), 34.
14. *HTS*, 39. Further references in this paragraph to "Oldstyle" are to *ibid.*, 40, 41.
15. Burstein, *The Original Knickerbocker*, 35–37.
16. See Irving's "European Journal," *CW-Journals*, 1:284–90. For "*gallop through Italy*," see PMI, 1:139.
17. STW, 1:44–46, 64–65. For more, see Pedro Galera Andreu, "Washington Irving, the Frustrated Painter," in *150 W.I.: Washington Irving and the Alhambra*, ed. Carmen Yusty Pérez (Granada: Patronato de la Alhambra y Generalife / Tf Editores [Madrid], 2009), 52–65, and, on portraits *of* Irving, 57–59.
18. Irving to Elias Hicks, May 4, 1805, *CW-Letters*, 1:186–87.
19. The portrait is reproduced in STW, vol.1, between 68–69, as well as in Burstein, *The Original Knickerbocker*, following p.198. Or else, view it at the Museum of Fine Arts, Boston, http://www.mfa.org/collections/object/portrait-of-washington-irving-157949, accessed March 3, 2014.
20. STW, 1:76–78, and Burstein, *The Original Knickerbocker*, 47–51. At the core of the group were James Kirke Paulding, Henry Brevoort, and Gouverneur Kemble. Other members included Kemble's younger brother, Peter Jr., Henry Ogden, Richard McCall, David Porter, and Peter Irving. Also sitting in from time to time were the staid Ebenezer Irving and William Jr., despite his stern rebuke of 1805, "Good company, I find, is the grand desideratum with you." Also noteworthy is that four of the Lads—Kemble, Ogden, and Peter and Washington Irving—never married.
21. Irving to Mrs. Amelia Foster, April-May 1823, *CW-Letters*, 1:739.
22. *HTS*, 49.
23. Paulding later complained that Longworth had bilked him and Irving out of as much as $15,000 (about $250,000 in

today's money). That was likely an exaggeration, but Paulding never admitted that the lost profits were due more to his and Irving's failure to secure their own copyright than to any duplicity on Longworth's part. See William Irving Paulding, *The Literary Life of James K. Paulding* (New York: Charles Scribner, 1867), 38–39.

24. Irving to Henry Brevoort, London, July 10, 1819, in *Letters of Washington Irving to Henry Brevoort*, ed. George S. Hellman (New York: Putnam's Sons, 1918), 311. In a similar vein, Irving later wrote to John Howard Payne: "It was a very juvenile work & one the republication of which I had always discouraged." Paris, January 7, 1824, qtd. in STW, 2:269.

25. See Ernest E. Leisy, "Irving and the Genteel Tradition," *Southwest Review* 21.2 (January 1936), 223–27. For a delineation of Knickerbocker's origins in Sterne, Fielding, and Swift, see James E. Evans, "The English Lineage of Diedrich Knickerbocker," *Early American Literature* 10 (1975), 3–13. For more, see Martin Roth, *Comedy and America: The Lost World of Washington Irving* (Port Washington, NY-London: Kennikat Press, 1976), and Joy S. Karson, *Artistic Voyagers: Europe and the American Imagination in the Works of Irving, Allston, Cole, Cooper, and Hawthorne* (Westport, CT: Greenwood Press, 1982).

26. On Irving as a master of public relations, see above, Chapter One, as well as the editors' introduction to *CW-History*, xxvi–xxix.

27. *CW-History*, 129–30. The passage is *not* in the original edition of 1809, which James W. Tuttleton used for the Library of America edition. Irving inserted the passage into the second American edition of 1812, published by Bradford & Inskeep, respectively in New York and Philadelphia (*ibid.*, 199–201; and see *CW-History*, xxvi, and Editorial Appendix, 409). The first *Newgate Calendar*, named for the famous London prison, is a record of notorious crimes from 1700, published in five volumes c.1774. Similar compilations appeared through 1826. Editorial note, HTS, 1086.

28. Theodor W. Adorno, *Negative Dialektik* (Frankfurt am Main: Suhrkamp, 1966), 356.

29. *CW-History*, 131.

30. Thomas Jefferson, too, Andrew Burstein notes, often displayed a remarkable delicacy and emotional softness. See *The Inner Jefferson: Portrait of a Grieving Optimist* (Charlottesville: University of Virginia Press, 1995), esp. chaps. 2 and 3. There was another facet to Jefferson's "effeminacy": Jefferson often was associated with France, and Frenchness was customarily considered to be "feminine," in contrast to the purported "manliness" of John Bull Englishness. For the explicitness of Irving's satire of the Jefferson administrations of 1801 to 1809, see Edwin A. Greenlaw, "Washington Irving's Comedy of Politics," *Texas Review* 1:4 (April 1916), 291–306. For a masterful analysis of Irving's anti-Jeffersonianism, see Robert A. Ferguson, "Hunting Down a Nation: Washington Irving's *A History of New York*," *Nineteenth-Century Fiction* 36:1 (June 1981), 22–46.

31. *CW-History*, xxvii.

32. HTS, 515–16.

33. Ibid., 517.

34. Ibid.

35. Ibid.

36. Ibid., 519. The ineffectualness of "fighting by proclamation" is described, in ARE, as "portentous" of the colony's future, "when the quiet Dutchman would be elbowed aside by the enterprising Yankee, and patient industry overtopped by windy speculation." *CW-History*, 141. On Irving's Yankee-bashing, see Donald A. Ringe, "New York and New England: Irving's Criticism of American Society," *American Literature* 38 (1967), 455–67; for more on the conflict, see Dixon Ryan Fox, *Yankees and Yorkers* (New York: New York University Press, 1940).

37. Burstein, *The Original Knickerbocker*, 77–81; STW, 1:99–101, 133–34; and PMI, 1:214–16. For a discussion of Jefferson's principles and policies in connection with the Embargo as an "experiment in peaceable coercion," see Leonard D. White, *The Jeffersonians: A Study in Administrative History* (1951; New York: Macmillan, 1959), especially chapters 29–30.

38. George Washington, "Farewell Address," *The Writings of George Washington*, ed. John Rhodehamel (New York: Library of America, 2011), 964, 965.

39. HTS, 548.

40. See *The Faces of Physiognomy: Interdisciplinary Approaches to Johann Caspar*

Lavater, ed. Ellis Shookman (Columbia, SC: Camden House, 1993), and Lorenzo Livianos-Aldana, Luis Rojo-Moreno, and Pilar Sierra-SanMiguel, "Gall and the Phrenological Movement," *American Journal of Psychiatry*, 164:3 (2007), 414, https://ajp.psychiatryonline.org/doi/full/10.1176/ajp.2007.164.3.414, retrieved March 31, 2020. It should be added that at Irving's time, both physiognomy and craniology were widely considered as pseudoscience.

41. *HTS*, 543.

42. Irving retained the history of the Long Pipes and Short Pipes for the Author's Revised Edition, as see *CW-History*, 150–52.

43. *HTS*, 550.

44. *Ibid.*, 551.

45. *Ibid.*, 694–95.

46. *Ibid.*, 696.

47. *PMI*, 1:187. The incident also caught the attention of Edward Wagenknecht, *Washington Irving: Moderation Displayed* (New York: Oxford University Press, 1962), 91 and 104–8, passim.

48. Henry Seidel Canby, *Classic Americans* (New York: Harcourt Brace & Co., 1931), 77.

49. *Ibid.*, 83.

50. *Ibid.*, 84. For similar views, largely following Canby, see Henry August Pochmann, "Irving's Politics as a Determining Factor," *Washington Irving: Representative Selections* (New York: American Book Company, 1934), xlii–lx.

51. *HTS*, 1123.

52. *Ibid.*, 699.

53. *Ibid.*; further references in this paragraph are to 655, 567, and 672. For the historical Stuyvesant, see Burstein, *The Original Knickerbocker*, 81–84.

54. See my *George Washington and Political Fatherhood: The Endurance of a National Myth* (Jefferson, NC: McFarland, 2020), Chapter 4.

55. *Ibid.*, Chapters 3, 5, and 7.

56. *HTS*, 710.

57. *Ibid.*, 711.

58. *Ibid.*, 686.

59. *Ibid.*, 717.

60. See Introduction to *CW-History*, lxii.

61. *Ibid.*, liii. On Irving's alterations, see Clarence M. Webster, "Irving's Expurgation of the 1809 *History of New York*," *American Literature*, 4 (November 1933), 293–95, and Michael L. Black, "*A History of New York*: Significant Revision in 1848," in *Washington Irving Reconsidered: A Symposium*, ed. Ralph M. Aderman (Hartford, CT: Transcendental Books, 1969), 40–47, based on "Washington Irving's *A History of New York* with Emphasis on the 1848 Revision," PhD dissertation, Columbia University, 1967.

62. A few references are less prominent, though, as see Introduction, *CW-History*, lvi.

63. *HTS*, 479; on Irving's racial stereotyping, see my "'Roman Countenances' and 'Abominations': Racial and Ethnic Stereotyping in the Writings of Washington Irving," in *The Polyphony of English Studies: A Festschrift for Allan James*, ed. Alexander Onysko, Eva-Maria Graf, Werner Delanoy, Nikola Dobrić, and Günther Sigott, AAA—Arbeiten aus Anglistik und Amerikanistik, Vol. 26 (Tübingen: Gunter Narr Verlag, 2017), 241–59.

64. For a loving tribute, by way of cultural history, to Irving's *A History of New York*, see Elizabeth L. Bradley, *Knickerbocker: The Myth behind New York* (Piscataway, NJ: Rivergate/Rutgers University Press, 2009).

65. *HTS*, 474; further references in this paragraph are to *ibid.*, 478, 479, and 486.

66. A charge of this kind had been made in 1837, on the basis of different prefaces for the American and British editions of *The Crayon Miscellany*. "'When Mr. Irving [...] prepares one preface for his countrymen, full of *amor patriae* and professions of American feelings, and another for the London market, in which all such professions are studiously omitted, he does what he has an undoubted right to do, whatever we may say of its spirit,'" wrote William Leggett, a Loco-Foco Democrat, in the *Plaindealer*. Qtd. in *PMI*, 3:103; for Irving's response, in a long public letter, see *ibid.*, 104–109.

67. *HTS*, 1105–06.

68. *Athenaeum*, October 14, 1829, qtd. in *STW*, 2:276.

69. *HTS*, 412.

70. For "Royal Brute," see Thomas Paine, "Thoughts on the Present State of American Affairs," in *Common Sense on the Origin and Design of Government in General ... together with The American Crisis* (New York: G. P. Putnam's Sons, 1912), 99. For "consent of the governed," see Thomas Jefferson, "The Declaration of Independence as Adopted

by Congress," *Concise Anthology of American Literature*, fourth edition, ed. George McMichael (Upper Saddle River, NJ: Prentice Hall, 1998), 375–78, quotation 376.

71. Ferguson, "Hunting Down a Nation," 23–24. For Irving's reading notes and ideas see his "Notes for Knickerbocker 1807-8," *CW-History*, xx–xxvi. Hugo Grotius was a seventeenth-century Dutch philosopher, best known for long, theory-laden treatises on, *inter alia*, liberal and international law; Samuel von Pufendorf was a seventeenth-century German philosopher and historian, whose classic book *De Officio Hominis et Civis* (*On the Duty of Man and Citizen*), appeared in 1682; Emer de Vattel, the Swiss philosopher and legal expert, is most famous for his 1758 work *Droit des gens* (*The Law of Nations* in the English translation of 1760); William Blackstone was an English jurist and politician, whose legacy and main work of renown is *Commentaries on the Laws of England*, published in 4 volumes 1766–1770.

72. *HTS*, 413–14; further references in this paragraph are to *ibid.*, 415, 416.

73. *Ibid.*, 416. The views Irving articulated in *A History of New York* reappear or are reflected in his two American Indian sketches, first published in the *Analectic Review* in 1814 and later republished in *The Sketch Book* in 1820. Irving's express purpose both in "Traits of Indian Character" and in "Philip of Pokanoket" was to correct the image of the Indigenous population, who he says had been wantonly dispossessed from the early years of colonization, and later grossly misrepresented through "vulgar prejudice and passionate exaggeration." *HTS*, 1004.

74. In earlier editions of *A History*, the Dutch are said to have cheated the Indigenous people in all sorts of trade, especially furs, but not in land. *CW-History*, lxiv.

75. *CW-History*, 88.

76. For a thorough discussion of what Irving knew and saw, what he didn't want to see or say, and what he couldn't see except belatedly, see Jerome McGann, "Washington Irving, *A History of New York*, and American History," *Early American Literature*, 47:2 (2012), 349–76.

77. PMI, 4:42.

78. *HTS*, 374.

79. *Ibid.*, 767.

80. *Ibid.*, 728; on Knickerbocker's views as "an essential part of Irving's complicated persona," see the Introduction to *CW-History*, xxix. For "strong, vigorous, and manly style," see the 1812 review of the second edition of *History*, qtd. in STW, 2:274.

81. Jones, *Washington Irving*, 190.

82. A fictional sketch is, then, like a picture in that it has no action; instead, a narrator communicates to the reader what he believes is of interest, usually in the first person. On this matter, see Jeffrey Rubin-Dorsky, "Washington Irving and the Genesis of the Fictional Sketch," in *Critical Essays on Washington Irving*, ed. Ralph M. Aderman (Boston, MA: G.K. Hall, 1990), 68–71, reprinted from *Early American Literature* 21 (Winter 1986/87), 226–47. On Irving's habit of using crayons to fill his notebooks, see Burstein, *The Original Knickerbocker*, 133 and 369n1.

83. On Irving's attraction to painters, see the extract from James T. Callow's book *Kindred Spirits: Knickerbocker Writers and American Artists, 1807–1855* (Chapel Hill: University of North Carolina Press, 1967), in Andrew B. Myers, ed., *A Century of Commentary on the Works of Washington Irving* (Tarrytown, NY: Sleepy Hollow Restorations, 1976), 412–19.

84. For "sordid dusty, and soul-killing" see Irving to Henry Brevoort, New York, May 15, 1811, *CW-Letters*, 1:316.

85. Jones, *Washington Irving*, 190–91.

86. John McWilliams, "'The Almighty [Unmentionable] Dollar': Washington Irving and Money," *Literature in the Early American Republic: Annual Studies on Cooper and His Contemporaries* 2 (2010), 214.

87. Ibid.

88. *CW-Traveller*, 256.

89. In a sermon delivered at Tarrytown less than a month after Irving's death, the Reverend John A. Todd eulogized about "*the wonderful magician*, who evoked from the realm of thought the spirit of romance and beauty." *Irvingiana: A Memorial of Washington Irving*, ed. Evert A. Duyckinck (New York: Charles B. Richardson, 1860), xliii–xliv, here xliii, emphases added.

90. On these issues, see Michael T. Gilmore, "The Literature of the Revolutionary and Early National Period," *The Cambridge History of American Literature*, vol. I, *1590–1820*, ed. Sacvan Bercovitch (Cambridge, UK: Cambridge University Press, 1994), 674.

91. The narratives of English lineage and primogeniture, Michael Warner remarked, might seem to be an odd aspect of feudalism for Irving—who came from a mercantile family in New York—to embrace. "And perhaps it is just because of Irving's persistent unease with his own relation to such structures that he kept narrating them with obsessively alienated longing." Warner, "Irving's Posterity," *ELH* (*English Literary History*) 67:3 (2000), 785.

92. Leonard Tennenhouse, *The Importance of Feeling English: American Literature and the British Diaspora, 1750–1850* (Princeton, NJ: Princeton University Press, 2007), 5. Irving was, of course, not alone in his infatuation with a world that seemed to him richer and older than his own. See Cushing Strout, *The American Image of the Old World* (New York: Harper & Row, 1963), and Elisa Tamarkin, *Anglophilia: Deference, Devotion, and Antebellum America* (Chicago: University of Chicago Press, 2008). On the conjunction of compensation and inscription, see Ann Bermingham, *Landscape and Ideology: The English Rustic Tradition, 1740–1860* (London: Thames and Hudsonia Press, 1987), 10–11.

93. *HTS*, 747.

94. Jeffrey Rubin-Dorsky, "The Value of Storytelling: 'Rip Van Winkle' and 'The Legend of Sleepy Hollow' in the Context of *The Sketch Book*," *Modern Philology* 84:2 (1985), 393–406, quotation 397.

95. *BTA*, 8.

96. E. Anthony Rotundo, *American Manhood: Transformations in Masculinity from the Revolution to the Modern Era* (New York: Basic Books, 1993), 3.

97. *HTS*, 793.

98. *Ibid.*, 925.

99. *Ibid.*, 744.

100. *Ibid.*, 796.

101. *Ibid.*, 800. For a thorough analysis of the country versus city topos, see Raymond Williams, *The Country and the City* (London: Chatto & Windus, 1973).

102. *HTS*, 799.

103. Linda Kerber, *Federalists in Dissent: Imagery and Ideology in Jeffersonian America* (Ithaca, NY: Cornell University Press, 1970), vii.

104. *HTS*, 924.

105. *Ibid.*, 937, 938; further references in this paragraph are to *ibid.*, 924, 944, 955, and 798.

106. *Ibid.*, 925.

107. *Ibid.*, 929.

108. *Ibid.*, 913.

109. *Ibid.*, 924–25.

110. *Ibid.*, 952.

111. *Ibid.*, 946.

112. See David S. Heidler and Jeanne T. Heidler, "Not a Ragged Mob; The Inauguration of 1829," *White House History* 15 (2004), 15–23, online, https://www.white househistory.org/not-a-ragged-mob-the-inauguration-of-1829, accessed January 6, 2021.

113. *HTS*, 945.

114. *Ibid.*, 830; further references in this paragraph are to 831, 832, 833.

115. *Ibid.*, 754, 755; further references in this paragraph are to 756.

116. *Ibid.*, 756.

117. David Anthony, "'Gone Distracted': 'Sleepy Hollow,' Gothic Masculinity, and the Panic of 1819," *Early American Literature* 40:1 (2005), 128. On Roscoe, see John Whale, "The Making of a City of Culture: William Roscoe's Liverpool," *Eighteenth-Century Life* 29:2 (2005), 91–107.

118. *HTS*, 896, 904.

119. *Ibid.*, 885; further references in this paragraph are to *ibid.*, 892, 893.

120. Raymond Williams, *Marxism and Literature* (Oxford-New York: Oxford University Press, 1977), 122–23.

121. *Ibid.*, 122.

122. *Ibid.*, 123.

123. *CW-Journals*, 2:64–65.

124. Richard Henry Dana, review of *The Sketch Book*, *North American Review*, September 1819, 348, quoted in *CW-SB*, xxviii, emphasis in original. It is worth noting that Dana's son, Richard Henry Dana, Jr., in 1840 became the author of *Two Years Before the Mast* (1840), which Michael S. Kimmel characterized as a "masculinist escape memoir." *Manhood in America: A Cultural History* (1996; 3rd edn. New York: Oxford University Press, 2012), 42.

125. Irving to Brevoort, London, March 3, 1819, *CW-Letters*, 1:543.

126. Ann Douglas, *The Feminization of American Culture* (1977; New York: Doubleday, 1988), 238.

127. *Ibid.*

128. Irving, "To the Reader," *BTA*, 384.

129. On the writing and publication of *Bracebridge Hall*, see *CW-BH*, xix–xxv, and 361.

130. BTA, 7.
131. Ibid., 11.
132. C. Michael Hurst "Reinventing Patriarchy: Washington Irving and the Autoerotics of the American Imaginary," *Early American Literature* 47:3 (2012), especially 671.
133. STW, 1:204-205, 2:284. It also has been suggested that the prototype for Bracebridge Hall may have been Brereton Hall in Cheshire or Walter Scott's Abbottsford. CW-BH, xv-xvii. On the historical Bracebridges, see John Burke, *A Genealogical and Heraldic History of the Commoners of Great Britain and Ireland* (London: Colburn and Bentley, 1834), 1:270-74.
134. BTA, 376.
135. Ibid., 8.
136. Ibid., 74-75.
137. Ibid., 74.
138. Anthony, "'Gone Distracted,'" 127. Allen Guttmann's position is even more pronounced, as he sees Irving as a Burkean Tory rather than a convinced Federalist. "Washington Irving and the Conservative Imagination," *American Literature* 36:2 (May 1964), 165-73. Guttmann is co-editor of the Irving's *Life of George Washington* for the Complete Works, vols. 19-21, and the author of *The Conservative Tradition in America* (New York: Oxford University Press, 1967), for which he worked the article into Chapter 2. Andrew Burstein's estimation of Irving's politics is more nuanced—"a moderate Federalist comfortable with moderate Republicans" (*The Original Knickerbocker*, 101, and see 252-54).
139. BTA, 9, 8.
140. Rubin-Dorsky, "The Value of Storytelling," 405.
141. Joseph Fichtelberg, *Critical Fictions: Sentiment and the American Market, 1780-1870* (Athens: University of Georgia Press, 2003), 8.
142. Hurst, "Reinventing Patriarchy," 665.
143. BTA, 192.
144. See STW, 2:8-9; for more, see Linda Colley, *Britons: Forging the Nation, 1707-1837* (New Haven, CT: Yale University Press, 1992), esp. 156-57.
145. BTA, 372.
146. Warner, "Irving's Posterity," 774. For Crayon as "the voice of early national bachelordom," see Bryce Traister, "The Wandering Bachelor: Irving, Masculinity, and Authorship," *American Literature* 74:1 (2002), 112.
147. Rotundo, *American Manhood*, 3, and 10-21; s. a. CW-History, xxiv-xxxv.
148. Warner, "Irving's Posterity," 776-77.
149. Gordon S. Wood, "Ideology and the Origins of Liberal America," *William and Mary Quarterly* 44:3 (July 1987) 628-40, here 635, 640.
150. Linda Hutcheon, "Irony, Nostalgia, and the Postmodern," January 1998, http://www.library.utoronto.ca/utel/criticism/hutchinp.html, §22, retrieved April 12, 2014.
151. David Lowenthal, *The Past Is a Foreign Country* (Cambridge: Cambridge University Press, 1985), 62.
152. CW-SB, xxix.
153. William Cobbett, *Rural Rides* (1830), ed. Ian Dyck (London: Penguin, 2001).
154. Irving to Brevoort, Birmingham, December 9, 1816, CW-Letters, 1:464-65.
155. See Irving's letters to Brevoort of March 1, 1831, as well as to Edward Livingston, August 6, 1831, CW-Letters, respectively 2:592-93 and 2:628-29. On the political struggles leading towards the Great Reform Bill, see Antonia Fraser, *Perilous Question: Reform or Revolution? Britain on the Brink, 1832* (New York: PublicAffairs, 2013).
156. Qtd. in CW-Traveller, xxiii.
157. *The Examiner*, October 1824, 563; quoted ibid., emphases added.
158. Irving, CW-Journals, 3:666. After his arrival in Dresden in November 1822, for instance, Irving became a favorite at the court of Frederick Augustus, King of Saxony. "I was introduced & [the King] spoke to me very flatteringly about my works," Irving wrote into his German journal on December 22, 1822. Ibid., 3:99.
159. Ibid., 3:494-95.
160. STW, 2:281.
161. Irving to Brevoort, April 4, 1827, PMI, 2:259.

Chapter Three

1. Irving, Manuscript Fragment, qtd. in STW, 1:144.
2. HTS, 747.
3. Michael Davitt Bell, *The Development of American Romance: The Sacrifice of Relation* (Chicago: University of Chicago Press, 1982), 66.

4. "P. & E." stands for Peter and Ebenezer, two of Washington's brothers.

5. Irving to Brevoort, Liverpool, March 15, 1816, *CW-Letters*, 1:432.

6. Philadelphia *Aurora*, January 24, 1818, qtd. in David Anthony, "'Gone Distracted': 'Sleepy Hollow,' Gothic Masculinity, and the Panic of 1819," *Early American Literature* 40:1 (2005), 121. For "monster" and "hydra of corruption," as Andrew Jackson called the bank, see my *The Monetary Imagination of Edgar Allan Poe* (Jefferson, NC: McFarland, 2013), 148. For more on the B.U.S., see Jean Alexander Wilburn, *Biddle's Bank: The Crucial Years* (New York: Columbia University Press, 1967).

7. See Charles Sellers, *The Market Revolution: Jacksonian America 1815–1846* (New York: Oxford University Press, 1994), 134–35.

8. For a useful history of the ensuing depression, see Samuel Reznek, "The Depression of 1819–1822: A Social History," *American Historical Review* 39:1 (1933), 28–47.

9. John Quincy Adams, *Memoirs of John Quincy Adams*, ed. Charles Francis Adams, 12 vols. (Philadelphia: Lippincott, 1874–77), 5:128.

10. Sellers, *The Market Revolution*, 137.

11. Scott A. Sandage, *Born Losers: A History of Failure in America* (Cambridge, MA: Harvard University Press, 2004), 22, 24.

12. Adams, *Memoirs*, 4:382.

13. Irving to Brevoort, London, July 10, 1819, *CW-Letters*, 1:549–50; for "humiliating alternative," see *ibid.*, 516, letter to Brevoort of January 28, 1818.

14. See STW, 1:149–54, and PMI, 1:341.

15. Irving, *CW-Letters*, 1:517n4, and letter to Brevoort, London, January 28, 1819, *ibid.*, 1:516.

16. Irving, "Notes while preparing Sketch Book," *CW-Journals*, 2:153.

17. *Ibid.*, 3:536; and see entries respectively for November 8 and November 15, 1825, *ibid.*, 541 and 543.

18. *Ibid.*, 4:202, entry for May 24, 1828.

19. Toby Ditz, "Shipwrecked; or, Masculinity Imperiled: Mercantile Representations of Failure and Gendered Self in Eighteenth-Century Philadelphia," *Journal of American History* 80:1 (June 1994), 51–80. Popular responses to economic failure habitually represented financial collapse in terms of a crisis of manhood. David Anthony in "'Gone Distracted,'" 122–24, discusses as examples Vermilye Taylor's three-act farce "The Banker; or, Things as They Have Been!" of 1819, and Thomas Holcroft's "The Road to Ruin," a five-act production performed in Philadelphia and New York in the same year.

20. For "murky cloud" and "wither & blight," see *CW-Letters*, 1:516. For "gloom," see STW, 153–55.

21. *CW-SB*, xi. For incapacitated for "literary exertion," see Irving to Henry Brevoort, London, July 10, 1819, *CW-Letters*, 1:549.

22. See Andrew Burstein, *The Original Knickerbocker: The Life of Washington Irving* (New York: Basic Books, 2007), 115, criticizing what he calls Stanley Williams's "overly dramatic terms."

23. *CW-Journals*, 2:99.

24. Irving to Henry Brevoort, Paris, March 10, 1821, PMI, 2:137.

25. *Ibid.*, 2:25.

26. Andrew Kopec, "Irving, Ruin, and Risk," *Early American Literature* 48:3 (2013), 709–35, here 711.

27. *Ibid.*

28. *CW-SB*, xi; see also *CW-Journals*, 2:172–202, and *Notes While Preparing Sketch Book &c., 1817*, ed. Stanley T. Williams (New Haven, CT: Yale University Press, 1927).

29. Irving to Brevoort, July 11, 1817, *CW-Letters*, 1:486.

30. Irving, *CW-Journals*, 3:584; the extract is from *Paradise Regained* (1671), Book IV, ll. 291–92.

31. See *CW-SB*, xxx–xxxiii.

32. David Anthony, *Paper Money Men: Commerce, Manhood, and the Sensational Public Sphere in Antebellum America* (Columbus: Ohio State University Press, 2009), here 41–43. Quite similarly, C. Michael Hurst observed, "No longer can one associate economic success or lack thereof with station in life; instead, success and, more importantly, failure redound to the individual." "Reinventing Patriarchy: Washington Irving and the Autoerotics of the American Imaginary," *Early American Literature* 47:3 (2012), 659. Dana D. Nelson further complicates the capitalist manhood emerging during this period. Arguing that the "radicalizing energy of local democratic practices" was "rerouted" during the early national and antebellum periods

into the psychological and affective energies of "market competition," she suggests that the white professional manhood came to embody a new and "corporate" form of national selfhood in which "the political and economic vicissitudes of the early nation" had to be "internalize[d] in terms of personal responsibility." *National Manhood: Capitalist Citizenship and the Imagined Fraternity of White Men* (Durham, NC: Duke University Press, 1998) 34, 15, 21, and 62.

33. Ditz, "Shipwrecked," 51.

34. For the impact of the Panic of 1819 on Irving's writing of the time, see Anthony, "'Gone Distracted,'" 119–39. For a discussion of Irving's *Sketch Book* in light of the social conditions of authorship, chiefly impacted by literary overproduction, see Edward Cahill, "The Other Panic of 1819," *Common-Place* 9:3 (April 2009), http://www.common-place.org/vol-09/no-03/cahill/, retrieved October 14, 2011.

35. In terms of the composition of "Rip Van Winkle," there is little of use in Irving's journals, including his "Notes while preparing *Sketch Book*."

36. *CW-SB*, 355.

37. Irving to Brevoort, London, March 3, 1819, *CW-Letters*, 1:543.

38. *STW*, 2:175, 176. For more on the reception of the *Sketch Book*, see *CW-SB*, xxiv–xxxii.

39. *CW-BH*, xxvn28. Putnam's Author's Revised Edition of 1848, for which Irving added seventeen pages of new material and made numerous revisions, also sold well. Within five years, 144,000 copies of all the fifteen titles had been sold, netting him another $22,464, about $500,000 today. See *STW*, 2:395n129.

40. *CW-SB*, 308, and Introduction, xiii. "Otmar" was a pseudonym used by Johann Karl Christoph Nachtigal, who in 1800 published some twenty-four texts as *Volcks-Sagen. Nacherzählt von Otmar*. Riesbeck's *Travels through Germany, in a Series of Letters* was published in an English translation by T. Cadell in London in 1787. See Burstein, *The Original Knickerbocker*, 117.

41. Carolyn L. Karcher, "Patriarchal Society and Matriarchal Family in Irving's 'Rip Van Winkle' and Child's 'Hilda Silfverling,'" *Legacy: A Journal of American Women Writers* 2:2 (1985), 31–44, quotation 33.

42. E. Anthony Rotundo, *American Manhood: Transformations in Masculinity from the Revolution to the Modern Era* (New York: Basic Books, 1993), 179.

43. *HTS*, 779.

44. *Ibid.*, 780. On Irving's intense awareness of social change and its impact on his writings, see Robert V. Wells, "While Rip Napped: Social Change in Late Eighteenth-Century New York," *New York History* 71 (1990), 4–23. To give just one example, 71 of the heads of households in New Rochelle [a small town to the south of Rip's village, on the east side of the Hudson River, settled in 1689 by French Huguenots] in 1771 had disappeared by 1790 and had been replaced by 80 new heads of households (*ibid.*. 15).

45. Perry Miller, "Afterword," *The Sketch Book of Geoffrey Crayon, Gent.* (New York: New American Library, 1981), 377.

46. *HTS*, 772. Dame Van Winkle, Carolyn Karcher argues, represents the "locus of the oppression that the capitalist ethos generates in the family." "Patriarchal Society and Matriarchal Family," 33. Judith Fetterley, commenting on Irving's misogynist achievement of the "creation of woman as villain," links Dame Van Winkle with the capitalist ethos à la Franklin: see *The Resisting Reader: A Feminist Approach to American Fiction* (Bloomington: Indiana University Press, 1978), 2–5, quotation 3. For additional meanings, see Burstein, *The Original Knickerbocker*, 128–29.

47. *HTS*, 771.

48. *Ibid.*, 773.

49. See Philip Young, "Fallen from Time: The Mythic Rip Van Winkle," *Kenyon Review* 22:4 (Autumn 1960), 547–73, following Joseph Campbell, *The Hero with a Thousand Faces* (1949; second edn. Princeton, NJ: Princeton University Press, 1968), especially Part II, Chapter iii, "Transformations of the Hero."

50. See David G. Pugh, *Sons of Liberty: The Masculine Mind in the Nineteenth Century* (Westport, CT: Greenwood Press, 1983), especially 6–9, drawing on, *inter alia*, Leslie Fiedler's classic study of 1960, *Love and Death in the American Novel*, second edn. (New York: Stein and Day, 1966). Andrew Burstein, on the suggestion of an eminent psychologist, offers a conclusion closer to Irving's own predicaments: "Rip's twenty-year sleep can be read as Irving's desire to escape normal adult relationships and resist those sexual impulses he finds uncomfortable." *The Original Knickerbocker*, 128.

51. *HTS*, 7778; further references in this paragraph to "Rip Van Winkle" are to *ibid.*, 781, 782.
52. *Ibid.*, 779; further references in this paragraph to "Rip Van Winkle" are to *ibid.*, 783.
53. Hurst, "Reinventing Patriarchy," 667.
54. *HTS*, 783.
55. Hurst, "Reinventing Patriarchy," 668.
56. *HTS*, 783–84.
57. Hurst, "Reinventing Patriarchy," 669.
58. *Ibid.*, 670.
59. Lloyd M. Daigrepont, "Ichabod Crane: Inglorious Man of Letters," *Early American Literature* 19:1 (Spring 1984), 68–81.
60. David Leverenz, *Manhood and the American Renaissance* (Ithaca, NY: Cornell University Press, 1989), 86.
61. *HTS*, 1058.
62. *CW-SB*, xiii, xx, 348, 349, and 353. By the time "Sleepy Hollow" was published, English papers had already published individual stories, and there were rumors that a British publisher wanted to issue an unauthorized volume. Irving therefore was under much pressure; when Murray declines, he published the first four numbers with John Miller in mid–February 1820, though thanks to Walter Scott, Murray eventually relented. *Ibid.*, xix.
63. *HTS*, 1062; further references in this paragraph to "Sleepy Hollow" are to *ibid.*, 1086, 1087.
64. *Ibid.*, 1088.
65. *Ibid.*, 1076.
66. It is tempting to see Thomas Cole's painting of 1828, *Expulsion, Moon and Firelight* as echoing the expulsion sequence of "The Legend of Sleepy Hollow." To view the painting, which renders the rise and fall of American civilization as a cautionary tale of its own kind, go to the Museo Nacional Thyssen-Bornemisza, Madrid, https://www.museothyssen.org/en/collection/artists/cole-thomas/expulsion-moon-and-firelight.
67. *HTS*, 1060.
68. For "intrusive male," see Laura Plummer and Michael Nelson, "'Girls Can Take Care of Themselves': Gender and Storytelling in Washington Irving's 'The Legend of Sleepy Hollow,'" *Studies in Short Fiction* 30:2 (1993), 175–84.
69. *HTS*, 1068.
70. *Ibid.*, 1067.
71. *Ibid.*
72. Hurst, "Reinventing Patriarchy," 660.
73. *HTS*, 1062; further references in this paragraph to "Sleepy Hollow" are to *ibid.*, 1067, 1060–61.
74. Irving to Brevoort, Birmingham, July 16, 1816, *CW-Letters*, 1:450.
75. Anthony, "'Gone Distracted,'" 131. On Ichabod Crane as "an exaggerated self-portrait—or self-satire," see Burstein, *The Original Knickerbocker*, 149.
76. Anthony, "'Gone Distracted,'" 133. References to "Sleepy Hollow" are to *HTS*, 1059.
77. *HTS*, 1071.
78. *Ibid.*, 1084.
79. Anthony, "'Gone Distracted,'" 133. For the Lover's dysfunctional shadow, see Robert L. Moore and Douglas Gillette, *King, Warrior, Magician, Lover: Rediscovering the Archetypes of the Mature Masculine* (New York: HarperCollins, 1991), 131–40.
80. Anthony, "'Gone Distracted,'" 116.
81. *Ibid.*, 139.
82. *CW-Journals*, 3:262–65, 280.
83. *Ibid.*, 3:310. Irving even played in the lottery, though as he wryly noted in his journal, his ticket had "drawn a blank." London, May 29, 1824, *CW-Journals*, 3:337. A year later, during his residence in Paris, he is offered shares of a copper mine, which he eagerly purchases, only to be faced with more financial worries. See his letters to Thomas Storrow, respectively of July 2, 1825 and July 12, 1826, and to Thomas Aspinwall, September 18, 1828: "As I entered into that speculation entirely through a confidence in Jones' judgment, I hope he will get me out of it without a loss." *Ibid.*, 3:488n153.
84. Irving, "To the Reader," *CW-Traveller*, 4. The changes were substantial, amounting to some 3,600 words, as see the textual commentary, *ibid.*, 308.
85. Irving to Catherine Paris, September 20, 1824, *CW-Letters*, 2:76, emphases added.
86. Irving to Henry Brevoort, December 11, 1824, *ibid.*, 2:90.
87. *CW-Traveller*, 4; further references in this paragraph to *Tales of a Traveller* are to *ibid.*, 211, 213.
88. "The Money Diggers" section "will live," *Blackwood's Edinburgh Magazine* wrote in September 1824, "the rest will die in three months." Qtd. in *STW*, 2:295.

89. See *Treasure in Literature and Culture*, ed. Rainer Emig, Regensburger Beiträge zur Genderforschung, vol. 6 (Heidelberg: Winter, 2013); Elias Canetti, *Crowds and Power*, trans Carol Stewart (1960; New York: Farrar, Straus and Giroux, 1981 / London: Gollancz, 1962), especially 397–98; and Margaret Atwood, *Payback: Debt and the Shadow Side of Wealth* (London: Bloomsbury, 2008), esp. 91–99.

90. "Money-digger," n., *Oxford English Dictionary*, Third Edition, June 2012.

91. *CW-Traveller*, 228; further references in this paragraph to "Wolfert Webber" are to *ibid.*, 229, 234.

92. In a satiric lithograph entitled "The Ghost of a Dollar or the Bankers Surprize," which probably dates from 1813, the powerful Philadelphia merchant and financier Stephen Girard, here called "Stephen Graspall," is represented as mesmerized by the ghostly image of a Spanish silver dollar hovering in front of him. For a discussion of the print, see Tschachler, *The Monetary Imagination of Edgar Allan Poe*, 22–23.

93. *CW-Traveller*, 229, 233, 239; further references in this paragraph to "Wolfert Webber" are to *ibid.*, 236, 237, 238, 240, 248.

94. *Ibid.*, 243–48; further references in this paragraph are to *ibid.*, 250, 254, 255.

95. Irving had ridiculed the Dutch for their eating, drinking, and smoking, their phlegmatic temperament, and their passion for scrubbing already in the *History of New York*, as see Edward Wagenknecht, *Washington Irving: Moderation Displayed* (New York: Oxford University Press, 1962), 172–74.

96. *CW-Traveller*, 259.

97. *Ibid.*, 261.

98. Karl Marx, *Capital*, trans. Ben Fowkes, ed. Ernest Mandel (New York: Vintage Books, 1977), 254.

99. *CW-Traveller*, 215, emphases added.

100. *Ibid.*, 264.

101. Anthony, "'Gone Distracted,'" 138.

102. *CW-Traveller*, 263.

103. Sandage, *Born Losers*, 5. For "land speculation," see John McWilliams, "'The Almighty [Unmentionable] Dollar': Washington Irving and Money," *Literature in the Early American Republic: Annual Studies on Cooper and His Contemporaries* 2 (2010), 220.

104. My reading of the "theft" of Webber's masculinity rests on Slavoj Žižek's notion of the "theft of enjoyment" in *Tarrying with the Negative: Kant, Hegel, and the Critique of Ideology* (Durham, NC: Duke University Press, 1993), 206.

105. *CW-Journals*, 3:327; Irving kept his French journal from 1823 to 1826.

106. *Ibid.*, 329, 334.

107. *CW-Traveller*, 223.

108. See Marc Shell, *Money, Language, and Thought. Literary and Philosophic Economies from the Medieval to the Modern Era* (Baltimore-London: Johns Hopkins University Press, 1982), 15.

109. *CW-Traveller*, 223.

110. Charles G. Zug III, "The Construction of 'The Devil and Tom Walker': A Study of Irving's Later Use of Folklore," *New York Folklore Quarterly* 24 (1968), 243–60, here 24–49.

111. *CW-Traveller*, 224.

112. Jennifer J. Baker, *Securing the Commonwealth: Debt, Speculation, and Writing in the Making of Early America* (Baltimore: Johns Hopkins University Press, 2008), 35.

113. Caroll Smith-Rosenberg, "Domesticating 'Virtue': Coquettes and Revolutionaries in Young America," *Literature and the Body: Essays on Persons and Populations*, ed. Elaine Scarry (Baltimore: Johns Hopkins University Press, 1986), 160–84, here 172.

114. *CW-Traveller*, 224.

115. See also James J. Lynch, "The Devil in the Writings of Irving, Hawthorne, and Poe," *New York Folklore Quarterly* VII: 2 (Summer 1952): 111–31.

116. Simon Aka, "George W. Bush's Great-Great-Great-Great-Grandfather Was a Slave Trader," *Slate*, June 20, 2013, https://slate.com/human-interest/2013/06/george-w-bush-and-slavery-the-president-and-his-father-are-descendants-of-thomas-walker-a-notorious-slave-trader.html, retrieved May 26, 2014.

117. *CW-Traveller*, 223.

118. *CW-History*, xlviii. For "distorted mirror image" see Jeffrey Rubin-Dorsky, *Adrift in the Old World: The Psychological Pilgrimage of Washington Irving* (Chicago: University of Chicago Press, 1988), 108.

119. *CW-Traveller*, 224, 225; further references in this paragraph to "The Devil and Tom Walker" are to *ibid.*, 224, 225, 226.

120. See Zug, "The Construction of 'The Devil and Tom Walker,'" 248, 255.

121. Anthony, "'Gone Distracted,'" 117.
122. *HTS*, 1066. In language strikingly similar to that offered here by Knickerbocker, Thomas Jefferson (himself a victim of the 1819 crash) wrote that speculative excitement had resulted in "a general demoralization of the nation, a filching from industry its honest earnings, *wherewith to build up palaces*, and raise gambling stock for swindlers and shavers, who are to close their career of piracies by fraudulent bankruptcy." Thomas Jefferson, *The Writings of Jefferson*, vol.10, ed. Paul Leicester Ford (New York: Putnam's Sons, 1892–99), 122, emphases added.
123. John Quincy Adams was the candidate of the newly formed National Republican Party, which later became the Whig Party and eventually, from its northern wing, the Republican Party, with Abraham Lincoln as its first president.
124. On these pivotal changes in the nation's political process, see Lynn Hudson Parsons, *The Birth of Modern Politics: Andrew Jackson, John Quincy Adams, and the Election of 1828* (New York: Oxford University Press, 2009).
125. *CW-Journals*, 3:550.
126. *Ibid.*, 3:240–44, and 274. For Irving's experience as Lieutenant Colonel of the militia, see STW, 1:142–53, and Burstein, *The Original Knickerbocker*, 99–101.
127. *CW-Journals*, 3:282. Further references in this paragraph are to *ibid.*, 284, 300.
128. *Ibid.*, 3:257; cf. a. *ibid.*, 427: "Glanced this evg in Exr. [the London *Examiner*]."
129. *Ibid.*, 3:268; "Dr Gall" probably was Franz Joseph Gall, the father of phrenology, who became a French citizen in 1819 (*ibid.*, n420). Further references in this paragraph are to *ibid.*, 268–69, 269.
130. *CW-Traveller*, 217.
131. Irving to Brevoort, Birmingham, December 9, 1816, *CW-Letters*, 1:464–65.
132. *Ibid.*, 3:665, 664.
133. *Ibid.*, 3:483n141.
134. *CW-Traveller*, 217.
135. *Ibid.*, 225.
136. William L. Hedges, *Washington Irving: An American Study, 1802–1832* (Baltimore: Johns Hopkins University Press, 1965; repr. Westport, Connecticut: Greenwood Press, 1980), 232.
137. Alexis de Tocqueville, *Democracy in America, 1835–1840*, ed. Thomas Bender (New York: Modern Library, 1981), vol.2, 2nd Book, Chapter XIII, 431.
138. Joyce Appleby, *Inheriting the Revolution: The First Generation of Americans* (Cambridge, MA: The Belknap Press of Harvard University Press, 2000), 11, 10.
139. William Charvat, *The Profession of Authorship in America,1800–1870*, ed. Matthew J. Bruccoli (New York: Columbia University Press, 1992), 64.
140. Kurt Müller, "'Progressive' and 'Conservative' Concepts of American Identity: Washington Irving's Response to the Franklinesque Model," *The Construction and Contestation of American Cultures and Identities in the Early National Period*, ed. Udo J. Hebel, American Studies: A Monograph Series (Heidelberg, Germany: Carl Winter, 1999), 137–53.
141. *CW-Traveller*, 226.
142. *Ibid.*, 219.
143. Once again, see Michael T. Gilmore, "The Literature of the Revolutionary and Early National Period," *The Cambridge History of American Literature*, vol. I, *1590–1820*, ed. Sacvan Bercovitch (Cambridge, UK: Cambridge University Press, 1994), 672.
144. Leverenz, *Manhood and the American Renaissance*, 74. For "communal manhood," see Rotundo, *American Manhood*, 2–3, 11–18.
145. *CW-Traveller*, 216.
146. Adam Smith, *An Inquiry into the Nature and Causes of the Wealth of Nations*, ed. Kathryn Sunderland (Oxford: Oxford University Press, 1993), 429–30. In this regard, Herman Melville's *Moby-Dick*, published in 1851, can be understood as a dithyramb to the destruction of work skills by industrial production, the de-skilling of the work, and the dehumanization of the workers and the workplace.
147. *HTS*, 1069.
148. *Ibid.*, 1060.
149. *Ibid.*, 1065.
150. Qtd. in Anthony, "'Gone Distracted,'" 129.
151. *CW-Traveller*, 226; further references in this paragraph to "The Devil and Tom Walker" are to *ibid.*, 212, 213, 217, 222, 224, 227.
152. Zug, "The Construction of 'The Devil and Tom Walker,'" 251.
153. "[D]as schauerliche Bild des gespenstisches Weltbeherrschers." Richard Wagner,

"Erkenne dich selbst," in *Gesammelte Schriften und Dichtungen*, 10 volumes (Leipzig: Siegel, 1887-1911), 10:343, my translation.
154. Hurst, "Reinventing Patriarchy," 649-50.
155. Irving to Catherine Paris, September 20, 1824, *CW-Letters*, 2:76; in a letter to John Murray of March 25, 1823, Irving had likewise self-advertised *Travellers* as "the best thing I have written." *Ibid.*, 2:41-42.
156. *CW-Journals*, 3:421.
157. *Ibid.*, 3:427.
158. Quoted respectively in *CW-Traveller*, xxi, and STW, 2:294, 296. For additional contemporary reviews, see *CW-Traveller*, xxi-xxiv, and STW, 2:294-96. Darrel Abel aptly summarizes contemporary critics by remarking that *Tales of a Traveller* is "one of his poorest ... a batch of hackwork pieced together" in an attempt to use "the German materials he had been accumulating." "The Rise of a National Literature," in *American Literature: Colonial and Early National Writing* (New York: Barron's Educational Series, 1963), 268-340, here 283.
159. Qtd. in STW, 2:294.
160. *CW-Journals*, 3:480.
161. STW, 2:295. See also Walter A. Reichart, "Washington Irving's Influence in German Literature," *The Modern Language Review* 52:4 (1957), 537-553.
162. *CW-Traveller*, 3.
163. *CW-Letters*, 2:90, emphases added.
164. *CW-Traveller*, 92.
165. Irving to Pierre Paris Irving, Paris, December 7, 1824, *CW-Letters*, 2:85.
166. STW, 1:207.
167. *Ibid.*, 217.
168. *Ibid.*, 2:21.
169. Irving to Murray, January 26, 1825, *CW-Letters*, 2:101.
170. Irving to Murray, August 19, 1825, *ibid.*, 128.
171. Henry A. Pochmann, Introduction to *Washington Irving: Representative Selections* (New York: American Book Company, 1934), xli, xlin89. On Irving's side is Pete Kyle McCarter, who noted that Irving considered his *Columbus* as a dignified work, and thus "a better foundation on which to build a literary reputation" than belles-lettres. "The Literary, Political, and Social Theories of Washington Irving" (Madison: University of Wisconsin, 1939), 191.

172. William L. Hedges, "Irving's *Columbus*: The Problem of Romantic Biography," *The Americas* 13:2 (October 1956), 129.
173. *CW-Columbus*, xlii-xliii.
174. *CW-Traveller*, xiii, and see xxv. For "second-hand miscellany," see STW, 1:263. On Irving's drift "from fancy towards fact," see Michael Davitt Bell's psychological study of Irving, *The Development of American Romance*. On "amplification" as a way of thinking that proceeds by way of analogy, parallel and imaginative elaboration, see above, Chapter One.
175. John Neal, "American Writers," *Blackwood's Edinburgh Magazine*, January 1825, 67, qtd. in *CW-Traveller*, xxiv.
176. Irving to Henry Brevoort, June 8, 1811, qtd. in STW, 1:128.
177. Irving, "Philip of Pokanoket: An Indian Memoir," *HTS*, 1013-1028, here 1027.
178. *The Journals of Washington Irving (July 1815—July 1842)*, ed. William P. Trent and George S. Hellman, 3 vols. (Boston: The Bibliophile Society, 1919), 2:120.
179. *Ibid.*, 125.

CHAPTER FOUR

1. *CW-WR*, 131, 132. See a. PMI, 3:153, and STW, 1:460, 2:325, 360.
2. *CW-Journals*, 3:471.
3. "Recd. letter from Mr Everett, attaching me to Embassy at Madrid. Inclosing passport and proposing <the> my translating voyage of Columbus." January 30, 1826, *CW-Journals*, 3:563. For Irving's letter to Everett, see *ibid.*, 3:503, 559-60.
4. *Ibid.*, 564.
5. *Ibid.*, 434-78.
6. *Ibid.*, 441.
7. Irving to Pierre Paris Irving, March 29, 1825, *CW-Letters*, 2:108.
8. Irving to Thomas Storrow, Bordeaux, December 2, 1825, *ibid.*, 2:151.
9. Irving to Amelia Foster, Bordeaux, January 9, 1826, *ibid.*, 2:163.
10. STW, 1:297.
11. James Perrin, "Presentation," *Washington Irving in the Columbus Memorial Places... August 1828*, ed. José Enrique Myro and Marta Hildebrandt (Huelva, Spain: Lubrizol Española, 1985), 8, as quoted in Celia M. Wallhead, *Washington Irving and Spain: The Romantic Movement, The Re/*

Creation of Islamic Andalusia and the Critical Reception (Bethesda, MD: Academica Press, 2010), 30. At the time of the publication of this collection, Perrin was cultural attaché to the U.S. Embassy in Madrid.

12. Michel Foucault calls the fields of discursive relations "fields of concomitance." *The Archeology of Knowledge*, trans. A. M. Sheridan Smith (New York: Pantheon, 1972), 58. On Irving's emotional attachment to Spain, see Rolena Adorno, "Washington Irving's Romantic Hispanism and Its Columbian Legacies," in *Spain in America: The Origins of Hispanism in the United States*, ed. Richard L. Kagan (Urbana: University of Illinois Press, 2002), 82–105.

13. *BTA*, 726.

14. *STW*, 1:370–76. Williams elsewhere calculated the considerable proportion of all Irving's writings that the books on Spain make up: "Altogether on Spain Irving wrote some three thousand pages and approximately one million words, amounting to about one third of his total writings." Moreover, Williams considers Irving's "sustained use of more than thirty years of materials collected in Spain." *The Spanish Background of American Literature* (New York: Archon Books, 1968), 2:38; originally published by Yale University Press in 1955.

15. Irving to Alexander H. Everett, Seville, April 23, 1828, PMI, 2:312–13.

16. Irving to Thomas Storrow, August 16, 1826, *CW-Letters*, 2:207.

17. Earl N. Harbert, Introduction to *Conquest of Granada*, *CW-Conquest*, xxii; reference is to Irving's letter to Peter Irving, September 4, 1823, *CW-Letters*, 2:5, in which Irving writes that "Scott's manner must likewise be avoided." What Irving meant by this is not entirely clear; most likely, Irving felt that instead of historical romances his line would be romantic history.

18. Irving to Thomas Storrow, December 1, 1827, *CW-Letters*, 2:256.

19. Another schoolbook, Caleb Bingham's *American Preceptor* (1794), likewise provided Irving with a biography of Columbus. There is no record, however, whether Irving was familiar with William Robertson's *History of America* (London, 1777), which contains a brief section on Columbus in its first volume. For a detailed study of Irving's preparatory reading, see Stanley T. Williams and Tremaine McDowell,

Diedrich Knickerbocker's *A History of New York*, ed. the same (New Haven: Yale University Press, 1927), xxxviii–lix, and Williams, *The Spanish Background of American Literature*, 2:3–45.

20. On the evolution of "Columbia," see Claudia L. Bushman, *America Discovers Columbus: How an Italian Explorer Became an American Hero* (Hanover, NH: University Press of New England, 1992), 41–53.

21. Andrew Burstein, *The Original Knickerbocker: The Life of Washington Irving* (New York: Basic Books, 2007), 197. For more, see the unpublished doctoral dissertation by William L. Hedges, "The Fiction of History: Washington Irving against a Romantic Transition" (Cambridge, MA: Harvard University, 1953), 66n1. Hedges' dissertation in all likelihood is the most thorough and learned discussion of Irving as a historian.

22. Nietzsche qtd. in Ann Douglas, *The Feminization of American Culture* (1977; New York: Doubleday, 1988), 212.

23. *HTS*, 744.

24. *CW-Columbus*, 3.

25. Ibid., 31.

26. Ibid., 565–66.

27. Ibid., 129.

28. Ibid., 379.

29. John D. Hazlett, "Literary Nationalism and Ambivalence in Washington Irving's *The Life and Voyages of Christopher Columbus*," *American Literature* 55.4 (1983), 567. For a similar estimation, see Bushman, *America Discovers Columbus*, 107–26.

30. *CW-Columbus*, 353.

31. Ibid., 566.

32. Ibid., 569.

33. Thomas Jefferson, "First Inaugural Address," The Avalon Project at Yale Law School, http://avalon.law.yale.edu/19th_century/jefinau1.asp, retrieved January 5, 2020.

34. *CW-Columbus*, 11.

35. Ibid., 84.

36. For "poetic elements" of Columbus' character, see William Cullen Bryant, "Life, Character, and Genius of Washington Irving," in Charles Dudley Warner, William Cullen Bryant, George Palmer Putnam, *Studies of Irving* (New York: Putnam's Sons, 1880), 77–128, here 105.

37. As Michael Stevens has pointed out, one of the key elements of Irving's *Colum-*

bus project "was the creation of a historical persona for Christopher Columbus that imagined his achievements as a logical and constitutive element in the emergence of the United States." Stevens, "Spanish Orientalism," 259. Quite similarly, John D. Hazlett treats *Columbus* as "American material," at which Irving arrived after having "written himself out" of Englishness and after the failure of *Tales of a Traveller*. Hazlett, "Literary Nationalism and Ambivalence," 560–75. It should also be noted that in 1825 Irving also was at work on "American essays"—which he later destroyed, as see STW, 1:292–94.

38. Hazlett, "Literary Nationalism and Ambivalence," 573.
39. *CW-Columbus*, 569.
40. *Ibid.*, 569. For "lofty and noble," see 565; for "naturally irritable and impetuous," see 566; for Columbus' superstitiousness, see for instance 466 and 567.
41. *Ibid.*, 563.
42. *Ibid.*, 566.
43. Irving, *History of the Life and Voyages of Christopher Columbus* (London: John Murray, 1828), 18. The passage, from Bk. I, Chap. ii, is not in the Complete Works edition, for which the editor relied chiefly on the third American edition, that is, Putnam's Author's Revised Edition, the only edition which Irving proof-read. See *CW-Columbus*, xliii, lxvi–lxvii, and, for the genesis of the text after its first publication, 606–607.
44. *CW-Columbus*, 564–68; as we'll see in Chapter 6, Irving would likewise defend George Washington against the charge of excess ambition. In this context, Andrew Burstein's suggestion that Irving "fashioned Columbus into a moderate Federalist" (*Original Knickerbocker*, 204) is much to the point.
45. *CW-Columbus*, 564. For a critique of such a reading as "ahistorical," see Jordan Wingate, "Irving's Columbus and Hemispheric American History," *American Literature* 89:3 (2017), 463–96, here 484.
46. *CW-Columbus*, 565; for Columbus' will, see *ibid.*, 319.
47. *Ibid.*, 567.
48. *Ibid.*, 167.
49. Hazlett, "Literary Nationalism and Ambivalence," 568.
50. Quotations are from *CW-Columbus*, 289. On the "two portraits" of Columbus, see Hazlett, "Literary Nationalism and Ambivalence," 564.
51. *CW-Columbus*, 493.
52. Hazlett, "Literary Nationalism and Ambivalence," 573.
53. *CW-Columbus*, 10, emphases added.
54. Gilbert Stuart Newton to Irving, October 8, 1827, qtd. in STW, 1:322.
55. Prescott, *History of Ferdinand and Isabella, the Catholic* (1849), 2:508, as qtd. in *CW-Columbus*, xc. Everett, as qtd. in Ralph Aderman, ed., *Critical Essays on Washington Irving* (Boston: G. K. Hall, 1990), 71.
56. *Columbus* made Irving over $20,000 for the two editions—British and American—and its abridgment (PMI, 2:268, 4:410). On the appeal of the biography to nineteenth-century readers, see *CW-Columbus*, xvi–xviii and lxxxvii–lxxxix. For "Christian warfare," see E. Anthony Rotundo, *American Manhood: Transformations in Masculinity from the Revolution to the Modern Era* (New York: Basic Books, 1993), 172–74.
57. Irving, diary entry for December 31, 1826, qtd. in *CW-Columbus*, Introduction, lii.
58. Irving to Henry Brevoort, Madrid, April 4, 1827, *CW-Letters*, 2:226.
59. For Irving's letter to Navarrete, see STW, 2:303. For Navarrete's letter to Irving, see *150 W.I.: Washington Irving and the Alhambra*, ed. Carmen Yusty Pérez (Granada: Patronato de la Alhambra y Generalife / Tf Editores [Madrid], 2009), 152–53.
60. For possible reasons for the ten-month delay in the delivery of the manuscript, see *CW-Columbus*, Introduction, li and lvi–lxvi. For an account of Irving's toilsome labor throughout, see also STW, 1:309–19.
61. According to Burstein, Irving's *Columbus* generally was "the most commonly owned book" in American libraries in the mid-nineteenth century and "undeniably influenced how American school-children were taught their country's origins" (*The Original Knickerbocker*, 196). For the 1833 recommendation, by the New York State Legislature, that Irving's *Columbus* be used as a textbook for the common schools, see Andrew B. Myers, *The Worlds of Washington Irving, 1783–1859* (Tarrytown, NY: Sleepy Hollow Restorations, 1974), 73.

62. Burstein, *The Original Knickerbocker*, 205. For a complete listing of the several editions, see *CW-Columbus*, Introduction, lxxxvi.

63. On the popularity of Irving's *Columbus*, see a. STW, 1:355, 2:304. By the time Morison's biography was published, the critical tide had changed against Irving, whose *Columbus* now was seen as failed history, neither very accurate nor original enough to count as historical scholarship. Stanley Williams even went so far as to say that Irving deserved censure for his "plagiarism, if such it may be called." STW, 2:298. Elsewhere, Williams dismisses Irving as nothing more than the interpreter, during his twenty-one months in Madrid, of materials the Spanish historian Navarrete had spent thirty-five years gathering. On Irving's debt to Navarrete, far beyond his candid allusions to the Spanish scholar's "most obliging assistance" (Preface to *CW-Columbus*, 4), see STW, 299–302; for critical discussions of Irving's diction, tone, and characterization in *Columbus*, see ibid., 296–308, 322–24. For a thorough analysis of Irving's "impeccable" research, which amounts to a complete rebuttal of the charge of plagiarism, see *CW-Columbus*, Introduction, lxviii–lxxvii and xciv. For criticism of Williams's inability (or unwillingness) to judge separately the virtues of compiler (Navarrete) and historian (Irving), see ibid., xcii–xciii.

64. PMI, 2:429–31; for membership in the Spanish Royal Academy, see Irving's letter to Prince Dmitri Dolgorouki, Seville, January 10, 1829, ibid., 2:366.

65. Ibid., 2:271. John Murray of London alone paid Irving the princely sum of three thousand guineas, about $300,000 today. Ibid., 365–66 and 428–41.

66. See Lindsay DiCuirci, "The Spanish Archive and the Remapping of U.S. History in Washington Irving's *Columbus*," in *Urban Identity and the Atlantic World*, ed. Elizabeth Fay and Leonard von Morzé (New York: Palgrave Macmillan, 2013), 175–92.

67. *CW-Columbus*, 3.

68. Hazlett, "Literary Nationalism and Ambivalence," 574.

69. Charles Lanman, "A Day with Washington Irving," *Daily National Intelligencer*, March 23, 1857, 2.

70. See William Hedges, "Irving's *Columbus*: The Problem of Romantic Biography," *The Americas* 13 (October 1956), 130, 134.

71. Irving to Philip J. Forbes, Sunnyside, October 25, 1852, qtd. in Adorno, "Washington Irving's Romantic Hispanism," 82–83. The letter was occasioned by Irving's recollection that Forbes's father had given him the entire series of *The World Displayed* (London, 1759, and numerous subsequent editions) as a boy.

72. Pete Kyle McCarter and William L. Hedges, respectively, both qtd. in Edward Wagenknecht, *Washington Irving: Moderation Displayed* (New York: Oxford University Press, 1962), 184.

73. Winsor as well as Pelayo, qtd. in *CW-Columbus*, Introduction, xcii.

74. STW, 1:324–25 and 2:297–308. In a 1991 article, Jack Shreve likewise criticizes Irving for his "active imagination," though he concedes that "despite" it, *Columbus* is "still readable today." Shreve, "Christopher Columbus: A Bibliographic Voyage," *Choice* 29 (1991), 703–11, here 704. I disagree with Shreve, arguing, instead, that *Columbus* is still readable today *because of* Irving's "active imagination."

75. Williams (STW, 1:480n141) provides himself a good example. Whereas a Spanish chronicle records simply the fortunes and final fate of an Indigenous chieftain, in Irving's versions the chieftain's death "is principally ascribed to the morbid melancholy of a proud but broken spirit." *CW-Columbus*, 311.

76. Irving, manuscript notebook, 1819–1823, *CW-Journals*, 3:594. The entry is not dated, though it was obviously copied during Irving's residence in Dresden. While in Germany, Irving bought an eleven-volume edition of Schiller's *Sämmtliche Werke* and other volumes, most of which he brought back to America. Moreover, Irving saw performances of two of Schiller's plays, read Schiller with the Fosters in Dresden, and continued such reading, as the journals of 1823 through 1825 show. *CW-Journals*, 3:112, 127–28, 148, 245, 246; 273, 274, 275; 441, 447, and Introduction, xx. Arndt's translation is quoted in Susanne Zantop, *Colonial Fantasies: Conquest, Family, and Nation in Precolonial Germany, 1770–1870* (Durham, NC: Duke University Press, 1997), 173.

77. Irving, *Columbus* (London: John Murray, 1828), 4:48–49, and 1:18. For "glory"

as "the great object of his ambition," see *CW-Columbus*, 434. In concluding his biography, however, Irving defended Columbus against the historical charge of excess ambition: "The charge is inconsiderate and unjust," Irving asserts (*CW-Columbus*, 564), as if he had felt compelled to already suggest the idealized character of his George Washington.
78. *CW-Columbus*, 565.
79. *Ibid.*, 452.
80. *Ibid.*, 567.
81. *Ibid.*, 565.
82. *Ibid.*
83. *Ibid.*, 566.
84. *Ibid.*, 565.
85. *Ibid.*, 22.
86. *Ibid.*
87. *Ibid.*, 30, 68–69, 155.
88. *Ibid.*, 160.
89. *Ibid.*, 165–66.
90. *Ibid.*, 182.
91. *Ibid.*, 341–42.
92. *Ibid.*, 323, 324.
93. Francisco Morales Padrón, "El descubrimiento de América según Washington Irving," in *Washington Irving (1859-1959)*, ed. Francisco Yndurain Hernández et al., *Anejos del Boletín de la Universidad de Granada. Conferencias XI* (Granada: University of Granada Press, 1959) 73, as qtd. in Wallhead, *Washington Irving and Spain*, 23.
94. Hedges, "Irving's *Columbus*, 137; for similar estimations of Irving's Columbus by other critics, see 133–37.
95. *CW-Columbus*, 270, 286, 296–97.
96. *Ibid.*, 418–25.
97. Bartolomé de Las Casas, *Historia de las Indias*, 1:393, as qtd. in Hedges, "Irving's *Columbus*," 135.
98. *CW-Columbus*, 341.
99. *Ibid.*, 425, 560.
100. For "naturally irritable and impetuous," see *ibid.*, 566.
101. *Ibid.*, 256–57; for delusions about gold, see 100–102; for vows for a pilgrimage, 145–46.
102. *Ibid.*,108; for a discussion of Columbus' delusions and visions as thoroughly quixotic, see Hedges, "Irving's *Columbus*," 134–39.
103. *CW-Columbus*, 568; further references in this paragraph are to *ibid.*, 568, 567, and 560; for "an instrument in the hands of providence," see 493.

104. *Ibid.*, 560.
105. *BTA*, 820. "Crayon" appeared as the author only in the first English edition, published by Colburn and Bentley in London in 1832, and in the Baudry's Foreign Library one-volume edition (Paris, 1832), titled *The Alhambra, or the New Sketch Book, by Geoffrey Crayon, Gent*. The title of the concurrent two-volume American edition of 1832 (Philadelphia: Carey & Lea) is *The Alhambra: A Series of Tales and Sketches of the Moors and Spaniards. By the Author of the Sketch Book*, which amounts pretty much to the same, as the "author" of the *Sketch Book* was given as "Geoffrey Crayon, Gent." (The copyright notice does, however, say that it was entered by Washington Irving.) Hints to Crayon were abandoned for the "Author's Revised Edition" published by Putnam (New York, 1851), as well as for all subsequent editions, including the Library of America edition I'm using here, which uses the text from the Twayne edition of the *Complete Works of Washington Irving*. See Edwin T. Bowden, comp., *Washington Irving: Bibliography, The Complete Works of Washington Irving*, vol. 30 (Boston: Twayne, 1989), 362–86. My own usage of "Crayon" follows Jeffrey Scraba, who consistently employs the original writer/persona duality. See "'Dear Old Romantic Spain': Washington Irving Imagines Andalucia," *Romanticism and the Anglo-Hispanic Imaginary*, ed. Joselyn M. Almeida (Amsterdam and New York: Rodopi, 2010), 275–95, passim.
106. *BTA*, 821.
107. *Ibid.*, 835.
108. *Ibid.*
109. Crayon (*ibid.*, 769) claims to have read de Hita by the banks of the Hudson in his youth. Indeed, Irving may have done just that, most likely in Thomas Rodd's English translation, *The Civil Wars of Granada* (London: Thomas Ostell, 1803). Other possible sources include Thomas Rodd's *Ancient Ballads from the Civil War of Granada* (London: Thomas Ostell,1803). Possibly also, Irving may have been familiar with John Dryden's *The Conquest of Granada* (1669–70), which had been inspired by de Hita. De Hita became Irving's main source for the *Chronicle of the Conquest of Granada*.
110. *BTA*, 820.
111. Scraba, "'Dear Old Romantic Spain,'" 294.

112. See Henry A. Pochmann and E. N. Feltskog, "Historical Note," *CW-Mahomet*, 520–21.
113. *CW-Mahomet*, 79.
114. *Ibid.*, 14.
115. Thomas Carlyle, *On Heroes, Hero-Worship and the Heroic in History* (New York: Frederick A. Stokes, 1893), 86. Irving, Stanley Williams writes (STW, 2:224), "probably saw" Carlyle's essay on Mahomet, first published in 1841. For a thorough discussion of the multiple images of Muhammad, see John V. Tolan, *Faces of Muhammad: Western Perceptions of the Prophet of Islam from the Middle Ages to Today* (Princeton, NJ: Princeton University Press, 2019).
116. *CW-Mahomet*, 192.
117. *Ibid.*, 193, 199.
118. *Ibid.*, 194, 197.
119. *Ibid.*, 195, 196.
120. *Ibid.*, 87.
121. *Ibid.*, 198.
122. *Ibid.*, 262.
123. *Ibid.*, 439.
124. *Ibid.*, 387.
125. For more, see *Washington Irving and Islam: Critical Essays*, ed. Zubeda Jalalzai (Lanham, MD: Lexington Books, 2018).
126. *The United States Magazine and Democratic Review* and *The Literary Gazette*, qtd. in Pochmann and Feltskog, "Historical Note," *CW-Mahomet*, 553–54. *Literary World* qtd. in Mary Weatherspoon Bowden, *Washington Irving*, Twayne's United States Authors Series; TUSAS 379 (Boston: Twayne Publishers, 1981), 175.
127. Qtd. in Pochmann and Feltskog, "Historical Note," *CW-Mahomet*, 556.
128. *Ibid.*, 557–58.
129. *CW-Mahomet*, 224.
130. Pochmann and Feltskog, "Historical Note," *CW-Mahomet*, 546. For the sources Irving actually used, see 535–37 and 539–40.
131. STW, 2:216.
132. Bowden, *Washington Irving*, 173.
133. *Ibid.*
134. Irving to Everett, Puerto Santa Maria, October 21, 1828, PMI, 2:348.
135. Irving to Brevoort, Paris, March 10, 1821, *CW-Letters*, 1:614.
136. *Ibid.*, emphases added.
137. Pochmann and Feltskog, "Historical Note," *CW-Mahomet*, 559.
138. Irving to Alexander H. Everett, Seville, February 14, 1829, *CW-Letters*, 2:382.
139. Irving to Peter Irving, Alhambra, July 25, 1829, PMI, 2:404.
140. Irving to John Wetherell, July 25, 1829, *CW-Letters*, 2:448.
141. Jenifer S. Banks, "Washington Irving, the Nineteenth-Century Bachelor," in *Critical Essays on Washington Irving*, ed. Ralph M. Aderman, Critical Essays on American Literature (Boston, MA: G. K. Hall, 1990), 253–65, here 263.
142. TBA, 745.
143. *Ibid.*, 726, 727.
144. STW, 1:335; for the painting, see Irving to R. C. Winthrop, Sunnyside, April 4, 1853, qtd. *ibid.*. For a representation of the painting, now in the possession of the New Walk Museum and Art Gallery, Leicester, England, see *Washington Irving and the Alhambra*, 158–59. For reproductions of the drawing, see STW, vol.1, between 334–35, and William Collins Watterson, "Vandyck's Image of Washington Irving," *Studies in the American Renaissance*, 22 (1992), 75–90, here 80 and 83, plate 10.
145. Byron's costume is now at Bowood in Wiltshire. The finished portrait met with a mixed reception, but the essayist and poet Leigh Hunt thought it "by far the best that has appeared; I mean the best of him at his best time of life, and the most like him in features as well as expression." The version on display at London's National Portrait Gallery was painted in about 1835. It is one of the most famous and enduring images of the poet at the height of his fame. To view the portrait, go to https://www.npg.org.uk/collections/search/portrait-list.php?search=sp&sText=Phillips Lord byron &firstRun=true.
146. Byron, *Childe Harold's Pilgrimage*, Canto I, qtd. in Alicia Laspra Rodriguez, "Fictionalizing History: British War Literature and the Austrian Uprising of 1808," in *Romanticism and the Anglo-Hispanic Imaginary*, ed. Joselyn M. Almeida (Amsterdam-New York: Rodopi, 2010), 109–32, here 123.
147. PMI, 2:68–69.
148. *Ibid.*, 2:25–26.
149. "Newstead Abbey," *CW-CM*, 171–238. For accounts of Irving's visits to Newstead Abbey, see his letters to Catherine Paris, respectively of October 29, 1831, and January 20, 1832, *CW-Letters*, 2:667–68 and 683–86.
150. BTA, 740, 741.
151. Irving to Thomas Storrow, Granada,

March 10, 1828, *CW-Letters*, 2:279; Irving to Antoinette Bolviller, Granada, March 15, 1828, *ibid.*, 2:280. Irving had copied the phrase, prophetically as it appears on hindsight, into his notebook of 1825, from a play by Calderón de la Barca: "Bellissima Granada / Ciudad de tantos rayos coronada ..." Qtd. in STW, 1:296.

152. The first English edition of *Voyages and Discoveries of the Companions of Columbus* was published by John Murray. The first American edition was published by Carey and Lea. Starting with Putnam's ARE in 1849, it was published together with *A History of the Life and Voyages of Christopher Columbus*.

153. Irving to Brevoort, Alhambra, May 23, 1829, *CW-Letters*, 2:424, emphases added.

154. Irving, "Recollections of the Alhambra," *Knickerbocker Magazine*, 13 (June 1839), 486.

155. BTA, 730-31, 744-46.
156. *Ibid.*, 746.
157. *Ibid.*, 728.
158. *Ibid.*, 729.
159. *Ibid.*, 769.
160. *Ibid.*, 1049, 1050.
161. Irving to Brevoort, August 10, 1829, *CW-Letters*, 2:460.

162. *A Chronicle of the Conquest of Granada* was published by Carey and Lea in Philadelphia in April 1829 and by John Murray in London in May 1829. And though it is not obvious from "The Journey," Irving was in fact also remembering his first trip to Andalusia of the spring of 1828.

163. *CW-Conquest*, 3.
164. Irving to Aspinwall, Seville, April 4, 1829, *CW-Letters*, 2:396.
165. Irving to Thomas W. Storrow, Puerto Santa Maria, October 22, 1828, *ibid.*, 2:349.
166. Unsigned essay from Irving's hand, *Quarterly Review* XLIII (May 1830), 57–58, qtd. in *CW-Conquest*, xxii. For "Detached Manipulator," see Robert L. Moore and Douglas Gillette, *King, Warrior, Magician, Lover: Rediscovering the Archetypes of the Mature Masculine* (New York: HarperCollins, 1991), 111–16.
167. Irving to Dolgorouki, Seville, January 10, 1829, *CW-Letters*, 2: 375.
168. *CW-Conquest*, 21.
169. *Ibid.*, 111.

170. *Ibid.*, 208, and see Scraba, "'Dear Old Romantic Spain,'" 286–89.
171. *CW-Conquest*, 281. On Irving's refusal to celebrate the victors uncritically, see Richard V. McLamore, "Postcolonial Columbus: Washington Irving and *The Conquest of Granada*," *Nineteenth-Century Literature* 48 (June 1993), 26–43.
172. *CW-Conquest*, 285.
173. *Ibid.*, 98. For the "Weakling," see Moore and Gillette, *King, Warrior, Magician, Lover*, 88–94.
174. *CW-Conquest*, 291; for "apostate," etc., see 107.
175. STW, 1:345.
176. Whether readers actually understood Irving's strategy is a matter of dispute. Readers did, however, fall for the romantic history. As the *Monthly Repository and Review* wrote in July 1829, *A Chronicle of the Conquest of Granada* appealed to bourgeois readers "whose age of chivalry is not yet gone." Qtd. in STW, 2:311.
177. BTA, 755; for a characterization of this "ragged philosopher," as Irving called Ximenes, see STW, 1:363–66.
178. BTA, 767.
179. *Ibid.*, 769.
180. *Ibid.*, 844.
181. *Ibid.*, 816. Borrowing from Foucault, we may see Irving's Alhambra as a space of non-hegemonic otherness, a "heterotopia" in which the set of relations that they ostensibly designate, mirror, or reflect, are questioned, neutralized, or inverted. Michel Foucault, "Of Other Spaces, Heterotopias," *Architecture, Mouvement, Continuité* 5 (1984), 46–49.
182. BTA, 1018.
183. Irving to Dolgorouki, Alhambra, June 15, 1829, PMI, 2: 393.
184. Irving to Peter Irving, Alhambra, June 13, 1829, *ibid.*, 391.
185. Irving to Bolviller, Granada, March 15, 1828, *ibid.*, 291.
186. See Wallhead, *Washington Irving and Spain*.
187. Scraba, "'Dear Old Romantic Spain,'" 277. For "soul of Granada," see Mario Méndez Bejerano, *Historia literaria; ensayo* (Madrid, 1902), qtd. in STW, 2:319.
188. El Legado Andalusí, "Route of Washington Irving," n.d., https://www.legadoandalusi.es/las-rutas/ruta-de-washington-irving/, accessed March 6, 2020.

189. *Washington Irving and the Alhambra.* Especially useful are the essays by María del Mar Villafranca Jiménez, "Washington Irving and the Alhambra," 10–15; Antonio Garnica Silva, "Washington Irving's Andalusian Itinerary," 17–29; José Antonio González Alcantud, "The Dream of Washington Irving in the Alhambra," 31–43; and Antonio Rodriguez Almodóvar, "The Fairytale Factor in the *Tales of the Alhambra*," 79–87.

190. Born in Madrid in 1930, Hernández then was a professor of sculpture at the Escuela de Artes y Oficios in Madrid; he also was a member of the Royal Society of Fine Arts of San Fernando, as see *The Alhambra and Generalife: Official Guide* (Granada: Patronato de la Alhambra y Generalife, Consejería de Cultura: TF Ediciones, n.d.), 37.

191. To see an image of what is now called the "Washington Irving Monument," go to https://www.alhambra-patronato.es/en/edificios-lugares/washington-irving-monument, accessed April 24, 2020.

192. *HTS*, 811.

193. *CW-Columbus*, 563.

194. *BTA*, 723.

195. Jeffrey Rubin-Dorsky, *Adrift in the Old World: The Psychological Pilgrimage of Washington Irving* (Chicago: University of Chicago Press, 1988), 216–231.

196. STW, 1:376.

197. Williams, *The Spanish Background of American Literature*, 2:19.

198. Irving had pitched *The Alhambra* as "my Spanish *Sketch Book*" to John Murray. See STW, 1:373.

199. Qtd. in STW, 1:374. Fernán Caballero was the *nom de plume* of Cecilia Böhl, the daughter of a German scholar and merchant Irving had befriended in Andalusia in 1828. *Ibid.*, 348–54.

200. Scraba, "'Dear Old Romantic Spain,'" 278.

201. *BTA*, 752; similarly, in the opening of "The Court of Lions," Crayon reflects on the "[t]he peculiar charms of this old dreamy palace [and of] its power of calling up vague reveries and picturings of the past, and thus [of] clothing naked realities with the illusions of the memory and imagination." (*Ibid.*, 816) On the duality of writer/persona both in *The Alhambra* and in nearly all of Irving's major works, see Scraba, "'Dear Old Romantic Spain,'" 275–95.

202. *BTA*, 728. Tellingly, there is nothing picturesque in the account of traveling that Irving offered in a letter to Anoinette Bolviller: "One is exhausted by incessant fatigue, and put out of all tune by the squalid miseries of the Spanish posadas. I am now so surrounded by dirt and villany of all kinds that I am almost ashamed to despatch a letter to your pure hands from so scoundrel a place." Granada, March 15, 1818, PMI, 2:285.

203. *BTA*, 734–35. An *alguazil* was a constable or court bailiff.

204. Irving, European Journal, 1804–1805, *CW-Journals*, 1:433. For discussion of Irving's use of picturesque description, see Beth Lynne Lueck, *American Writers and the Picturesque Tour: The Search for National Identity, 1790–1860* (New York: Garland, 1997), 91–102.

205. "The Balcony," *BTA*, 810–11.

206. For the entry in *Sketch Book*, see "The Author's Account of Himself," *HTS*, 735, 743. On Irving's posturing on the prairies, see Richard H. Cracroft, "The American West of Washington Irving: The Quest for a National Tradition" (PhD thesis, University of Wisconsin, Madison, WI, 1970), 68. Just as revealing is Irving's letter to Mrs. Foster, sent from Prague on June 1, 1823, in which he writes about his habit of "contemplating" people and things "from a distance, and my imagination lending [them] tints." PMI, 2:157.

207. Ann Bermingham, *Landscape and Ideology: The English Rustic Tradition, 1740–1860* (London: Thames and Hudsonia Press, 1987), 10–11.

208. *CW-Columbus*, 567.

209. *BTA*, 1020. Subsequent references to "The Legend of Don Munio" are to *ibid.*, 1021, 1022, 1023, and 1025.

210. *Ibid.*, 725, 726.

211. Irving, "Recollections of the Alhambra," 485.

212. See Michael S. Stevens, "Spanish Orientalism: Washington Irving and the Romance of the Moors," *History Dissertations*, Paper 8 (Georgia State University, 2007). The classic accounts of "orientalism" are Edward W. Said, *Orientalism* (New York, NY: Pantheon, 1978), and Ziauddin Sardar, *Orientalism* (Buckingham, UK: Open University Press, 1999).

213. Irving, "Recollections of the Alhambra," 485, emphases added. *CW-WR*, List of Emendations, 308, and lv–lvi.

214. *CW-WR*, lvi.
215. *Ibid.*, 230.
216. Irving to William Irving Jr., August 1, 1804, *CW-Letters*, 1:44.
217. STW, vol.2, chapter XVIII; for America's ideals becoming Irving's own, see 2:52.
218. For "unsettled condition ...," see Hedges, *Washington Irving*, 116; for "failed and ineffectual masculinity," see Bryce Traister, "The Wandering Bachelor: Irving, Masculinity, and Authorship," *American Literature* 74:1 (2002), 116.
219. Irving to PMI, April 14, 1847, in PMI, 4:14–16.
220. *Ibid.*, 2:367 and 2:389n.
221. *Ibid.*, 4:14–16.
222. Irving to PMI, April 15, 1847, *ibid.*, 17.
223. *CW-CM*, xlvii–xlviii.
224. Irving, Preface to "Legends," *ibid.*, 242.
225. *Ibid.*, 247. Subsequent references to "The Legend of Don Roderick" in this paragraph are to *ibid.*, 291, 260–63, and 293, 295.
226. *Ibid.*, 242.
227. Irving, Notebook, 1829, qtd. in STW, 1:367.

CHAPTER FIVE

1. Qtd. in Michael S. Kimmel, *Manhood in America: A Cultural History* (1996; 3rd edn. New York: Oxford University Press, 2012), 24.
2. Qtd. in Marvin Meyers, *The Jacksonian Persuasion: Politics and Belief* (Stanford, CA: Stanford University Press, 1957), 161.
3. Qtd. in David Pugh, *Sons of Liberty: The Masculine Mind in the Nineteenth Century* (Westport, CT: Greenwood Press, 1983), 28.
4. Terence Martin, "Rip, Ichabod and the American Imagination," *American Literature* 31:2 (1959), 137–49, quotation 139.
5. Howard Horwitz, "'Rip Van Winkle' and Legendary National Memory," *Western Humanities Review* 58:2 (2004), 34–47, quotation 37.
6. I am here using the rhetoric of John Adams, who posed the question about how to prevent the creation of a new aristocracy in a letter to Thomas Jefferson of December 21, 1819: "Will you tell me how to prevent riches becoming the effects of temperance and industry? Will you tell me how to prevent riches from producing luxury? Will you tell me how to prevent luxury from producing effeminacy, intoxication, extravagance, vice and folly?" *The Adams-Jefferson Letters: The Complete Correspondence between Thomas Jefferson and Abigail and John Adams*, ed. Lester J. Cappon (1959; Chapel Hill-London: University of North Carolina Press, 1988), 550–51.
7. Irving, Fort Gibson, Arkansas, October 9, 1832, *CW-Letters*, 2:727.
8. Irving, *CW-CM*, 32.
9. "We send Americans to cities to educate them. Send them to the Country." Notebook entry, 1825, *CW-Journals*, 3:661.
10. Kimmel, *Manhood*, 38; for more, see David Pugh, *Sons of Liberty*, and Ann Douglas, *The Feminization of American Culture* (1977; New York: Doubleday, 1988).
11. Qtd. in Kimmel, *Manhood*, 25.
12. *Ibid.*, 43.
13. STW, 2:353n87.
14. Irving copied the account of Boone's exploration from Filson into a Notebook section titled "Extracts from Travels 1817." See editorial notes, *CW-Journals*, 2:203, 261, 262. For the Boone sketch, see *ibid.*, 247–52. On Boone, see John Mack Farragher, *Daniel Boone: The Life and Legend of an American Pioneer* (New York: Henry Holt, 1992).
15. *CW-Journals*, 2:249, 252.
16. *Ibid.*, 260.
17. On the "hero's welcome" Irving received from his native city, see Andrew Burstein, *The Original Knickerbocker: The Life of Washington Irving* (New York: Basic Books, 2007), 247–51.
18. *The Diary of William Dunlap*, September 26, 1833, qtd. in Van Wyck Brooks, *The World of Washington Irving* (1944; New York: Dutton—London: Dent, 1950), 438n.
19. Peter Antelyes, *Tales of Adventurous Enterprise: Washington Irving and the Poetics of Western Expansion* (New York: Columbia University Press, 1990), 48–50. See also Richard H. Cracroft, "The American West of Washington Irving: The Quest for a National Tradition" (PhD thesis, University of Wisconsin, Madison, WI, 1970); a shortened version appeared as *Washington Irving: The Western Works*, Boise State University Western Writers Series, 14 (Boise, ID: Boise State University Press, 1974). For a

thorough analysis of Irving's Western writings (mostly based on Cracroft's PhD thesis of 1970), see Heiner Bus, *Studien zur Reiseprosa Washington Irvings* (Frankfurt am Main: P. Lang, 1982).

20. Irving to Peter Irving, Granada, April/May 1829, *CW-Letters*, 2:412.

21. *North American Review*, April 1835, qtd. in PMI, 3:67.

22. Stanley T. Williams and Ernest E. Leisy, "'Polly Holman's Wedding': Notes by Washington Irving," *Southwest Review* 19 (1934), 449–54, here 449. For similarly unkind twentieth-century comments, see Heiner Bus, "Geoffrey Crayon 'Lighting Out for the Territory' and for Cultural Nationalism: A Reevaluation of Washington Irving's Western Writings," in *The Construction and Contestation of American Cultures and Identities in the Early National Period*, ed. Udo J. Hebel, American Studies: A Monograph Series (Heidelberg: Winter, 1999), 157.

23. STW, 2:45.

24. Instructions by Secretary of War Lewis Cass, qtd. in J. F. McDermott, ed., *The Western Journals of Washington Irving* (Norman: University of Oklahoma Press, 1966), 9. For a vivid narration of Irving's tour in its entirety see Burstein, *The Original Knickerbocker*, 257–71. For full chronicles of the tour, see McDermott, *Western Journals*.

25. On Indian removal see Anthony Wallace, *The Long Bitter Trail: Andrew Jackson and the Indians* (New York: Hill & Wang, 1993), and John Ehle, *Trail of Tears: The Rise and Fall of the Cherokee Nation* (New York: Doubleday, 1988). For Irving's—fairly inexpert—position on Indian removal, see Burstein, *The Original Knickerbocker*, 258–59.

26. *CW-CM*, 36. The Rangers had been added to the United States Army only in June 1832 to serve on the frontier. McDermott, *Western Journals*, 28.

27. December 18, 1832, *CW-Letters*, 2:733–34, emphases added.

28. *CW-CM*, 26.

29. *CW-History*, 36.

30. *CW-CM*, 26. Irving also welcomed the Indian sketches of his nephew John Treat Irving. "We have not yet had much of the true Indian character," he commented, as "writers have all represented the Indians according to a conventional and artificial model." Irving to Thomas Aspinwall, May 31, 1835, *CW-Letters*, 2:828; see a. Irving's letter to the same of June 20, 1837, *ibid.*, 908.

31. *CW-Letters*, 2:723.

32. *CW-Journals*, 5:64; *CW-Letters*, 2:273.

33. *CW-Letters*, 2:734, emphases added.

34. *CW-CM*, 15, emphases added.

35. Burstein, *The Original Knickerbocker*, 387n23. "Anthropological correctness" is inherent to the method of "natural history": observing a single adult Osage, for example, permitted the natural historian to classify all adult Osages who had ever lived. The practice, needless to say, was equally applied to Africans as well as to other "races."

36. *CW-CM*, 15.

37. Colonel Matthew Arbuckle's instructions to Captain Jesse Bean, commander of a company of Rangers, as qtd. in McDermott, ed., *Western Journals*, 32. For "friendly Indians," see *CW-Letters*, 2:727.

38. Irving had heard that the Pawnee could match any white marksman with their deadly bows and arrows. As he retells it in *Tour on the Prairies*, "the Pawnee ... could shoot with unerring aim three hundred yards, and send his arrow clean through and through a buffalo ..." *CW-CM*, 53.

39. *Ibid.*, 9.

40. *Ibid.*, 15, 20, 24, 26.

41. Christopher Hussey, *The Picturesque: Studies in a Point of View* (1927; repr. Hamden, CT: Archon Books, 1967), 1.

42. "I look chiefly with an eye to the picturesque," Irving wrote while traveling in Europe in 1805. European Journal, 1804–1805, *CW-Journals*, 1:433.

43. For discussion of Irving's romantic engagement with Spain, see above, Chapter Four. For discussion of Irving's use of picturesque description, see Beth Lynne Lueck, *American Writers and the Picturesque Tour: The Search for National Identity, 1790–1860* (New York: Garland, 1997), 91–102; for discussion of his romantic enthusiasm for primitivism, see Albert Keiser, *The Indian in American Literature* (New York: Oxford University Press, 1933), Chap. VII, 52–64.

44. *CW-CM*, 51, 60.

45. Irving to Lanman, Sunnyside, March 2, 1857, PMI, 4:226.

46. *CW-CM*, 21.

47. *Ibid.*, 10–11.

48. Cracroft, "The American West of Washington Irving," 68.
49. See my "'Roman Countenances' and 'Abominations': Racial and Ethnic Stereotyping in the Writings of Washington Irving," in *The Polyphony of English Studies: A Festschrift for Allan James*, ed. Alexander Onysko, Eva-Maria Graf, Werner Delanoy, Nikola Dobrić, and Günther Sigott, AAA—Arbeiten aus Anglistik und Amerikanistik, Vol. 26 (Tübingen: Gunter Narr Verlag, 2017), 241–59.
50. For discussion of Native Americans as proxies for an *American* civilization, one not to be colonized and subjugated by Europeans, see Myra Jehlen, "The Dispute of the New World," in *Cambridge History of American Literature*, vol.1, *1590-1820*, ed. Sacvan Bercovitch (Cambridge, UK: Cambridge University Press, 1994), 109–125, here 121–25. For "*our* aboriginal tribes" see Irving to Catherine Paris, September 2, 1832, *CW-Letters*, 2:717–18, emphasis added. Irving's comment was occasioned by his observing, en route to the Oklahoma territory, a number of Indigenous earth mounds and ramparts along the Miami River in Ohio.
51. Burstein, *The Original Knickerbocker*, 261–63; on the reassessment of the Indigenous population in histories and novels during the antebellum period, see Richard Slotkin, *Regeneration through Violence: The Mythology of the American Frontier, 1600-1860* (Middletown, CT: Wesleyan University Press, 1973), 354–59; on the transformation of "savages" into "noble savages," see Hoaxie Neale Fairchild, *The Noble Savage: A Study in Romantic Naturalism* (New York: Columbia University Press, 1928), esp. chapters I and II; Roy Harvey Pearce, *The Savages of America: A Study of the Indian and Civilization* (Baltimore, MD: Johns Hopkins University Press, 1953); Stelio Cro, *The Noble Savage: Allegory of Freedom* (Waterloo, Ontario: Wilfried Laurier University Press), 1990; and *Der Alteritätsdiskurs des edlen Wilden*, ed. Monika Fludernik et al. (Würzburg, Germany: Eon, 2002).
52. Edward Everett, in Andrew B. Myers, ed., *A Century of Commentary on the Works of Washington Irving* (Tarrytown, NY: Sleepy Hollow Restorations, 1976), 181. For similar estimations see Bus, "Geoffrey Crayon 'Lighting Out for the Territory,'" 170–71, and Mark Bernhardt, "Washington Irving's Western Adventure: Masculinity, Race, and the Early American Frontier," *Journal of the West* 52:1 (Winter 2013), 17–24.
53. Laura J. Murray, "The Aesthetic of Dispossession: Washington Irving and Ideologies of (De)Colonization in the Early Republic," *American Literary History* 8 (Summer 1996), 205–231, here 221–26, which contrasts Irving to William Apess, a Pequot, who treats Philip of Pokanoket in a strikingly different way, as living *in* history.
54. HTS, 1014.
55. See Guy Reynolds, "The Winning of the West: Washington Irving's *A Tour on the Prairies*," *Yearbook of English Studies* 34 (January 2004), 88–99, here 95.
56. Irving, "Philip of Pokanoket," *Analectic Magazine* 3 (June 1814), 502–15; "Traits of Indian Character," *Analectic Review* 3 (February 1814), 145–56.
57. Donald A. Ringe, "New York and New England: Irving's Criticism of American Society," *American Literature* 38 (1967), 463, 467.
58. HTS, 744. On Irving's ambivalent attitude towards westward expansion, see also Bus, "Geoffrey Crayon 'Lighting Out for the Territory,'" 169–70.
59. "Philip of Pokanoket," 1013, 1014.
60. Daniel F. Littlefield, Jr. "Washington Irving and the American Indian," *American Indian Quarterly* 5:2 (May 1979), 141–52.
61. HTS, 1011.
62. Irving, "remnants […] about to disappear," letter to his brother Peter, December 18, 1832, *CW-Letters*, 2:733–34. "[T]he right thing to do," Robert Musil, *The Man without Qualities*, vol.2, *Into the Millennium*, trans. Sophie Wilkins, *From the Posthumous Papers*, trans. Burton Pike (New York: Knopf / London: Picador, 1995), 1754. My thanks to Fabjan Hafner (†), Walter Fanta, and Angelika Rossak from the Musil-Institut for their help in identifying this elusive passage. In the German original the passage reads, "*Das Richtige wäre herüberzuretten.*" Robert Musil, *Der Mann ohne Eigenschaften*, ed. Adolf Frisé (Reinbek: Rowohlt, 1952 / Zürich: Buchklub Ex Libris, n.d.), 2:1578.
63. McDermott, *Western Journals*, 63.
64. *CW-Journals*, 5:103, 105.
65. Ibid., 84, 105.
66. Ibid., 133.
67. Ibid., 97.

68. Editor's introduction, *CW-Journals*, 5:xxxvi, emphases added. For the writings of Irving's fellow-travelers, see Henry L. Ellsworth, *Washington Irving on the Prairie or, A Narrative of a Tour of the Southwest in the Year 1832*, ed. Stanley T. Williams (New York: American, 1937); Charles J. Latrobe, *The Rambler in North America, 1832-1833*, 2 vols. (London: Seeley & Burnside, 1836; American edn. New York: Harper & Bros., 1835); and, incomplete as it is, Albert de Pourtalès, *On the Western Tour with Washington Irving: The Journal and Letters of Count de Pourtalès*, ed. George F. Spaulding (Norman: University of Oklahoma Press, 1968).

69. *CW-Journals*, 5:109; *CW-CM*, 20.

70. *CW-CM*, 21.

71. *CW-Journals* 5:105, 106.

72. Qtd. in McDermott, *Western Journals*, 44.

73. *CW-CM*, 19, 20.

74. *Ibid.*, 20-21.

75. *Ibid.*, 27.

76. *Ibid.*, 18, 11.

77. *Ibid.*, 32.

78. Bus, "Geoffrey Crayon 'Lighting Out for the Territory,'" 173. See also Bernhardt, "Irving's Western Adventure," 22-23.

79. Peter Antelyes even considers the bee hunt episode in Chapter IX of *A Tour on the Prairies* as a satire of American capitalism and its bustling protagonists. See *Tales of Adventurous Enterprise*, 125-27. Within the context of Irving's loyalty to traditional values and heritage, it is significant that *Crayon Miscellany* combined *A Tour on the Prairies* with two European pieces, "Abbotsford" (an essay on Walter Scott) and "Newstead Abbey" (a much longer piece that looks back nostalgically, *inter alia*, on Robin Hood and Sherwood Forest). Social order, hierarchy, patrician ideals, and America's European heritage are also important in "A Virginia Mansion" (*CW-Journals* 2:206ff.), and, of course, throughout Irving's final work, *Life of George Washington*.

80. *CW-CM*, 102. For Thomas Jefferson, it was not the Pawnees but the Osages who were the greatest potential adversary in the vast Louisiana Territory. See Burstein, *The Original Knickerbocker*, 265.

81. *CW-CM*, 110, 120.

82. See Irving to Peter Irving, October 28, 1833 and November 8, 1833, *CW-Letters*, 2:780, 781. For "the terror of the frontier," see *CW-Journals*, 5:97.

83. Irving to Peter Irving, November 24, 1834, *CW-Letters*, 2:804.

84. Irving to Peter Irving, January 8, 1835, *ibid.*, 806.

85. *North American Review*, qtd. in Ralph M. Aderman, *Critical Essays on Washington Irving* (Boston: G. K. Hall, 1990), 105. For sales figures, see *ibid.*, 103, 207. For more on the reception of Irving's *Tour*, see Dahlia Kirby Terrell, Introduction to *CW-CM*, xxx-xxxi.

86. On the "literariness" of *Tour on the Prairies* as well as on Irving's consciousness of the marketability of western narratives, see Antelyes, *Tales of Adventurous Enterprise*, 81-84, and Bus, "Geoffrey Crayon 'Lighting Out for the Territory,'" 157-63.

87. See Burstein, *Original Knickerbocker*, 282-89, and Peter Jaros, "Irving's Astoria and the Forms of Enterprise," *American Literary History* 30:1 (2018), 1-28. *Bonneville* was originally titled *The Rocky Mountains; Or, Scenes, Incidents, and Adventures in the Far West*.

88. Irving to Thomas Aspinwall, February 9, 1837, *CW-Letters*, 2:897.

89. *CW-Bonneville*, 11, 12.

90. Irving to Gouverneur Kemble, New York, January 10, 1838, *CW-Letters*, 2:919-20.

91. STW, 2:52; for "citizen of the republic," see Chapter XVIII.

92. Irving to Gouverneur Kemble, New York, January 10, 1838, *CW-Letters*, 2:920.

93. *CW-Astoria*, 7, 130.

94. *CW-Bonneville*, 36, 181.

95. *CW-Astoria*, 208. Further references to *Astoria* in this paragraph are to *ibid.*, 152, 158, 13.

96. *Ibid.*, 158.

97. Qtd. in PMI, 3:93.

98. *CW-Astoria*, "Introduction," 3.

99. *Ibid.*, 13.

100. Littlefield, "Irving and the American Indian," 144-47, quotation 145. For "national point of view," see *CW-Astoria*, 355. The "supineness [...] apathy, and neglect" (*CW-Bonneville*, 206) on the part of the U.S. government during the War of 1812 may well have been the reason why in "The Empire of the West," published anonymously in *Knickerbocker* magazine in 1840, Irving hailed the settlement of Oregon, much as he obligingly helped negotiate the settlement of the boundary dispute with England in 1845-1846.

101. *CW-Astoria*, 78. For a systematic study of the incident, see James P. Ronda, *Astoria and Empire* (Lincoln: University of Nebraska Press, 1990), 94–95.
102. *CW-Bonneville*, 269, 270.
103. *Ibid.*, 159. For "ingrafted ...," see Introductory Notice, 3. For "midway between ...," see Peter Irving to Washington Irving, March 6, 1837, PMI, 3:113.
104. *CW-Bonneville*, 4.
105. Stephanie LeMenager, "Trading Stories: Washington Irving and the Global West," *American Literary History* 15:4 (2003), 683–708, here 685. For an evaluation of Irving's involvement with the literature of American expansion, see a. Bus, "Geoffrey Crayon 'Lighting out for the Territory," and Reynolds, "The Winning of the West," 88–99.
106. LeMenager, "Trading Stories," 687.
107. Burstein, *The Original Knickerbocker*, 343; on *Astoria*, see 286–87; on *Bonneville*, see 288–89.
108. Herman Melville, *Selected Tales and Poems*, ed. Richard Chase (New York: Holt, Rinehart and Winston, 1950), 93. The words are spoken by the story's attorney-narrator.
109. Qtd. in Van Wyck Brooks, *The World of Washington Irving*, 438n223.
110. *CW-Astoria*, 23.
111. Antelyes, *Tales of Adventurous Enterprise*, 154–62, 167. For a less flattering view of Astor's career, see Richard E. Oglesby, "John Jacob Astor—'a better businessman than the best of them'," *Journal of the West* 25 (1986), 8–14.
112. Antelyes, *Tales of Adventurous Enterprise*, 76. The term is fitting in another respect as well. The new wealthy like Astor were no longer the landed gentry but the new merchants and industrialists. And they had risen to considerable power. While in 1774 the richest tenth of all Americans held slightly less (49.6 percent) than half the wealth, they held 73 percent in 1860, and the richest one percent more than doubled their share of the wealth, from 12.6 to 29 percent, and then to about 50 percent by mid-century. Charles Sellers, *The Market Revolution: Jacksonian America 1815-1846* (New York: Oxford University Press, 1994), 152, 238.
113. *CW-Astoria*, 15–16.
114. Antelyes, *Tales of Adventurous Enterprise*, 168–70. Nevertheless, John Jacob Astor was "greatly gratified" with the work.

Irving to Pierre Munro Irving, December 12, 1836, *CW-Letters*, 2:884.
115. Antelyes, *Tales of Adventurous Enterprise*, 162–85; quotations 119, 186, 191–92, 250. Irving had read Cooper's *The Pioneers* of 1827 before he set out on his tour. See *ibid.*, 37.
116. *Ibid.* 182, and see Irving to Pierre Munro Irving, September 15, 1834, *CW-Letters*, 2:798–99.
117. Irving to Pierre Munro Irving, October 29, 1834, *CW-Letters*, 2:802.
118. *CW-Bonneville*, 5.
119. Irving to Major James H. Hook, March 27, 1835, *CW-Letters*, 2:865.
120. Irving to Thomas Aspinwall, March 29, 1835, *ibid.*, 904.
121. *New York Review*, October 1837, qtd. in *Critical Essays on Washington Irving*, ed. Ralph M. Aderman (Boston, MA: G. K. Hall, 1990), 111–12. The lone exception seems to have been Hubert Howe Bancroft, historian of the American West, who slashed the book savagely, implying that in his portrayal of Bonneville, Irving had whitewashed a scoundrel. See STW, 2:89–91. For modern critics who see value in Irving's *Bonneville*, see Burstein, *The Original Knickerbocker*, 391n24.
122. *Literary Gazette*, qtd. in *Critical Essays on Washington Irving*, ed. Aderman, 110–11. Generally on British reviewers, see Burstein, *The Original Knickerbocker*, 288.
123. *CW-Misc.*, 2:115–119. On Irving's adopted role as a cultural ambassador of sorts, always wary of "national myopia," see Jordan Wingate, "Irving's Columbus and Hemispheric American History," *American Literature* 89:3 (2017), 463–96, especially 471.
124. *CW-WR*, 3–16.
125. *Ibid.*, 182.
126. Littlefield, "Irving and the American Indian," 151. For a harrowing account of the consequences of this "tidal wave" on the Indigenous population, see Jeffrey Ostler, *Surviving Genocide: Native Nations and the United States from the American Revolution to Bleeding Kansas* (New Haven: Yale University Press, 2020).
127. One of the earliest critics to do so was Jason Alma Russell, "Irving. Recorder of Indian Life," *Journal of American History* 25 (1931), 184–95. On "receptivity" as the premier attitude of an anima persona, see Emma Jung, *Animus and Anima*, 55.

128. "Traits of Indian Character," 145.
129. Edward Wagenknecht, *Washington Irving: Moderation Displayed* (New York: Oxford University Press, 1962), 111.
130. PMI, 1:57, 58. Emphases in original.
131. HTS, 224.
132. CW-History, 43, 35.
133. For a thorough discussion of Irving's explanation of this aspect of American history, see Jerome McGann, "Washington Irving, *A History of New York*, and American History," *Early American Literature*, 47:2 (2012), 349–76.
134. Qtd. in Ronald Takaki, "*The Tempest* in the Wilderness: The Racialization of Savagery," *Journal of American History* 79:3 (December 1992), 892–912, here 902, 903.
135. James Kent, *Commentaries on American Law*, 4 vols., 1826–1830 2nd edn. (New York: O. Halsted, 1832), 3:386.
136. See Alden T. Vaughan, "From White Man to Redskin: Changing Anglo-American Perceptions of the American Indian," *American Historical Review* 87 (1982), 917–53.
137. HTS, 1007.
138. Ibid. 1014, 1028.
139. Ibid., 1002.
140. Ibid., 1009.
141. Significantly, the reviewer for the *Analectic* generously credits Irving with awareness both "that Indian behavior was not motivated by the same cultural traditions that motivated the behavior of the transplanted European" and "that Indian cultural traditions were adequate to produce a character of heroic proportions." Qtd. in Wagenknecht, *Washington Irving*, 111.
142. HTS, 1004. Further references in this paragraph to "Traits of Indian Character" are to *ibid.*, 1003 and 1011.
143. Ibid., 1011.
144. Ibid., 1014.
145. Ibid., 1018–19, 1028.
146. *Analectic Review* 3 (February 1814), 145.
147. Jackson's Indian policy was, if anything, more topical than ever: "It is high time," he told Secretary of War John C. Calhoun, "to do away with the farce of treating with Indian tribes." Andrew Jackson, September 2, 1820, *Papers of Andrew Jackson*, ed. Sam B. Smith (Knoxville: University of Tennessee Press, 1980), 4:388. Jackson also dismissed the director of the BIA, Thomas McKenney. The BIA, the Bureau of Indian Affairs, had been founded in 1816, under the control of the Department of War. For a fuller treatment of Irving's Indian sketches in the context of the Creek war, see Burstein, *The Original Knickerbocker*, 258–59. For a detailed analysis of Jackson's actions as a war hawk, see David S. Heidler and Jeanne T. Heidler, *Old Hickory's War: Andrew Jackson and the Quest for Empire* (Baton Rouge: Louisiana State University Press, 1996).
148. Irving "heavily revised" both "Traits" and "Philip" for the *Sketch Book*. See the editor's introduction to CW-SB, xxi, n30, and textual commentary, 360–64.
149. HTS, 1014.
150. All qtd. in Takaki, "*The Tempest* in the Wilderness," 898, 907.
151. HTS, 1020.
152. Ibid., 1028.
153. See Philip Gould, "Remembering Metacom: Historical Writing and the Culture of Masculinity," in *Sentimental Men: Masculinity and the Politics of Affect in American Culture*, ed. Mary Chapman (Berkeley: University of California Press, 1999), 112–24, here 117.
154. The *Analectic Review* not only printed Irving's Indian sketches but also gave prominent place to his triumphalist portraits of America's emerging naval heroes such as James Lawrence, William Burrows, David Porter, Stephen Decatur, and Commodore Oliver Hazard Perry, who had distinguished himself in naval battles along the U.S.-Canadian border. In addition, Irving in August 1814 had reprinted in its pages Francis Scott Key's poem "Defense of Fort M'Henry." See STW, 1:135–40, Elsie Lee West, "Washington Irving, Biographer," *Washington Irving Reconsidered: A Symposium*, ed. Ralph M. Aderman (Hartford, CT: Transcendental Books, 1969), 48–49, Burstein, *The Original Knickerbocker*, 96–99, and CW-Misc., 1:132.
155. STW, 1:294.
156. CW-Columbus, 126.
157. CW-CM, 49–50, 93–94.
158. CW-Journals, 5:86, 88; CW-CM, 93. Irving saw fit not to include the chief's burial in the printed work, presumably because he would have been afraid it would offend the delicate tastes of his eastern readers.
159. Irving to Van Buren, New York, April 30, 1838, CW-Letters, 2:926.

160. George Santayana, *The Genteel Tradition: Nine Essays by George Santayana* (Cambridge, MA: Harvard University Press, 1967), 439–40.

161. "The Creole Village," which is subtitled "A Sketch from a Steamboat," may have been intended for insertion in *A Tour on the Prairies* (1835) but was withdrawn and was first published in Henry Herbert's annual, *The Magnolia*, in 1837, at the height of the financial crisis following Jackson's war on the Second Bank of the United States. In 1855, the sketch was republished in *Wolfert's Roost*.

162. *CW-WR*, 22. Further references to the sketch in this paragraph are to *ibid*., 23, and 24.

163. As Edward Wagenknecht noted, in Irving's time, "genteel" was not yet a dirty word. See *Washington Irving: Moderation Displayed*, 188.

164. *CW-WR*, 23.

165. *Ibid*., 27. Further references to the sketch in this paragraph are to *ibid*. For the 1855 republication, Irving made only minor changes, except for one major addition in the form of a footnote at the end of the story: "This phrase [the almighty dollar] used for the first time, in this sketch, has since passed into current circulation, and by some has been questioned as savoring of irreverence. The author, therefore, owes it to his orthodoxy to declare that no irreverence was intended even to the dollar itself; which he is aware is daily becoming more and more an object of worship" (*CW-WR*, 27n.). In other words, Irving means no disrespect for religion, but expresses his contempt for those who treat money, or rather the wrong kind of money, as if it were God and thus an object of devotion.

166. The quotations by Blake as well as the New York college student are from E. Anthony Rotundo, *American Manhood: Transformations in Masculinity from the Revolution to the Modern Era* (New York: Basic Books, 1993), 335, 336.

167. Irving to Sarah Storrow, Honesdale, July 31, 1841, *CW-Letters*, 3:145.

168. *CW-WR*, 95–119. "Mississippi Bubble" was republished in 1855 in volume XV in Putnam's edition of *The Works of Washington Irving*, and again in 1883 in *The Crayon Papers* (New York: J. W. Lovell); the sketch is also accessible online at www.online-literature.com/irving/crayon-papers/2/. For "usurped by the plodder & moneymaker," see *CW-Journals*, 3:665.

169. Antelyes, *Tales of Adventurous Enterprise*, 60–64.

170. *CW-WR*, 95.

171. See my *The Greenback: Paper Money and American Culture* (Jefferson, NC: McFarland, 2010), 33, 48.

172. *CW-WR*, 95.

173. See Jessica M. Lepler, *The Many Panics of 1837: People, Politics, and the Creation of a Transatlantic Financial Crisis* (New York: Cambridge University Press, 2013), and Heinz Tschachler, *The Monetary Imagination of Edgar Allan Poe* (Jefferson, NC: McFarland, 2013), 14–15, 34–37, and passim.

174. John Kenneth Galbraith, *A Short History of Financial Euphoria* (1990; New York: Whittle Books in association with Penguin Books, 1994), 45–46.

175. David Leverenz, *Manhood and the American Renaissance* (Ithaca, NY: Cornell University Press, 1989), 223.

176. Dwight, *Travels in New-England and New-York* (New-Haven: T. Dwight, 1821), 2:460; Crèvecoeur qtd. in Roderick Nash, *Wilderness and the American Mind* (New Haven, CT: Yale University Press, 1967), 30.

177. Kimmel, *Manhood*, 41–42, Leverenz, *Manhood and the American Renaissance*, esp. 217–26; for a modern edition, see *The Oregon Trail*, ed. David Levin (Harmondsworth, UK: Penguin, 1982).

178. *CW-CM*, 102.

179. Qtd. in STW, 2:48.

180. *Ibid*., 2:51; other references in this paragraph are to *ibid*., 48 and 59. On Irving's narrative strategy in *Life of George Washington*, see C. Michael Hurst, "Reinventing Patriarchy: Washington Irving and the Autoerotics of the American Imaginary," *Early American Literature* 47:3 (2012), esp. 671. For "a liberal infusion of *stronger* material," see Leverenz, *Manhood and the American Renaissance*, 170, quoting from an 1845 essay by William Kirkland, "British and American Monthlies," in *Godey's Lady's Book*, emphasis in original. William Kirkland was Caroline M. Kirkland's husband.

CHAPTER SIX

1. Irving, "Preface," *Life of George Washington* (New York: Putnam, 1855–1859), V:iii.

2. Linda Kerber, *Federalists in Dissent: Imagery and Ideology in Jeffersonian America* (Ithaca, NY: Cornell University Press, 1970), vii.

3. For "symbolically fatherless sons," see E. Anthony Rotundo, *American Manhood: Transformations in Masculinity from the Revolution to the Modern Era* (New York: Basic Books, 1993), 25. For "attended [...] through life," see Charles Lanman's "A Day with Washington Irving," *Daily National Intelligencer*, March 23, 1857, 2.

4. David Leverenz, *Manhood and the American Renaissance* (Ithaca, NY: Cornell University Press, 1989), 4, 73.

5. *CW-Goldsmith*, 3–4. For an eBook version of the 1849 edition of *Goldsmith*, go to http://www.gutenberg.org/files/7993/7993-h/7993-h.htm.

6. *CW-Journals*, 3:306.

7. Qtd. in *CW-Goldsmith*, xxxiv.

8. *The Gentleman's Magazine*, 32 (December 1849), 617, qtd. in Elsie Lee West, "Washington Irving, Biographer," in *Washington Irving Reconsidered: A Symposium*, ed. Ralph M. Aderman (Hartford, CT: Transcendental Books, 1969), 47–52, here 51.

9. George W. Greene, *Christian Review*, April 1850, in PMI, 4:57–58.

10. James Hillman, *anima, an anatomy of a personified notion* (Putnam, CT: Spring Publications, 1985), 81.

11. *CW-Goldsmith*, xv–xvi.

12. *Ibid.*, 5.

13. *Ibid.*, xxi.

14. *Ibid.*, 5.

15. John McWilliams, "'The Almighty [Unmentionable] Dollar': Washington Irving and Money," *Literature in the Early American Republic: Annual Studies on Cooper and His Contemporaries* 2 (2010), 215.

16. *CW-Goldsmith*, 239; other quotations in this paragraph are from *ibid.*, 237 and 94. Charles Dickens, who met with Irving in 1842, may have been the first to suggest that Goldsmith was Irving's "own brother." See Edward Wagenknecht, *Washington Irving: Moderation Displayed* (New York: Oxford University Press, 1962), 95.

17. *CW-Goldsmith*, xxxvi–xxxvii.

18. Irving, it seems, wanted to rewrite every book he'd written. When Theodore Tilton, an editor at the New York *Independent*, visited him on November 7, 1859, and asked which of his books he looked back upon "with most pleasure," Irving responded: "I scarcely look with full satisfaction upon any; for they do not seem what they might have been. I often wish that I could have twenty years more, to take them down from the shelf one by one, and write them over." PMI, 4:319.

19. *JCW*, 14: §749, and see above, Chapter 1.

20. Irving to Theodore Tilton, Sunnyside, June 7, 1859, PMI, 4:321.

21. *Ibid.*, 4:198.

22. "[I] have determined immediately to undertake ... a Life of Washington." Washington Irving to Peter Irving, London, December 18, 1829, *CW-Letters*, 2:494–95.

23. *CW-Journals*, 5:395n2.

24. Lanman, "A Day with Washington Irving," 2.

25. *CW-Journals*, 2:282.

26. *Ibid.*, 288.

27. *Ibid.*, 355.

28. *Ibid.*, 3:506; see a. PMI, 2:238, and STW, 1:283. Irving later acknowledged Marshall's *Life* as a source in his own account of the touching farewell at Fraunces Tavern. *Washington*, IV:441.

29. Irving to Constable, August 19, 1825, *CW-Letters*, 2:126–27, emphases added. On the notes Irving made for *Life of George Washington*, see *CW-Journals*, 5:394–99; on subsequent notes in the years until the end of his life, see the editorial notes in *CW-Washington*, 5:395n2.

30. Editorial note in *CW-Letters*, 2:127.

31. Nevertheless, Marshall's *The Life of Washington*, published between 1804 and 1807, was widely read, confirming Thomas Jefferson's forebodings that it would dominate the popular view of American history for generations to come. Which indeed it did, until George Bancroft's *History of the United States* was published in Boston in 1839.

32. *CW-Journals*, 4:41.

33. Journal entry, February 18, 1829, *ibid.*, 254. The dinner was probably prompted by Washington's birthday.

34. See David Pugh, *Sons of Liberty: The Masculine Mind in the Nineteenth Century* (Westport, CT: Greenwood Press, 1983), 13–38.

35. Irving to Alexander H. Everett, Seville, February 14, 1829, *CW-Letters*, 2:382. A journal entry of February 19, 1824, also testifies to Irving's long-standing admira-

tion of Jackson: "Col[onel] Thornton speaks of the handsome manner in which Genl Jackson sent back watches & Epaulettes that had been taken from officers at N Orleans." *CW-Journals*, 3:292. Sir William Thornton had distinguished himself at the Battle of New Orleans in January 1815. Irving retold the episode of Jackson's "chivalrous act" in a letter to Virginia lawyer W. M. Blackford, whose strong Whig position he also knew. The letter is dated New York, October 27, 1833 (*CW-Letters*, 2:778–79; a. in STW, 2:346n111). And when Irving was invited to a White House dinner in June 1832, a guest observed that he "came out a Jackson man." Qtd. in Peter Antelyes, *Tales of Adventurous Enterprise: Washington Irving and the Poetics of Western Expansion* (New York: Columbia University Press, 1990), 49 and 211–12n2. The observation was not inaccurate. As Irving wrote to his brother Peter in Paris, "I have been most kindly received by the old general, with whom I am much pleased as well as amused. As his admirers say, he is truly an *old Roman*—to which I would add, *with a little dash of the Greek*; for I suspect he is as *knowing*; and I believe he is *honest*." Irving to Peter Irving, Washington, DC, June 16, 1832, *CW-Letters*, 2:705; PMI, 3:22. Irving also would never forget that Jackson, in 1841, had reimbursed him for expenses he had incurred during his time with the Legation at St. James. Although there was no law then providing for such claims, Jackson ordered that Irving should receive the pay of his charge—to the amount of more than twice what he had asked for. See Lanman, "A Day with Washington Irving," 2.

36. See Irving's letter to Gouverneur Kemble, January 10, 1838, *CW-Letters*, 2:918–921.

37. Irving to Ebenezer Irving, February 16, 1842, *ibid.*, 3:181.

38. On February 1, 1855, Irving attended the wedding of his grandniece Henrietta Eckford Irving, granddaughter of John Treat Irving, to Smith Thompson Van Buren, son of the former president. In early September 1855, Irving visited Van Buren at his Kinderhook home, where Irving had written part of *A History of New York*, when it belonged to the Van Ness family. Andrew Burstein, *The Original Knickerbocker: The Life of Washington Irving* (New York: Basic Books, 2007), 320–21, and Irving to Van Buren, September 4, 1855, in *CW-Letters*, 4:549. For more on the intimate connections between Irving and Van Buren, see Ted Widmer's biography, *Martin Van Buren*, American Presidents Series (New York: Times Books, 2005).

39. STW, 2:363n159. Williams does not cite from this letter, dated Boston, May 10, 1842, nor does he give documentation.

40. PMI, 3:133–34. In a letter to Pierre Munro Irving, Irving later wrote that renouncing the Mexican project had been a great "sacrifice." As in his other bio-histories, he had intended the story of the discoverers and conquistadors to bring out "in strong relief ... the different characters of the dramatis personae." March 24, 1844, PMI, 3:143, 145.

41. Irving to Sarah Storrow, Madrid, February 27, 1845, qtd. in STW, 2:190; for "his literary passion had atrophied," see *ibid.*, 197.

42. STW, 1:156.

43. Sunnyside, April 15, 1847, PMI, 4:64–65.

44. Irving to Sarah Storrow, Sunnyside, July 5, 1849, *ibid.*, 4:52. For "hack writer," see STW, 2:212.

45. James Tuttleton, HTS, 1117.

46. Jared Sparks, qtd. in Ann Douglas, *The Feminization of American Culture* (1977; New York: Doubleday, 1988), 188.

47. Andrew Myers, "The New York Years in Irving's *Life of George Washington*," *Early American Literature* 11 (1976), 68–83, here 75.

48. PMI, 4:130.

49. Irving, Preface to *Washington*, I:iv.

50. Washington Irving to William Irving Jr., August 1, 1804, *CW-Letters*, 1:44.

51. Myers, "Irving's *Life*," 76.

52. Tuttleton, HTS, 1119.

53. *Ibid.* Irving gratefully acknowledged the assistance in the preface to the fifth volume: " ... kindly assisted by his nephew, who had previously aided him in the course of his necessary researches, and who now carefully collated the manuscript with the works, letters, and indited documents from which the facts had been derived." *Washington*, V: iv.

54. These exercises in life-writing would serve the nephew well in preparing the first official biography of his uncle, a mere three years after Irving's death in 1859. See Wayne R. Kime, *Pierre M. Irving and*

Washington Irving: A Collaboration in Life and Letters (Waterloo, Ontario: Wilfrid Laurier University Press, 1977), 132-33. For "empire," see Irving's letter to Mrs. John P. Kennedy, March 11, 1853, PMI, 4:137.

55. PMI, 4:332.

56. Sunnyside, February 15, 1847, qtd. in STW, 2:212.

57. *Ibid.*, 227.

58. William Alfred Bryan, *George Washington in American Literature 1775-1865* (New York: Columbia University Press, 1952; repr. Westport, CT: Greenwood Press, 1970), 96-120. For a discussion of Washington biographies through Irving, see a. Jeff Smith, *The Presidents We Imagine: Two Centuries of White House Fictions on the Page, on the Stage, Onscreen, and Online* (Madison: University of Wisconsin Press, 2009), 28-31.

59. Bryan, *Washington in American Literature*, 92-96. On Weems, see my *George Washington and Political Fatherhood: The Endurance of a National Myth* (Jefferson, NC: McFarland, 2020), chapter 2, 34-36.

60. John Adams to Thomas Jefferson, July 1813, qtd. in Bryan, *Washington in American Literature*, 14; for further discussion of Marshall's *Life*, see *ibid.*, 89-91, and William A. Foran, "John Marshall as a Historian," *American Historical Review* 43:1 (October 1937), 51-64.

61. Bryan, *Washington in American Literature*, 98-100. Sparks had done even worse damage working towards his twelve-volume edition of *The Writings of George Washington*, completed in 1837.

62. According to Bernard Bailyn, "heroic history" marks the first phase in modern historiography. It is followed by "Whig history," in which the personalities recede, and the flow of events is presented through a chain of inevitable causation; lastly comes what Bailyn calls "tragic history," a neutral type of historiography in which the historian has no stake in the outcome of events. For more, see the preface to *The Ordeal of Thomas Hutchinson* (Cambridge, MA: Belknap Press/Harvard University Press, 1974).

63. *Washington*, I:46.

64. *Ibid.*, 74.

65. Max Weber, "The Nature of Charismatic Authority and its Routinization," in *Max Weber on Charisma and Institution Building. Selected Papers*, ed. S. N. Eisenstadt (Chicago: University of Chicago Press,

1968), 48-65, quotations 48, 49, and 161 (for "adepts"). Weber's essay was originally published in 1922 in German as *Wirtschaft und Gesellschaft*. An earlier attempt at "charisma" is his 1917 newspaper article "Parliament and Government in a Reconstructed Germany," in which he tries to come to terms with the leadership of Otto von Bismarck. See, *inter alia*, Thomas E. Dow, Jr., "An Analysis of Weber's Work on Charisma," *British Journal of Sociology* 29:1 (1978), 83-93, and Christopher Adair-Toteff, "Max Weber's Charisma," *Journal of Classical Sociology* 5:2 (2005), 189-204.

66. *Washington*, II:448.

67. *Ibid.*, V:320.

68. William L. Hedges, "Irving's *Columbus*: The Problem of Romantic Biography," *The Americas* 13:2 (October 1956), 127-40, here 129.

69. *Washington*, I:1. Irving may have got it all wrong, though. For a different pedigree, see *The Writings of George Washington*, ed. Worthington Chauncey Ford, vol. XIV, 1798-1799 (New York-London: Putnam, 1893), Appendix, "The Washington Family", 317-31, also available on archive.org, https://archive.org/stream/cu31924092900400#page/n337/mode/2up, retrieved November 5, 2013.

70. *Washington*, I:309-24, quotation 311.

71. On Washington's use value in the antebellum period, see my *George Washington and Political Fatherhood*, 121-26. On the persistence of the Southern aristocracy in Southern literature, see Emmeline Gros, "The Southern Gentleman and the Idea of Masculinity: Figures and Aspects of the Southern Beau in the Literary Tradition of the American South," Georgia State University and Université Versailles St. Quentin-en-Yvelines, 2010, *English Dissertations*, Paper 64, http://digitalarchive.gsu.edu/english_diss, accessed March 10, 2013.

72. Mary Weatherspoon Bowden, *Washington Irving* (Boston: Twayne, 1981), 180; additionally, according to Bowden, Irving points out "every instance, in the French and Indian War and in the Revolutionary War, when the different colonies, or states, cooperated to relieve one another."

73. See Donald A. Ringe, "New York and New England: Irving's Criticism of American Society," *American Literature* 38 (1967), 455-67.

74. Myers, "Irving's *Life*," 69.

75. *Washington*, IV:440; emphasis in original.

76. Irving does not identify the lady, which is all too typical of his gentlemanly decorum. This vagueness did not bother Douglas Southall Freeman too much, as he repeats the testimony in his own seven-volume biography of George Washington. Andrew Myers, too, thinks that it rings true, and even suggests that the details could have come from one of Irving's own sisters, two of whom, Ann Sarah Dodge (1770–1832) and Catherine Rodgers Paris (1774–1873), were indeed "very young" in 1783 yet could have remembered clearly the end of British occupation. Myers, "Irving's *Life*," 79, and STW, vol.2, following 254.

77. *Washington*, IV:517. For more on the comparison between Washington and the Roman soldier-farmer Cincinnatus, see Gary Wills, *Cincinnatus: George Washington and the Enlightenment* (New York: Doubleday & Co., Inc., 1984).

78. *Washington*, I:310, IV:215.

79. *Ibid.*, III:485. Irving had noticed plenty of "sectional spirit" already during the Nullification crisis of the 1830s. Writing to his brother Peter in early 1833, he laments "so many elements of sectional prejudice, hostility, and selfishness stirring and increasing in activity and acrimony in this country, that I begin to doubt strongly of the long existence of the general Union." PMI, 3:46.

80. *Washington*, V:319.

81. Andrew Delbanco, *The War Before the War: Fugitive Slaves and the Struggle for America's Soul from the Revolution to the Civil War* (New York: Penguin Random House, 2018).

82. *Washington*, IV:181, emphases added.

83. I have drawn here on William Casey King's remarkable book *Ambition, a History: From Vice to Virtue* (New Haven, CT: Yale University Press, 2013).

84. *Washington*, I:457.

85. *Ibid.*, 28. The manuscript that Irving consulted was printed, in part, in Sparks's *Writings of George Washington*, *ibid.*, 2:412–15. The "Rules" have been reprinted in George Washington, *Writings*, ed. John Rhodehamel (New York: Library of America, 1997), 3–10. According to Rhodehamel's editorial note, the rules derived from a 1595 Jesuit treatise, "Bienséance de la Conversation entre les Hommes." Washington's text was probably based on the translation by Francis Hawkins (1628–81), which was published in England in more than ten editions between 1640 and 1672 (*ibid.*, 1094). Modern scholarship, however, no longer talks of Washington "harnessing" his ambition but rather of "screening" it by all means available. Thus, see Stephen Brumwell, *George Washington: Gentleman Warrior* (New York-London: Quercus, 2012), and John Ferling, *The Ascent of George Washington: The Hidden Political Genius of an American Icon* (London-New York: Bloomsbury Press, 2009).

86. Irving also had defended Columbus against the historical charge of excess ambition: "The charge is inconsiderate and unjust," the author asserts (*CW-Columbus*, 564), in a gesture that already suggests the idealized character of George Washington.

87. See Bertram Wyatt-Brown, *Southern Honor: Ethics and Behavior in the Old South* (New York: Oxford University Press, 1982), 14–15, 45–47, 155–58.

88. *Washington*, I:103. Altogether, Irving uses words like "slaves," "slavery," or "slaveholding" only most sparingly, a clear index to what extent he sanitized his language so as not to offend Southern readers. He does, however, emphasize the fact that in his will, George Washington freed his slaves.

89. *Ibid.*, III:306, and IV:518.

90. In February 1852, Leutze came to dinner at Sunnyside. Dinner was "pleasant," wrote Irving, adding that he had been "much pleased with Leutze." PMI, 4:103. On Leutze's painting, see my *George Washington and Political Fatherhood*, 138–40.

91. Barry Schwartz, *George Washington: The Making of an American Symbol* (New York: Free Press, 1987), 195.

92. George Washington Greene, in *North American Review* for April 1858, qtd. in *Critical Essays on Washington Irving*, ed. Ralph M. Aderman (Boston, MA: G. K. Hall, 1990), 143.

93. Douglas, *The Feminization of American Culture*, 169–70. For more, see George H. Callcott, *History in the United States 1800–1860: Its Practice and Purpose* (Baltimore, MD-London: Johns Hopkins University Press, 1970).

94. Myers, "Irving's *Life*," 81–82n3; praise

for Irving's biography also comes in Edward H. O'Neill's *A History of American Biography, 1800–1935* (Philadelphia: University of Pennsylvania Press, 1935), 7–8, 164–66. The outside wrapper for part 12 of the "Illustrated Edition" (1857) of Irving's biography showed a reproduction of a medal featuring a Roman-looking portrait of George Washington. Andrew B. Myers, *The Worlds of Washington Irving, 1783–1859* (Tarrytown, NY: Sleepy Hollow Restorations, 1974), 122.

95. See Bryan, *Washington in American Literature*, 103–105, and STW, 1:10 and 2:227–31.

96. Bryan, *Washington in American Literature*, 100–101. For the quote from Paulding, see *Washington*, V:309.

97. *Washington*, I:vi. On Irving's narrative strategy, see C. Michael Hurst "Reinventing Patriarchy: Washington Irving and the Autoerotics of the American Imaginary," *Early American Literature* 47:3 (2012), 671.

98. On this subject, see Jeffry H. Morrison, *The Political Philosophy of George Washington* (Baltimore, MD: Johns Hopkins University Press, 2009).

99. Ann Douglas, *The Feminization of American Culture*, 176–77.

100. *Washington*, I:99, 158.

101. Brumwell, *Gentleman* Warrior, 11.

102. PMI, 4:195.

103. For "magnitude of theme," see Irving to Frederick S. Cozzens, Sunnyside, May 22, 1857, *ibid.*, 4:230.

104. *Washington*, IV:416; Irving here quotes from Josiah Quincy's *Memoir of Major Shaw* (1847). Major Samuel Shaw was later appointed as the first American consul at Canton.

105. *Washington*, III:9–10.

106. David Ramsay, *Life of George Washington*, 3rd edn. (Baltimore, MD: J. Cushing, 1814), 236; John Marshall, *The Life of George Washington*, 5 vols. (Philadelphia: C. P. Wayne, 1804–7), 2:19–20; James K. Paulding, *A Life of Washington*, 2 vols. (New York: Harper & Brothers, 1835), 1:216; Caroline M. Kirkland, *Memoirs of Washington* (New York: Appleton & Co., 1837), 55. For "battlefield code," see Leverenz, *Manhood and the American Renaissance*, 73

107. See my *George Washington and Political Fatherhood*, 50–51, 95–98.

108. To view the lithograph, go to Library of Congress Prints and Photographs Division, LC-USZC2-2419, https://www.loc.gov/item/2001700074/.

109. *Washington*, I:20.

110. Ron Chernow, *Washington: A Life* (New York: Penguin, 2010), 196; for "a just pretension," see Washington's letter to Governor Patrick Henry, October 5, 1776, Founders Online, National Archives, http://founders.archives.gov/documents/Washington/03-06-02-0367, retrieved October 26, 2016.

111. *Washington*, IV:451–52.

112. *Ibid.*, 497, emphases added.

113. *Ibid.*, I:227.

114. James Fenimore Cooper, *The Spy: A Tale of the Neutral Ground* (1831; New York: Charles Scribner's, 1931), 8. For a discussion of the representation of Washington in Cooper's novel, see Bryan, *Washington in American Literature*, 195–200.

115. "Gentleman," *Oxford English Dictionary*, Third Edition, June 2012, 1a and 3a. Also useful are Edwin Harrison Cady, *The Gentleman in America: A Literary Study in American Culture* (Syracuse: Syracuse UP, 1949; repr. New York: Greenwood Press, 1969), and Christine Berberich, *The Image of the Gentleman in Twentieth-Century Literature: Englishness and Nostalgia* (Aldershot, Hampshire and Burlington, VT: Ashgate, 2007).

116. *Ibid.*, I:350. On Washington's "Englishness," see also Paul K. Longmore, *The Invention of George Washington* (Berkeley: University of California Press, 1988), 7–10.

117. See Leonard Tennenhouse, *The Importance of Feeling English: American Literature and the British Diaspora, 1750–1850* (Princeton, NJ: Princeton University Press, 2007), quotation 17, and Richard Gravil, *Romantic Dialogues: Anglo-American Continuities, 1776–1862* (New York: St. Martin's, 2000; Basingstoke: Macmillan, 2001).

118. Burke, *Reflections on the Revolution in France* (New York: Holt, Rinehart and Winston, 1959), 91.

119. Alexis de Tocqueville, *Democracy in America*, 1835–1840, ed. Thomas Bender (New York: Modern Library, 1981), vol.2, 2nd Book, Chapter XIII, 464.

120. William Ellery Channing, *Self-Culture. An Address Introductory to the Franklin Lectures* (Boston: Dutton & Wentworth, 1838, repr. New York, 1969), 5, 36. For an excellent overview of the various movements to reform American lives, see

Joshua D. Rothman, *Reforming America, 1815–1860* (New York: W. W. Norton, 2009).
121. *Washington*, I:28.
122. *Ibid.*, IV:487.
123. *Ibid.*, II:514; I:23 and 28.
124. George L. Mosse has demonstrated how the new bourgeoisie, faced with a bewildering, rapidly industrialized world, latched onto the knightly ideal of chivalry. *The Image of Man: The Creation of Modern Masculinity* (New York: Oxford University Press, 1998), esp. chapters 2 and 7. For outbursts of chivalry in postbellum America, see John Fraser, *America and the Patterns of Chivalry* (New York: Cambridge University Press, 1982).
125. *HTS*, 924.
126. On Peacham, see Alan R. Young, *Henry Peacham* (Boston: Twayne, 1979).
127. *Washington*, I:16.
128. *Ibid.*, 99. For Washington as a true "Virginia Gentleman" see also Longmore, *The Invention of George Washington*, 1–16.
129. *Washington*, I:103.
130. Thomas Jefferson to John Adams, October 28, 1813, in *The Writings of Thomas Jefferson*, Definitive Edition, ed. Andrew A. Lipscomb and Albert Ellery Bergh (Washington, DC: The Thomas Jefferson Memorial Association, 1905), 13:396.
131. Qtd. in William R. Taylor, *Cavalier and Yankee: The Old South and American National Character* (New York: Braziller, 1961), 334.
132. *Washington*, I:454.
133. *Ibid.*, 315. For more, see Edward G. Lengel, *First Entrepreneur: How George Washington Built His—and the Nation's—Prosperity* (New York: Da Capo Press, 2016).
134. *Pennsylvania Gazette*, qtd. in Schwartz, *George Washington*, xiii.
135. Bryan, *George Washington in American Literature*, vii. And see Karsten Fitz, *The American Revolution Remembered, 1830s to 1850s: Competing Images and Conflicting Narratives* (Heidelberg: Universitätsverlag Winter, 2010).
136. *Washington*, V:320, emphases added.
137. *Ibid.*
138. Bowden, *Washington Irving*, 179.
139. See Karal Ann Marling, *Washington Slept Here: Colonial Revivals and American Culture, 1876–1986* (Cambridge, MA: Harvard University Press, 1988), 77–84. On George Washington as "national property," see Matthew Costello, *The Property of the Nation: George Washington's Tomb, Mount Vernon, and the Memory of the First President* (Lawrence: University Press of Kansas, 2020). For *"lieu de mémoire,"* see Pierre Nora, "Between Memory and History: *Les lieux de mémoire* [1984]," *Representations* 26 (Spring 1989), 7–25.
140. PMI, 4:250, emphases added.
141. George Washington to the Secretary of War, July 27, 1795, in *The Writings of George Washington, from the Original Manuscript Sources, 1745–1799*, ed. John C. Fitzpatrick, 39 vols. (Washington, DC: Government Printing Office, 1931–1944), 34: 251, emphases added.
142. Sean Wilentz, "The Mirage: The Long and Tragical History of Post-Partisanship, from Washington to Obama," *The New Republic*, November 17, 2011, 25–33.
143. George Washington, "Farewell Address," in *Writings*, ed. John Rhodehamel, 968, 976.
144. Irving to Gouverneur Kemble, New York, January 10, 1838, *CW-Letters*, 2:918, 919. Kemble was then a member of Congress.
145. *Ibid.*
146. Irving to Sarah Storrow, Sunnyside, July 18, 1850, PMI, 4:73. Of Taylor, who had been elected president in 1849, it was said that his education on the frontier had developed his manly character. Michael S. Kimmel, *Manhood in America: A Cultural History* (1996; 3rd edn. New York: Oxford University Press, 2012), 27. If Taylor has been struggling to win manhood, he proved himself a true descendant of Andrew Jackson, who used to see his military exploits as a strategy to overcome his own "indolence" (qtd. *ibid.*, 25.)
147. Irving to Peter Irving, Washington, DC, April 1, 1833, PMI, 3:50.
148. Irving to Brevoort, Washington, DC, February 7, 1811, PMI, 1:267.
149. *Ibid.*, 3:119, emphases added.
150. One of the earliest studies was Pete Kyle McCarter's PhD thesis, "The Literary, Political, and Social Theories of Washington Irving" (Madison: University of Wisconsin, 1939); see also Allen Guttmann, "Washington Irving and the Conservative Imagination," *American Literature* 36:2 (May 1964), 165–73; Donna Hagensick, "Irving: A Littérateur in Politics," in *Critical Essays on Washington Irving*, ed. Ralph M. Aderman (Boston, MA: G.K. Hall, 1990), 178–91;

and Wagenknecht, *Washington Irving*, 104–8.

151. Vernon Louis Parrington, *The Romantic Revolution in America, 1800–1860, Main Currents in American Thought*, vol. II (1927; New Brunswick, NJ-London, UK: Transaction Publishers, 2012), 209.

152. Brian Jay Jones, *Washington Irving: An American Original* (New York: Arcade Pub., 2008), 65.

153. Irving to Catherine Paris, March 22, 1838; Irving to Gouverneur Kemble, March 12, 1838; Irving to Kemble, June 2, 1838, *CW-Letters*, 2, respectively 925, 923, 929.

154. Irving to Helen Dodge Irving, wife of his nephew Pierre Munro Irving, February 28, 1853, *CW-Letters*, 4:378; Irving to Storrow, March 28, 1853, *ibid.*, 385.

155. Lanman, "A Day with Washington Irving," 2. It is also a matter of record that Irving tinkered with the passages on Washington's character to the very last moment. Pierre M. Irving, February 15, 1859, PMI, 4:274.

156. Irving to Frederick Cozzens, as qtd. in STW, 2:230.

157. George Washington Greene, Review of *Life of George Washington*, Volumes 1–4, *North American Review* 86 (April 1858), 330–58, in *Critical Essays on Washington Irving*, ed. Aderman, 152; other quotations are from 142, 151.

158. *Washington*, V:320.

159. *Ibid.*, 334; Irving reprinted the "Farewell Address" in full in the Appendix. See a. Washington, *Writings*, ed. John Rhodehamel, 963–64.

160. Daniel Webster, "The Character of Washington," in *The Works of Daniel Webster*, 6 vols. (Boston: Little and Brown, 1851), 1:227, 229.

161. "The Bunker Hill Monument," and "Completion of the Bunker Hill Monument," *ibid.*, 78 and 87.

162. "The Addition to the Capitol," *ibid.*, 2:599, 618, 619.

163. *Washington*, V:320.

164. *Ibid.*, IV:517–18.

165. Andrew Burstein, *The Original Knickerbocker: The Life of Washington Irving* (New York: Basic Books, 2007), 325.

166. As if with foresight, Irving had written into his 1850 will that if he should die prematurely, his *Life of George Washington* would be managed by his nephew Pierre Munro Irving. Kime, *Pierre M. Irving and Washington Irving*, 252–54.

167. Myers, "Irving's *Life*," 70.

168. Qtd. in Haskell Springer, *Washington Irving: A Reference Guide* (Boston: G. K. Hall, 1976), 74.

169. See, for instance, "Washington Irvings Biographie George Washingtons," *Blätter für literarische Unterhaltung*, August 6, 1857, 585–89, and "Lebensgeschichte George Washingtons," *Magazin für die Literatur des Auslands*, 56 (November 18, 1859), both cited in Springer, *Washington Irving: A Reference Guide*, 76. And see Walter A. Reichart, "Washington Irving's Influence in German Literature," *The Modern Language Review* 52:4 (1957), 537–553.

170. See David Anthony, "'Gone Distracted': 'Sleepy Hollow,' Gothic Masculinity, and the Panic of 1819," *Early American Literature* 40:1 (2005), 127, 126.

171. Leverenz, *Manhood*, 16. On Irving's downfall, see Alice Hiller, "'An Avenue to Some Degree of Profit and Reputation': The Sketch Book as Washington Irving's Entree and Undoing," *Journal of American Studies* 31:2 (1997), 275–93.

172. Hedges, "Irving's *Columbus*," 127–40, here 137.

173. *CW-Columbus*, 323, 324; for "lofty and noble," see *ibid.*, 565.

174. *Washington*, III:340–41. Martyrdom then was the standard mode of interpretation, and Irving deferred to it. Biographers like John Marshall and Jared Sparks were particularly adept at representing George Washington as wounded innocence. Marshall pitted Washington's "purity of mind" against "a highly increased degree of acrimony." John Marshall, *The Life of George Washington ...* (Philadelphia: C. P. Wayne, 1807), 3:339, 5:409. Sparks, for his part, spoke of "a station, in which patriotism, the purest intentions, hardships, and sacrifice, were rewarded only with calumny and reproach." Jared Sparks, *The Life of George Washington ...*, 2 vols. (London: Henry Colburn, 1839), 1:81.

175. *Washington*, IV:516, 517. Subsequent quotations in this paragraph are from *ibid.*, 516, 517.

176. Catherine L. Albanese, *The Sons of the Fathers: The Civil Religion of the American Revolution* (Philadelphia: Temple University Press, 1976), 155.

177. PMI, 4:232.

178. Ibid., 230.
179. "Irving," in Andrew B. Myers, ed., *A Century of Commentary on the Works of Washington Irving* (Tarrytown, NY: Sleepy Hollow Restorations, 1976), 118-33, here 132. George Haven Putnam was the son and successor of Irving's last publisher and had known Irving as a boy.
180. Dixon Wecter, *The Hero in America* (1941; Ann Arbor: University of Michigan Press, 1963), 141. For more on the reception of Irving's *Washington*, see Bryan, *George Washington in American Literature*, 103-107.
181. Daniel J. Boorstin, *The Americans: The National Experience* (New York: Random House / Vintage Books, 1965), 345.
182. James T. Flexner, *George Washington*, 4 vols. (Boston: Little, Brown, 1965-1972), I:358. Flexner also published a one-volume condensation as *Washington: The Indispensable Man* (Boston: Little, Brown, 1974).
183. Ralph Ketcham, *From Colony to Country: The Revolution in American Thought, 1750-1820* (New York: Macmillan, 1974), 254.
184. Washington Irving, *George Washington: A Biography*, ed. and abr. Charles Neider (Boston: Da Capo Press, 1994), xliii. Another historian, Andrew Burstein, too thinks highly of Irving, the literary giant, as his masterful biography of 2007 demonstrates.
185. Myers, "The New York Years in Irving's *Life of George Washington*," 69. "Bedside reading" has since been provided, in the form of a one-volume version, edited by Jess Stein with an introduction by Richard B. Morris, and published by Sleepy Hollow Restorations, Tarrytown, New York, in 1975, as well as of Charles Neider's abridged edition, first published by Doubleday in 1976 and re-issued by Boston's Da Capo Press in 1994.
186. George S. Hellman, "Irving's *Washington* and an Episode in Courtesy," *The Colophon* 1 (New York, 1930), 53-60; Elsie Lee West, "Washington Irving, Biographer," 47-52. Ms West's article was also published in the *American Transcendental Quarterly* no.5:1 (1970); it is probably derived from "Gentle Flute: Washington Irving as Biographer," PhD thesis, New York: Columbia University, 1965, *Dissertation Abstracts* 27 (1966), 463A-64A.

187. Bowden, *Washington Irving*, 9, 179-82.
188. Schwartz, *George Washington*, 190; for "reverent," see *ibid.*, 2.
189. Mark E. Thistlethwaite, *The Image of George Washington: Studies in Mid-Nineteenth-Century American History Painting* (New York: Garland, 1979), 26, emphases in original.
190. STW, 1:10.
191. George Washington Parke Custis, *Recollections and Private Memoirs of Washington* (New York: Derby & Jackson, 1860), 172.
192. PMI, 1:30.
193. Lanman, "A Day with Washington Irving," 2. This is the text which Stanley T. Williams refers to as an "unidentified newspaper clipping in my possession," STW, 1:409n30; Wayne R. Kime erroneously dates it March 20, 1857, *Pierre M. Irving and Washington Irving*, 162n95.
194. STW, 1:10 and 382n70.
195. Ibid., 1:10.
196. *Washington*, V:320.
197. STW, 2:216, 221.
198. Washington Irving to Peter Irving, London, December 18, 1829, *CW-Letters*, 2:494. Irving begins the letter by saying that he had "abandoned the idea of the History of the United States" and had determined to undertake the *Life of Washington* "in lieu of it."
199. George Bancroft to Washington Irving, May 9, 1859, PMI, 4:281.
200. For this, see the editors' introduction to *CW-Washington*, xxvii-xxxi.
201. *Washington*, V:196. Jefferson's remarks are from his letter to Walter Jones, January 2, 1814. See *Founders Online*, National Archives, last modified June 13, 2018, http://founders.archives.gov/documents/Jefferson/03-07-02-0052. Jefferson had also found words of praise in the years following the success of the War of Independence, that is, before the two men became estranged one from the other: "In war, we have produced a Washington, whose memory will be adored while liberty shall have votaries, whose name will triumph over time, and will in future ages assume its just station among the most celebrated worthies of the world." Thomas Jefferson, *Notes on the State of Virginia* (1785), ed. William Peden (New York-London: W. W. Norton, 1982), 64.

202. Qtd. in Springer, *Washington Irving: A Reference Guide*, 74.
203. *Harper's New Monthly Magazine*, April 1851, qtd. in Burstein, *The Original Knickerbocker*, 315.

Epilogue

1. Irving to Sarah Storrow, March 28, 1853, PMI, 4:140.
2. STW, 2:231, 237.
3. See my *George Washington and Political Fatherhood: The Endurance of a National Myth* (Jefferson, NC: McFarland, 2020).
4. Irving, "Spanish Romance," *BTA*, 1018, 1019. For "master of the obsolete in times and substance," see *Times Literary Supplement*, March 21, 1936, qtd. in Andrew B. Myers, ed., *A Century of Commentary on the Works of Washington Irving* (Tarrytown, NY: Sleepy Hollow Restorations, 1976), 199.
5. The "King" archetype, Robert L. Moore and Douglas Gillette claim, is the "central archetype," the one to have incorporated the archetypes of Lover, Magician, and Warrior. See *King, Warrior, Magician, Lover: Rediscovering the Archetypes of the Mature Masculine* (New York: HarperCollins, 1991), 44, 49, 52, 99.
6. STW, 2:107.
7. *Times Literary Supplement*, March 21, 1936, qtd. in Myers, *A Century of Commentary*, 203.
8. Washington Irving to William Irving Jr., August 1, 1804, *CW-Letters*, 1:44.
9. Irving to Sarah Storrow, Madrid, October 8, 1842, *ibid.*, 3:350.
10. *JCW*, 14: §753.
11. STW, 2:218, 229.
12. Irving to Sarah Storrow, Madrid, March 27, 1845, PMI, 3:374.
13. Stoddard, "Abraham Lincoln, a Horatian Ode," qtd. in William Alfred Bryan, *George Washington in American Literature 1775-1865* (New York: Columbia University Press, 1952; repr. Westport, CT: Greenwood Press, 1970), 166. For "Prairie King," see Michael Butter, *Der "Washington-Code": Zur Heroisierung amerikanischer Präsidenten, 1775-1865*, Figurationen des Heroischen, vol. 3 (Göttingen: Wallstein Verlag, 2016), 95.
14. "Ode on the Death of President Lincoln" (1865), qtd. in Butter, *Der "Washington-Code,"* 96.
15. Qtd. in Barry Schwartz, *George Washington: The Making of an American Symbol* (New York: Free Press, 1987), 197.
16. "Columbia's Noblest Sons" is the title of a lithograph by Kimmel & Forster, ca. 1865, now in the Fraunces Tavern Museum, New York. See Library of Congress Prints and Photographs Division, LC-DIG-pga-01775, https://www.loc.gov/item/2004665370/.
17. See Helen Vendler, "'No Poetry You Have Read'" [review of *Herman Melville: Complete Poems*, ed. Hershel Parker (New York: Library of America, 2019)], *The New York Review of Books*, December 5, 2019, 29, 32–34, here 33.
18. See STW, 1:180, 217, 223, 225, 360, and passim; and Jeffrey Rubin-Dorsky, *Adrift in the Old World: The Psychological Pilgrimage of Washington Irving* (Chicago: University of Chicago Press, 1988), passim.
19. "To the Reader," *CW-Traveller*, 4.
20. Michael M. Mason, "The Cultivation of the Senses for Creative Nostalgia in the Essays of W. H. Hudson," *ARIEL* 20:1 (1989), 23. For more on the deep connection between loss and desire, see Jacques Lacan, *Écrits: A Selection*, trans. Alan Sheridan (New York: W. W. Norton, 1977), 150–55.
21. *Times Literary Supplement*, March 21, 1936, qtd. in Myers, *A Century of Commentary*, 200.
22. Michael Warner, "Irving's Posterity," *ELH* (*English Literary History*) 67:3 (2000), 790.
23. *Ibid.*
24. William Shakespeare, *A Midsummer Night's Dream*, V:i, *The Yale Shakespeare*, ed. Wilbur L. Cross and Tucker Brooke (New York: Barnes & Noble, 1993), 125–51, here 145. For "atemporal stasis," see C. Michael Hurst "Reinventing Patriarchy: Washington Irving and the Autoerotics of the American Imaginary," *Early American Literature* 47:3 (2012), 665.
25. Henry Wadsworth Longfellow, "Address on the Death of Washington Irving," *Poems and Other Writings* (New York: Library of America, 2000), 802, and *Harper's New Monthly Magazine*, April 1851, as qtd. in Andrew Burstein, *The Original Knickerbocker: The Life of Washington Irving* (New York: Basic Books, 2007), 315.
26. *New-York Mirror*, September 25, 1824, as qtd. in STW, 2:294, emphases added.

Notes—Epilogue 259

27. Brian Jay Jones, *Washington Irving: An American Original* (New York: Arcade Publishing, 2008), 409.

28. On the distinction between "conventionally engaging" and "conventionally distancing" modes of writing, see Robyn R. Warhol, "Toward a Theory of the Engaging Narrator: Earnest Interventions in Gaskell, Stowe, and Eliot," *PMLA* 101:5 (October 1986), 811–818.

29. On the issue of the anti-mimetic bias, see Nina Baym's acerbic remarks on the politics of women's literature in *Novels, Readers, and Reviewers: Responses to Fiction in Antebellum America* (Ithaca, NY: Cornell University Press, 1984), esp. 53–54, 98–100, 170–71, 257–58. For "sweet and wholesome," see Henry A. Bates, 1891, as cited in Myers, *A Century of Commentary*, xviii.

30. Henry Seidel Canby, *Classic Americans* (New York: Harcourt Brace & Co., 1931). Canby treats Irving at length in chap. II, 67–96.

31. Vernon Louis Parrington, *The Romantic Revolution in America, 1800–1860, Main Currents in American Thought*, vol. II (1927; New Brunswick, NJ-London, UK: Transaction Publishers, 2012), 204.

32. Carl Van Doren, "Toward a New Canon," *The Nation*, February 29, 1932, 429–30, qtd. in Myers, *A Century of Commentary*, xxix; what also impacted on Irving's low reputation was market pressure: Putnam's interest had elapsed, and Irving's works came into the public domain.

33. Stanley T. Williams's *Life of Irving* is full of hostile remarks of this kind; more concise—and better known—is Williams's Introduction to *Washington Irving: Selected Prose* (New York: Reinhart, 1950).

34. I have listed the scholarship in the bibliography. Donna Campbell, a professor of English at Washington State University, Pullman, maintains a Washington Irving Bibliography, at http://www.wsu.edu/~campbelld/amlit/irvingbib.html (regrettably, though, the last update is from 2013).

35. To learn more about the society, go to https://washingtonirvingsociety.org/.

36. William Charvat, *The Profession of Authorship in America, 1800–1870*, ed. Matthew J. Bruccoli (New York: Columbia University Press, 1992), 241.

37. Melville to Hawthorne, June 1, 1851, in *The Letters of Herman Melville*, ed. Merrell R. Davis and William H. Gilman (New Haven, CT: Yale University Press, 1960), 128.

38. David Leverenz, *Manhood and the American Renaissance* (Ithaca, NY: Cornell University Press, 1989), 13.

39. *Ibid.*, 15.

40. Take, for instance, an 1836 commentary according to which an American man "is never ... so uneasy as when seated by his fireside; for he feels, while conversing with his kindred, that he is making no money. And as for fireside reading ... 'he reads no book but his ledger.'" Artemis B. Muzzey, *The Young Man's Friend* (Boston, 1836), 102, qtd. in E. Anthony Rotundo, *American Manhood: Transformations in Masculinity from the Revolution to the Modern Era* (New York: Basic Books, 1993), 175–76.

41. Charvat, *The Profession of Authorship*, esp. chapter 2, and Ann Douglas, *The Feminization of American Culture* (1977; New York: Doubleday, 1988). For "the mediocre & the dull," see Ralph Waldo Emerson's journal entry for April 5, 1847, in *Emerson in His Journals*, ed. Joel Porte (Cambridge, MA: Belknap Press of Harvard University Press, 1982), 369.

42. "To the Reader," *BTA*, 384.

43. Irving to Brevoort, London, March 3, 1819, *CW-Letters*, 1:543.

44. Burstein, *The Original Knickerbocker*, 154.

45. Canby, *Classic Americans*, 71. See a. George S. Hellman, *Washington Irving, Esquire: Ambassador at Large from the New World to the Old* (New York: Knopf, 1925), 65–67.

46. For the full story, see Ben Harris McClary, *Washington Irving and the House of Murray* (Knoxville: University of Tennessee Press, 1969), 191–95. For the letters Irving sent *to* Murray, see *CW-Letters*, 4:218–19, 222. For a definitive Irving genealogy, see STW, 2:241–54.

47. Irving to his niece Sarah, now Mrs. Storrow, Honesdale, July 31, 1841, *CW-Letters*, 3:145. On the notion that Irving had "written himself out," see STW, 1:207 and 2:21.

48. Irving to Pierre Paris Irving, Paris, March 29, 1825, *CW-Letters*, 2:106.

49. Qtd. in Rotundo, *American Manhood*, 336. I have also drawn here on Leverenz, *Manhood*, 168–70.

50. On Irving as an observer, a "mere spectator of other men's fortunes and

adventures," see above, Chapters One, Three, and Four. On Howells and James as "sissies," see Alfred Habegger, *Gender, Fantasy, and Realism in American Literature* (New York: Columbia University Press, 1982), chap. 7, 56–65. I have also drawn here on Douglas, *The Feminization of American Culture*, 6–10 and passim.

51. Irving to Helen Dodge Irving, Sunnyside, April 30, 1847, *CW-Letters*, 4:131.

52. Irving to Pierre Munro Irving, London, December 30, 1830, *ibid.*, 2:577, emphases added.

53. Irving to Pierre Paris Irving, Paris, December 7, 1824, *ibid.*, 2:85. A few months before, Irving had written a similar letter to Pierre Paris' mother. Letter to Catherine Paris, Paris, September 20, 1824, 1824, *ibid.*, 2:80.

54. *Ibid.*, 84.

55. *Ibid.*,106.

56. Charvat, *The Profession of Authorship*, 61–62.

57. For "moderation," see Edward Wagenknecht, *Washington Irving: Moderation Displayed* (New York: Oxford University Press, 1962). On Irving's "moderate" politics, see Burstein, *The Original Knickerbocker*, 101.

58. Qtd. in *Wagenknecht, Moderation Displayed*, 188.

59. Emily Fuller to Pierre Munro Irving, March 10, 1860, PMI, 2:128.

60. *Ibid.*, 4:387.

61. See *Washington Irving and His Literary Friends at Sunnyside*, an 1863 painting by F. O. C. Darley and Christian Schussele. For a reproduction of the painting, which now is in the possession of Historic Hudson Valley, see the exhibition catalog *150 W.I.: Washington Irving and the Alhambra*, ed. Carmen Yusty Pérez (Granada: Patronato de la Alhambra y Generalife / Tf Editores [Madrid], 2009), 58.

62. John McWilliams, "'The Almighty [Unmentionable] Dollar': Washington Irving and Money," *Literature in the Early American Republic: Annual Studies on Cooper and His Contemporaries* 2 (2010), 214. Today Sunnyside is being preserved as a National Historic Landmark. Operated by Historic Hudson Valley, Sunnyside is open to visitors between May and November, as see http://www.hudsonvalley.org/historic-sites/washington-irvings-sunnyside and https://en.wikipedia.org/wiki/Sunnyside_(Tarrytown,_New_York), last accessed May 3, 2019.

63. Irving to Pierre Munro Irving, December 12, 1834, *CW-Letters*, 2:884.

64. Irving to his niece Sarah Storrow, Madrid, December 12, 1842, *ibid.*, 3:437; Irving to his sister Catherine Paris, May 29, 1842, *ibid.*, 303.

65. Warner, "Irving's Posterity," 773, 775. On Irving's life at Sunnyside, see Harold Dean Cater, "Washington Irving and Sunnyside," *New York History* 38:2 (April 1957), 123–66.

66. To view the daguerreotype, which was taken by John Plumbe c.1855, go to Library of Congress, Prints and Photographs Division, LC-USZ62-110044, https://www.loc.gov/item/2004664004/; it is also reproduced in Washington Irving, *Mr. Bryant's Address on His Life and Genius* (New York: G. P. Putnam, 1860), opposite p.38, STW, vol.2, between 232–33, and Burstein, *The Original Knickerbocker*, between 198–99. William Collins Watterson dates the Brady daguerreotype to 1849, a few years after Irving's return from the Spanish court. See "Vandyck's Image of Washington Irving," *Studies in the American Renaissance*, 22 (1992), 75–90, here 80, 86, plate 13. An undated oil portrait by Henry F. Darby, which closely resembles the Brady photograph, is reproduced as frontispiece in Myers, *A Century of Commentary*.

67. "Sunnyside, the Home of Washington Irving," *Harper's New Monthly Magazine* 79 (December 1856), 1–21, qtd. in Burstein, *The Original Knickerbocker*, 326.

68. In 1851, the Irving Bank of the City of New York was founded. The bank indeed was named after Washington Irving. Its notes, in various denominations, were graced by portraits of the writer and, on occasion, a vignette of his Sunnyside cottage, which certainly contributed to their wide appeal. James A. Haxby lists notes from the Irving Bank, classified as "NY-1665," in denominations of $1, $2, $3, $5, $10, $20, $50, and $100. See *Standard Catalog of United States Obsolete Bank Notes, 1782–1866* (Iola, WI: Krause Publications, 2009), 3:1637–38. On June 29, 2010, Stack's of New York sold an uncirculated $10 note at auction for $2,990.00.

69. George P. Putnam, "Recollections of Irving," in Charles Dudley Warner, William Cullen Bryant, George Palmer Putnam,

Studies of Irving (New York: Putnam's Sons, 1880), 131–59, quotation 137. Putnam's essay was originally published in the *Atlantic Monthly*, November 1860.
70. Francis Grund, qtd. in Michael S. Kimmel, *Manhood in America: A Cultural History* (1996; 3rd edn. New York: Oxford University Press, 2012), 21. Grund's *The Americans in Their Moral, Social, and Political Relations* was first published by Marsh, Capen and Lyon in Boston in 1837.
71. *CW-Columbus*, 22.
72. Irving to Charles Lanman, in Lanman, "A Day with Washington Irving," *Daily National Intelligencer*, March 23, 1857, 2.
73. Mitchell, "Preface of 1863," qtd. in Burstein, *The Original Knickerbocker*, 318, emphasis in original. Reference is to the essayist Donald Grant Mitchell, with whom Irving struck up an acquaintance in the 1850s. For "genial humor" and "kindly nature," see John W. Francis, "Characteristics of Washington Irving," in *Irvingiana: A Memorial of Washington Irving*, ed. Evert A. Duyckinck (New York: Charles B. Richardson, 1860), xxxii–xxxvi, here xxxv.
74. Burstein, *The Original Knickerbocker*, 88.
75. Irving to Ebenezer Irving, London, March 3, 1819, *CW-Letters*, 1:540.
76. Irving, Tour in Scotland, 1817, qtd. in Wagenknecht, *Moderation Displayed*, 38. For a general discussion of the "vein of iron" in Irving, see Part 2, "The Man," esp. 25–39.
77. Fredrika Bremer to her sister, Brooklyn, November 5, 1849, qtd. in STW, 2:203.
78. Klaus Theweleit, *Male Fantasies*, trans. Chris Turner, Carter Erica, and Stephen Conway, Foreword by Jessica Benjamin and Anson Rabinbach, 2 vols. (Minneapolis: University of Minnesota Press, 1987). The German original, *Männerphantasien*, was first published by Verlag Roter Stern of Frankfurt am Main in 1977–1978 and was reissued by Matthes & Seitz of Berlin in 2019. For a more sober discussion of the fascist ideals of masculinity, see George L. Mosse, *The Image of Man: The Creation of Modern Masculinity* (New York: Oxford University Press, 1998), chapter 8.
79. On this topic, see Sara Martin, *Representations of Masculinity in Literature and Film: Focus on Men* (Newcastle upon Tyne, UK: Cambridge Scholars Publishing, 2020), and *Masculinity and Patriarchal Villainy in the British Novel: From Hitler to Voldemort* (New York: Routledge, 2019).
80. For "distant Europe" and "native country," see Irving's letter to Henry Brevoort, Madrid, April 4, 1827, PMI, 2:259.

Bibliography

All of Washington Irving's writings are available in the *Complete Works* edition under the general editorship of Henry A. Pochmann. Due to the Covid-19 pandemic of 2020, however, I was unable to access a number of volumes in that edition from libraries (interlibrary loans also were suspended). I therefore relied on other available editions and, in particular, on the volumes in the Library of America edition which, in most instances, print the texts from the *Complete Works*.

Aderman, Ralph M., ed. *Critical Essays on Washington Irving*. Boston: G. K. Hall, 1990.

Antelyes, Peter. *Tales of Adventurous Enterprise: Washington Irving and the Poetics of Western Expansion*. New York: Columbia University Press, 1990.

Anthony, David. "'Gone Distracted': 'Sleepy Hollow,' Gothic Masculinity, and the Panic of 1819." *Early American Literature* 40:1 (2005): 111–144.

———. *Paper Money Men: Commerce, Manhood, and the Sensational Public Sphere in Antebellum America*. Columbus: Ohio State University Press, 2009.

Banks, Jenifer S. "Washington Irving, the Nineteenth-Century Bachelor." *Critical Essays on Washington Irving*. Ed. Ralph M. Aderman. Critical Essays on American Literature. Boston, MA: G. K. Hall, 1990. 253–65.

Bernhardt, Mark. "Washington Irving's Western Adventure: Masculinity, Race, and the Early American Frontier." *Journal of the West* 52:1 (Winter 2013): 17–24.

Bowden, Edwin T., comp. *Washington Irving: Bibliography*. The Complete Works of Washington Irving, vol. 30. Boston: Twayne, 1989.

Bowden, Mary Weatherspoon. *Washington Irving*. Twayne's United States Authors Series; TUSAS 379. Boston: Twayne Publishers, 1981.

Brooks, Van Wyck. *The World of Washington Irving*. 1944; New York: Dutton—London: Dent, 1950.

Brumwell, Stephen. *George Washington: Gentleman Warrior*. New York-London: Quercus, 2012.

Burstein, Andrew. *The Original Knickerbocker: The Life of Washington Irving*. New York: Basic Books, 2007.

Bus, Heiner. "Geoffrey Crayon 'Lighting Out for the Territory' and for Cultural Nationalism: A Reevaluation of Washington Irving's Western Writings." *The Construction and Contestation of American Cultures and Identities in the Early National Period*. Ed. Udo J. Hebel. American Studies: A Monograph Series. Heidelberg: Winter, 1999. 156–79.

Campbell, Joseph. *The Hero with a Thousand Faces*. 1949; second edn. Princeton, NJ: Princeton University Press, 1968.

Carlyle, Thomas. *On Heroes, Hero-Worship and the Heroic in History*. New York: Frederick A. Stokes, 1893.

Charvat, William. *The Profession of Authorship in America,1800–1870*. Ed. Matthew J. Bruccoli. New York: Columbia University Press, 1992.

DiCuirci, Lindsay. "The Spanish Archive and the Remapping of US History in

Washington Irving's *Columbus." Urban Identity and the Atlantic World*. Ed. Elizabeth Fay and Leonard von Morzé. New York: Palgrave Macmillan, 2013. 175–92.

Douglas, Ann. *The Feminization of American Culture*. 1977; New York: Doubleday, 1988.

Ellenberger, Henri F. *The Discovery of the Unconscious: The History and Evolution of Dynamic Psychiatry*. New York: Basic Books, 1970.

Engler, Bernd, and Oliver Scheiding, *Key Concepts in American Cultural History: From the Colonial Period to the End of the 19th Century*. Trier, Germany: WVT Wissenschaftlicher Verlag Trier, 2007.

Ferguson, Robert A. "Hunting Down a Nation: Washington Irving's *A History of New York*." *Nineteenth-Century Fiction* 36:1 (June 1981): 22–46.

Gilmore, David D. *Manhood in the Making: Cultural Concepts of Masculinity*. New Haven, CT: Yale University Press, 1990.

Guttmann, Allen. "Washington Irving and the Conservative Imagination." *American Literature* 36:2 (May 1964): 165–73.

Hagensick, Donna. "Irving: A Littérateur in Politics." *Critical Essays on Washington Irving*. Ed. Ralph M. Aderman. Boston, MA: G.K. Hall, 1990. 178–91.

Hedges, William L. "Irving's *Columbus*: The Problem of Romantic Biography." *The Americas* 13:2 (October 1956): 127–40.

_____. *Washington Irving: An American Study, 1802–1832*. Baltimore: Johns Hopkins University Press, 1965; repr. Westport, CT: Greenwood Press, 1980.

Heller, André. *Anima*. Wien: Brandstätter Verlag, 2018.

Hillman, James. *anima, an anatomy of a personified notion*. Putnam, CT: Spring Publications, 1985.

Hurst, C. Michael. "Reinventing Patriarchy: Washington Irving and the Autoerotics of the American Imaginary." *Early American Literature* 47:3 (2012): 649–78.

Irving, Pierre M. *The Life and Letters of Washington Irving*. 4 vols. New York: G. P. Putnam, 1862–1864.

Irving, Washington. *The Adventures of Captain Bonneville*. Ed. Robert A. Rees and Alan Sandy. Boston: Twayne, 1977.

_____. *Astoria, or Anecdotes of an Enterprize beyond the Rocky Mountains*. Ed. Richard Dilworth Rust. Boston: Twayne, 1976.

_____. *Bracebridge Hall or The Humourists. A Medley by Geoffrey Crayon, Gent*. Ed. Herbert F. Smith. Boston: Twayne, 1977.

_____. *Bracebridge Hall, Tales of a Traveller, The Alhambra*. New York: Library of America, 1991.

_____. *A Chronicle of the Conquest of Granada*. Ed. Miriam J. Shillingsburg. Boston: Twayne, 1988.

_____. *Crayon Miscellany*. Ed. Dahlia Kirby Terrell. Boston: Twayne, 1979.

_____. *George Washington: A Biography*. Ed. and abr. Charles Neider. Boston: Da Capo Press, 1994.

_____. *A History of New York*. Ed. Michael L. Black and Nancy B. Black. Boston: Twayne, 1984.

_____. *History, Tales and Sketches*. New York: Library of America, 1983.

_____. *Journals and Notebooks*. Ed. Nathalia Wright et al. 5 vols. Madison and Boston: University of Wisconsin Press and Twayne Publishers, 1969–1981.

_____. *Letters*. Ed. Ralph M. Aderman, Herbert L. Kleinfield, and Jenifer S. Banks. 4 vols. Boston: Twayne, 1978–1982.

_____. *The Life and Voyages of Christopher Columbus*. Ed. John Harmon McElroy. Boston: Twayne, 1981.

_____. *Life of George Washington*. 5 vols. New York: G. P. Putnam, 1855–1859.

_____. *Life of George Washington*. Ed. Allen Guttmann and James A. Sappenfield. 3 vols. Boston: Twayne, 1982.

_____. *Mahomet and His Successors*. Ed. Henry A. Pochmann and E. N. Feltskog. Madison: University of Wisconsin Press, 1970.

_____. *Miscellaneous Writings*. Ed. Wayne R. Kime. 2 vols. Boston: Twayne, 1981.

_____. *Oliver Goldsmith: A Biography / Biography of the Late Margaret Miller Davidson*. Ed. Elsie Lee West. Boston: Twayne, 1978.

_____. "Philip of Pokanoket." *Analectic Review* 3 (June 1814): 502–515.

_____. "Recollections of the Alhambra." *Knickerbocker Magazine* 13 (June 1839): 485–94.

_____. *The Sketch Book of Geoffrey Crayon, Gent*. Ed. Haskell Springer. Boston: Twayne, 1978.

_____. *Tales of a Traveller by Geoffrey Crayon, Gent*. Ed. Judith Giblin Haig. Boston: Twayne, 1987.

_____. "Traits of Indian Character." *Analectic Review* 3 (February 1814): 145–156.

Bibliography 265

———. *Wolfert's Roost*. Ed. Roberta Rosenberg. Boston: Twayne, 1979.

———. "The Works of Robert Treat Paine." *Analectic Review* 1 (1813): 249–66.

Jaros, Peter. "Irving's Astoria and the Forms of Enterprise." *American Literary History* 30:1 (2018): 1–28.

Jung, C.G. *Aion: Researches into the Phenomenology of the Self. The Collected Works of C. G. Jung*, trans. R. F. C. Hull. Bollingen Series XX, vol. 9, Part II. Princeton, NJ: Princeton University Press, 1969.

———. *Alchemical Studies. The Collected Works of C. G. Jung*, trans. R. F. C. Hull. Bollingen Series XX, vol. 13. Princeton, NJ: Princeton University Press, 1967.

———. *The Archetypes of the Collective Unconscious. The Collected Works of C. G. Jung*, trans. R. F. C. Hull. Bollingen Series XX, vol. 9, Part I. Princeton, NJ: Princeton University Press, 1959.

———. *Civilization in Transition. The Collected Works of C. G. Jung*, trans. R. F. C. Hull. Bollingen Series XX, vol. 10. 1964; Princeton, NJ: Princeton University Press, 1970.

———. *Mysterium Coniunctionis. The Collected Works of C. G. Jung*, trans. R. F. C. Hull. Bollingen Series XX, vol. 14. Princeton, NJ: Princeton University Press, 1970.

———. *The Practice of Psychotherapy. The Collected Works of C. G. Jung*, trans. R. F. C. Hull. Bollingen Series XX, vol. 16. Princeton, NJ: Princeton University Press, 1966.

———. *Psychological Types. The Collected Works of C. G. Jung*, trans. R. F. C. Hull. Bollingen Series XX, vol. 6. Princeton, NJ: Princeton University Press, 1971.

———. *Psychology and Religion. The Collected Works of C. G. Jung*, trans. R. F. C. Hull. Bollingen Series XX, vol. 11. Princeton, NJ: Princeton University Press, 1969.

———. *Structure and Dynamics of the Psyche. The Collected Works of C. G. Jung*, trans. R. F. C. Hull. Bollingen Series XX, vol. 8. Princeton, NJ: Princeton University Press, 1970.

———. *The Symbolic Life. The Collected Works of C. G. Jung*, trans. R. F. C. Hull. Bollingen Series XX, vol. 18. 1950; Princeton, NJ: Princeton University Press, 1976.

———. *Symbols of Transformation. The Collected Works of C. G. Jung*, trans. R. F. C. Hull. Bollingen Series XX, vol. 5. Princeton, NJ: Princeton University Press, 1956.

———. *Two Essays on Analytic Psychology. The Collected Works of C. G. Jung*, trans. R. F. C. Hull. Bollingen Series XX, vol. 7. 1953; Princeton, NJ: Princeton University Press, 1966.

Jung, Emma. *Animus and Anima*. Trans. Cary F. Baynes and Hildegard Nagel. 1957; Putnam, CT: Spring Publications, 2008.

Kime, Wayne R. *Pierre Munro Irving and Washington Irving: A Collaboration in Life and Letters*. Waterloo, Ont.: Wilfrid Laurier University Press, 1977.

Kimmel, Michael S. *Manhood in America: A Cultural History*. 1996; 3rd edn. New York: Oxford University Press, 2012.

Kopec, Andrew. "Irving, Ruin, and Risk." *Early American Literature* 48:3 (2013): 709–35.

Lanman, Charles. "A Day with Washington Irving." *Daily National Intelligencer* (March 23, 1857): 2.

LeMenager, Stephanie. "Trading Stories: Washington Irving and the Global West." *American Literary History* 15:4 (2003): 683–708.

Leverenz, David. *Manhood and the American Renaissance*. Ithaca, NY: Cornell University Press, 1989.

Littlefield, Daniel F., Jr. "Washington Irving and the American Indian." *American Indian Quarterly* 5:2 (May 1979): 135–154.

Longfellow, Henry Wadsworth. "Address on the Death of Washington Irving." *Poems and Other Writings*. New York: Library of America, 2000. 800–802.

Martin, Sara. *Masculinity and Patriarchal Villainy in the British Novel: From Hitler to Voldemort*. New York: Routledge, 2019.

———. *Representations of Masculinity in Literature and Film: Focus on Men*. Newcastle upon Tyne, UK: Cambridge Scholars Publishing, 2020.

McDermott, John Francis, ed. *The Western Journals of Washington Irving*. Norman: University of Oklahoma Press, 1966.

McGann, Jerome. "Washington Irving, 'A History of New York,' and American History." *Early American Literature* 47:2 (2012): 349–76.

McWilliams, John. "'The Almighty [Unmentionable] Dollar': Washington Irving and Money." *Literature in the Early American Republic: Annual Studies on Cooper and His Contemporaries* 2 (2010): 203–27.

Moore, Robert L., and Douglas Gillette. *King, Warrior, Magician, Lover: Redis-*

covering the Archetypes of the Mature Masculine. New York: HarperCollins, 1991.
Murray, Laura J. "The Aesthetic of Dispossession: Washington Irving and Ideologies of (De)Colonization in the Early Republic." *American Literary History* 8 (Summer 1996): 205–231.
Myers, Andrew. "The New York Years in Irving's *Life of George Washington*." *Early American Literature* 11 (1976): 68–83.
Neumann, Erich. *The Great Mother: An Analysis of the Archetype*, trans. Ralph Mannheim. Bollingen Series. Princeton, NJ: Princeton University Press, 1955.
150 W. I.: Washington Irving and the Alhambra: 150th Anniversary 1859-2009. Exhibition catalog. Ed. Carmen Yusty Pérez. Granada: Patronato de la Alhambra y el Generalife / Tf Editores [Madrid], 2009.
Pearce, Roy Harvey. *Savagism and Civilization: A Study of the Indian and the American Mind*. Berkeley: University of California Press, 1988.
Reynolds, Guy. "The Winning of the West: Washington Irving's *A Tour on the Prairies*." *Yearbook of English Studies* 34 (January 2004): 88–99.
Ringe, Donald A. "New York and New England: Irving's Criticism of American Society." *American Literature* 38 (1967): 455–67.
Roth, Martin. *Comedy and America: The Lost World of Washington Irving*. Port Washington, NY-London: Kennikat Press, 1976.
Rotundo, E. Anthony. *American Manhood: Transformations in Masculinity from the Revolution to the Modern Era*. New York: Basic Books, 1993.
Rubin-Dorsky, Jeffrey. *Adrift in the Old World: The Psychological Pilgrimage of Washington Irving*. Chicago: University of Chicago Press, 1988.
Sanford, John A. *The Invisible Partners: How the Male and Female in Each of Us Affects Our Relationships*. New York-Mahwah, NJ: Paulist Press, 1980.
Scraba, Jeffrey. "'Dear Old Romantic Spain': Washington Irving Imagines Andalucia." *Romanticism and the Anglo-Hispanic Imaginary*. Ed. Joselyn M. Almeida. Amsterdam and New York: Rodopi, 2010. 275–95.
Sellers, Charles. *The Market Revolution: Jacksonian America 1815-1846*. New York: Oxford University Press, 1994.
Takaki, Ronald. "*The Tempest* in the Wilderness: The Racialization of Savagery." *Journal of American History* 79:3 (December 1992): 892–912.
Traister, Bryce. "The Wandering Bachelor: Irving, Masculinity, and Authorship." *American Literature* 74:1 (2002): 111–37.
Tschachler, Heinz. *George Washington and Political Fatherhood: The Endurance of a National Myth*. Jefferson, NC: McFarland, 2020.
_____. *The Greenback: Paper Money and American Culture*. Jefferson, NC: McFarland, 2010.
_____. *The Monetary Imagination of Edgar Allan Poe*. Jefferson, NC: McFarland, 2013.
_____. "'Roman Countenances' and 'Abominations': Racial and Ethnic Stereotyping in the Writings of Washington Irving," *The Polyphony of English Studies: A Festschrift for Allan James*, ed. Alexander Onysko, Eva-Maria Graf, Werner Delanoy, Nikola Dobrić, and Günther Sigott. AAA—Arbeiten aus Anglistik und Amerikanistik, Vol. 26. Tübingen: Gunter Narr Verlag, 2017. 241–59.
Vaughan, Alden T. "From White Man to Redskin: Changing Anglo-American Perceptions of the American Indian." *American Historical Review* 87 (1982): 917–953.
Wagenknecht, Edward C. *Washington Irving: Moderation Displayed*. New York: Oxford University Press, 1962.
Wallhead, Celia M. *Washington Irving and Spain: The Romantic Movement, The Re/Creation of Islamic Andalusia and the Critical Reception*. Bethesda, MD: Academica Press, 2010.
Warner, Michael. "Irving's Posterity." *ELH (English Literary History)* 67:3 (2000): 773–99.
Washington, George. "Farewell Address." *The Writings of George Washington*. Ed. John Rhodehamel. New York: Library of America, 2011. 962–77.
West, Elsie Lee. "Washington Irving, Biographer." *Washington Irving Reconsidered: A Symposium*. Ed. Ralph M. Aderman. Hartford, CT: Transcendental Books, 1969. 47–52.
Williams, Stanley T. *The Life of Washington Irving*. 2 vols. New York: Oxford University Press, 1935.
Wingate, Jordan. "Irving's Columbus and Hemispheric American History." *American Literature* 89:3 (2017): 463–96.

Index

"Abbotsford" 222n161, 246n79
"acting 'as if'" 20–22; see also "active imagination"; admiration"; "amplification"; "invocation"
"active imagination" (C.G. Jung) 20–22, 42, 170, 217n52, 217n54, 238n74; see also "acting 'as if'"; "admiration"; "amplification"; "invocation"
Adams, John 95
Adams, John Quincy 75, 76, 95, 138, 234n123
Addison, Joseph: *Cato* (1712) 54
"admiration" 20–22; see also "acting 'as if'"; active imagination"; "amplification"; "invocation"
"The Adventure of the Black Fisherman" 89
The Adventures of Captain Bonneville 136, 151–56, 246n87; manliness in 154
African Americans 145; see also slavery, slaves
Agapida see Fray Antonio Agapida
The Alhambra 33, 37, 118–19, 125–27, 129–36, 219n100, 239n105; see also individual stories, by title
Alhambra (Granada Palace) 33, 107, 126, 130; see also "Recollections of the Alhambra"
Allston, Washington 47, 59
ambition 49, 77, 111, 116, 178–79, 185–86, 191, 239n77, 253n83
American Indians see Native Americans
American Revolution 82, 139, 167, 187, 255n135; see also War of Independence
amplification (C.G. Jung) 20–21, 167; see also "acting 'as if'"; active imagination"; admiration"; "invocation"
Analectic Magazine 147, 158, 248n141, 248n154
androgyny 15, 140, 161, 215n15
"The Angler" 36
anima 2–8, 14–19, 24, 33–36, 60, 67, 101, 104, 124, 131, 140, 156, 161–62, 166, 169–70, 189, 197, 200, 214n7, 220n132, 221n149; see also animus; archetypes; Hillman, James; Irving, Washington, anima-consciousness; Jung, C.G.; Sanford, John A.

anima-consciousness 2, 15, 19, 29, 70, 83, 162, 197
anima-ego 8, 17, 35, 42, 124, 131, 164–66, 170, 189, 209
ANIMA GARDEN 2–3, 5, 6, 212n7; see also Heller, André
animus 4, 6–8, 16, 19, 22, 26, 31, 140, 161, 196, 197, 215n15; see also animus; archetypes; Hillman, James; Jung, C.G.; Sanford, John A.
"Annette Delarbre" 36
archetypes 7, 14, 16, 22, 31–32, 42, 99, 105, 120, 148, 199, 210; see also Gillette, Douglas; Hillman, James; Irving, Washington, archetypes in his writings; Jung, C.G.; Moore, Robert L.; Sanford, John A.
artisan paradigm (David Leverenz) 99, 222n169
Aspinwall, Col. Thomas 40, 95, 122
Aston Hall 69
Astor, John Jacob 30, 114, 154–55; as American Columbus 154; solicits Irving authorship of *Astoria* 155
Astoria 151–55; Pierre Munro Irving and 155
"The Author's Account of Himself" 62, 147; see also *The Sketch Book*
"The Author's Farewell" 69; see also *Bracebridge Hall*

Bachelard, Gaston 221n149
bachelorhood and sexuality 216n33, 216n38; see also "gay bachelor"; Irving, Washington, bachelorhood and; as sexual orientation
"Bachelors" 18
"A Bachelor's Confessions" 36
Bailyn, Bernard 176, 252n62; see also Carlyle, Thomas; Great Men theory of history; "heroic history"
Bancroft, George 114, 140, 180–81, 193, 196
Barlow, Joel 108
Benton, Thomas Hart 57
Bergh, Mme. de 18
Bibliothèque universelle des romans 219n101

267

Index

Biography and Poetical Remains of the Late Margaret Miller Davidson 5
Black Hawk (Chief) 143
Blackwood's Edinburgh Magazine 102
Boabdil 118–19, 128
Böhl von Faber, Cecilia *see* Caballero, Fernán
Bolviller, Antoinette 18, 130, 242*n*202
Bonaparte, Napoleon 2
Bonneville, Benjamin Louis Eulalie du 155–56
Boone, Daniel 81, 140–41
Bordeaux, Irving in 106
Bowden, Mary Weatherspoon 122–23, 188, 194, 202
Bracebridge, Squire 8, 63–64, 70–71, 103, 185–86
Bracebridge Hall 22, 61, 68–73, 103
Brady, Matthew M.: daguerreotype of Irving 208, 260*n*66
Bremer, Fredrika 209
Brevoort, Henry 13, 23, 33, 38, 40, 73–74, 76, 77, 79, 86, 88, 96, 102–103, 113, 123, 126, 127, 157, 158, 189, 204, 224*n*20
Britain, Great Britain *see* England
"The Broken Heart" 36
"Buckthorne, or the Young Man of Great Expectations" 26–27, 218*n*98
buffalo hunting, Irving and 151, 166
Burke, Edmund 184
Burr, Aaron 2, 44; duel with Hamilton 46–47
Burr, Theodosia 18
Burstein, Andrew (biographer of Irving) 18, 113, 154, 191, 216*n*29, 216*n*33, 219*n*102, 231*n*50
Bush, George H.W. 93
Bush, George W. 93
business *see* Irving, Washington, attitude toward; business investments
Butter, Michael *see* "Washington-Code"
Byron, Lord (George Gordon) 30, 34, 35, 125

Caballero, Fernán (Cecilia Böhl von Faber) 132
Calderón de la Barca, Pedro 241*n*151
Calhoun, John C. 123
Campbell, Joseph: *The Hero with a Thousand Faces* 32; *see also* archetypes
Campbell, Thomas 204
Canby, Henry Seidel 53, 204
capitalism 9, 37–38, 61–65, 70, 80, 82–85, 88, 90–92, 111, 134, 154–55, 164, 167, 206
Carey, Lea and Blanchard (publishers) 142
Carlyle, Thomas 212*n*2, 240*n*115; *see also* Bailyn, Bernard; Great Men theory of history; "heroic history"
Carvill, G. & C. (publishers) 113
Cass, Lewis 57

Cato: A Tragedy see Addison, Joseph
Chaucer, Geoffrey 58
Cherry Tree legend (George Washington) 175
Chesterfield, P.D. Stanhope, 4th Earl of 45, 63, 185
"Christmas" 61, 63; *see also The Sketch Book*
A Chronicle of the Conquest of Granada 33, 107, 118, 126–27, 129–31, 171; *see also* Agapida, Fray Antonio
Cincinnatus, Lucius Quinctus 138, 178, 253*n*77; *see also* Washington, George: as C.
Civil War, American 10, 123, 177–79, 186, 199; *see also Life of George Washington*; North; South
Clark, William 58, 143, 148, 152; *see also* Lewis, Meriwether
Clay, Henry 222*n*168
Coleridge, Samuel Taylor 3, 13, 34, 215*n*15; *see also* "What if you slept"
"The Columbiad" (Joel Barlow) 108
"Columbia's Noblest Sons" (lithograph) 200
Columbus, Christopher *see History of the Life and Voyages of Christopher Columbus*
Common Sense see Paine, Thomas
Confederacy 152; *see also* Civil War, American
The Conquest of Granada see A Chronicle of the Conquest of Granada
Constable, Archibald 30, 171
Constitution *see* United States Constitution
Cooper, James Fenimore 42, 109, 163; on Irving 28; *The Spy* (1821) 183
Corbin, Henry 221*n*149
Crane, Ichabod 5, 6, 61, 77, 83–87, 99, 100, 232*n*75; *see also* "The Legend of Sleepy Hollow"
craniology 51, 143, 226*n*40
Crayon, Geoffrey (Irving pseudonym) 2, 4, 22, 25, 31, 33, 35, 37, 41, 58–72, 74, 88, 99, 109, 118–19, 125–36, 169, 196, 198, 203, 229*n*146, 239*n*105
The Crayon Miscellany 41, 125, 136, 226*n*66
"The Creole Village" 135, 162–63, 249*n*161

Dana, Richard Henry 68
Davidson, Margaret Miller (Irving's biography) *see Biography and Poetical Remains of the Late Margaret Miller Davidson*
Decatur, Stephen 2, 212*n*4, 248*n*154
Declaration of Independence 57, 191
de Hita *see* Pérez de Hita, Ginés
de las Casas, Fray Bartolomé 106, 108, 115, 117, 118
Democratic Republicans 48, 95, 100; *see also* Federalism; Jefferson, Thomas; republicanism
"depersonalization," "derealization" 29, 219*n*117

Index 269

"The Devil and Tom Walker" 1, 91–99; class bias in 97–98
Dolgorouki, Prince Dmitri 130, 132
"Dolph Heyliger" 16, 61
dreaming, dreams, daydreaming 15, 21, 22, 33, 34, 48, 77, 86, 100, 113–15, 121, 124–29, 135, 202, 210, 214n37, 217n554, 242n201
Dresden *see* Irving, Washington, in Dresden

Edinburgh Magazine 102, 232n88
effeminacy, effeminate 8, 13, 15, 16, 19, 24, 25, 50, 63, 64, 78, 86, 114, 121, 124, 131, 138–40, 153, 186, 205, 225n30; *see also* Irving, Washington, effeminacy and; "manliness and independence of character" (Irving)
elections *see* presidential elections
Ellenberger, Henri F. 217n72, 219n117, 221n150
Ellsworth, Henry 142, 145
Embargo Act (1807) 51; *see also* Jefferson, Thomas
Emerson, Ralph Waldo, on Irving 166
England 62, 64–71, 135, 157, 160, 166, 168, 184, 198; Irving's early interest in 69, 103; *see also* London
"English Country Gentlemen" 71
"English Writers on America" 4, 62
erythema multiforme 219n105; *see also* Irving, Washington, health issues
Espartero, Baldomero (regent of Spain) 2, 212n3
Everett, Alexander 106, 107, 112, 123
Everett, Edward 146, 180, 245n52
Evergreen, Anthony (Irving pseudonym) 204

Fairlie, Mary 18, 42, 52
family business: bankruptcy 11, 15, 39, 87, 205; Irving's role in 25, 76, 77, 218n86
"Farewell Address" 51, 188, 190, 256n159; *see also* Washington, George
Father of His Country: Washington as *see* Washington, George: as Father of His Country
Federalist Party 52, 53, 95; *see also* Democratic Republicans; Hamilton, Alexander; Irving, Washington, political views; republicanism
feminization, of American culture 35, 76, 140, 161, 203, 209, 221n158
"The Field of Waterloo" 105
Fillmore, Willard 190
Flexner, James Thomas: *George Washington* 193, 257n182
Der fliegende Holländer (Richard Wagner) 14
folklore 34, 79, 94, 202
Foster, Amelia 28, 29, 219n100; Irving's confessional letter to 17, 216n39, 242n206
Foster, Emily 16, 17, 29, 207, 219n118
Foster, Flora 16, 220n118

Franklin, Benjamin 97, 231n46
Fray Antonio Agapida (Irving pseudonym) 2, 33, 107, 127–31, 197
Freeman, Douglas Southall: *George Washington* 193, 253n76
Der Freischütz (Carl Maria von Weber) 14
Freneau, Philip 108

Galignanis (publishers) 30, 95–96, 113, 142
gentleman (definition) 45, 59, 69, 145, 179, 182–84, 186, 204
Germany *see* Irving, Washington, in Germany
ghost stories 101, 201
Gillette, Douglas 32; *see also* Moore, Robert L.
Goldsmith, Oliver 5, 22, 119; Irving's biography 31, 124, 168–70, 174; *see also Life of Oliver Goldsmith*
Gor, Duke of 53, 137
gothic 13, 67, 87, 93, 117
Granada: Irving in 38, 126–27, 132, 133; *see also* Alhambra (palace); *The Alhambra*; *The Conquest of Granada*; Spain
Gratz, Rebecca 18
Great Britain *see* England
Great Men theory of history *see* Carlyle, Thomas; *see also* Bailyn, Bernard; "heroic history"
Grimm, Brothers 28, 34, 147
Grund, Francis 208, 209

Haddon Hall 69, 171
Hamilton, Alexander 46–47; *see also* federalism; Jefferson, Thomas
Harrison, William Henry 138, 172
Hawthorne, Nathaniel 192, 203, 206
Hedges, William 97, 103, 104, 117, 176, 192, 202, 236n21
Hegel, Georg Wilhelm Friedrich (*"Weltgeist,"* "World Spirit") 35, 49, 191, 201
hegira 119; *see also Mahomet and His Successors*
Hell Gate 88, 155
Heller, André 2–3, 4, 5; *see also ANIMA GARDEN*
"heroic history" 56, 104, 176, 252n62; *see also* Bailyn, Bernard; Carlyle, Thomas; Great Men theory of history; *Life of George Washington* as
Hillman, James 2, 41, 68, 215n15; *see also* anima; animus; archetypes
A History of New York: conception and evolution 17; critique of Indian policy in 56–57, 157–58, 227n73; Dutch New Amsterdam spoofed in 53, 56–58, 227n74, 233n95; Jefferson and his policies satirized in 8, 50; publicity for 40; reception 48, 56; revisions 50, 55, 226n61

History of the Life and Voyages of Christopher Columbus 30, 104, 106; Columbus as American hero 108, 110–11, 114; Columbus as hero-saint 108–109, 115–16; Columbus's appearance 116–17; Columbus's character and conduct 112; conception and evolution 104–108; double standard in 109, 112; reception 112–15
Hoffman, Josiah Ogden 13, 47, 51, 52, 53
Hoffman, Matilda 13, 15; impact of death on Irving 17, 216n30

Indian Removal Act 142, 148, 154, 156, 244n25
Indian Sketches (John Treat Irving) 244n30
Indians *see* Native Americans
"individuation" (C.G. Jung) 20
Innskeep & Bradford (publishers) 40
"integration" (C.G. Jung) 20, 22, 210; *see also* "recognition"
"invocation" 20, 22, 217n54; *see also* "acting 'as if'"; "active imagination"; "admiration"; "amplification"
Irving, Catherine *see* Paris, Catherine Irving
Irving, Ebenezer 26, 27, 38, 41, 78, 83, 172, 209, 218n94, 230n4
Irving, John T. 244n30, 251n38
Irving, Peter 3, 13, 21, 26, 33, 44, 48, 51, 76, 124, 143, 151, 251n35, 253n79
Irving, Pierre Munro 15, 23, 26, 41, 47, 107, 172, 218n96; hired to help write *Astoria* 155; hired for Washington biography 195, 206, 219n118; role at end of Irving's life 173–74, 256n166
Irving, Pierre Paris (Irving's nephew) 29, 103, 205
Irving, Sarah (Irving's sister) *see* Van Wart, Sarah
Irving, Sarah Sanders (Irving's mother) 26
Irving, Washington: admiration for Walter Scott 53, 222n161; and Andrew Jackson 2, 51, 124, 171–72, 188, 251n35; Anglophilia 69, 103, 184, 228n92; anima-consciousness 2, 15, 19, 29, 70, 83, 162, 197; and archetypes in writings 7, 22, 32–33, 42, 99, 105, 120, 148, 199, 209–10; bachelorhood and 17–19, 36, 58, 71–72, 136, 216n33, 216n38, 216n39, 229n146; business and commerce, attitude toward 4, 9, 13, 29, 38, 39, 40, 44, 59, 63, 68, 70–71, 77, 86, 103, 152, 164, 206, 218n88; business investments 39, 76, 165, 172; career, indecision and self-doubt about 13, 24–25, 29, 38, 68, 74, 104, 105, 112, 200–201, 206; celebrity status 31, 56, 68, 77, 112–13, 130, 157; class bias 11, 35, 42, 44, 48, 50, 52–53, 55, 70, 72, 73, 94, 97–98, 140, 203, 205; as Columbus's biographer 104–108, 112–115; Cooper's criticism 28; on copyright 39–40, 223n187; courtship of Emily Foster 28–29, 219n118; Dana's criticism 68; death 174; and death of Matilda Hoffman 17, 216n30; as diplomat 56, 72, 139, 164, 172, 246n100, 251n35; in Dresden 17, 28, 229n158, 238n76; early encounter with Native Americans 157; and effeminacy 8, 13, 15–16, 19, 24–25, 50, 63–64, 86, 114, 121, 124, 131, 138–40, 205; evaluated by biographer Stanley T. Williams 21, 24, 30, 41, 44, 73, 103–106, 115, 122, 129, 131, 166, 172–74, 197, 199, 203, 238n63; fear of criticism 2, 27, 46, 68, 73, 169; as Federalist 8, 48, 50–53, 70, 86, 94, 99, 161, 167, 172, 205, 229n138; financial difficulties 14, 18, 25, 28, 30, 39, 76, 87, 106, 165, 172, 174, 209, 223n182, 232n83; as "gay bachelor" 17; in Germany 28, 119, 192, 215n9, 238n76; health issues 27, 47, 74, 174, 219n105; as historian 9, 21, 107, 113, 115, 119, 123, 127, 131, 151, 158, 175–76, 180–81, 190, 192, 194, 201, 222n162, 236n21, 238n63; history, attitude toward and view 1, 10, 17, 30, 31, 49, 56, 57, 66, 103–104, 108, 110–11, 117, 124, 129, 139, 146, 166, 252n62; income from writing 40, 41, 79, 223n192, 225n23, 231n39, 237n56, 238n65; as lawyer 13, 47–48, 57; literary success and 31, 41, 48, 56, 59, 68, 77, 79, 102, 112–13, 122, 130, 136, 169, 180–81; and manliness 10, 19, 64, 66, 78, 105, 121, 135, 138, 139, 154, 173, 182, 183, 199, 200, 208, 209, 225n30; as Minister to Spain 31, 139, 164, 172, 207; opinion of Jeffersonian democracy 8, 42, 48–53, 198; as "Patriarch of American Letters" 38, 196, 201; as *"pere de famille"* 207; personal crisis of 1825 28–29, 97, 104; physical description 8, 15–16, 124–25, 207–209, 215n16, 215n17, 215n20; his "pilgrimage" 24–25, 200, 218n85; political attitude and views 34, 51–53, 66, 163, 172, 188–89, 224n199, 225n30, 226n50, 229n38, 260n57; prairie tour 30, 114, 139–46, 150–51, 161–62; public persona 4, 11, 15–16, 23, 27, 58–59, 197; his "quest" 24–25, 77–78, 81, 87, 104, 105, 109, 112, 113, 123, 139, 144–45, 172, 192, 197, 200; relations with nephew Pierre Munro Irving 23, 107, 155, 172–74, 218n96, 251n54, 256n166; relations with publisher John Murray 28, 33, 77, 79, 103, 113, 119, 128, 204, 223n192, 232n62; as Romantic 9, 15, 53, 124–27, 133, 142, 181, 202; sensibility and sensitiveness 4, 16, 22, 25, 27, 161, 162, 169, 200, 207, 213n14, 219n100; sexual orientation 17–19, 136, 216n33, 216n38, 231n50; his "softened masculinity" 16, 200, 204, 216n26; Spanish legacy 130–31; "Spanish orientalism" 134, 242n212; Sterne's influence on 47; views concerning Native Americans 16, 142–46, 156–61, 247n126; as Washington's biographer 104, 167, 170–78,

181–82, 187–88, 191–96; welcomed back from Europe 30, 141, 243n17; and women 5–6, 13, 17–19, 29, 35–36, 124, 216n34, 216n36, 218–19n99; *see also* Alhambra; anima; animus; archetypes; Burstein, Andrew (biographer of Irving); Crayon, Geoffrey; dreaming, dreams, daydreaming; England; Evergreen, Anthony; family business; Fray Antonio Agapida; Granada; "heroic history"; Knickerbocker, Diedrich; "Lads of Kilkenny"; Langstaff, Launcelot; Longfellow, Henry Wadsworth; Madrid; "manliness and independence of character"; New York (city), and Washington Irving; Oldstyle, Jonathan; picturesque, Irving's use of; Seville; Spain; Sunnyside (The Roost); Washington, George, encounter with Irving; Williams, Stanley T.; individual works, by title
Irving, William (Irving's father) 25, 169, 196; death 25
Irving, William, Jr. (Irving's brother) 15, 26, 48, 157, 218n96; comments on Irving's travels 19, 47

Jackson, Andrew 53, 55, 65, 95, 138, 140, 165; Irving's admiration 2, 51, 124, 171–72, 188, 251n35; and Native Americans 57, 142, 144, 148, 157, 160, 248n147
Jarvis, John Wesley 59; portrait of Irving 15, 16
Jefferson, Thomas 8, 42, 52, 110, 198, 225n30, 226n70; as classical republican 51, 186, 225n37, 239n122; on George Washington 196, 257n201; satirized in *A History of New York* 8, 49–55; *see also* Democratic Republicans; republicanism
"The Journey" 127, 241n162; *see also The Alhambra*
Jung, C.G. 7, 14–21, 29, 31, 170, 215n15, 221n150; *see also* "active imagination"; "amplification"; anima; animus; archetypes
Jung, Emma 31, 214n7, 217n46; *see also* anima; animus; archetypes

Kemble, Gouverneur 188, 224n20
Kidd, Captain (Kidd's treasure) 88, 90, 93–97, 100, 101
Kieft, Wilhelm (Irving's lampoon of Jefferson) 8, 49–52; *see also* William the Testy
"King" archetype 32, 44, 45, 54, 121, 199, 220n135, 258n5
Kirkland, Caroline Matilda: *Memoirs of Washington* 180, 182
Knickerbocker, Diedrich (Irving pseudonym) 2, 5, 8, 17, 36, 40, 41, 48, 58–60, 84, 89, 197, 198, 204, 263
Knickerbocker Magazine 40, 60, 92, 134, 164, 173, 192, 246n10

Knickerbocker's History see *A History of New York*

"Lads of Kilkenny" 47
Langstaff, Launcelot (Irving pseudonym) 48, 197, 204
Lanman, Charles 114, 145, 170, 190, 195
Latrobe, Charles Joseph 145, 246n68
Lavater, Johann Kaspar 51, 226n40
Lea & Blanchard (publishers) 142
Legado Andalusí, El (The Legacy of Andalusia) 130
"The Legend of Don Munio Sancho de Hinojosa" 133–34
"The Legend of Don Roderick" 136–37
"Legend of Prince Ahmed Al Kamel" 217n59
"The Legend of Sleepy Hollow" 1, 61, 83–87, 232n66; *see also* Crane, Ichabod
Legends of the Conquest of Spain 30, 107, 136–37, 171
Leslie, Charles Robert 15, 59, 69, 171; portrait of Irving 15, 215n20
Letters of Jonathan Oldstyle, Gent. 44–45, 61
Leutze, Emanuel Gottlieb: *Washington Crossing the Delaware* 180, 253n90
Lewis, Meriwether 143, 152; *see also* Clark, William
Life of George Washington: and civic virtue 176, 191; conception and evolution 29, 126, 166–67, 170–74; as "gentleman warrior" 182; as "heroic history" 176; importance of "Union" in 177, 187–88, 190–91; as Irving's "crowning labor" 1, 170, 196; Irving's political views in 171–72, 188–89; as "King" archetype 199; and masculine perfection 104, 192, 196–97, 210; as nonpartisan 188; as patriarch 186–87; reception 190–94, 196; as slaveowner 179–80; as Southerner 186–87; success 180; as symbol of national unity 177, 200; timeliness 178; as Virginia aristocrat 179–80; Washington as Cincinnatus 178, 253n77; Washington's character and conduct 182–86; Washington's charisma 176; Washington's "Englishness" 184; Washington's personal appearance 183–84; *see also* Irving, Washington, as Washington's biographer; Washington, George, biographies
Life of Oliver Goldsmith (Irving) 31, 168, 170, 174
Lincoln, Abraham 187, 234n123; and George Washington 200
Lindaraxa 3, 33; *see also* Alhambra
The Literary Gazette (London) 79, 122, 156
London (Irving in) 19, 47, 72, 124, 129, 131, 172, 219n100
Longfellow, Henry Wadsworth 4, 39 201; relations with Irving 213n14

272 Index

Longworth, David 39, 48, 224–25n23
"Lover" archetype 32, 86, 99, 108, 199, 220n135, 258n5

Mackenzie, Henry: *The Man of Feeling* 16, 22, 198
Madrid (Irving in) 30, 106–108; *see also* Navarrete, Martín Fernández de; Rich, Obadiah; Spain
"Magician" archetype 32, 46, 99, 128, 129, 199, 220n135, 258n5
Mahomet and His Successors 107, 119, 122–23, 173–74; Mahomet's appearance 119
"manhood, communal" (E. Anthony Rotundo) 62, 71–72, 222n169
"manliness and independence of character" (Irving) 19, 135, 173, 199, 200
Maria Louisa, Empress (Napoleon's second wife) 18
Marshall, John: *Life of Washington* 22, 30, 104, 170–71, 175, 182, 250n31, 256n174
Marx, Karl: *Capital* 88
masculinity crisis 37
Melville, Herman 38, 154, 192, 200, 203
Men's Movement 32; *see also* Gillette, Douglas; Moore, Robert L.
Mexican War 189
middle classes: rise 38, 110, 185
"Mississippi Bubble, The Great" *see* "'A Time of Unexampled Prosperity.' The Great Mississippi Bubble"
Mitchell, Donald Grant 23, 213n13, 261n73
money digger, def. 88
"The Money Diggers" 61, 88–91, 99–101, 232n88
Monroe, James 95
Moore, Robert L. 32; *see also* archetypes; Gillette, Douglas; "King," "Lover," "Magician," and "Warrior" archetypes; Men's Movement
Moore, Thomas: *Life of Byron* 125
Morning Chronicle: Irving's contributions to 44–46
"Mother, Great" (Erich Neumann) 36, 221n157
Mount Vernon *see* Washington, George, and Mount Vernon
Murray, John II (publisher) 28, 33, 77, 79, 103, 119, 125, 128, 223n192, 232n62, 238n65, 242n198; and Columbus biography 112–13, 241n132; *see also* Irving, Washington, relations with publisher John Murray
Murray, John III (publisher) 204, 223n192
Musil, Robert 148

Napoleon *see* Bonaparte, Napoleon
Narváez, Joaquin (Spanish prime minister) 2
"National Nomenclature" 156

Native Americans 16, 30, 57–58, 141–53, 156–61, 176, 245n50, 247n126; *see also* Irving, Washington, early encounter with; Irving, views concerning; Jackson, Andrew, and Native Americans; Osage; Pawnee
naval biographies 2, 248n154; *see also* War of 1812
Navarrete, Martín Fernández de 106, 107, 113, 114, 238n63
Neal, John 104
Nelson, Adm. Horatio 2
New York (city) 44, 54, 55, 84, 89, 99, 156, 165, 177; and Washington Irving 13, 30, 34, 40–42, 47–48, 59, 108, 141, 173, 189, 199, 220n127, 226n64, 245n62, 260n68; *see also* Yankees and Yorkers
New York Evening Post 40
New-York Mirror 102
"Newstead Abbey" 240n149, 246n79
Newstead Abbey (Byron's former home) 125
Newton, Gilbert Stuart 15, 59; portrait of Irving 8, 15–16, 215n17
Non-Importation Act (Thomas Jefferson) 51
North *see* Civil War, American
North American Review 112, 192
nostalgia, nostalgic 9, 38, 53, 70, 72, 101, 131, 135, 152, 160, 163, 167, 180, 191, 192, 201, 218n88, 229n150
"Notes While Preparing Sketch Book" 77, 231n35
Nullification Crisis 172, 253n79

Ogden, Henry A. 224n20
Oklahoma Territory 30, 142
Oldstyle, Jonathan (Irving pseudonym) 2, 5, 8, 44–46, 61, 197, 198, 204, 224n5
150 W.I.: Washington Irving and the Alhambra (exhibition and catalog) 130, 215n17, 216n33, 266
Osage 135, 144–46, 148–51, 161, 244n35, 246n80; *see also* Native Americans
Outre-Mer (Longfellow) 213n14
Oxford University (awards honorary doctorate to Irving) 114

P. & E. Irving (family business) 74, 76, 230n4
Paine, Thomas 57
Panic of 1819 75, 87, 165, 231n34, 234n122
Panic of 1837 55, 92, 164–65, 247n173
Paris, Catherine Irving 88, 139, 143
Paris, Sarah *see* Storrow, Sarah Paris
Paris, France: Irving in 14, 19, 28, 38, 47, 68, 95–97, 106, 140, 171
Parkman, Francis, Jr. 166
Patriae Pater, portrait of Washington (Rembrandt Peale) 29
patriarchy 6, 10, 37–38, 61–73, 80, 82, 89, 91, 98–101, 139, 151, 166, 168, 174, 186, 196, 205–

208, 213n22, 222n169, 230n32; Irving as "patriarch of American letters" 38–39, 196, 201
"patrician paradigm" (David Leverenz) 204, 222n169
Paulding, James Kirke: contribution to *Salmagundi* 40, 48, 224n20, 224–25n23; *Life of Washington* 180–81, 182
Pawnee 144, 151, 244n38, 246n80; *see also* Native Americans
Payne, John Howard 87, 219n115, 225n24
Peacham, Henry (*Peacham's Compleat Gentleman*) 63, 185–86
Pérez de Hita, Ginés 118, 128, 129, 239n109
Perry, Oliver Hazard 2, 248n154
"Peter Klaus" (inspiration for "Rip Van Winkle") 79
"The Phantom Ship" 14
"Philip of Pokanoket" 146–47, 159, 227n73; *see also* "Traits of Indian Character"
physiognomy *see* Lavater, Johann Kaspar
picturesque, Irving's use of 115, 126, 132–33, 136, 140, 144–45, 181, 202, 242n204, 244n42
Pierce, Franklin 189–90
planter aristocracy *see* Virginia aristocracy
Pochmann, Henry A. 97, 103–104, 124, 222n162
Poe, Edgar Allan 154, 181
"Poor Devil Author" 103; *see also Tales of a Traveller*
populism 34, 66; *see also* Jackson, Andrew
Pourtalès, Albert-Alexandre de (Conte) 145, 245n68
Prescott, William Hickling 39, 112, 114, 172, 181, 193
presidential elections 94–95
"The Pride of the Village" 36
"protective mimicry" (James Hillman) 2, 14, 41
providence 18, 97, 110, 158; Columbus's belief in 118, 239n103
Putnam, George P. (publisher) 41, 172, 180, 208, 260n69

Quandt, Mme. de 96
Quarterly Review 102, 126
Quixote, Don 46, 126, 127, 132
Quoz, Andrew 44–46; *see also Letters of Jonathan Oldstyle, Gent.*

Real Academia de la Historia (makes Irving a member) 114
"recognition" (C.G. Jung) 20, 176; *see also* "integration"
"Recollections of the Alhambra" 134–35
Renwick, Jean Jeffrey 18
republicanism 55, 72, 161, 177, 188, 200; *see also* Democratic Republicans; Federalism; Jefferson, Thomas
Rich, Obadiah 108; *see also History of the Life and Voyages of Christopher Columbus*, conception and evolution; Madrid
"Rip Van Winkle" 78–83, 94, 101, 231n35; cultural significance 80–83, 94; masculinity in 79–80
Rocky Mountains 151–52, 155, 246n87
romance, historical 9, 22, 36, 106, 110, 119, 122, 127, 129, 131, 177, 193, 221n152, 222n162, 236n17
Romanticism, romantic, Romantics 9, 10, 13, 15, 21, 31, 33–36, 46, 53, 62, 93, 107, 108, 115, 116, 123–29, 132, 134–35, 142–46, 149, 151, 153, 180–81, 198, 202, 221n150, 236n17, 241n176; *see also* Irving, Washington, as Romantic
"Roscoe" 65, 66
Roscoe, William 228n117
Rubin-Dorsky, Jeffrey 24, 61, 202
"Rural Life in England" 63

Salmagundi 8, 15, 18, 39, 42, 48, 49, 61, 119, 157, 204; reissue in 1820 48
Sanford, John A. 215n15; *see also* anima; animus; archetypes
Santayana, George 162–63
Schiller, Friedrich 115, 117, 238n76
Schlegel, Friedrich 34
Scott, Sir Walter 34, 36, 53, 108; Irving's admiration 53, 222n161; Irving's visit to Abbotsford 246n79
Scraba, Jeffrey 119, 239n105, 242n201
self-made man 37, 38, 71, 79, 84, 89, 97–98, 167, 177, 222n168, 222n169
A Sentimental Journey (Sterne) 47
sentimentalism, sentimentalization 7, 8, 18, 24, 35, 36, 48, 68, 103, 131, 140, 142, 146, 151, 161, 169, 175, 203–204
Seville: Irving in 124–26
sexuality *see* bachelorhood and sexuality; Irving, Washington: sexual orientation
"shadow" (C.G. Jung) 8, 19–20, 45, 46, 54, 86, 93, 128, 185, 198, 210, 220n135
Shakespeare, William: *Hamlet*, quoted by Irving 20; *A Midsummer Night's Dream* 22
Shelley, Mary Godwin 18
The Sketch Book 4, 9, 28, 33, 36, 40, 58, 60–63, 68–72, 74–79, 87, 101, 102, 108, 131, 133–34, 147, 158, 160, 185, 218n88, 231n35; *see also* individual stories, by title
"Sketches in Paris in 1825" 105
slavery, slaves 93, 118, 178; Irving, Washington on 179–80, 253n88; *see also* African Americans
Sleepy Hollow 84–86, 99–100; *see also* "The Legend of Sleepy Hollow"
Smith, Adam: *Wealth of Nations* 99

South see Civil War, American
South Sea Bubble 92
Southern Literary Messenger 181
Spain: Irving as Minister to 31, 139, 164, 172; Irving attached to Legation in 106–107; Irving's interest in 6, 9, 21, 30, 125–26, 134–37, 236n12, 236n14
Spanish Papers (Irving) 107, 136
"Spanish Romance" (Irving) 129
Sparkle, Sophy 18
Sparks, Jared: *Life of Washington* 173, 175, 176, 181, 256n174
Spectator (Addison, Steele) 22, 45
"The Spectre Bridegroom" 66–67, 68
The Spy (Cooper) 183
Staël, Mme. de 18
Sterne, Laurence: *A Sentimental Journey* 47
Storrow, Sarah Paris (Irving's niece, wife of Thomas W. Storrow, Jr.) 163, 173, 174, 190, 199
Stuyvesant, Peter 52–55; see also *A History of New York*
Sunnyside (The Roost) 31, 41, 60, 139, 164, 174, 207, 260n62, 260n65
Súspiro del Moro, el ultimo 119, 129; see also *The Alhambra*
Swift, Jonathan 8, 49, 225n25
"syzygy" (C.G. Jung) 19

Tales of a Traveller 4, 26, 60–61, 72–73, 87–94, 200, 203; reception 22, 29, 88, 102–104, 171, 235n158; writing 28, 87–88; see also individual stories, by title
Tales of the Alhambra see *The Alhambra*
Tarrytown 25, 31, 41, 164, 207, 227n89; see also Sunnyside (The Roost)
Taylor, Zachary 58; Irving's admiration 188
Theweleit, Klaus (*Male Fantasies*) 209, 261n78
Tilton, Theodore 170, 174, 250n18
"'A Time of Unexampled Prosperity.' The Great Mississippi Bubble" 92, 164, 249n168
The Times (London) 73, 76
Tocqueville, Alexis de 38, 61, 97, 140, 185
Tompkins, Daniel D. 95
Tonish (Deshetres, Antoine) 150; see also *A Tour on the Prairies*
Tonquin (ship) 153; see also *Astoria*
A Tour on the Prairies 41, 142–51: contrast to journals 148–50; manliness in 114, 139–40, 145, 150; publication 151; reviews 142, 146; as western adventure narrative 151; see also Indian Removal Act
"Traits of Indian Character" 147, 159–60, 227n73; see also "Philip of Pokanoket"
Trumbull, John: *The Death of General Mercer at the Battle of Princeton* 182; *General George Washington at Trenton* 182
Tyler, John 165, 172

Union: George Washington as symbol of 187–88, 190–91, 194
United States Constitution 185, 188, 190
United States Literary Gazette 102
United States Magazine and Democratic Review 122

Van Buren, Martin 55, 124, 138, 162, 165, 172; Irving breaks with 172
Vanderlyn, John 47
Van Tassel, Baltus 63, 85, 91, 94; see also "The Legend of Sleepy Hollow"
Van Tassel, Katrina 83, 85, 100; see also "The Legend of Sleepy Hollow"
Van Twiller, Wouter 56; see also *History of New York*
Van Wart, Henry 69
Van Wart, Sarah Irving (Irving's sister) 18, 69, 78
Van Winkle, C.S. (publisher) 78
Van Winkle, Dame 5, 80, 82, 93, 231n46; see also "Rip Van Winkle"
Van Winkle, Rip 5, 9, 32, 66, 77, 80–82, 94, 145, 197; see also "Rip Van Winkle"
Virginia aristocracy 138, 177, 179, 186, 255n128; see also *Life of George Washington*
virtue, republican 42, 161, 179, 184, 191; see also *Life of George Washington*
The Vision of Columbus (Barlow) 108
"The Voyage" 74; see also *The Sketch Book*
The Voyages and Discoveries of the Companions of Columbus 30, 107, 126, 171, 241n152
Voyages of Columbus (Navarrete) 106

Wagner, Richard: *Der fliegende Holländer* 14
Walker, Thomas "Beau" ("The Devil and Tom Walker") 93
War of 1812 2, 15, 95, 153, 160, 198, 246n100; see also naval biographies
Warner, Charles Dudley 4
"Warrior" archetype 32, 99, 105, 108, 121, 181–82, 199, 220n135
Washington, George: biographies 22, 174–75, 180–81, 187, 252n58; centennial of birth 175, 190–91; encounter with Irving 195–96; "Farewell Address" 51, 188, 190, 256n159; as Father of His Country 178, 181, 191, 197, 258n3; as Irving's shadow-self 198; and Lincoln 187, 200; and Mount Vernon 139; see also Flexner, James Thomas; Freeman, Douglas Southall; Irving, Washington, as Washington's biographer; Kirkland, Caroline Matilda; Leutze, Emanuel Gottlieb; *Life of George Washington* (Irving's biography); Marshall, John; *Patriae Pater*, portrait (Peale); Paulding, James Kirke;

Sparks, Jared; Trumbull, John; Weems, "Parson" Mason L.
"Washington-Code" (Michael Butter) 258n13
Washington Crossing the Delaware see Leutze, Emanuel Gottlieb
Waterloo, Battle of 2, 105
Weber, Carl Maria von: *Der Freischütz* 14
Weber, Max: "charismatic authority" 176
Webster, Daniel 172; on George Washington 190–91, 256n160
Weems, "Parson" Mason L.: *The Life of Washington* 175, 180, 181, 252n59
"Westminster Abbey" 66
Westminster Review 73
"What if you slept" (Coleridge) 3
Whig Party 42, 138, 172, 189, 234n123
"The Widow and Her Son" 36
"The Wife" 5, 35, 36, 222n159
Wilkie, David 59; drawing and painting of Irving 124–24
Will Wizard, Esq. (Irving pseudonym) 8

William the Conqueror 2, 212n3
William the Testy (Irving's lampoon of Jefferson) 23, 49; *see also* Kieft, William
Williams, Raymond 67
Williams, Stanley T. 14, 27, 69, 152, 195, 236n14; *see also* Irving, Washington, evaluated by biographer Stanley T. Williams
"Wolfert Webber" 60, 89–91
Wolfert's Roost *see* Sunnyside
Wolfert's Roost 105, 135, 156, 173, 249n161
"the woman within" 24, 27, 69, 70, 81, 140; *see also* Irving, Washington, and effeminacy

Ximenes (Jiménez), Mateo 125, 129–30, 241n177; *see also The Alhambra*; Granada

Yancey, William Lowndes 186; *see also* Civil War, American; North; South
Yankees 21, 50, 90, 98, 177, 186, 186, 198; Irving's attitude toward 177, 198, 225n36; and Yorkers 50, 225n36

www.ingramcontent.com/pod-product-compliance
Lightning Source LLC
Chambersburg PA
CBHW021349300426
44114CB00012B/1146